Cracknell's

Law Students' Companion

Contract

Ayo Adelani SODIMU
University of Westminster
Law School
Red Lion Square
London WC1R 4SR

Cracknell's
Law Students' Companion

Contract

Tenth Edition

D G CRACKNELL, LLB
of the Middle Temple, Barrister

Series Editor
D G Cracknell, LLB
of the Middle Temple, Barrister

OLD BAILEY PRESS

OLD BAILEY PRESS LIMITED
The Gatehouse, Ruck Lane, Horsmonden, Kent TN12 8EA

First published 1961
Tenth Edition 1997

© Old Bailey Press Ltd 1997

ISBN 1 85836 058 7

British Library Cataloguing-in-Publication.

A CIP Catalogue record for this book is available from the British Library.

Printed and bound in Great Britain.

Contents

Preface
to the Tenth Edition

There have been many important developments in this branch of the law since December 1994, the effective date of the previous edition.

Summaries of twenty recent cases have been added, including four decisions of the House of Lords (or Privy Council) and twelve Court of Appeal decisions.

If only to illustrate the range and significance of the new material, the additional cases include *Barber* v *NSW Bank plc* [1996] 1 All ER 906 (Court of Appeal: rescission), *Credit Lyonnais Bank Nederland NV* v *Burch* (1996) The Times 1 July (Court of Appeal: undue influence) and *Slater* v *Finning Ltd* [1996] 3 All ER 398 (House of Lords: implied conditions as to fitness for purpose).

In the statutes section, account has been taken of changes made by (amongst others) the Sale of Goods (Amendment) Act 1995 which amended the law relating to the sale of unascertained goods forming part of an identified bulk and the sale of undivided shares in goods.

I trust that students will continue to find it helpful to have this book at their side.

D G CRACKNELL
September 1996

Preface
to the First Edition

This work is not intended to compete with other legal textbooks, but it is hoped that it will be of use as a companion to textbooks, lecture notes and correspondence courses. It is intended primarily for the student who does not have access to or time to take full advantage of a law library and finds it difficult to ascertain the facts of cases or the wording of Acts of Parliament to which he has been referred in the course of his studies. Other students are more fortunate in so far as they have the opportunity to make full use of a law library, but it is thought that even they might find it to be of assistance to have this work at hand, especially when revising for examinations.

An attempt has been made to include those cases and statutory provisions which are of importance to students. The statutes speak for themselves and the case notes contain an outline of the facts and a summary of those points in the judgement which are vital from a student's point of view. Cross-references have been made in order that the student who refers to one case will have little difficulty in finding others in which the same or a similar point arose. There is also a short glossary of Latin words and phrases that a student is likely to encounter during his reading.

This volume is concerned with the general principles of the Law of Contract. In all this work, the author is greatly indebted to the publishers for their patience, encouragement and painstaking preparation of the manuscript for press, including the compilation of the indices.

D G CRACKNELL
July 1961

Cases

Adams v Lindsell (1818) 1 B & Ald 681 **[1]**

The defendants wrote to the plaintiff to offer to sell some wool and asked for a reply 'in course of post'. The letter containing the offer was wrongly addressed and because of this the letter of reply was posted and received two days later than it would have been reasonable for the defendants to expect. On the day previous to the receipt of the letter of acceptance the defendants sold the wool to a third person, but the letter of acceptance had been posted before the day on which the wool was sold. The plaintiff sued for breach of contract. *Held,* the plaintiff was entitled to recover as the contract was concluded when the letter of acceptance was posted. (See also *Household Fire, etc, Insurance Co Ltd v Grant.*)

Addis v Gramophone Co Ltd [1909] AC 488 (House of Lords) **[2]**

Addis was wrongfully dismissed from his employment by the defendants, and claimed (a) damages for the manner of his dismissal, and, (b) damages for his injured feelings. *Held,* such damages are not recoverable. Addis was entitled to recover only the commission and salary which he had lost. (See also *Shove* v *Downs Surgical plc, Cox* v *Phillips Industries Ltd, Ruxley Electronics and Construction Ltd* v *Forsyth* and *O'Laoire* v *Jackel International Ltd.*)

Adler v Dickson [1954] 3 All ER 396 (Court of Appeal) **[3]**

A sailing ticket issued to the plaintiff provided 'Passengers... are carried at passengers' entire risk' and 'The company will not be responsible for and shall be exempt from all liability in respect of any ... injury ... of any passenger ... whether such injury ... shall occur on land, on shipboard or elsewhere ... and whether the same shall arise from or be occasioned by the negligence of the company's servants ... in the discharge of their duties, or whether by the negligence of other persons directly or indirectly in the employment or service of the company ... under any circumstances whatsoever ...' The plaintiff was injured and she alleged that her injuries were caused by the negligence of the master and boatswain of the ship. *Held,* the shipping company were protected by the terms of the contract but the plaintiff could proceed with her action against their employees who received no protection, expressly or by implication, under the contract. (See also *Scruttons Ltd* v *Midland Silicones Ltd.*)

Affréteurs Réunis Société Anonyme, Les v Leopold **[4]**
Walford (London) Ltd [1919] AC 801 (House of Lords)

A charterparty provided that commission was due to the charterers' brokers on the signing of the charter whereas by custom commission was only payable if hire was earned. *Held,* commission was payable on the signing of the charter as the custom was entirely inconsistent with the plain words of the agreement and therefore, in the circumstances of the case, of no effect. The charterers, as trustees for the brokers, could enforce this provision against the shipowners. (See also *Royal Exchange Assurance* v *Hope.*)

Aiken v Stewart Wrightson Members' Agency Ltd   [5]
[1995] 3 All ER 449

The plaintiff Lloyd's names sought, inter alia, damages for breach of contract from the defendant agents. Certain of the contracts between the parties were under seal. Were these plaintiffs entitled to the benefit of the 12-year limitation period under s8(1) of the Limitation Act 1980? *Held,* they were since an 'action upon a specialty' included an action based on a contract under seal. There was no warrant for confining the application of the expression to actions for specific performance of the obligations created by the contract.

Ailsa Craig Fishing Co Ltd v Malvern Fishing Co Ltd   [6]
[1983] 1 All ER 101 (House of Lords)

The appellants' fishing boat sank while berthed in Aberdeen harbour and the vessel was a complete loss. At the time, the respondent security company were required by contract to provide continuous security cover and the appellants' loss resulted from the respondents' negligence and breach of this contract. However, the contract provided, inter alia, that in the event of the respondents incurring liability 'for any loss or damage of whatever nature arising out of ... or [the] failure in [the] provision of the services' contracted for, such liability was to be limited to £1,000. *Held,* this clause effectively limited the respondents' liability to £1,000 because, inter alia, it applied where there had been a total (as well as a partial) failure to provide the contracted services. 'Whether a condition limiting liability is effective or not is a question of construction of that condition in the context of the contract as a whole. If it is to exclude liability of negligence, it must be most clearly and unambiguously expressed, and, in such a contract as this, must be construed contra proferentem ... I venture to add one further qualification, or at least clarification: one must not strive to create ambiguities by strained construction ... The relevant words must be given, if possible, their natural plain meaning. Clauses of limitation are not regarded by the courts with the same hostility as clauses of exclusion; this is because they must be related to other contractual terms, in particular to the risks to which the defending party may be exposed, the remuneration which he receives and possibly also the opportunity of the other party to insure' (*per* LORD WILBERFORCE). (But see *Mitchell (George) (Chesterhall) Ltd* v *Finney Lock Seeds Ltd.*)

Ajayi v R T Briscoe (Nigeria) Ltd [1964] 3 All ER 556   [7]
(Privy Council)

By two hire-purchase agreements the defendant hired from the plaintiffs 11 lorries valued at over £24,000. The defendant fell into arrears and over £11,000 was still unpaid. He wrote to the plaintiffs saying that he had to withdraw the lorries from use because of lack of repair and servicing facilities, but he did not wish to forfeit the sums already paid, and would contribute for all essential repairs carried out by the plaintiffs' repair organisation, the repairs to be debited to his account and paid for when the lorries were again in service. The plaintiffs wrote back promising to provide these facilities and confirming that they were agreeable to the defendant 'withholding instalments due ... as long as they are withdrawn from active service'. The defendant then returned eight of the lorries for repair. Two years later the plaintiffs brought an action for payment of the outstanding instalments, and the defendant pleaded the equitable defence of promissory estoppel, on the basis of the plaintiffs' letter. *Held,* the defendant had failed to establish the defence of promissory estoppel for, on the evidence, it had not been proved that the lorries were not made available to him after they had been repaired and he had not altered his position, after receipt of the letter, by not putting forward counter-proposals or by organising his business in a different way, and it could not be inferred that such reorganisation was necessary. (See also *Central London Property Trust Ltd* v *High Trees House Ltd, Combe* v *Combe* and *Tool Metal Manufacturing Co Ltd* v *Tungsten Electric Co Ltd.*)

Akerhielm v De Mare [1959] 3 All ER 485 (Privy Council) [8]

The appellants decided to form a company in Kenya to manufacture 'cold process tiles' and issued a prospectus which stated that: 'About a third of the capital has already been subscribed in Denmark.' This statement was untrue but the appellants honestly believed it to be true at the time at which it was made. The prospectus induced the respondents to subscribe for shares in the appellants' company but when the company went into liquidation they sought damages for deceit in respect of the alleged fraudulent misrepresentation contained in the prospectus. *Held,* their action would fail as, when it was made, the appellants honestly believed the representation to be true. (See also *Derry* v *Peek*).

Akerib v Booth Ltd [1961] 1 All ER 380 (Court of Appeal) [9]

The defendants let to the plaintiff rooms on the second and third floors but retained in their possession a water closet on the fourth floor. The agreement stipulated that the plaintiff should give the whole of his packing and forwarding business to the defendants and provided that the defendants 'shall not in any circumstances be responsible for damage caused by ... water ... to any goods whether in the possession of the [defendants] or not'. Due to the negligence of the defendants or their servants, water escaped from a cistern in the water closet and damaged the plaintiff's goods. *Held,* the defendants were liable because words, however wide, must be construed in relation to the subject-matter about which they are used and the words upon which the defendants relied applied only to goods which came into their possession for packing and forwarding. 'In a document of this class ... if there is any doubt as to its meaning ... the proper construction must be against the defendants' *(per* DANCKWERTS LJ). (But see *Alderslade* v *Hendon Laundry Ltd.*)

Albazero, The [1976] 3 All ER 129 (House of Lords) [10]

The plaintiffs chartered a vessel from the defendants under a five-year time charter, and a cargo of crude oil was shipped on board in Venezuela for discharge at Amsterdam. The bill of lading named the plaintiffs as consignees. In the course of the voyage the vessel and her cargo became a total loss. At the time of the loss the property in the cargo was no longer vested in the plaintiffs but in endorsees of the bill of lading, who were now the cargo owners. The plaintiffs claimed damages against the defendants for breach of the charterparty which had resulted in loss, and the question was whether the plaintiffs were entitled to substantial damages, since they had no proprietary interest in the goods. *Held,* the plaintiffs' claim must fail. The general principle that, apart from nominal damages, a party to a contract could only recover the actual loss he had himself sustained, was subject to an exception in the case of a commercial contract concerning goods where it was in the parties' contemplation that the proprietary interest in the goods might be transferred from one owner to another after the contract had been entered into and before the breach, but that exception could not be extended to a contract for

3

the carriage of goods which contemplated that the carrier would also enter into separate contracts of carriage with whomsoever became owner of the goods carried pursuant to the original contract. This was such a contract and the plaintiffs were entitled only to nominal damages. (Applied in *Linden Gardens Trust Ltd* v *Lenesta Sludge Disposals Ltd.*)

Alder v Moore [1961] 1 All ER 1 (Court of Appeal) [11]

The defendant, a professional footballer, received an injury to his right eye and everyone concerned believed that he would never again be able to participate in professional football. In view of this, the plaintiff insurer paid him £500 under a policy of insurance which provided: 'No claim shall be paid hereunder for permanent total disablement unless the claimant shall have given to underwriters a signed declaration to the effect that he will take no part as a playing member of any form of professional football in the future and that in the event of infringement of this condition he will be subject to a penalty of the amount paid him in settlement of his claim.' The defendant made such a declaration, but within four months was a professional with another club. The plaintiff sought to recover £500 from the defendant. *Held,* the plaintiff would succeed as his claim was for the repayment of a sum in circumstances which were entirely equitable.

Alderslade v Hendon Laundry Ltd [1945] 1 All ER 244 [12]
(Court of Appeal)

One of the terms on which the appellants accepted articles for laundering was that: 'The maximum amount allowed for lost or damaged articles is 20 times the charge made for laundering.' Certain of the respondent's handkerchiefs were lost as a result of the appellants' negligence and the respondent claimed damages. *Held,* the appellants had successfully excluded liability for such loss and the claim must fail. (But see *Davies* v *Collins* and *Smith* v *South Wales Switchgear Ltd.*)

Alec Lobb (Garages) Ltd v Total Oil GB Ltd [13]
[1985] 1 All ER 303 (Court of Appeal)

The plaintiffs were a company and a mother and her son who were the shareholders and directors of the company. In 1964 the company borrowed £15,000 from the defendants, on security of a legal charge which contained a tie covenant by the company to purchase the defendants' petrol exclusively for the period of the loan (18 years) and for a further period thereafter; the charge was irredeemable during the loan period. By November 1968 the company was under pressure from other creditors and the parties entered into negotiations, the plaintiffs receiving independent advice. Reluctantly, but in order to preserve the garage as a sales outlet for its petrol, the defendants agreed a lease and leaseback transaction whereby the garage was leased to the defendants for 51 years in return for the payment to the company of a premium of £35,000 and there was an immediate lease-back to the son and mother for a term of 21 years at a rent of £2,250 per annum. This transaction extinguished the existing charge and it was completed in July 1969. The sublease (the lease-back) could be terminated by either party after seven or 14 years; it contained an absolute prohibition on assignment and tie provisions as to the sale only of the defendants' petrol. The plaintiffs sought – in 1979 – to set aside the lease and leaseback arrangements. *Held,* they could not succeed. Although the doctrine of restraint of trade applied, on the facts the restraint constituted by the lease and sublease was not unreasonable and it was accordingly valid. Further, again on the facts, the defendants' conduct had not been unconscionable or oppressive and, in any case, the plaintiffs' claim in equity was barred by laches. (Applied: *Esso Petroleum Co Ltd v Harper's Garage (Stourport) Ltd*; distinguished: *Lloyds Bank Ltd v Bundy*; but see *Vancouver Malt and Sake Brewing Co Ltd v Vancouver Breweries Ltd*.)

Alexander v Rayson [1936] 1 KB 169 (Court of Appeal)   [14]

Mrs Rayson agreed to take a flat in Piccadilly at a rent of £1,200 pa and this rent was to include the provision of certain services. Mr Alexander, the owner of the flat, sent her two documents, one being a lease of the flat at a rent of £450 and the other was an agreement for the rendering of certain services in consideration of the payment of £750 pa and the services specified in this document were almost identical to those referred to in the earlier agreement. A dispute arose as to whether certain of the services had been carried out and when Mrs Rayson refused to pay an instalment under the service agreement, Mr Alexander brought an action to recover that amount and one quarter's rent payable under the lease which had been tendered but refused. By her defence Mrs Rayson contended that the service agreement was void for illegality as its purpose was to lower the rental value and enable the owners to obtain a reduction in the rateable value which was, in fact, achieved. *Held,* the transaction was fraudulent and Mr Alexander could not enforce either the lease or the service agreement. (See also *Berg v Sadler Moore* and *Miller v Karlinski*; but see *Tinsley v Milligan*.)

Allan (JM) (Merchandising) Ltd v Cloke   [15]
[1963] 2 All ER 258 (Court of Appeal)

The defendants owned a club and hired from the plaintiffs a roulette-wheel, a roulette table and a croupier's rake. Upon the defendants failing to make the second quarterly payment in accordance with the terms of the contract of hire the plaintiffs sued for its recovery, but the defendants maintained that the contract was illegal. It was envisaged by the parties that the equipment hired would be used for the playing of roulette-royale and, although at the time at which the contract was made neither party knew that the game was unlawful, the court found that roulette-royale as it was played to the knowledge of both parties was an unlawful game. *Held,* the contract of hire was illegal and no action lay for the recovery of arrears of rent. 'Where two people together have the common design to use a subject-matter for an unlawful purpose, so that each participates in the unlawful purposes, then that contract is illegal in its formation; and it is no answer for them to say that they did not know the law on the matter' (*per* LORD DENNING MR). (See also *Snell v Unity Finance Ltd*.)

Allcard v Skinner (1887) 36 Ch D 145 (Court of Appeal)   [16]

When Miss Allcard was about 35 years of age she felt a desire to devote her life to good works. She became associated with the Sisters of the Poor and after a few years became a professed member of that sisterhood and bound herself to observe the rules of poverty, chastity and obedience. The rule as to poverty required a member to surrender all her property either to her relatives, the poor or to the sisterhood itself. The rules also provided that no sister should seek advice from anyone outside the order without the consent of the lady superior. Within a few days of becoming a member Miss Allcard made a will bequeathing all her property to Miss Skinner, the lady superior, and in succeeding years made gifts to the value of about £7,000 to the same person. When Miss Allcard left the sisterhood about eight years later she immediately revoked her will but waited a further six years before commencing an action to recover what was left of the money given to Miss Skinner. *Held,* if she had sued to recover the amount of her gifts which had not been expended on the fulfilment of the purposes of the sisterhood at an earlier date she would have succeeded on the ground of undue influence, but as it was her acquiescence rendered her claim barred by laches. (But see *Morley* v *Loughman*.)

Allen v Rescous (1676) 2 Lev 174   [17]

The plaintiff gave the defendant £1 in return for his promise to beat a third person but if he failed to carry out the assault the defendant was to pay the plaintiff £2. The defendant failed to fulfil his mission and the plaintiff sued to recover £2. *Held*, the action must fail as the consideration for the whole contract was illegal and void. (See also *Fores* v *Johnes*.)

Alliance Bank Ltd v Broom (1865) 34 LJ Ch 256   [18]

A bank required security from a customer in respect of an overdrawn account. The customer promised to give certain security but later refused to carry out his promise. *Held*, the court would assume that there was some forbearance to sue on the part of the bank and this was sufficient consideration for the customer's promise to give security. (See also *Horton* v *Horton*.)

Alpenstow Ltd v Regalian Properties plc [1985] 2 All ER 545   [19]

Following negotiations, the plaintiffs wrote to the defendants agreeing that if, following the grant of planning permission, they wished to sell any part of their interest in the property (a) they would give notice to the defendants of their willingness to sell to the defendants at a stated price, (b) within 28 days of the notice the defendants would inform them of their acceptance of the notice, subject to contract, and within seven days thereafter the plaintiffs would submit a draft contract for approval by the defendants and (c) within 28 days of receipt of the draft contract the defendants would approve the contract and exchange contracts within seven days thereafter. The letter concluded by stating that the plaintiffs were awaiting confirmation of acceptance of the agreement set out in the letter. The defendants duly accepted the agreement. Subsequently planning permission was granted and the plaintiffs gave notice of their willingness to sell part of their interest to the defendants. The defendants accepted the contract but, on request for a draft contract as agreed, the plaintiffs contended that the letter setting out the agreement was 'subject to contract' and accordingly was not a binding contract. The defendants sought specific performance of the agreement and registered cautions against the land concerned in order to protect their position. The plaintiffs moved to have the cautions removed, and the question arose as to the effect of the words 'subject to contract' in the circumstances. *Held*, the motion would be dismissed. Although the words 'subject to contract' have a clear prima facie meaning, being in themselves merely conditional, here there was a very strong and exceptional context which would induce the court not to give them that meaning. (But see *A-G of Hong Kong* v *Humphreys Estate (Queen's Gardens) Ltd*.)

Amar Singh v Kulubya See Mistry Amar Singh v Kulubya

Amoco Australia Pty Ltd v Rocca Bros Motor Engineering   [20]
Co Pty Ltd [1975] 1 All ER 968 (Privy Council)

The plaintiffs were refiners and distributors of petrol, and the defendants operated petrol stations. They entered into an agreement whereby the defendants would build a service station on their own land and at their own expense, the plaintiffs to provide the necessary plant and equipment. In return, the defendants granted a lease to the plaintiffs for 15 years at £1 a year, plus 3p a gallon for all petrol delivered by the plaintiffs, who in turn granted an underlease to the defendants at £1 a year for 15 years less one day. Both deeds were executed together, but the lease provided that it was not dependent on any other agreement. In the underlease, the defendants covenanted not to cease carrying on the business of a petrol station during its term, and that they would buy all petrol from the plaintiffs, with a stipulated minimum. Some five years later, the defendants began to remove the plaintiffs' pumps and replace them with others. *Held,* the contract was not severable and, despite the provisions of the lease, the two documents were part of the same transaction. The covenant was in unreasonable restraint of trade. (See also *Esso Petroleum Co Ltd* v *Harper's Garage (Stourport) Ltd.*)

Anderson Ltd v Daniel [1924] 1 KB 138 **[21]**

The parties contracted for the sale and purchase of 10 tons of artificial manure. The plaintiff sued to recover the purchase price and the defendant maintained that he should not succeed as certain statutory requirements as to an invoice stating the contents of the manure had not been complied with. The statute provided that where fertiliser was sold and the seller failed to give an invoice, he should be liable to a penalty. *Held,* the fact that no invoice had been given entitled the defendant to refuse to pay the purchase price as non-compliance with the statutory provision rendered the contract illegal. The object of the statute was not merely to impose a penalty but also to protect the purchasers of fertilisers. (But see *Marles* v *Philip Trant & Sons Ltd.*)

Andrews v Hopkinson [1956] 3 All ER 422 **[22]**

The defendant was a dealer in second-hand cars and his sales manager assured the plaintiff that a 1934 Standard saloon was a 'good little bus' and added: 'I would stake my life on it. You will have no trouble with it.' The plaintiff decided to buy the vehicle and entered into a hire-purchase agreement with a finance company to whom the defendant sold the car. The plaintiff acknowledged in a delivery note that he was satisfied as to the car's condition, but a week later the steering mechanism failed and, as a result, the plaintiff was seriously injured in a collision with a lorry. The defective condition of the steering was of long standing and could have been easily discovered by a competent mechanic. *Held,* the plaintiff was entitled to damages for breach of warranty, including damages for personal injuries, as the words of the defendant's sales manager amounted to a warranty that the car was in good condition and reasonably safe for use on the highway. (See also *Shanklin Pier Ltd* v *Detel Products Ltd.*)

Anglia Television Ltd v Reed **[23]**
[1971] 3 All ER 690 (Court of Appeal)

The plaintiffs decided to make a film for television and engaged Reed as leading actor. Before doing this, the plaintiffs had incurred expenses in employing a director, a designer and others, amounting to £2,750. Later Reed found that he could not take the part and repudiated the contract. Unable to find a substitute, the plaintiffs accepted the repudiation and abandoned the film. They then sued Reed for breach of contract (for which he admitted liability) claiming as part of the damages the wasted expenditure incurred before the contract was made with Reed. *Held,* the plaintiffs were entitled to succeed. 'If the plaintiff claims the wasted expenditure, he is not limited to the expenditure incurred *after* the contract was concluded. He can claim also the expenditure incurred *before* the contract, provided that it was such as would reasonably be in the contemplation of the parties as likely to be wasted if the contract was broken' *(per* LORD DENNING MR). (Distinguished in *C & P Haulage* v *Middleton*; see also *CCC Films (London) Ltd* v *Impact Quadrant Films Ltd.*)

Appleby v Myers (1867) LR 2 CP 651   [24]

The plaintiffs contracted to erect certain machinery on the defendant's premises. When the work was nearly completed the premises and the machinery were destroyed by an accidental fire. The plaintiffs claimed payment in respect of that part of the work which had been carried out. *Held,* their claim would fail as they were not entitled to recover anything until the whole of the work was finished. (See also *Cutter* v *Powell*; but see s1(3) of the Law Reform (Frustrated Contracts) Act 1943.)

Archbolds (Freightage) Ltd v S Spanglett Ltd   [25]
[1961] 1 All ER 417 (Court of Appeal)

The defendants were furniture manufacturers and they had five vans which had 'C' licences, which entitled them to carry only their own goods. However, the defendants contracted with the plaintiffs to transport a consignment of whisky from Leeds to London and, due to the defendants' negligence, the whisky was stolen in transit. The plaintiffs sought to recover damages and it was shown that at all material times they did not know and should not have known that the defendants had only 'C' licences and were therefore not entitled to carry the whisky on their behalf, although this fact was known to the defendants. *Held,* the plaintiffs should succeed. The contract for the carriage of whisky was 'collateral' and not as such prohibited by statute, expressly or by implication, as the statute merely regulated the means by which carriers should carry goods. Further, it was not a rule of law that 'where a contract is on the face of it legal and is not forbidden by statute, but must in fact produce illegality by reason of a circumstance known to one party only, it should be held illegal so as to debar the innocent party from relief' *(per* PEARCE LJ). (See also *St John Shipping Corporation* v *Joseph Rank Ltd*; but see *Allan (JM) (Merchandising) Ltd* v *Cloke* and *Bedford Insurance Co Ltd* v *Instituto de Resseguros do Brasil.*)

Archer v Brown [1984] 2 All ER 267   [26]

Having already sold the share capital in a company several times over to other unsuspecting victims, the defendant sold the shares to the plaintiff for £30,000, the plaintiff borrowing the money from a bank. The plaintiff also entered into a service agreement with the company whereby he was to be joint managing director, with the defendant, at a salary of £16,750 per annum. On discovering the fraud, the plaintiff claimed the return of the £30,000, damages resulting from the defendant's deceit (including bank interest), damages for deceit or breach of contract and exemplary damages. The defendant (who had been convicted and imprisoned) conceded that the plaintiff was entitled to rescission and the return of the £30,000. *Held,* the defendant's concession as to rescission could not deprive the plaintiff of damages in deceit. Even if the plaintiff was restricted to claiming relief for misrepresentation, he was entitled to damages as well as rescission because the misrepresentation was fraudulent; even if it had been innocent, the plaintiff would have been entitled to damages under s2 of the Misrepresentation Act 1967. The plaintiff was also entitled to bank interest (the defendant being aware of the loan and that the plaintiff could not repay it immediately), damages for loss of employment (£2,500) and expenses incurred in seeking new employment (£1,000) and moderate aggravated damages for injured feelings (£500). However, the plaintiff was not entitled to exemplary damages, even if they could be awarded in deceit, because the defendant had already been punished (imprisoned) for his fraud. (See also *Redgrave* v *Hurd*.)

Ardennes (Cargo Owners) v Ardennes (Owners)   [27]
[1950] 2 All ER 517

The defendants orally promised that their ship would proceed direct to London and in reliance upon this promise the plaintiffs agreed to the shipment of 3,000 cases of their mandarines for sale in the London market. The bill of lading provided that the defendants were able to carry the goods to London 'proceeding by any route, and whether directly or indirectly to such port' and were permitted 'to carry the goods beyond their port of destination'. The ship did not sail straight to London but went first to Antwerp and as a result the cargo was delivered later than could have reasonably been expected. The plaintiffs obtained a lower price for their fruit, had to pay a higher import duty and claimed damages for breach of contract in respect of this loss. *Held,* they were entitled to succeed as the bill of lading was not, in itself, the contract between the parties but merely evidence of its terms. The promise to proceed direct to London was part of the contract and the plaintiffs were awarded damages for breach of this provision. (See also *De Lassalle* v *Guildford*; but see *Pilkington* v *Wood*.)

Ashbury Railway Carriage and Iron Co v Riche   [28]
(1875) LR 7 HL 653 (House of Lords)

The memorandum of association of the appellant company stated that its objects were 'to make, and sell, or lend on hire, railway carriages and waggons, and all kinds of railway plant, fittings, machinery, and rolling-stock; to carry on the business of mechanical engineers and general contractors; to purchase, lease, work, and sell mines, minerals, land, and buildings; to purchase and sell, as merchants, timber, coal, metals, or other materials, and to buy and sell any such materials on commission or as agents'. The directors of the appellant company agreed to purchase a concession for making a railway in Belgium and afterwards contracted to assign the concession to a company formed in that country. *Held,* such an agreement was ultra vires and void as it was of a nature not included in the memorandum of association and as such could not be ratified even by the whole body of shareholders. (But see ss35, 35A and 35B of the Companies Act 1985.)

Ashmore, Benson, Pease & Co v Dawson   [29]
[1973] 2 All ER 856 (Court of Appeal)

The defendants agreed to carry a load for the plaintiffs. As the plaintiffs' transport manager watched, the defendants overloaded their lorries in breach of statutory regulations. One of the lorries toppled over, and the vehicle and its load were damaged. The plaintiffs claimed damages. *Held,* although the contract was lawful in its inception, it was illegal in its execution to the knowledge of the plaintiffs. Damages were not, therefore, recoverable. (See also *Allan (JM) Merchandising Ltd* v *Cloke*.)

Associated Distributors Ltd v Hall and Hall   [30]
[1938] 1 All ER 511 (Court of Appeal)

A hire-purchase agreement in respect of a tandem bicycle made provision for its determination by the hirer and, in the event of the hirer's default, by the owner.

Clause 7 of the agreement stipulated that in the event of its determination for any cause whatsoever there would be payable by the hirer 'by way of compensation for depreciation ... such sums as with the amount previously paid for rent shall make up a sum equivalent to not less than one-half of the total amount'. The hirer elected to terminate the hiring and the court was asked to decide whether the sum which the owners claimed under clause 7 was liquidated damages or a penalty. *Held,* the hirer had exercised an option on the terms of clause 7 and the question whether sums payable under that clause constituted liquidated damages or a penalty did not arise. It followed that the hirer had to pay the amount which he had made himself liable to pay under that clause. (But see *Cooden Engineering Co Ltd* v *Stanford.*)

Associated Japanese Bank (International) Ltd v Crédit [31] du Nord SA [1988] 3 All ER 902

Under a sale and leaseback transaction, the plaintiffs bought four machines from Bennett for £1,021,000 and leased them back to him, Bennett's obligations being guaranteed by the defendants. Bennett defaulted and it was found that the machines did not exist. Following Bennett's bankruptcy, the plaintiffs sued the defendants on their guarantee. *Held,* the plaintiffs' claim would fail as, inter alia, the guarantee contained an implied condition precedent that the lease related to existing machines. (See also *Moorcock, The*). STEYN J added: 'For both parties the guarantee of obligations under a lease with non-existent machines was essentially different from a guarantee of a lease with four machines which both parties at the time of the contract believed to exist ... the stringent test of common law mistake is satisfied; the guarantee is void ab initio.' (But see *Bell* v *Lever Brothers Ltd.*)

Atlantic Baron, The See North Ocean Shipping Co Ltd v Hyundi

Atlas Express Ltd v Kafco (Importers and Distributors) Ltd [32] [1989] 1 All ER 641

The defendants had entered into an agreement to supply their imported basketware to Woolworth shops and they contracted with the plaintiffs for the deliveries. Before this contract was concluded, the plaintiffs' depot manager had seen a sample of the defendants' goods at their warehouse and calculated the price (£1.10 a carton) on the basis of transporting a minimum of 400 cartons on each trailer. In the event, the first load contained only 200 cartons, so the plaintiffs' manager told the defendants that they could not carry any more cartons unless the defendants agreed to pay a minimum price of £440 a load. As they were heavily dependent on the Woolworth contract and unable at that time to find another carrier, the defendants agreed but later refused to pay the new rate. *Held,* the plaintiffs' claim to recover the amount owing according to the new rate would be dismissed as the defendants' apparent consent to the new terms was vitiated by economic duress. In any case, there was no consideration for the new agreement. (See also *Barton* v *Armstrong*; but see *Pao On* v *Lau Yiu Long.*)

A-G v Barker [1990] 3 All ER 257 (Court of Appeal) [33]

A person employed in the royal household had given a contractual undertaking, on a perpetual and worldwide basis, not to disclose information obtained there. He proposed to write a book about his royal household service: the Attorney-General sought an interlocutory injunction. *Held,* the injunction would be granted. The covenant was not void on any ground of public policy and the balance of justice required an interlocutory injunction having extra-territorial effect.

A-G of Hong Kong v Humphreys Estate (Queen's Gardens)   [34]
Ltd [1987] 2 All ER 387 (Privy Council)

The appellants and a group including the respondents agreed in principle but subject to contract that the government would grant the group a Crown lease for development in exchange for 83 of the group's flats. The government took possession of the flats and fitted them out; senior civil servants moved in and the government disposed of their previous residences. For its part, the group paid the government the agreed difference in value between the flats and the Crown property, but before the contract was executed the group purported to withdraw and terminate the government's right to occupy the flats. The appellants maintained that the respondents were estopped from withdrawing from the transaction. *Held,* this was not the case. In order to succeed, the appellants had to show not only that they had acted to their detriment, but also that the group had created and encouraged a belief or expectation that they would not withdraw and that the government had relied on that belief or expectation: on the facts, the group had not encouraged or allowed such a belief or expectation. '... the government acted in the hope that a voluntary agreement in principle expressly made "subject to contract" and therefore not binding would eventually be followed by the achievement of legal relationships in the form of grants and transfers of property. It is possible but unlikely that in circumstances at present unforeseeable a party to negotiations set out in a document expressed to be "subject to contract" would be able to satisfy the court that the parties had subsequently agreed to convert the document into a contract or that some form of estoppel had arisen to prevent both parties from refusing to proceed with the transactions envisaged by the document. But in the present case the government chose to begin and elected to continue on terms that either party might suffer a change of mind and withdraw' (*per* LORD TEMPLEMAN). (See also *Cohen* v *Nessdale Ltd.*)

Attwood v Lamont [1920] 3 KB 571 (Court of Appeal)   [35]

The plaintiff, who was a draper, tailor and general outfitter at Kidderminster, employed the defendant as a cutter and head of the tailoring department. The defendant's contract of employment contained a covenant that he would not engage in 'the trade or business of a tailor, dressmaker, general draper, milliner, hatter, haberdasher, gentlemen's, ladies' or children's outfitter at any place within a radius of 10 miles of the [plaintiff's] place of business' at Kidderminster. This restraint referred to business carried on in other departments of the plaintiff's business with which the defendant was not concerned. The defendant subsequently set up business as a tailor at Worcester, which is more than 10 miles from Kidderminster, but he did business with several of the plaintiff's customers and took orders in Kidderminster. The plaintiff sought an injunction to restrain this activity and the defendant maintained that the agreement upon which the plaintiff relied was invalid as it was in restraint of trade and too wide in its terms to be reasonable. The plaintiff argued that the covenant relating to business as a tailor should be severed from the rest and enforced because it was reasonable. *Held,* the provisions formed a single covenant for the protection of the plaintiff's entire business and not several covenants for the protection of his several businesses and therefore could not be severed. The plaintiff was not entitled to an injunction. (But see *Putsman* v *Taylor*; see also *Petrofina (Great Britain) Ltd* v *Martin.*)

Attwood v Small (1838) 6 Cl & Fin 232 (House of Lords)   [36]

The appellant negotiated with the respondents for the sale of certain mines and iron works. The respondents asked questions as to the capabilities of the property and the appellant's answers were verified on inspection by persons appointed by the respondents. Six months after the sale was completed the respondents discovered that the statements had been inaccurate and sought to rescind the contract on the grounds of misrepresentation. *Held,* their action must fail as the respondents had not relied upon the appellant's statements, but tested their accuracy, and after having knowledge, or the means of knowledge, declared that they were satisfied that the statements were correct. (See also *Jennings* v *Broughton.*)

Australian Hardwoods Pty Ltd v Commissioner for Railways [1961] 1 All ER 737 (Privy Council) [37]

The appellant company was engaged in the timber business and the respondents held an occupation permit which entitled them to occupy certain lands and to operate a sawmill. The parties entered into an agreement under which, inter alia, the appellants were to take over the sawmill and sell sleepers to the respondents at a fixed price. The agreement was to run for ten years, subject to determination on three months' notice by either side if there had been a breach on the other side of 'any clause or provision of this agreement'. The appellants defaulted and the respondents gave notice of termination, but the appellants sought specific performance of certain terms of the agreement containing an option to purchase which they had purported to exercise after the giving of notice of termination by the respondents. *Held,* their claim would fail. 'A plaintiff who asks the courts to enforce by mandatory order in his favour some stipulations of an agreement which itself consists of interdependent undertakings between the plaintiff and the defendant cannot succeed in obtaining such relief if he is at the time in breach of his own obligations ... Secondly, where the agreement is one which involves continuing or future acts to be performed by the plaintiff, he must fail unless he can show that he is ready and willing on his part to carry out those obligations, which are in fact part of the consideration for the undertaking of the defendant that the plaintiff seeks to have enforced. Here, the appellant could never show that it was ready and willing to perform its share of the agreement ... ; for its breaches had brought on it the notice of determination which precluded it for good from doing anything more in furtherance of that agreement' *(per* LORD RADCLIFFE).

Avon Finance Co Ltd v Bridger [1985] 2 All ER 281 (Court of Appeal) [38]

An elderly couple purchased a house for their retirement, the arrangements being undertaken by their son. Part of the money was to be provided by the son and, in order to raise it and without telling his parents, he obtained a loan from the plaintiff finance company on the security of the house, the son undertaking to procure the execution by his parents of the legal charge. This he did by telling his parents that the documents they were signing were connected with a building society mortgage which was the principal means of financing the purchase. The son's payments fell into arrears and the plaintiffs sought possession of the house. *Held,* their action could not succeed. Although the parents could not rely on non est factum as they had not exercised reasonable care in signing the charge (applied in *Saunders* v *Anglia Building Society),* the transaction was voidable in equity as the plaintiffs had appointed the son to procure the security, they should have been aware that the son would exercise influence over his parents and they (the parents) had not received independent legal advice. (Applied: *Lloyds Bank Ltd* v *Bundy*; distinguished in *Bank of Baroda* v *Shah*; approved in *Barclays Bank plc* v *O'Brien.*)

Bainbridge v Firmstone (1838) 8 Ad & El 743 **[39]**

The plaintiff gave the defendant permission to weigh two of his boilers and the defendant promised that 'he would, within a reasonable time... leave and give up the boilers in as perfect and complete a condition' as when he borrowed them. The defendant broke his promise and when sued for breach of contract maintained that there was no consideration to support it. *Held*, he was liable, as the consideration could be found in the benefit which the defendant derived and the detriment which the plaintiff suffered in parting with possession of the boilers. (See also *Coggs* v *Bernard*.)

Baldry v Marshall [1925] 1 KB 260 (Court of Appeal) **[40]**

The plaintiff asked the defendant motor dealers for a car 'suitable for touring purposes'. The defendants recommended a 'Bugatti', which the plaintiff ordered. The car was unsuitable for touring, and the plaintiff claimed to reject it and recover the price. The written contract contained a clause excluding 'guarantees or warranties, statutory or otherwise'. *Held,* the stipulation as to suitability was a condition, not a guarantee or warranty, and was not therefore excluded. (See also s14 of the Sale of Goods Act 1979, as amended.)

Balfour v Balfour [1919] 2 KB 571 (Court of Appeal) **[41]**

The defendant, who was about to go abroad, promised to pay his wife £30 per month in consideration of her agreeing to support herself without calling on him for any further maintenance. The wife contended that the defendant was bound by this promise. *Held,* there was no legally binding contract between the parties as it was an ordinary domestic arrangement which was not intended to create legal relations. (See also *Spellman* v *Spellman*.)

Ballett v Mingay [1943] 1 All ER 143 (Court of Appeal) **[42]**

The appellant, a minor, borrowed an amplifier and microphone from the respondent but failed to return the goods as he himself had parted with possession of them. The respondent brought an action in detinue. *Held,* the respondent should succeed as the parting with possession of the goods by the appellant was outside the purview or contemplation of the bailment. (But see *Johnson* v *Pye*.)

Bank Line Ltd v Arthur Capel & Co [1919] AC 435 **[43]**
(House of Lords)

The parties entered into an agreement by which the defendants agreed to let a steamer to the plaintiffs for a period of 12 months. The ship was requisitioned by the government before it was delivered and the plaintiffs claimed damages for non-delivery. *Held,* the plaintiffs would not succeed as the requisitioning had destroyed the character of the chartered service, the charter had therefore been frustrated and the letting was at an end. (But see *Maritime National Fish Ltd* v *Ocean Trawlers Ltd* and *Finelvet AG* v *Vinava Shipping Co Ltd, The Chrysalis*.)

Bank of Baroda v Shah [1988] 3 All ER 24 (Court of Appeal) **[44]**

By a legal charge in favour of the plaintiff bank the defendants charged their property with the payment to the plaintiffs of all moneys at any time owed to the plaintiffs by Seasonworth Ltd. The defendants took this step as the result of misrepresentation and undue influence exerted by the second defendant's brother, a director of Seasonworth, whose solicitors acted for the defendants in connection with the charge although they (the defendants) had not instructed them to do so. Seasonworth having defaulted, the bank sought possession of the defendants' property. *Held,* they were entitled to succeed. There was no legal obligation on the bank to ensure that the defendants received entirely independent advice before executing the charge and the bank was not infected with the brother's conduct or the solicitors' misrepresentation to the bank that they had authority to act for the defendants. (Followed: *Coldunell Ltd* v *Gallon*; distinguished: *Avon Finance Co Ltd* v *Bridger.*)

Bannerman v White (1861) 10 CB (NS) 844   **[45]**

The parties negotiated for the sale of hops and previously to this the defendants had made it known that they did not wish to buy hops to which sulphur had been applied. When samples were produced the defendants inquired as to whether any sulphur had been used and they were assured that it had not. It appeared that five acres of the crop out of a total of 300 acres had been sulphured and the defendants repudiated the contract. *Held,* the plaintiff's statement that the hops had not been treated with sulphur entitled the defendants to repudiate the contract. (But see *Heilbut, Symons & Co* v *Buckleton.*)

Barber v NWS Bank plc [1996] 1 All ER 906 (Court of Appeal)   **[46]**

In October 1989 the plaintiff decided to buy a car apparently owned by a garage. The garage sold the car to the defendant bank which then agreed to sell the vehicle to the plaintiff under a conditional sale agreement. Until the plaintiff had completed the agreed payments, the car was to remain vested in the defendants. The plaintiff paid the agreed instalments until May 1991. He then decided to sell the car, only to find that it was subject to a prior finance agreement on which there were moneys outstanding. *Held,* in view of the provision in the agreement that the car was to remain vested in the defendants until all payments under the agreement had been made, it was an express condition, fundamental to the transaction, that the defendants were, at the date of the agreement, owners of the car. Since this was not the case, the plaintiff was entitled to rescind the agreement and recover all the moneys (ie, his deposit and instalments) which he had paid under it. (But see *Hong Kong Fir Shipping Co Ltd* v *Kawasaki Kisen Kaisha Ltd.*)

Barclays Bank plc v Fairclough Building Ltd   **[47]**
[1995] 1 All ER 289 (Court of Appeal)

The defendant contractors were in breach of certain of their obligations under a standard form of building contract. The trial judge found that the plaintiff employers were guilty of contributory negligence in failing to supervise the manner in which the defendants executed the work and reduced the plaintiffs' damages by 40 per cent. The plaintiffs appealed against this decision. *Held,* the appeal would be allowed since the provisions of the Law Reform (Contributory Negligence) Act 1945 do not entitle a defendant to raise in his defence contributory negligence by the plaintiff where – as here – liability arose from breach of a contractual provision which does not depend on a failure to take reasonable care. 'It ought to be a cause of general concern that the law should have got into such a state that a contractor who is in breach of two of the main obligations expressly undertaken by him in a standard form building contract was able to persuade the judge in the court below that the building owner's damages should be reduced by 40 per cent because of his own negligence in not preventing the contractor from committing the breaches. In circumstances such as these, release, waiver, forbearance or the like are the only defences available to a party to a contract who wishes to assert that the other party's right to recover damages for its breach has been lost or diminished' (*per* NOURSE LJ). (But see *Forsikringsaktieselskapet Vesta* v *Butcher.*)

Barclays Bank plc v O'Brien [1994] 1 AC 180   [48]
(House of Lords)

A company in which Mr O'Brien, an accountant, held shares was granted an overdraft facility by the plaintiff bank. By way of security, Mr O'Brien guaranteed the company's indebtedness and his liability under the guarantee was secured by a second charge on Mr and Mrs O'Brien's matrimonial home which was jointly owned by them. Although the bank manager gave instructions that Mr and Mrs O'Brien should be made fully aware of the effect of the relevant documents and that they should seek independent legal advice if they had any doubts, these instructions were not carried out by the staff who dealt with the matter. The bank sought to enforce the guarantee and to obtain possession of the matrimonial home. It was found that Mr O'Brien had falsely represented to his wife the effect of the charge. *Held*, Mrs O'Brien was entitled to set aside the charge. 'I can ... summarise my views as follows. Where one cohabitee has entered into an obligation to stand as surety for the debts of the other cohabitee and the creditor is aware that they are cohabitees: (1) the surety obligation will be valid and enforceable by the creditor unless the suretyship was procured by the undue influence, misrepresentation or other legal wrong of the principal debtor; (2) if there has been undue influence, misrepresentation or other legal wrong by the principal debtor, unless the creditor has taken reasonable steps to satisfy himself that the surety entered into the obligation freely and in knowledge of the true facts, the creditor will be unable to enforce the surety obligation because he will be fixed with constructive notice of the surety's right to set aside the transaction; (3) unless there are special exceptional circumstances, a creditor will have taken such reasonable steps to avoid being fixed with constructive notice if the creditor warns the surety (at a meeting not attended by the principal debtor) of the amount of her potential liability and of the risks involved and advises the surety to take independent legal advice ... Applying those principles to this case, ... the bank (having failed to take reasonable steps) is fixed with constructive notice of the wrongful misrpresentation made by Mr O'Brien to Mrs O'Brien. Mrs O'Brien is therefore entitled as against the bank to set aside the legal charge on the matrimonial home securing her husband's liability to the bank' (*per* LORD BROWNE-WILKINSON). (Approved: *Avon Finance Co Ltd* v *Bridger*; see also *Credit Lyonnais Bank Nederland NV* v *Burch*; but see *CIBC Mortgages plc* v *Pitt.*)

Barton v Armstrong [1975] 2 All ER 465 (Privy Council)   [49]

A and B were major shareholders in a company. B signed a deed agreeing to buy A's shares on terms set out. B later claimed that the agreement was void on the *Duress* grounds that he had been coerced into signing by threats made by A. It was found as a fact that the threats were made, but that the main reason for the contract was commercial necessity. *Held*, B's action should succeed. It was for A to show that the threats made to B contributed nothing to his decision to sign. In the circumstances the proper inference was that duress had played a part. (See also *Atlas Express Ltd* v *Kafco (Importers and Distributors) Ltd.*)

Basildon District Council v J E Lesser (Properties) Ltd   [50]
[1985] 1 All ER 20

The first defendants, system builders, submitted a tender, including design drawings, to complete site works and sub-structures of some dwellings for the plaintiffs, subject, amongst other things, to the completion of a formal contract; the standard-term contract was concluded after further exchanges between the parties. Subsequently, defects developed in some of the buildings, necessitating repairs, and the plaintiffs sued, inter alia, for damages. *Held,* they were entitled to succeed. It was an implied term that the buildings would be fit for habitation, not least because the plaintiffs had relied on the expertise of the first defendants, as system builders, to produce habitable dwellings. Even if this term had not been implied, there would have been implied the lesser term that the first defendants were to design the buildings with the skill and care to be expected of system builders. (Distinguished: *Lynch* v *Thorne.*)

Batty v Metropolitan Property Realisations Ltd   [51]
[1978] 2 All ER 445 (Court of Appeal)

The plaintiffs purchased a newly built leasehold house from the first defendants, a development company. The house had been built by the second defendants. The house was built on a steep hillside which subsequently proved wholly unsuitable for building. The plaintiffs claimed against the development company in tort for negligence and for breach of contract and against the builders for negligence. They also claimed against the local authority for negligence or breach of statutory duty in respect of the council's duty to inspect the foundations. *Held,* the defects lay not in the construction of the house, but in the nature of the land on which it was built. The fault could have been detected by experts and the development company was therefore liable for breach of the contractual warranty that the house was fit for habitation. Additionally, they were liable in tort for failing properly to inspect the site before taking the decision to build. The builders were also held liable in tort, but the local authority was not liable. (See also *Esso Petroleum Co Ltd* v *Mardon.*)

Beale v Taylor [1967] 3 All ER 253 (Court of Appeal)   [52]

The defendant advertised a car for sale as a 'Herald convertible, white, 1961, twin carbs.' The plaintiff answered the advertisement, went to the defendant's home, and having inspected the car there, bought it. In fact, though neither realised it at the time, the rear half of the car was from a 1961 Herald convertible, and the front half from an earlier model, the two halves having been welded together. No one could see from an ordinary examination of the car that it was anything other than the defendant had advertised it as being. On discovering the true position, the plaintiff bought an action against the defendant for damages under s13 of the Sale of Goods Act 1893 for breach of condition. The defendant contended that the plaintiff had seen the car before buying it and had then bought it on his own assessment of its value. *Held,* the plaintiff was entitled to damages because, although the description of the car was not false to the knowledge of either party, yet fundamentally the seller was selling a car of the description advertised. (See also *Nicholson and Venn* v *Smith Marriott.*)

Beaumont v Reeve (1846) 8 QB 483   [53]

The defendant seduced the plaintiff and induced her to live with him for five years as his mistress. The plaintiff alleged that she had suffered great injury to her character and reputation and had been deprived of the means of earning an honest living and in consideration of this and by way of compensation the defendant promised to pay the plaintiff an annuity of £60. The plaintiff did not receive any money and she sued for breach of contract. *Held,* the defendant's promise could not be enforced as the consideration was moral and not legal and it was also past. (See also *Benyon* v *Nettlefold.*)

Bedford Insurance Co Ltd v Instituto de Resseguros do [54] Brasil [1984] 3 All ER 766

The plaintiffs, a Hong Kong insurance company, authorised London brokers to act as their agents up to a specified limit and neither the plaintiffs nor the brokers were authorised, as required by statute, to carry on business in marine insurance. It was an offence to carry on insurance business in contravention of the relevant Act of Parliament. Contracts of marine insurance were written by the brokers on the plaintiffs' behalf and reinsured with the defendants. Claims having been settled by the plaintiffs, they sought an indemnity from the defendants. *Held,* their action could not succeed. The contracts written by the brokers were illegal and void ab initio and they could not therefore form the basis of a reinsurance contract with the defendants. (But see *Archbolds (Freightage) Ltd v S Spanglett Ltd.*)

Behn v Burness (1863) 3 B & S 751 [55]

It was agreed that the plaintiff's ship, 'then in the port of Amsterdam, and being tight, staunch, strong and every way fitted and ready for the voyage, should, with all possible dispatch proceed to Newport, Monmouthshire, and the defendant should there load her with a full cargo of coals, which she should carry to Hong Kong'. In fact the ship concerned was not in Amsterdam at the date of the contract but was four days' sail away. The defendant refused to load the cargo of coals. *Held,* he was entitled to do so as the words 'now in the port of Amsterdam' amounted to a condition precedent, the breach of which entitled the defendant to repudiate the contract. (See also *Bentsen v Taylor, Sons & Co.*)

Behzadi v Shaftesbury Hotels Ltd [56] [1991] 2 All ER 477 (Court of Appeal)

The defendants contracted with the plaintiff for the sale to her of their hotel business, but they were unable to deliver the abstract of title by the contract date because of difficulties with the Land Registry. The plaintiff's solicitors gave the defendants' solicitors notice making time of the essence and requiring title to be deduced within seven days, failing which the contract would be rescinded. The defendants' solicitors were unable to comply and the plaintiff sought a declaration that she had been entitled to rescind the contract and was entitled to the return of her deposit. *Held,* the plaintiff's summons had properly been dismissed. Although she had not had to wait until there had been an unreasonable delay before serving a notice making time of the essence, she had to allow a reasonable time for the performance of the outstanding obligation and, in all the circumstances, this she had failed to do. (See also *British and Commonwealth Holdings plc v Quadrex Holdings Inc*; but see *Rickards (Charles) Ltd v Oppenheim.*)

Bell v Lever Brothers Ltd [1932] AC 161 (House of Lords) [57]

The appellant was employed for a fixed term as chairman of a company in which the respondents had a controlling interest. When this contract of employment still had a substantial time to run, owing to the amalgamation of the company of which the appellant was chairman, which meant that the appellant's services were no longer required, the respondents agreed to the payment of a certain sum to the appellant by way of compensation and this amount was actually paid. It afterwards appeared that during the course of his employment the appellant had made certain speculative deals in cocoa on his own account which would have entitled the respondents to dismiss him summarily without the payment of compensation, although at the time that the settlement was negotiated neither of the parties applied their minds to this possibility. The respondents contended that they had paid the compensation on the mistaken belief that they were legally bound to do so and sought to recover the amount which the appellant had actually received. *Held,* the mistake in question was not one which would entitle the respondents to recover the amount of compensation paid to the appellant. (But see *Strickland* v *Turner, Sybron Corpn* v *Rochem Ltd* and *Associated Japanese Bank (International) Ltd* v *Crédit du Nord SA.*)

Belvoir Finance Co Ltd v Stapleton [58]
[1970] 3 All ER 664 (Court of Appeal)

The plaintiffs bought cars from dealers and, by a separate contract, let them on hire-purchase to X Ltd who took delivery direct from the dealers. The hire-purchase contracts were illegal because they contravened statutory regulations. The contracts with the dealers were also tainted with illegality because the dealers knew of the illegal arrangement. Stapleton, as agent of X Ltd, sold the cars to third parties without the plaintiffs' consent. X Ltd went into liquidation and the plaintiffs sued Stapleton for conversion. *Held,* property transferred by one person to another, in pursuance of a conspiracy to effect an illegal purpose, remains vested in the transferee, despite its illegal origin. Therefore, although the plaintiffs had obtained the cars under illegal contracts, as the contracts had been executed and the property in the cars had passed to the plaintiffs, they were able to claim against the defendant who, as X Ltd's agent, was liable to them in conversion. (See also *Bowmakers Ltd* v *Barnet Instruments Ltd* and *Sajan Singh* v *Sardara Ali.*)

Bentley (Dick) Productions Ltd v Harold Smith [59]
(Motors) Ltd [1965] 2 All ER 65 (Court of Appeal)

The plaintiff told the defendant dealer that he was on the look-out for a well vetted Bentley car and the defendant truthfully assured the plaintiff that he (the defendant) was in a position to find out the history of cars. Later, the defendant informed the plaintiff that he had just purchased 'one of the nicest cars we have had in for quite a long time', that it had been fitted with a replacement engine and gearbox and (falsely but not fraudulently) that it had done twenty thousand miles only since it had been so fitted (the speedometer read twenty thousand miles). The plaintiff purchased the car for £1,850 but it was a considerable disappointment to him and he brought an action for breach of warranty. *Held,* he was entitled to succeed as the inference that the representation was intended as a warranty had not been rebutted. 'If a representation is made in the course of dealings for a contract for the very purpose of inducing the other party to act on it, and it actually induces him to act on it by entering into the contract, that is prima facie ground for inferring that the representation was intended as a warranty ... But the maker of the representation can rebut this inference if he can show that it really was an innocent misrepresentation, in that he was in fact innocent of fault in making it, and that it would not be reasonable in the circumstances for him to be bound by it' (*per* LORD DENNING MR). (See also *Esso Petroleum Co Ltd* v *Mardon*; but see *Hopkins* v *Tanqueray.*)

Bentsen v Taylor, Sons & Co [1893] 2 QB 274 [60]
(Court of Appeal)

A charterparty described a certain ship as 'now sailed or about to sail from a pitch pine port to the United Kingdom'. In fact the ship did not sail until nearly one month after the date of the charterparty. *Held,* the description of the ship as 'now sailed or about to sail' was of substance to the contract. It was a condition precedent and not a mere warranty and the charterers would have been entitled to repudiate the contract. (See also *Behn* v *Burness* and *Cie Commerciale Sucres et Denrées* v *C Czarnikow Ltd, The Naxos.)*

Benyon v Nettlefold (1850) 3 Mac & G 94   **[61]**

A man covenanted to pay Miss Caroline Nettlefold an annuity of £200 pa. On the face of it, the deed was valid but it afterwards appeared that the real consideration for the promise was an agreement between the man and Miss Nettlefold that they should thereafter live together as man and wife. Miss Nettlefold sued to enforce payment of the annuity. *Held,* she would not succeed as the contract upon which she based her claim was founded upon an immoral consideration. (But see *Nye* v *Moseley.)*

Berg v Sadler and Moore [1937] 1 All ER 637   **[62]**
(Court of Appeal)

The parties had entered into a price-maintenance agreement with the Tobacco Trade Association. The plaintiff was found to have broken the terms of the agreement and as a 'cut-price retailer' was placed on the stop list which meant that he would not be supplied with goods by members of the Association. The plaintiff persuaded another member of the Association to obtain goods on his behalf from the defendants. The plaintiff paid the defendants £72 19s for 39,500 cigarettes through the good offices of the third member but the defendants became suspicious and refused to supply the goods or refund the amount paid. The plaintiff claimed the return of the money. *Held,* the plaintiff's claim would fail as he had attempted to obtain the cigarettes by false pretences, an illegal act. (See also *Bigos* v *Bousted* and *St John Shipping Corpn* v *Joseph Rank Ltd.)*

Bernstein v Pamson Motors (Golders Green) Ltd   **[63]**
[1987] 2 All ER 220

The plaintiff bought a new Nissan Laurel from the defendants: three weeks and 140 miles later its camshaft seized up on a motorway. Next day the plaintiff purported to reject the car on the ground that it was not of merchantable quality within s14 of the Sale of Goods Act 1979. The car was repaired under warranty at no cost to the plaintiff, but he refused to have it back. He argued that he was entitled to recover damages and to rescind the contract of sale. *Held,* the car had not been of merchantable quality within s14(6) of the 1979 Act but, on the facts and in the light of s35(1) of the 1979 Act, he had lost the right to reject it. Consequently, he was entitled only to damages for, inter alia, five days' loss of use of the car. (But see *Rogers* v *Parish (Scarborough) Ltd;* see now s14 of the 1979 Act, as amended.)

Berry v Berry [1929] 2 KB 316   **[64]**

By a deed of separation a husband agreed to pay his wife a certain allowance. The parties purported to vary the terms of the deed by an agreement in writing. *Held,* the written variation would be enforced. (But see *Goss* v *Lord Nugent.)*

Bessler, Waechter, Glover & Co v South Derwent Coal   **[65]**
Co Ltd [1937] 4 All ER 552

There was a written agreement for the delivery of 70,000 tons of coal over a certain period. At that time statute required such a contract to be in writing but the parties orally agreed that the date on which the coal was to be delivered should be put forward. *Held,* this oral provision was binding as it did not constitute a variation of the contract but a mere voluntary forbearance to insist on delivery or acceptance and as such did not need to be in writing. (But see *Morris* v *Baron & Co.*)

Beswick v Beswick [1967] 2 All ER 1197 (House of Lords)   [66]

By a written agreement P.B. assigned his business as a coal merchant to his nephew, J.B. In consideration, J.B. agreed to employ P.B. as a consultant at £6 10s 0d a week for the rest of his life, and further to pay P.B.'s wife an annuity of £5 a week for her life, after P.B.'s death. P.B.'s wife was not a party to the contract. After P.B.'s death, J.B. paid one sum of £5 to the widow, but refused to pay any more. The widow sought an order for specific performance of the agreement in her capacity as administratrix of her husband's estate and in her personal capacity. *Held,* the widow as administratrix was entitled to enforce the agreement by an order for specific performance in her own personal favour. However, the House of Lords rejected the argument that s56 of the Law of Property Act 1925 applied to such an agreement, and hence the widow would be unable to enforce the agreement in her personal capacity. (See also *Smith and Snipes Hall Farm Ltd* v *River Douglas Catchment Board.*)

Bettini v Gye (1876) 1 QBD 183   [67]

The plaintiff entered into a contract to sing for the defendant for a certain period and at a fixed salary and agreed to be in London six days before the commencement of his engagement for the purpose of rehearsal. In fact, due to illness, he arrived four days later than he had promised and the defendant refused to proceed with the engagement. *Held,* the provision as to rehearsal was not a condition precedent as it did not go to the root of the matter and for this reason the defendant was not entitled to avoid the contract. (But see *Poussard* v *Spiers & Pond.*)

Bigg v Boyd Gibbins Ltd [1971] 2 All ER 183   [68]
(Court of Appeal)

The parties were negotiating for the sale of some freehold property belonging to the plaintiffs. The plaintiffs wrote to the defendants stating: 'As you are aware that I paid £25,000 for this property, your offer of £20,000 would appear to be at least a little optimistic. For a quick sale I would accept £26,000 ...' The defendants replied: 'I accept your offer' and asked the plaintiffs to contact the defendants' solicitors. In their final letter the plaintiffs said: 'I am putting the matter in the hands of my solicitors. My wife and I are both pleased that you are purchasing the property.' The plaint alleged that this exchange of correspondence constituted an agreement for the sale of property and sought specific performance. *Held,* although an agreement on price did not necessarily mean an agreement for sale and purchase, nor did the use of the word 'offer' always amount to an offer in law, on the facts it was clear from the terms of correspondence that the plaintiffs' first letter constituted an offer the acceptance of which by the defendants constituted a binding agreement. Specific performance would be granted. (But see *Harvey* v *Facey* and *Clifton* v *Palumbo,* both of which were distinguished, and s2 of the Law of Property (Miscellaneous Provisions) Act 1989.)

Bigos v Bousted [1951] 1 All ER 92   [69]

Bousted's young daughter suffered from pleurisy and he was advised to send her abroad before the winter. Owing to currency restrictions his daughter's allowance was restricted to £40, which was quite inadequate, and he entered into an oral agreement with Mrs Bigos whereby she would make available £150 in Italian money for the use of Bousted's daughter and Bousted agreed to repay this amount in English currency in England. Bousted deposited a share certificate with Mrs Bigos as security for the repayment of the £150. Both parties knew that the agreement was unlawful. Mrs Bigos failed to make the promised £150 available in Italy and Bousted claimed the return of the share certificate. *Held,* the claim would fail as the agreement providing for the deposit of the share certificate was tainted with illegality. This was not a case where the agreement had not been performed because of the repentance of the party seeking to enforce it. (See also *Boissevain* v *Weil* and *Miller* v *Karlinski*; but see *Taylor* v *Bowers.*)

Bisset v Wilkinson [1927] AC 177 (Privy Council)   [70]

The appellant sought to recover the purchase money under an agreement for the sale of certain land but the respondents claimed to be entitled to rescind the contract on the ground of misrepresentation. It was shown that the appellant had stated that it was his belief that the land in question would carry 2,000 sheep if properly worked but in fact it had never been able to support that number. *Held,* the contract would not be rescinded on the ground of misrepresentation as the statement as to the carrying capacity of the land was merely an opinion which the appellant honestly entertained. (But see *Smith* v *Land and House Property Corporation.*)

Blackpool and Fylde Aero Club Ltd v Blackpool Borough   [71]
Council [1990] 3 All ER 25 (Court of Appeal)

Having been granted the concession to operate pleasure flights from Blackpool airport on the three previous occasions, the plaintiffs were one of seven parties invited by the defendants, the owners of the airport, to tender in common form for the next concession. Tenders had to be received by 12 noon on 17 March. The plaintiffs' tender was put in the Town Hall letter box at 11 am on that day but, as the box was not cleared by the defendants' staff (as it was supposed to be) at noon, the plaintiffs' tender was not considered. The plaintiffs claimed damages for breach of contract. *Held,* their action would be successful as, in all the circumstances, it was to be implied that if an invitee submitted a conforming tender before the deadline he had a contractual right to have his tender considered. '... the council's invitation to tender was ... an offer [to consider] and the club's submission of a timely and conforming tender an acceptance' (*per* BINGHAM LJ). (But see *Spencer* v *Harding.*)

Boast v Firth (1868) LR 4 CP 1   [72]

An apprentice chemist and druggist was bound to his master by the terms of the apprenticeship deed for a period of five years. Before his apprenticeship was completed the apprentice contracted a permanent illness which prevented him from doing his work and his master claimed damages to compensate him for the loss of his services. *Held,* the master's action would fail as the illness, an act of God, was a sufficient excuse for the non-performance of the contract. (See also *Poussard* v *Spiers & Pond.*)

Boissevain v Weil [1950] 1 All ER 728 (House of Lords)   [73]

A Dutchman lent an Englishwoman a sum of money in French currency while both were resident in enemy occupied Monaco. The Englishwoman gave a cheque and certain other security for the money but the whole transaction was prohibited by statute. The Dutchman sought to recover the amount of the loan. *Held*, his action would fail as in these circumstances the contract of loan was illegal. (See also *Bigos* v *Bousted*.)

Bolton v Madden (1873) LR 9 QB 55 [74]

The parties were subscribers to a charity the objects of which were determined by members who had votes according to the amount of their subscription. It was agreed that if the plaintiff would give 28 votes for an object favoured by the defendant, at the next election the defendant would use 28 votes in accordance with the wishes of the plaintiff. The defendant refused to vote as requested by the plaintiff. *Held*, the plaintiff was able to recover the amount which he had subscribed in order to obtain 28 additional votes to be used in lieu of those promised by the defendant; the fact that the consideration for the defendant's promise may not have been adequate was the concern of the parties and not of the court.

Bolton v Mahadeva [1972] 2 All ER 1322 (Court of Appeal) [75]

The plaintiff agreed to instal central heating and do other work in the defendant's house. The contract price for the central heating was a lump sum of £560. On completion, the defendant complained that the work was defective and refused to pay. The trial judge found that there were serious defects, the cost of remedying which was £174.50, and gave judgment for the balance, i.e., £431.50. The defendant appealed. *Held*, a plaintiff was only entitled to recover on a lump sum contract, subject to set-off in respect of defects, where the contract had been substantially performed. In considering this, it was relevant to take into account the nature of the defects and the proportion between the cost of rectifying them and the contract price. As installed, the central heating system failed to heat the house adequately, and taking into account the cost of repairs, it was impossible to say that the contract had been substantially performed. (Distinguished: *Dakin (H) & Co Ltd* v *Lee*.)

Bowler v Lovegrove [1921] 1 Ch 642 [76]

Bowler and Blake, the plaintiffs, were in partnership as auctioneers and estate agents at Portsmouth and Gosport and employed the defendant as an outside canvassing and negotiating clerk. The defendant promised that he would not for one year after the termination of his employment 'carry on or be interested in carrying on the business of auctioneers and estate agents ... within the borough of Portsmouth or in the town of Gosport'. The defendant left the plaintiffs' employment and immediately commenced business on his own account as an estate agent within the prohibited area. *Held*, the plaintiffs could not enforce this agreement as it was against public policy. The restrictive provision was wider than was reasonably necessary for the protection of the plaintiffs' business as in the great majority of cases customers were customers for one transaction only. (But see *Fitch* v *Dewes*.)

Bowmakers Ltd v Barnet Instruments Ltd [77]
[1944] 2 All ER 579 (Court of Appeal)

The appellants hired some machine tools from the respondents under certain hire purchase agreements. The respondents had bought the tools from one Smith, but this sale was illegal as it was made in contravention of a statutory instrument. The appellants sold the tools, thus converting them to their own use, and the respondents claimed damages for conversion. The appellants maintained that as the sale by Smith to the respondents was illegal, the hire-purchase agreements were affected by that illegality and should not, on the ground of public policy, be enforced. *Held,* the respondents could recover as their right to the tools and their cause of action was unaffected by and wholly independent of the previous illegal sale. (See also *Mistry Amar Singh* v *Kuluby, Sajan Singh* v *Sardara Ali* and *Tinsley* v *Milligan*; but see *Taylor* v *Chester.*)

Branca v Cobarro [1947] 2 All ER 101 (Court of Appeal) [78]

The parties negotiated for the sale of a mushroom farm and signed a document containing the terms of their agreement which concluded: 'This is a provisional agreement until a fully legalised agreement drawn up by a solicitor and embodying all the conditions herewith stated is signed.' The purchaser sued for the return of his deposit and the vendor contended that their 'provisional agreement' was a binding contract. *Held,* there was an immediately binding contract 'until' the document was replaced by one expressed in more precise and formal language. If the parties had used the word 'tentative' instead of 'provisional' it would probably have been held otherwise, but each case depends on the intention of the parties as found by the court. (But see *Chillingworth* v *Esche.*)

Bridge v Campbell Discount Co Ltd [79]
[1962] 1 All ER 385 (House of Lords)

By a hire-purchase agreement the respondent finance company agreed to let and the appellant agreed to hire a used Bedford Dormobile. Clause 6 of the agreement provided that the appellant could terminate the hiring by giving the respondents written notice of termination and that thereupon the provisions of clause 9 should apply. Clause 9 provided, inter alia, that in the event of such termination the appellant should pay to the respondents 'all arrears of hire rent due and unpaid at the date of termination ... with interest thereon ... and by way of agreed compensation for depreciation of the vehicle such further sum as may be necessary to make the rentals paid and payable hereunder equal to two-thirds of the hire-purchase price.' Within two months of the date of the agreement and after paying only the initial and the first monthly rentals the appellant wrote to the respondents: 'Owing to unforeseen personal circumstances I am very sorry but I will not be able to pay any more payments on the Bedford Dormobile. Will you please let me know when and where I will have to return the car.' The appellant returned the vehicle to the dealers concerned in the transaction within the following two weeks and the respondents sought to recover the sum payable under clause 9 of the hire-purchase agreement. *Held,* by a majority, the appellant had not exercised his option under clause 6, but had simply declared his inability to go on with the contract. The respondents' claim would fail as the sum stipulated in clause 9 was a penalty and not a genuine pre-estimate of the loss which would be suffered by the respondents in the event of the termination of the hiring. The respondents' remedy was to claim from the appellant any damage that they could show themselves to have actually suffered by reason of his breach of contract. (See also *Jobson* v *Johnson.*)

Bridge v Savage (1885) 15 QBD 363 [80]

The plaintiff employed the defendant on a commission basis to make bets on horses on his behalf. The defendant carried out his instructions and made the bets but refused to pay the winnings to the plaintiff. In an action for money had and received the defendant relied upon s18 of the Gaming Act 1845. *Held,* the plaintiff could recover as s18, although rendering void all wagering transactions, did not prevent the plaintiff recovering the amount of the winnings from the defendant. (But see *Cohen* v *Kittell.*)

Briggs v Oates [1991] 1 All ER 407 [81]

The plaintiff entered into a partnership agreement with another solicitor, the plaintiff being the senior partner and sole proprietor of the firm's goodwill. The firm engaged the defendant as a salaried partner and the agreement contained a clause in restraint of trade. When the partnership came to an end, in accordance with the partnership agreement, during the period of the defendant's contract, he regarded his employment as having been terminated and he commenced practice on his own account nearby. The plaintiff sought to enforce the restraint of trade clause. *Held*, his action would be dismissed as the dissolution of the partnership constituted a breach and the termination of the defendant's contract of employment. (See also *General Billposting Co Ltd* v *Atkinson.*)

Brinkibon Ltd v Stahag Stahl und [82]
Stahlwarenhandelsgesellschaft mbH [1982] 1 All ER 293
(House of Lords)

Following negotiations regarding the sale of steel bars to be delivered to Egypt, the buyers, an English company, accepted by telex sent from London to Vienna the terms of sale offered by the sellers, an Austrian company. The contract was never performed and the buyers claimed damages for breach of contract. Had the contract been made within the court's jurisdiction? *Held*, it had not – it had been made where (and when) acceptance of the offer was received by the offeror, that is, in Austria. (Approved: *Entores Ltd* v *Miles Far East Corporation.*)

British and Commonwealth Holdings plc v [83]
Quadrex Holdings Ltd [1989] 3 All ER 492 (Court of Appeal)

An agreement provided for the sale of shares in unquoted private companies trading in a volatile sector, completion to take place 'as soon as reasonably practicable' after a certain event. That event having occurred and the defendant having failed to complete the purchase because of financing difficulties, the plaintiffs gave formal notice to complete. Completion having failed to take place by the stated date, the plaintiffs maintained that the contract had been repudiated and they claimed damages for breach of contract. The judge gave summary judgment for the plaintiffs. *Held*, in such circumstances, if a completion date had been stated in the agreement time would have been of the essence. Further, if the plaintiffs had not themselves been in breach of contract, they could give notice to complete within a reasonable time and the time specified here had been reasonable. However, as it was arguable that the plaintiffs had been in breach of contract the defendants would be given leave to defend. (See also *Behzadi* v *Shaftesbury Hotels Ltd.*)

British Bank for Foreign Trade Ltd v Novimex Ltd [84]
[1949] 1 KB 623 (Court of Appeal)

The defendants contracted to pay the plaintiffs 'an agreed commission on any other business transacted with your friends'. The plaintiffs introduced some of their friends to the defendants and the plaintiffs claimed commission on two sales of oilskin suits which were transacted as a result. The defendants argued that they were not bound to pay commission as the amount of commission had not been agreed. *Held,* a contract to pay a reasonable sum by way of commission would be implied from the conduct of the parties. (See also *Powell* v *Braun.*)

British Crane Hire Corp Ltd v Ipswich Plant Hire Ltd   [85]
[1974] 1 All ER 1059 (Court of Appeal)

A crane was hired under an oral agreement between two large companies who were both engaged in the plant hire business. The owner's usual printed conditions of hire, which were standard in the trade, were sent on later. *Held,* the conditions of hire were part of the contract notwithstanding that there had been no 'course of dealing'. The standard conditions were fair and reasonable and the hirers knew that conditions were always applied.

British Movietonews Ltd v London and District Cinemas   [86]
Ltd [1951] 2 All ER 617 (House of Lords)

There was a contract for the supply of newsreels determinable by four weeks' notice but in view of a certain Order restricting the supply of film made under the Defence Regulations the parties entered into a supplemental agreement dated May 1943; this modified some of the terms of the original agreement but provided that the original agreement was in all other respects to 'remain in full force and effect until such time as the Order is cancelled'. In 1948, when film was again in plentiful supply, but the Order was still in force, the defendants gave four weeks' notice to determine the agreement and the plaintiffs sued for breach of contract. *Held,* the plaintiffs were entitled to recover as the supplemental agreement had expressly provided that the original contract was to remain in force 'until such time as the Order is cancelled' and as the Order was still in force the original agreement could not be validly determined. (See also *Davis Contractors Ltd* v *Fareham Urban District Council.*)

British Reinforced Concrete Engineering Co Ltd v   [87]
Schelff [1921] 2 Ch 563

The plaintiffs engaged in the manufacture and sale of BRC road reinforcements and the defendants, who had a much smaller business, sold loop reinforcements. The defendants covenanted to sell their business to the plaintiffs and agreed that they would not, for a certain period, be concerned in the manufacture or sale of road reinforcements. One of the defendants entered employment in breach of this agreement and the plaintiffs sued upon the covenant. *Held,* their action must fail as the covenant was wider than that reasonably necessary for the protection of the plaintiffs in respect of the particular business sold, i.e., the restraint would only be justifiable and valid if it had been confined to the restriction of the sale of loop road reinforcements. (See also *Vancouver Malt and Sake Brewing Co Ltd* v *Vancouver Breweries Ltd.*)

British Russian Gazette and Trade Outlook Ltd v   [88]
Associated Newspapers Ltd [1933] 2 KB 616 (Court of Appeal)

One Talbot, a director of the plaintiff company, sued the defendants in respect of an alleged libel. A representative of the defendants met Talbot and terms of a settlement were arranged whereby Talbot agreed to accept 1,000 guineas in full discharge and settlement of his claims and of that of the plaintiff company and undertook to discontinue the action against the defendants. Before the agreed amount was paid Talbot proceeded with the action in breach of the agreement. *Held,* he was not entitled to do so as he was bound by the terms of the settlement, consideration for which was to be found in executory promises by the defendants. (But see *Foakes* v *Beer*.)

Brodie v Brodie [1971] P 271 [89]

Immediately before their marriage the parties entered into an agreement in writing which provided that they would live apart and this agreement was confirmed by an indorsement immediately after the marriage ceremony. *Held,* the agreement was void as it was contrary to public policy to contract with a view to a future separation. (But see *Wilson* v *Wilson*.)

Brogden v Metropolitan Railway Co (1877) 2 App Cas 666 [90]
(House of Lords)

The appellant supplied the respondents with coal and after a number of years suggested that they should enter into a formal contract. A draft of the contract was submitted to the appellant who completed certain details, introduced a new term by adding the name of an arbitrator, wrote 'approved' at the end of the paper, signed his name and returned the draft to the respondents. The contract was never executed but for some time coal was supplied and payment made in accordance with the terms contained in the draft agreement. *Held,* while mere mental assent to the terms of the draft would not be sufficient, because the parties had acted upon the draft, there was, from the time when the respondents first ordered coal after the return of the draft or at latest when the appellant completed delivery of the order, a valid contract between them. (See also *Stevenson, Jaques & Co* v *McLean*.)

Brooke (Lord) v Rounthwaite (1846) 5 Hare 298 [91]

Particulars of sale described an estate as containing 'upwards of sixty-five acres of fine oak timber trees, the average size of which approached fifty feet'. There was a conflict of evidence as to whether the average size of the trees was thirty-five or twenty-two feet but both parties agreed that fifty feet was an over-statement. *Held,* the representation in the particulars of sale having been proved to be incorrect, the contract for the purchase of the estate would not be specifically enforced. (But see *Scott* v *Hanson*.)

Bunge Corp v Tradax SA [1981] 2 All ER 513 [92]
(House of Lords)

A contract for the sale and purchase of soya bean meal provided that one shipment was to be in June and that the buyers, who were to provide the vessel, should give at least 15 days' notice of its probable readiness. They did not give such notice until 17 June and the sellers maintained that the late notice was a breach of contract amounting to a repudiation and they claimed damages. *Held,* the sellers should succeed. '... the statement ... appears to me to be correct, in particular in asserting (1) that the court will require precise compliance with stipulations as to time wherever the circumstances of the case indicate that this would fulfil the intention of the parties, and (2) that broadly speaking time will be considered of the essence in "mercantile" contracts ... The relevant clause falls squarely within these principles, and such authority as there is supports its status as a condition' (*per* LORD WILBERFORCE). (Distinguished: *Hong Kong Fir Shipping Co Ltd* v *Kawasaki Kisen Kaisha Ltd*; see also *Cie Commerciale Sucres et Denrées* v *C Czarnikow Ltd, The Naxos*.)

Burnard v Haggis (1863) 14 CB (NS) 45 [93]

The defendant, who was under age, went to the stables of the plaintiff and hired a horse to ride on the road. The plaintiff stipulated that the horse was not to be ridden by anyone but the defendant and was not to be used for jumping. The defendant let his friend ride the horse and the friend forced the animal to attempt a fence but the jump was unsuccessful, the horse falling and being transfixed by a hedge-stake. *Held,* the plaintiff was entitled to damages in tort as such conduct was not contemplated by the contract and had in fact been specifically forbidden. (But see *Jennings* v *Rundall.*)

Bushwall Properties Ltd v Vortex Properties Ltd [94]
[1976] 2 All ER 283 (Court of Appeal)

A contract for the sale of land provided that the purchase price of £500,000 was 'to be phased as to £250,000 upon first completion, as to £125,000 twelve months thereafter and as to the balance of £125,000 a further twelve months thereafter' and 'on the occasion of each completion a proportionate part of the land shall be released forthwith to' the plaintiffs. In breach of the agreement, the defendants conveyed the land to X, who offered to sell it to the plaintiffs for £500,000 payable immediately. The plaintiffs accepted the offer and completed the sale on those terms. They then sued the defendants for breach of the original contract of sale. The defendants argued that there was no binding contract since the reference to 'a proportionate part of the land' was too uncertain in that the agreement did not provide whether the plaintiffs or the defendants were to have the power to select 'a proportionate part' of the land. *Held,* the contract was void for uncertainty in the absence of any express term as to how the land to be included in each phase was selected.

Butler Machine Tool Co Ltd v Ex-cell-o Corp Ltd [95]
[1979] 1 All ER 965 (Court of Appeal)

The plaintiffs offered to sell machine tools to the defendants subject to their own terms and conditions which included a price variation clause. The defendants replied purporting to accept the offer on their own terms, which did not include a price variation clause. The plaintiffs acknowledged the order by returning to the defendants a tear-off slip. After delivery, the plaintiffs claimed increased costs, which the defendants refused to pay. *Held,* the transaction must be analysed in terms of offer and acceptance. The defendants' order was not an acceptance of the plaintiffs' offer but was a counter-offer which was tantamount to a rejection. The contract had been concluded on the defendants' terms and conditions by the plaintiffs' acknowledgment of the order.

Byrne & Co v Leon Van Tienhoven & Co [96]
(1880) 5 CPD 344

The defendants, who carried on business in Cardiff, wrote to the plaintiffs, whose office was in New York, offering to sell certain goods at a fixed price. On the day on which they received the offer the plaintiffs telegraphed their acceptance, but three days previously the defendants had sent a letter withdrawing the offer; this did not arrive until after the acceptance had been confirmed by post. The plaintiffs sought damages for breach of contract. *Held,* the plaintiffs were entitled to damages as there was a binding contract from the moment the offer was accepted and the withdrawal was of no effect as it was not received by the plaintiffs until after acceptance. (See also *Henthorn* v *Fraser.*)

C & P Haulage v Middleton [1983] 3 All ER 94   [97]
(Court of Appeal)

The appellant self-employed motor engineer was granted by the respondents a contractual licence to occupy a yard on a renewable six-monthly basis. He spent money on the premises even though the licence provided 'Any fixtures you put in are left'. Ten weeks before the end of the initial six months the appellant was unlawfully ejected and, as a temporary measure, the local authority allowed him to use his home for the purpose of his business. He claimed the cost of the improvements effected by him to the yard. *Held,* his claim could not succeed as he was no worse off than if the contract had been fully performed. He was, however, awarded nominal damages of £10. (Distinguished in *Anglia Television Ltd v Reed.*)

CCC Films (London) Ltd v Impact Quadrant Films Ltd   [98]
[1984] 3 All ER 298

The defendants granted the plaintiffs a licence to distribute three films in 26 countries and the plaintiffs asked the defendants to insure and send by recorded delivery video tapes of the films to be used for marketing purposes. In breach of this agreement the defendants sent the tapes uninsured by ordinary post in the course of which they were lost. The defendants also failed to perform subsequent agreements to send replacement tapes. The plaintiffs were unable to produce evidence of loss of profits so they sued to recover $12,000 as wasted expenditure. *Held,* they were entitled to succeed as they had an unfettered choice whether to claim for loss of profits or for wasted expenditure. The onus of proving that the plaintiffs would not have recouped their outlay of $12,000 if they had received the tapes and exploited the films lay on the defendants and they had not discharged that burden. (See also *Anglia Television Ltd v Reed.*)

CHT Ltd v Ward [1963] 3 All ER 226   [99]

The defendant was a member of Crockfords, a club owned by the plaintiffs, and her account was debited with the total face value of the chips handed to her. The chips were used in playing poker under conditions in which it was lawful gaming and also for the purchase of food, liquor and cigarettes. An account was sent to the defendant on a weekly basis and if at any time her account was in credit (ie she had paid in more chips in any week than she had received) the plaintiffs paid her the credit balance by cheque. In common with other members, when she won she had the choice of having her account credited with her winnings or drawing cash for any credit balance standing on her account. The plaintiffs sued to recover the amount of a debit balance. *Held,* the plaintiffs had in fact paid the defendant's gaming losses and it followed that under the provisions of s1 of the Gaming Act 1892 the action was brought on a promise made by the defendant to the plaintiffs to pay them sums paid by them in respect of contracts rendered null and void by the Gaming Act 1845 and that the plaintiffs could not recover the sums so paid. (See also *M'Kinnell v Robinson.*)

CIBC Mortgages plc v Pitt [1994] 1 AC 200   [100]
(House of Lords)

Wishing to buy shares on the stock market, Mr Pitt proposed to borrow money from the plaintiff mortgagee, charging the matrimonial home (which was in the joint names of Mr Pitt and his wife) by way of security. Mrs Pitt was not happy with this suggestion, but under pressure from her husband, she eventually agreed and both of them signed the legal charge which was prepared by the plaintiffs' solicitors. The wife did not receive independent advice and nobody suggested that she should. In their loan application they had stated that the money would be used to pay off their existing mortgage and to buy a holiday home. The balance of the loan (after the discharge of their existing mortgage) was paid into their joint account. The husband bought shares, the market crashed and, as they were unable to keep up the mortgage payments, the plaintiffs sought possession of the matrimonial home. The judge found that Mr Pitt had exercised actual undue influence in procuring his wife's agreement to the charge. *Held*, nevertheless, the plaintiffs' claim would be successful. While a person who proves actual undue influence is not also required to prove that the transaction was manifestly disadvantageous, here the plaintiffs were not affected by the husband's undue influence because he had not, in a real sense, acted as their agent in procuring Mrs Pitt's agreement and the plaintiffs had no actual or constructive notice of the undue influence. So far as they were aware, the transaction consisted of a joint loan to the husband and wife for the purposes stated on the loan application. The loan was advanced to them jointly and there was nothing to indicate to the plaintiffs that the loan was anything other than a normal advance to a husband and wife for their joint benefit. The mere fact that there was a risk of there being undue influence because one of the borrowers was the wife was, in itself, not sufficient to put the plaintiffs on inquiry. (Overruled: *Bank of Credit and Commerce International SA v Aboody* [1990] 1 QB 923; but see *Barclays Bank plc v O'Brien*.)

CTN Cash and Carry Ltd v Gallaher Ltd [1994] 4 All ER 714   **[101]**
(Court of Appeal)

The defendants, sole distributors of certain popular brands, supplied cigarettes for sale in the plaintiffs' six warehouses. They were not contractually bound to sell them any cigarettes: separate contracts were made from time to time. The defendants granted the plaintiffs credit facilities, but these could be withdrawn at any time. The manager of one of the plaintiffs' warehouses placed an order; by mistake they were delivered to the wrong one. The defendants agreed to collect the cigarettes and deliver them to the right one: before they could do so, the goods were stolen. Although property in the stolen cigarettes had not passed to the plaintiffs, the defendants invoiced them for them. The defendants thought (mistakenly but in good faith) that the cigarettes were, at the time of the robbery, at the plaintiffs' risk. The plaintiffs rejected the invoice but, after the defendants had made it clear that they would not in future be granted credit facilities, they paid it, believing it to be the lesser of two evils. The plaintiffs now claimed repayment on the ground that the money had been paid under duress. *Held*, their action would fail since the defendants' conduct had not amounted to duress. The common law does not recognise the doctrine of inequality of bargaining power in commercial dealings (see *National Westminster Bank plc v Morgan*): the defendants had merely exerted commercial pressure, and followed commercial self-interest, with a view to recovering a sum which, at the time, they bona fide considered to be due to them. '… the basis on which the defendant had sought and insisted on payment was then shown to be false … on the sketchy facts before us … it does seem to me that prima facie it would be unconscionable for the defendant company to insist on retaining the money now. It demanded the money when under a mistaken belief as to its legal entitlement to be paid. It only made the demand because of its belief that it was entitled to be paid. Then money was then paid to it by a plaintiff which, in practical terms, had no other option. In broad terms, in the end result the defendant may be said to have been unjustly enriched. Whether a new claim for restitution now, on the facts as they have since emerged, would succeed is not a matter I need pursue. I observe, as to that, only that the categories of unjust enrichment are not closed' (*per* SIR DONALD NICHOLLS V-C).

Callisher v Bischoffsheim (1870) LR 5 QB 449   **[102]**

The plaintiff alleged that certain moneys were due to him from the Government of Honduras and was about to institute proceedings to enforce payment. The defendant promised to deliver certain debentures to the plaintiff and the consideration for this promise was the plaintiff's forbearance to sue the Honduras Government. In fact the plaintiff did not have a claim which he could prosecute successfully and the defendant argued that there was therefore no consideration for his promise to deliver the debentures. *Held,* the defendant was bound as the fact that the plaintiff could not have maintained a successful action against the Honduras Government did not vitiate the contract and destroy the validity of the consideration. The plaintiff entertained a bona fide belief that he could bring a successful action but if he had known his claim to be unfounded there would have been no contract between the parties. (But see *Wade* v *Simeon.*)

Car and Universal Finance Co Ltd v Caldwell   **[103]**
[1964] 1 All ER 290 (Court of Appeal)

Caldwell, the vendor of a car, was induced to part with possession of it on payment by cheque. The cheque was not met, and the fraudulent purchaser avoided communication with Caldwell, who informed both the police and a national motoring organisation. Some time later, the purchaser sold the car to X, from whom Caldwell sought possession. *Held,* as Caldwell had, by overt conduct, effectively rescinded the contract, the fraudulent buyer could not pass a good title, and Caldwell was entitled to succeed. (See also *Reese River Silver Mining Co Ltd* v *Smith.*)

Carlill v Carbolic Smoke Ball Co [1893] 1 QB 256   **[104]**
(Court of Appeal)

The plaintiff bought a medical preparation called 'The Carbolic Smoke Ball' on the faith of an advertisement issued by the defendants in which they offered to pay £100 to any person who contracted influenza after using one of their smoke balls in a specific manner and for a specified period. 'To show their sincerity' the defendants deposited £1,000 with their bankers. The plaintiff bought one of the smoke balls and used it as prescribed but never the less contracted influenza and sued for £100. The defendants contended that there was no binding agreement. *Held,* (i) an offer may be made to the world at large and the advertisement was such an offer which was accepted by any person who bought the smoke ball and complied with the conditions as to manner and period of use (see also *Shipton* v *Cardiff Corporation*); (ii) there was no need for the plaintiff to communicate acceptance of the offer as the defendants had made no mention of the necessity for communication in the advertisement and had impliedly intimated that it would be sufficient acceptance to act upon the offer, that is, to use the smoke ball as prescribed (but see *Powell* v *Lee*); (iii) the offer was not 'mere puff' as the fact that they had deposited £1,000 was sufficient evidence of their intention to create legal relations with users of the smoke ball. (But see *Balfour* v *Balfour.*)

Carlton Hall Club Ltd v Laurence [1929] 2 KB 153   **[105]**

The plaintiffs were proprietors of a club which met for social purposes and for the playing of cards, billiards and other games. Members taking part in games for money were supplied with 'chips' upon which were marked their value and the members paid for their 'chips' by cheque. The defendant borrowed £26 7s 3d in 'chips' for the purpose of playing snooker and poker and paid for them by cheques which were not met. The plaintiffs did not sue upon these cheques as securities for money knowingly lent for gaming are rendered void by the Gaming Acts, but sought to recover by suing on the agreement for the loan. *Held*, their action must fail as the combined effect of s1 of the Gaming Act 1710 and s1 of the Gaming Act 1835, is to render void not only a security for money knowingly lent for gambling but by implication the consideration for a contract for the loan of money for this purpose, whether the gaming was legal or illegal. (See also *Macdonald* v *Green*.)

Carney v Herbert [1985] 1 All ER 438 (Privy Council) [106]

The appellant and the three respondents between them owned the shares of Airfoil Ltd and were the directors of that company and of its subsidiary, Newbridge Ltd. The respondents agreed to sell their shares in Airfoil to Ilerain Ltd, a company controlled by the appellant, and the appellant and Newbridge guaranteed the payment of the purchase price, Newbridge's guarantee being secured by mortgages on its land. The appellant contended that he was not liable on the guarantee since the sale agreement was illegal and unenforceable because the mortgages amounted to the provision of security by a subsidiary of the company whose shares were being purchased, contrary to the provisions of a local statute. *Held*, this was not the case. The illegal mortgages could not be said to go to the heart of the transaction and they could therefore be severed from the remainder of the contract. There was no public policy arising from the nature of the illegality which prevented the enforcement of the severed contract. (See also *Nicolene Ltd* v *Simmonds*.)

Carpenters Estates Ltd v Davies [1940] 1 All ER 13 [107]

The plaintiffs bought some land from the defendant for building purposes and the defendant covenanted that he would construct certain roads and sewers. The defendant made the roads but neglected to make the sewers. The plaintiffs claimed specific performance of the defendant's promise. *Held*, an order for specific performance would be made as an award of damages would not be a sufficient remedy.

Cartwright v Hoogstoel (1911) 105 LT 628 [108]

The defendant offered the plaintiff the lease of some premises and said that his offer would remain open for seven days. The plaintiff purported to exercise this option within the period specified but before acceptance he was informed of conduct on the part of the defendant which was quite inconsistent with the offer and consistent only with an absolute withdrawal of the offer. *Held*, the plaintiff was not entitled to specific performance as the conduct of the defendant which had come to the notice of the plaintiff was a sufficient retraction of the offer. (See also *Dickinson* v *Dodds*.)

Casey's Patents, Re [1892] 1 Ch 104 (Court of Appeal) [109]

The joint owners of certain patents informed C that in consideration of services rendered they would give him a one-third share of the patents. The defendants contended that this promise was not binding as the consideration was past. *Held*, the plaintiff would succeed in his action on the defendants' promise as there was an implication at the time of rendering the services that they would be paid for and the share in the patents would be regarded as such payment. (See also *Lampleigh* v *Brathwait* and *Pao On* v *Lau Yiu*.)

Central London Property Trust Ltd v High Trees [110]
House Ltd [1947] KB 130

In 1937 the plaintiffs let a block of flats to the defendants for a term of 99 years at a ground rent of £2,500 pa. In 1940, as few of the flats were occupied because of the war, the plaintiffs agreed to reduce the rent to £1,250 as from the beginning of the term. The defendants continued to pay the reduced rent until 1945 when all the flats were let and the plaintiffs claimed that the full rent was again payable. *Held,* the plaintiffs were entitled to recover the full rent from the time when the flats were again occupied; had they sued for the full rent between 1940 and 1945 they would have been estopped from asserting their strict legal right to demand payment in full, as when parties enter into an arrangement which is intended to create legal relations and in pursuance of such arrangement one party makes a promise to the other which he knows will be acted on and which is in fact acted on by the promisee, the promise is binding on the promisor to the extent that it will not allow him to act inconsistently with it, although the promise may not be supported by consideration in the strict sense. 'I ... apply the principle that the promise, intended to be binding, intended to be acted on and in fact acted on, is binding so far as its terms properly apply. It is binding as covering the period down to 1945, and from that time full rent is payable' (*per* DENNING J). (But see *Combe* v *Combe.*)

Central Railway Company of Venezuela v Kisch (1867) [111]
LR 2 HL 99 (House of Lords)

The appellants issued a prospectus which contained representations which were untrue and deceptive but the respondent was given the opportunity of inspecting certain reports and plans which would have supplied the correct information, the lack of which he afterwards alleged entitled him to rescind the contract. *Held,* no mis-statement or concealment of any material fact or circumstances would be permitted in a prospectus and as there had been such a misrepresentation in reliance upon which the respondent had agreed to buy the shares he was entitled to be relieved from the contract. It was no answer to his claim that he could have discovered the true position if he had carried out the inspections open to him. (See also *Redgrave* v *Hurd.*)

Chapelton v Barry Urban District Council [112]
[1940] 1 All ER 356 (Court of Appeal)

Deck chairs were stacked up on the beach and beside them was a notice which said 'Barry Urban District Council. Cold Knap. Hire of chairs, 2d per session of 3 hours ...' The appellant paid for the hire of two chairs and was given two tickets on the back of which was a condition which purported to exclude the respondents' liability for any injury which the hirer should sustain. The appellant did not read this condition. The canvas on one of the chairs was defective and the appellant claimed damages in respect of the injuries which resulted. *Held,* damages would be awarded as the appellant was entitled to assume that the conditions of hire were to be found in the notice near the stack of chairs. The ticket was a mere voucher or receipt to prove payment or the time of commencement of hire. (See also *Olley* v *Marlborough Court Ltd.*)

Chaplin v Hicks [1911] 2 KB 786 (Court of Appeal) [113]

The plaintiff accepted the defendant's offer to apply for selection for employment by him as an actress for a term of three years. Twelve such engagements were offered and the plaintiff was one of the 50 applicants from whom the 12 were to be selected. The plaintiff was given insufficient notice of the interview at which the final choice was to be made and thereby lost her chance of selection. The plaintiff claimed damages for breach of contract. *Held,* she was entitled to succeed as the damage which she had suffered (ie loss of opportunity) was within the contemplation of the parties as the possible direct outcome of the defendant's breach of contract and therefore not too remote. Although it was difficult, if not impossible, to arrive at an accurate assessment of the amount of damages which should be awarded, the question had rightly been left to the jury who had concluded that the plaintiff had been deprived of something which had a monetary value and decided that the plaintiff should receive £100. 'I ... wish to deny with emphasis that, because precision cannot be arrived at, the jury has no function in the assessment of damages' (*per* VAUGHAN WILLIAMS LJ).

Chaplin v Leslie Frewin (Publishers) Ltd [114]
[1965] 3 All ER 764 (Court of Appeal)

C, the son of the famous film actor, was a minor, and in need of money. He and his wife, who was of full age, entered into two contracts, to have his life story written by two ghost writers, and published by the defendants. The copyright in the book was to vest in C and his wife, who warranted that the book contained nothing defamatory or objectionable, and agreed to indemnify the publishers against claims in consequence of any breach of the warranty. Although told by the defendants to get independent legal advice, neither C nor his wife did so. A few months later, C and his wife passed the proofs, having made certain amendments to passages that might be defamatory. Later, C consulted solicitors, who on his behalf repudiated the agreement on grounds of his minority. C now objected to the book on grounds that included its unpleasantness and that there were libellous passages in it. He sought an injunction restraining the defendants from printing and publishing the book. *Held,* his claim must fail. The question whether the contract was for C's benefit must be judged at the date when it was made and, so considered, it was prima facie for C's benefit, since the publishers alleged that the allegedly defamatory passages were justifiable and since C benefited financially. (See also *Doyle* v *White City Stadium Ltd.*)

Chappell & Co Ltd v Nestlé Co Ltd [115]
[1960] 2 All ER 701 (House of Lords)

The plaintiffs owned the copyright in a dance tune. X made records of the tune which they sold to the defendants for 4d each. The defendants advertised these records to the public for 1s 6d each but required, in addition, three wrappers from Nestlé products. The plaintiffs sued the defendants for breach of copyright. The defendants pleaded s8 of the Copyright Act 1956 which provided that recordings of musical work may be made for retail sale providing the copyright owner is paid a royalty of 64 per cent of 'the ordinary retail selling price'. The question was whether this statutory royalty was to be based on the 1s 6d a record, or whether the wrappers (which were thrown away) were part of the consideration. *Held,* the plaintiffs' claim should succeed. 'A contracting party can stipulate for what consideration he chooses. A peppercorn does not cease to be good consideration if it is established that the promisee does not like pepper and will throw away the corn' (*per* LORD SOMERVELL).

Chapple v Cooper (1844) 13 M & W 252 [116]

Anne Cooper's husband died and she placed an order with an undertaker for the conduct of his funeral. When the undertaker sued to recover his charges Anne relied on the fact that she was a minor and the undertaker contended that she was liable as the contract into which she had entered was one for 'necessaries'. *Held,* the undertaker would succeed as the decent Christian burial of his wife and lawful children is a personal advantage and reasonably necessary to a husband and there was no reason why the decent burial of her husband should not likewise be regarded as of advantage and necessary to Anne. (But see *Nash* v *Inman.*)

Charnock v Liverpool Corporation   [117]
[1968] 3 All ER 473 (Court of Appeal)

The plaintiff took his car to X's garage for repair. At a meeting at the garage between the plaintiff, X's manager, and an assessor employed by the plaintiff's insurers, it was agreed that the insurance company would pay the cost of repairs, this being confirmed by them in writing. The garage took eight weeks to repair the car. The plaintiff was awarded damages against X for the failure to repair the car within a reasonable time. X appealed against this judgment on the ground that there was no contract between them and the plaintiff, and that their only contract was with the insurance company. *Held,* although there was a contract by the insurers with the repairers, there was also a contract between X and the plaintiff to carry out the repairs. It was an implied term of that contract that the repairs would be carried out within a reasonable time, and as this had not been done, X was liable in damages. (See also s14 of the Supply of Goods and Services Act 1982.)

Cheese v Thomas [1994] 1 WLR 129   [118]
(Court of Appeal)

The 86-year-old plaintiff and the defendant, his great-nephew, agreed to buy a house for £83,000 to provide a home for the plaintiff for the rest of his life. The plaintiff contributed £43,000 and the defendant (by means of a mortgage) £40,000. The house was purchased in the defendant's name. The defendant having failed to keep up the mortgage payments, the plaintiff sought repayment of his £43,000 contribution and the setting aside of the transaction on the ground of undue influence. The judge agreed that the transaction had been manifestly disadvantageous to the plaintiff and ordered that the house be sold and that the proceeds be divided in the same proportions as the parties had contributed to the purchase price, ie 43-40. The house was sold for £55,000. Both parties appealed. *Held,* the appeals would be dismissed. The transaction had indeed been disadvantageous to the plaintiff, but practical justice should be achieved for both parties and the whole of the loss resulting from the fall in market value should not be borne by the defendant. The judge's division of the proceeds of sale had been correct. (But see *National Westminister Bank plc* v *Morgan.*)

Chichester and Wife v Cobb (1866) 14 LT 433   [119]

The two plaintiffs had agreed to marry one another and the defendant wrote to the female plaintiff and promised to give her £300 when all the arrangements for the marriage were completed. The plaintiffs married but the £300 was never paid. *Held,* there was a binding contract founded on a sufficient consideration. (See also *Shadwell* v *Shadwell.*)

Chillingworth v Esche [1924] 1 Ch 97 (Court of Appeal)   [120]

The plaintiffs agreed to purchase the defendant's nursery for £4,800 'subject to a proper contract to be prepared by the vendor's solicitors'. The purchasers refused to sign a contract which had been approved by their solicitors and executed by the vendor and did not complete the transaction. *Held,* the consent was conditional upon a 'proper contract' being signed and the plaintiffs were entitled to recover their deposit. (But see *Branca* v *Cobarro.*)

Cie Commerciale Sucres et Denrées v C Czarnikow Ltd, [121]
The Naxos [1990] 3 All ER 641 (House of Lords)

The parties contracted for the sale and purchase of 12,000 metric tons of sugar. It was found, in accordance with the contract, that the sellers should have had the sugar available to load onto The Naxos immediately the ship arrived at Dunkirk, but it was not so available. *Held,* the sellers were in breach of a condition of the contract. Accordingly, the buyers had been entitled to terminate the contract and, by way of damages, they were entitled to recover the difference between the cost of the replacement cargo and the original contract price and loss of despatch which would have been earned had the ship not remained idle while awaiting cargo. (See also *Bunge Corpn* v *Tradax SA* and *Bentsen* v *Taylor, Sons & Co.*)

Citibank NA v Brown Shipley & Co Ltd [1991] 2 All ER 690 [122]

A bank was deceived into issuing a banker's draft to a receiving bank which then paid the amount of the draft in cash to a fraudster who claimed to have an account with the issuing bank and who had forged the signature of persons authorised to operate the account. *Held,* the issuing bank had to bear the loss as the delivery of the banker's draft from the issuing bank to the receiving bank, with the authority of the issuing bank, established a contract between the banks under which title to the draft passed directly to the receiving bank. In these circumstances the fraudster's identity was not of fundamental importance and the issuing bank could not therefore claim that title had not passed. (Distinguished: *Cundy* v *Lindsay.*)

City Index Ltd v Leslie [1991] 3 All ER 180 (Court of Appeal) [123]

The plaintiffs accepted wagers on stock market movements and, after a number of such bets, the defendant owed them £34,580. When sued, the defendant relied on s18 of the Gaming Act 1845. *Held,* the plaintiffs' action would be successful as transactions of this kind were excluded by s63 of the Financial Services Act 1986 from being void or unenforceable as a gaming debt. (See also *Universal Stock Exchange Ltd* v *David Strachan.*)

Clark v Uruquhart See Smith New Court Securities Ltd v Scrimgeour Vickers (Asset Management) Ltd

Clarke v Dunraven, The Satanita [1897] AC 59 [124]
(House of Lords)

Two yachts were entered by their respective owners for a club race and each owner had undertaken to be bound by the club rules, one of which provided that an owner was to be liable for any damage which arose from a breach of the rules. In breach of a rule one yacht ran into and sank the other and the offended owner brought an action for damages. *Held,* there was a contract between the owners on which the owner of the damaged yacht could bring a successful action because by entering for the race and agreeing to be bound by the rules there was created by inference a contractual obligation to make good any damage caused in breach of the rules. (But see *Gibson* v *Manchester City Council.*)

Clarke v Newland [1991] 1 All ER 397 (Court of Appeal)   [125]

The plaintiff general medical practitioner took the defendant as a salaried partner and the defendant undertook 'not to practise in the practice area' (which was defined) within three years after the termination of the agreement. The agreement was duly terminated and the defendant decided to set up practice as a general medical practitioner within the practice area. *Held*, the plaintiff was entitled to an injunction. In all the circumstances, the covenant 'not to practise' would be construed as an undertaking not to practise as a general medical practitioner and as such it was enforceable as it was not unreasonably wide. (Distinguished: *Routh* v *Jones*.)

Clay v Yates (1856) 1 H & N 73   [126]

The plaintiff, a printer, orally agreed to print for the defendant 500 copies of a book entitled 'Military Tactics', to which a dedication, which had not at that time been written, was to be prefixed. After printing had begun the plaintiff saw the dedication, which contained libellous matter, for the first time and refused to complete the work. The plaintiff sought to recover for work, labour and materials. *Held*, the plaintiff was justified in refusing to complete the printing of the book and was entitled to be paid for that part of the work which he had carried out. (See also *Cowan* v *Milbourn*.)

Clements v London and North Western Railway Co   [127]
[1894] 2 QB 482 (Court of Appeal)

The plaintiff, who was a minor, entered the service of the defendants as a porter and agreed to become a member of the defendants' insurance scheme, to the funds of which the defendants contributed, and to forfeit his right to sue the defendants under the Employers' Liability Acts. The insurance scheme did not restrict the payment of compensation to those cases for which the employers would otherwise be liable, but the amount of benefit payable under the scheme was rather less than that which could be recovered under the Employers' Liability Acts. The scheme also provided that claims should be forfeited in certain circumstances and that all disputes should be settled by arbitration. The plaintiff was injured in the course of his employment and sued to recover damages from the defendants. *Held*, the action must fail as the plaintiff's contract of service, which contained a clause prohibiting the institution of proceedings of this kind, was binding upon him as it was, taken as a whole, advantageous to him. (See also *Doyle* v *White City Stadium Ltd*.)

Cleveland Petroleum Co Ltd v Dartstone Ltd   [128]
[1969] 1 All ER 201 (Court of Appeal)

S, the fee simple owner of a garage, leased the premises to the plaintiffs for 25 years. The plaintiffs granted an underlease to X Ltd, who covenanted, inter alia, not to sell or distribute motor fuels other than those supplied by the plaintiffs. Subsequently, the underlease was assigned to the defendants, who undertook to perform the covenants. The defendants challenged the validity of the tie. *Held*, the tie was valid and not an unreasonable restraint of trade because the defendants, not having been in possession previously, took possession under a lease and knowingly accepted the covenant. They thereby bound themselves to it. (See also *Esso Petroleum Co Ltd* v *Harper's Garage (Stourport) Ltd*.)

Clifford Davis Management Ltd v WEA Records Ltd [129]
[1975] 1 All ER 237 (Court of Appeal)

The plaintiff was manager of a 'pop group', two of whose members were talented composers who wanted to get their songs published. He persuaded them to sign publishing agreements with him. Although they were experienced performers and were of full age, they were not experienced in business. The agreements were professionally drafted in standard form and neither of the young men took independent advice before signing. The terms of the agreements were somewhat one-sided, and bound the defendants to assign copyrights to the plaintiff for a nominal sum, subject to a royalty payment if the plaintiff chose to exploit the songs. Subsequently the plaintiff and the group split up, and the two young men wrote new songs for the group which were recorded. The plaintiff brought an action for an injunction to restrain the defendant distributors from infringing his copyright in the songs. *Held,* the defendants had established a prima facie case that the agreements were unenforceable in that they had been made in circumstances where there was inequality of bargaining power. The plaintiff's application would be refused. (See also *Schroeder* v *Macaulay* and *Lloyds Bank Ltd* v *Bundy.*)

Clifton v Palumbo [1944] 2 All ER 497 (Court of Appeal) [130]

The defendant was negotiating for the purchase of a large estate owned by the plaintiff who wrote 'I am prepared to offer you ... my ... estate for £600,000 ... I also agree that a reasonable and sufficient time shall be granted to you for the examination and consideration of all the data and details necessary for the preparation of the Schedule of Completion.' *Held,* in the circumstances of the case, this letter did not amount to an offer to sell but was a preliminary statement as to price to enable negotiations to proceed. (See also *Harvey* v *Facey* and *Bigg* v *Boyd Gibbins Ltd.*)

Clubb v Hutson (1865) 18 CB (NS) 414 [131]

The plaintiff sought to enforce payment of a promissory note and the defendant contended that he should not succeed as, before making the note, the plaintiff had preferred a charge of obtaining by false pretences against the defendant and the note was given in consideration of the plaintiff consenting to withdraw the charge. *Held,* the plaintiff would fail as it was in the interest of the public that the suppression of a prosecution should not be made a matter of private bargain. (But see *Fisher & Co* v *Apollinaris Co.*)

Clyde Cycle Co v Hargreaves (1898) 78 LT 296 [132]

An apprentice, who was a minor, earned 21s per week and lived with his parents, bought a racing bicycle for £12 10s. The plaintiff, from whom the machine was purchased, brought an action against the apprentice to recover the balance of the price. There was evidence that the defendant had used the bicycle for racing (for which he had won several prizes) and occasionally on the road. *Held,* in the circumstances of the case and remembering that it was a common practice for persons in the defendant's position to use bicycles, the plaintiff would succeed as the machine was necessary to the defendant. (See also s2 of the Sale of Goods Act 1979; but see *Peters* v *Fleming.*)

Coggs v Bernard (1703) 2 Ld Raym 909   **[133]**

The defendant undertook to carry several hogsheads of brandy from one cellar to another but through neglect many gallons of brandy were spilt. It was not alleged that the defendant was a common carrier or suggested that he had been paid anything for his pains. *Held,* although no one could have compelled the defendant to remove the hogsheads, the plaintiff's trusting him with the goods was sufficient consideration to make him liable for any damage that they might sustain. (See also *Bainbridge* v *Firmstone.*)

Cohen v Kittell (1889) 22 QBD 680   **[134]**

The plaintiff employed the defendant to bet on commission. The defendant failed to carry out the plaintiff's instructions to make certain bets and the plaintiff claimed damages for breach of contract by the defendant as the plaintiff's agent. The plaintiff claimed as damages the excess of gains over losses which would have been received by the defendant if the bets had been made, less the amount of his agreed commission. *Held,* the action must fail as the bets themselves, the subject-matter of the agency, would not have been recoverable by reason of s18 of the Gaming Act 1845. (But see *De Mattos* v *Benjamin.*)

Cohen v Nessdale Ltd [1982] 2 All ER 97 (Court of Appeal)   **[135]**

The defendant landlord offered, 'subject to contract', to sell his plaintiff statutory tenant a long lease of his flat for £20,000. Negotiations continued for two months, but the tenant then broke them off as the landlord had applied to increase the rent. Six months later the parties orally agreed the sale and purchase of a 99-year lease for £17,000; later that day the landlords confirmed the agreement in writing 'subject to contract'. The plaintiff sought specific performance of the oral contract claiming that his making of the first payment of rent under the new lease was part performance. *Held,* his claim could not succeed as a 'subject to contract' qualification, once introduced into negotiations, can only cease to apply to the negotiations if the parties expressly or by necessary implication agree that it should be expunged and this was not the case here. (But see *Alpenstow Ltd* v *Regalian Properties plc.*)

Coldunell Ltd v Gallon [1986] 1 All ER 429 (Court of Appeal)   **[136]**

A son in his fifties needed money for his business and his father offered to help him; the son arranged for the plaintiff moneylenders to lend his father £20,000 who, as the plaintiffs knew, would then give the money to the son. The loan was secured by a charge on the father's house with the son a surety. In completing the transaction, the plaintiffs' solicitors dealt solely with and through the son. They sent the parents a letter advising them to seek independent legal advice but they never received it. The parents' signatures were procured by the son in the presence of his own solicitor but he (the solicitor) did not advise them as to the nature and effect of the transaction. The son forged his father's signature on the cheque and kept the money. Neither the loan nor the interest was repaid and the plaintiffs sought to enforce the charge on the house. *Held,* they were entitled to succeed. Although the son had exercised undue influence, he had not been the plaintiffs' agent. The plaintiffs' only duty was to point out the desirability of taking independent legal advice. (Distinguished: *Kingsnorth Trust Ltd* v *Bell*; followed in *Bank of Baroda* v *Shab.*)

Collins v Godefroy (1831) 1 B & Ad 950 [137]

An attorney had attended a trial of a civil action for six days on the defendant's subpoena and the defendant afterwards promised to pay him a fee of six guineas. *Held,* the promise could not be enforced as the plaintiff, having been subpoenaed, was under a duty to attend and there was no consideration for the defendant's promise to pay him a fee. (But see *England* v *Davidson.*)

Combe v Combe [1951] 1 All ER 767 (Court of Appeal) [138]

A wife had obtained a decree nisi and her solicitors wrote to the husband's solicitors to ask them to confirm that he would allow her £100 pa and they confirmed that this was the case. The wife did not apply to the court for maintenance and the husband did not observe his promise to pay her £100 pa. *Held,* as the husband had not requested the wife to refrain from making an application to the court there was no consideration for his promise; even if he had made such a request there would have been no consideration, as the wife's promise not to apply for an order would not be binding on her so as to preclude her from applying for an order for permanent maintenance. The principle stated in *Central London Property Trust Ltd* v *High Trees House Ltd* must be 'used as a shield and not as a sword' (*per* BIRKETT LJ). (But see *Tool Metal Manufacturing Co Ltd* v *Tungsten Electric Co Ltd.*)

Commercial Plastics Ltd v Vincent [1964] 3 All ER 546 [139]
(Court of Appeal)

The plaintiffs manufactured thin PVC calendered sheeting and one of the many ways in which this was used was in the manufacture of adhesive tape. In this field the plaintiffs had about twenty per cent of the United Kingdom market and they had five principal rivals, although they (the plaintiffs) manufactured about eighty per cent of the market for plastic sheeting used to make adhesive tape and this represented about twenty per cent of the plaintiffs' total production. The defendant was employed by the plaintiffs to co-ordinate research and development work in connection with adhesive tape production and his contract of service provided that he would not 'seek employment with any of our competitors in the PVC calendering field, for at least one year after leaving our employ'. The defendant gave one month's notice in accordance with the terms of his contract of service and entered the employment of one of the plaintiffs' competitors in the PVC calendering field. The plaintiffs sought to enforce the restrictive provision contained in the defendant's contract of service with them. *Held,* they would fail because the restriction was void as it was wider than was reasonably necessary for the protection of the plaintiffs' trade secrets. There was no evidence to prove that the plaintiffs needed for their protection a restriction that was potentially world-wide and the plaintiffs had failed to show that it was necessary for the restrictive provision to apply to the whole of the PVC calendering field, as opposed to the production of sheeting for adhesive tape. (See also *Strange (SW) Ltd* v *Mann.*)

Commission for the New Towns v Cooper (GB) Ltd [140]
[1995] 2 All ER 929 (Court of Appeal)

Following a meeting at which they discussed the assignment of a leasehold interest in land, the parties subsequently set out the agreement which they had reached in an exchange of letters which were, in substance, an offer and an acceptance. The question arose, inter alia, as to whether the requirements of s2 of the Law of Property (Miscellaneous Provisions) Act 1989 had been satisfied. *Held,* they had not. '... when there has been a prior oral agreement, there is only an "exchange of contracts" within s2 when documents are exchanged which set out or incorporate all of the terms which have been agreed and when, crucially, those documents are intended, by virtue of their exchange, to bring about a contract to which s2 applies ...The letters exchanged ... were not documents of the kind described as contracts in s2 of the 1989 Act, and therefore no contract meaning a legally enforceable agreement was made ...' (*per* EVANS LJ). (See also *Firstpost Homes Ltd* v *Johnson*.)

Compagnie de Commerce et Commission SARL v   [141] Parkinson Stove Co Ltd [1953] 2 Lloyd's Rep 487 (Court of Appeal)

The appellants negotiated with the respondents for the purchase of steel sheets and the respondents stipulated that the appellants should accept their offer on a certain form and that no other method of acceptance, verbal or written, would be valid. The appellants tendered their acceptance by letter but subsequently purported to cancel the order. *Held,* there had been no valid acceptance of the respondents' offer and there was no binding contract but in such cases it would be possible to hold that the respondents had waived the condition as to mode of acceptance, expressly or by conduct. (See also *Eliason* v *Henshaw*.)

Compania Naviera Maropan SA v Bowaters Lloyd   [142] Pulp and Paper Mills Ltd [1955] 2 All ER 241 (Court of Appeal)

A charterparty in respect of the steamship Stork provided that: 'Charterers have the right to order the ship to load at two safe berths or loading places.' The charterers directed the ship to load at a place on the east coast of Newfoundland but during a heavy gale she dragged her anchors and was severely damaged. *Held,* the owners were entitled to damages for breach of contract as the charterers had ordered the vessel to load at an unsafe place. The damages flowed naturally from the charterers' breach of contract. (But see *Hadley* v *Baxendale*.)

Constantine (Joseph) Steamship Line Ltd v Imperial   [143] Smelting Corp Ltd [1941] 2 All ER 165 (House of Lords)

The respondents chartered a steamship from the appellants but on the day before she was due to load her cargo an explosion occurred in the neighbourhood of her auxiliary boiler which made it impossible for the ship to undertake the voyage. The respondents claimed damages for failure to load the cargo and the appellants maintained that they were not liable as performance of the contract had been frustrated. *Held,* the case would be decided in favour of the appellants as the party denying frustration had to prove negligence on the part of the party relying on that defence and this the respondents had been unable to do. (See also *Jackson* v *Union Marine Insurance Co Ltd*.)

Cooden Engineering Co Ltd v Stanford   [144] [1952] 2 All ER 915 (Court of Appeal)

A hire-purchase agreement in respect of a motor car provided that upon the determination of the agreement by the owners the car should be returned and the hirer should pay the instalments which were outstanding at the date of such determination and, by way of compensation for depreciation, 40 per cent of the instalments which had not yet fallen due. *Held,* this sum was a penalty and could not therefore be recovered. (But see *Stockloser* v *Johnson*.)

Cooper v Phibbs (1867) LR 2 HL 149 (House of Lords)   **[145]**

The appellant sought to be relieved from an agreement whereby he contracted to take from the respondent a three-year lease of a salmon fishery. At the time of making the agreement the appellant believed that the fishery belonged to the respondent but it afterwards appeared that the fishery was the property of the appellant himself. *Held,* the appellant was entitled to have the agreement for the lease set aside subject to the respondent having a lien on the property in respect of money spent on purchasing certain fishing rights and improving the fishery. (See also *Huddersfield Banking Co Ltd* v *Henry Lister & Son Ltd.*)

Cooper v Willis (1906) 22 TLR 582   **[146]**

The parties entered into a settlement in respect of certain racing debts. The debtor, the defendant, agreed to give the plaintiff two cheques payable at a future date and not to set up a defence under the Gaming Acts if the plaintiff should need to sue upon the cheques. One cheque was dishonoured and the defendant, in breach of the terms of the settlement, relied upon the Gaming Acts by way of defence. *Held,* his defence would succeed; the agreement whereby the defendant purported to prevent himself from taking advantage of the statutory defence under the Gaming Acts was illegal and void as it prejudiced the administration of justice. (See also *Keir* v *Leeman.*)

Coral v Kleyman [1951] 1 All ER 518   **[147]**

The plaintiff was a bookmaker to whom the defendant's son had lost, but not paid, £355 15s. The defendant signed an undertaking to the effect that he would pay the amount due in consideration of the plaintiff not reporting his son to the Committee of Tattersalls. The plaintiff sued to enforce payment under the agreement. *Held,* the action would fail. The undertaking was merely a device to contravene s18 of the Gaming Act 1845 under which the debt could not be recovered from the son. The plaintiff knew that he could not succeed against the son so his forbearance to report him to Tattersalls was not a consideration sufficient to support the contract. (See also *Hill* v *Hill (William) (Park Lane) Ltd.*)

Cornish v Midland Bank plc [1985] 3 All ER 513   **[148]**
(Court of Appeal)

The plaintiff bank customer signed a second mortgage in favour of the bank without being aware that it secured not only a loan of £2,000 for renovations to a farmhouse jointly owned with her husband, but also unlimited further advances made to the husband. *Held,* inter alia, the bank had assumed a duty to give the plaintiff proper advice as to the effect of the mortgage; it had been negligent in the way it had discharged that duty and the plaintiff was therefore entitled to damages against it. However, the mortgage itself would not be set aside; the only relationship existing between the plaintiff and the bank was that of banker and customer and no unfair advantage had been taken of her and no presumption of undue influence had arisen. (Followed: *National Westminster Bank plc* v *Morgan.*)

Couchman v Hill [1947] 1 All ER 103 (Court of Appeal)   **[149]**

The plaintiff bought a heifer at an auction and the catalogue described it as 'unserved'. The conditions of sale provided that the auctioneers gave no warranty in respect of the condition or description of any of the animals but before the sale and when the heifer was in the ring, the plaintiff asked the defendant and the auctioneer to confirm that it was 'unserved'. This confirmation was given but within eight weeks of the sale the heifer died as a result of carrying a calf at too young an age for breeding. *Held,* the statements that the heifer was 'unserved' constituted a warranty which over-rode the conditions of sale and the plaintiff was able to recover damages for breach of this warranty. (But see *Routledge* v *McKay.*)

Couturier v Hastie (1852) 8 Exch 40 [150]

The plaintiffs, who were merchants, shipped 1,180 quarters of Indian corn and the defendants, their del credere agents, successfully negotiated a sale. The corn had to be sold before the voyage was completed because tempestuous weather had made it heated and fermented but the plaintiffs nevertheless sought to recover the price of the cargo. The implied guarantee on the part of the defendants as to the due performance of the contract which arose from the special relationship of the parties had not been reduced to writing and the defendants maintained that they were protected under the provisions of s4 of the Statute of Frauds. *Held,* the defendants were liable by reason of the payment of del credere commission and not solely because of their implied guarantee and for this reason their liability was not one to pay the debt of another within the meaning of the section. (See also *Sutton & Co* v *Grey.*) On appeal to the House of Lords (1856) 5 HL Cas 673. *Held,* the contract contemplated that there was an existing something to be sold and bought and capable of transfer but as the corn had been sold at the time of the sale by the defendants this was not the case and the defendants were not liable. (See also *Scott* v *Coulson;* but see *McRae* v *Commonwealth Disposals Commission.*)

Cowan v Milbourn (1867) LR 2 Exch 230 [151]

The defendant agreed to let certain assembly rooms to the plaintiff, but on discovering that it was intended to use the rooms for the purpose of delivering lectures which were to be blasphemous in content the defendant withdrew his consent to the letting. The plaintiff claimed damages for breach of contract. *Held,* the plaintiff could not recover. The purpose for which the rooms were let was illegal and for this reason the contract between the parties could not be enforced at law. (See also *Clay* v *Yates.*)

Cowern v Nield [1912] 2 KB 419 [152]

The defendant was a minor who carried on business as a hay and straw merchant. The plaintiff ordered some clover and hay and sent his cheque in settlement. The goods were never delivered and the plaintiff brought an action to recover the amount which he had paid. *Held,* the plaintiff's claim must fail as the transaction in question was a trading contract and whether or not it was for the benefit of the defendant, in the absence of fraud, he could not be liable under such an agreement. (But see s3 of the Minors' Contracts Act 1987.)

Cox v Philips Industries Ltd [1976] 3 All ER 161 [153]

The plaintiff claimed damages from his employers for breach of contract as they had removed him to a position of less responsibility where the duties were very vague. As a result he had become frustrated, depressed and ill. When he complained about the situation, he was made redundant and was given five months' salary in lieu of notice. He claimed damages for the vexation and frustration caused by the breach. The employers claimed that damages for emotional distress were limited to contracts for pleasure and enjoyment. *Held,* it was within the contemplation of the employers when they had originally given the plaintiff a position of responsibility that a breach of the contract would lead to frustration and distress. Consequently he was entitled to compensation for the emotional distress caused by the breach. Damages for emotional distress arising from a breach of contract were not limited to contracts for giving pleasure and enjoyment. (See also *Jarvis* v *Swans Tours Ltd* and *Addis* v *Gramophone Co Ltd*.)

Credit Lyonnais Bank Nederland NV v Burch   [154]
(1996) The Times 1 July (Court of Appeal)

The defendant's employer, with whom and with whose family she had close links, encountered financial difficulties and he asked her to put up her flat as collateral security for his company's overdraft with the plaintiff bank. If she failed to do so, he explained, the company would collapse and she would be out of a job. The employer did not explain to the defendant the company's financial position and, although the plaintiffs advised the defendant to take independent legal advice, she did not do so and duly entered into the mortgage, guaranteeing without limit repayment of the company's borrowings. *Held*, the mortgage would be set aside. NOURSE LJ said that the unconscionability of the transaction was of direct materiality to the case based on undue influence. Since it was so manifestly disadvantageous to the defendant, the plaintiffs could not be said to have taken reasonable steps to avoid being fixed with constructive notice of the employer's undue influence over her when neither the potential extent of her liability had been explained to her nor had she received independent advice. It was not enough for the defendant to have been told by the plaintiffs repeatedly that the mortgage was unlimited in time and amount nor to have been advised by the bank to take independent legal advice. It was at the least necessary that she should receive such advice. (See also *Barclays Bank plc* v *O'Brien*.)

Cricklewood Property and Investment Trust Ltd v   [155]
Leightons Investment Trust Ltd [1945] 1 All ER 252
(House of Lords)

A building lease was entered into in 1936 for a term of 99 years whereby the tenants were to erect a number of shops to form a shopping centre. War came before the work was completed and the tenants refused to pay the rent reserved by the lease on the ground that the lease had been frustrated by restrictions imposed by the Government on building and the supply of materials. *Held*, the tenants' view would not be supported as the interruption of building did not destroy the identity of the arrangement or make it unreasonable to carry out the work as soon as the restrictions were lifted. (See also *Eyre* v *Johnson* and *National Carriers Ltd* v *Panalpina (Northern) Ltd*.)

Criminal proceedings against Bernáldez (Case C–129/94)   [156]
(1996) The Times 6 May (European Court of Justice)

The defendant caused a road accident while driving while intoxicated and he had been ordered to make reparation for the damage to property he had caused. However, the insurance company, with which the defendant had taken out a policy covering damage caused by his vehicle, was absolved from liability since a Spanish law excluded from cover damage to property caused where the driver was intoxicated. *Held*, art 3(1) of Council Directive 72/166/EEC was to be interpreted as meaning that, without prejudice to the provisions of art 2(1) of Council Directive 84/5/EEC, a compulsory insurance contract could not provide that in certain cases, in particular where the driver of the vehicle was intoxicated, the insurer was not obliged to pay compensation for the damage to property and personal injuries caused to third parties by the insured vehicle. On the other hand, such a contract could provide that in such cases the insurer was to have a right of recovery against the insured.

Crow v Rogers (1724) 1 Stra 592   **[157]**

John Hardy owed the plaintiff £70 and it was agreed between Hardy and the defendant that the defendant would pay the plaintiff £70 in return for a promise by Hardy that he would convey his house to the defendant. The plaintiff sought to recover £70 from the defendant. *Held,* the action must fail as the plaintiff was a stranger to the consideration. (See also *Price* v *Easton.*)

Cumber v Wane (1721) 1 Stra 426   **[158]**

The defendant gave the plaintiff a promissory note for £5 in satisfaction of a debt of £15. *Held,* the plaintiff could recover the balance. (See also *D & C Builders Ltd* v *Rees.*)

Cundy v Lindsay (1878) 3 App Cas 459 (House of Lords)   **[159]**

Messrs Lindsay & Co were linen manufacturers in Belfast and Alfred Blenkarn, who occupied a room in a house looking into Wood Street, Cheapside, wrote to them and proposed buying a quantity of their goods. Blenkarn used the address '37, Wood Street, Cheapside' and signed the letters, without using an initial or Christian name, in such a way that his signature appeared to be 'Blenkiron & Co'. There was a highly respectable firm of W. Blenkiron & Son carrying on business at 123, Wood Street and Messrs Lindsay & Co, who knew of this firm's reputation but not the number of the premises where they carried on business, supplied the goods ordered by Blenkarn and addressed them to Messrs Blenkiron & Co, 37, Wood Street, Cheapside. Blenkarn did not pay for the goods but disposed of them to the defendants who were sued by Messrs Lindsay & Co for unlawful conversion. *Held,* no contract had been concluded with Blenkarn, who therefore had no property in the goods to transfer to the defendants; consequently the defendants were liable to the extent of their value. (But see *Henderson & Co* v *Williams* and *Citibank NA* v *Brown Shipley & Co Ltd.*)

Curtis v Chemical Cleaning and Dyeing Co Ltd   **[160]**
[1951] 1 All ER 631 (Court of Appeal)

The plaintiff took a white satin wedding dress to the defendants for cleaning. She was asked to sign a document which contained a clause that the dress 'is accepted on condition that the company is not liable for any damage howsoever arising' but, before she signed, she was told that the effect of the document which she was about to sign was to exclude liability for damage to beads or sequins. Without reading all the terms of the document the plaintiff then signed as she was asked. The dress was stained due to the negligence of the defendants. *Held,* the defendants were liable as the innocent misrepresentation as to the extent of the exception clause had the effect of excluding the clause from the contract between the parties. (See also s13 of the Supply of Goods and Services Act 1982; but see *L'Estrange* v *F Graucob Ltd.*)

Cutter v Powell (1795) 6 Term Rep 320   **[161]**

The defendant agreed to pay Cutter 30 guineas 'provided he proceeds, continues and does his duty as second mate' on a voyage from Kingston, Jamaica, to Liverpool. Cutter began the journey but died when the ship was about one week's sail from Liverpool. His administratrix sought to recover a proportion of the agreed wage in respect of that part of the journey for which Cutter had acted as a second mate. *Held,* she was unable to succeed as Cutter had not performed his part of the contract. (See also *Appleby* v *Myers*.)

D & C Builders Ltd v Rees [1965] 3 All ER 837   [162]
(Court of Appeal)

The plaintiffs had carried out work for the defendant to the value of £482 13s 1d. For months they pressed for payment. Finally, the defendant's wife, who knew that the plaintiffs were in financial difficulties, offered £300 in settlement of the debt, saying that if the offer were not accepted, nothing would be paid. The plaintiffs accepted a cheque for £300 and gave a receipt 'in completion of the account'. Later, they sued for the balance, and the question arose whether the action was barred by accord and satisfaction. *Held,* the plaintiffs were not barred from recovering the balance. There was no true accord because the plaintiffs' consent had been obtained under pressure, nor was there any equitable ground disentitling them to recover. (See also *Pinnel's Case* and *Foakes* v *Beer*.)

Dakin (H) & Co Ltd v Lee [1916] 1 KB 566 (Court of Appeal)   [163]

The plaintiffs, who were builders, sought to recover the balance of the price of certain repairs carried out at the defendant's house. The defendant resisted their claim as concrete underpinning a wall was 2 ft thick instead of 4 ft as specified in the contract, columns of solid iron 4 in in diameter had been used instead of hollow iron 5 in in diameter and certain joists over the bay window had not been bolted as stipulated. *Held,* the plaintiffs were entitled to recover the balance of their charges, less an amount in respect of that part of the work which had been carried out contrary to the specification, as the defendant could only withhold payment if he could show that the total work carried out by the plaintiffs was of no benefit to him, that it was entirely different to that which they contracted to do or that they had abandoned the work and left it unfinished. (Distinguished in *Bolton* v *Mahadeva*; but see *Sumpter* v *Hedges*.)

David (Lawrence) Ltd v Ashton [1991] 1 All ER 385   [164]
(Court of Appeal)

The contract of employment of the defendant, the plaintiffs' sales director, contained covenants against disclosure of information regarding the plaintiffs or their customers and trade secrets or competition for a period of two years after termination of the contract. The plaintiffs dismissed the defendant and he was immediately offered employment by a direct competitor. In proceedings to enforce the covenants, the plaintiffs sought an interlocutory injunction. *Held*, the injunction would not be granted in respect of confidential information or trade secrets because the plaintiffs had been unable to define with any precision what it was that they were seeking to protect. However, the injunction would be granted to enforce the covenant in restraint of trade because the plaintiffs had shown that there was a serious issue to be tried and that damages would not be an adequate remedy and, as a speedy trial was possible, it would not operate for any great length of time. (See also *Michael (John) Design plc* v *Cooke*; but see *Lansing Linde Ltd* v *Kerr*.)

Davies v Collins [1945] 1 All ER 247 (Court of Appeal)   [165]

The respondent took his uniform to the appellants for cleaning and repair. He was handed a docket which stipulated that 'Whilst every care is exercised cleaning and dyeing garments, all orders are accepted at owner's risk entirely and we are unable to hold ourselves responsible for damage, shrinkage, colour or defects developed in necessary handling. The proprietors' liability for loss is limited to an amount not exceeding 10 times the cost of cleaning.' The uniform was sent to a sub-contractor but was never returned and the respondent claimed the full value of the uniform. *Held,* he was entitled to recover the amount for which he claimed as the mere presence of a limitation clause in this form was sufficient to exclude the appellants' right to send the uniform to another contractor and therefore when they did allow another to perform the work they were in breach of their contract and denied such protection as it may have otherwise afforded. (See also *Woolmer v Delmer Price Ltd.*)

Davies v London and Provincial Marine Insurance Co   [166]
(1878) 8 Ch D 469

In the belief that the retention of money by one of their agents amounted to a felony, the company ordered his arrest. Friends of the suspected person offered to deposit a sum of money by way of security for his defaults but while the offer was being considered the company was advised that the agent had not committed a felony and the directions for his arrest were withdrawn. At a second interview on the same day, the friends agreed to deposit the money as a security for any deficiency but they were not told that the directions for the arrest of their friend had been withdrawn. *Held,* this agreement should be rescinded as the agent's friends ought to have been told of the change of circumstances. (See also *Williams v Bayley.*)

Davis Contractors Ltd v Fareham Urban District   [167]
Council [1956] 2 All ER 145 (House of Lords)

The plaintiffs contracted to build the defendants 78 council houses within eight months for a fixed price. Through no fault on the part of the plaintiffs there was a scarcity of skilled labour and the work took 22 months to complete. The plaintiffs maintained that by reason of the scarcity of labour the contract had been brought to an end and that they were entitled to recover a sum in excess of the contract price on the basis of a quantum meruit. *Held,* their claim should fail, as the scarcity of labour had not frustrated the contract and the plaintiffs had not been released from its terms as regards price. (See also *Tsakiroglou & Co Ltd v Noblee & Thorl GmbH.*)

Deacons v Bridge [1984] 2 All ER 19 (Privy Council)   [168]

The plaintiffs were a large firm of solicitors in Hong Kong and, before he resigned to set up his own practice there, the defendant was the partner in charge of the intellectual property and trade marks department which, like the other departments, was largely self-contained. The partnership agreement provided, inter alia, that if a partner ceased to be a partner he was not to act as a solicitor in Hong Kong for a period of five years for any client of the firm or any person who had been a client in the preceding three years. *Held,* the plaintiffs were entitled to an injunction to enforce the restrictive covenant the terms of which, in all the circumstances, were not unreasonable. It was reasonable, as between the parties, for the firm to protect itself against the appropriation by the defendant of any part of the firm's goodwill, notwithstanding the division of the firm's practice into self-contained departments. (See also *Kerr v Morris.*)

De Francesco v Barnum (1890) 45 Ch D 430   **[169]**

A minor and her mother executed a deed whereby the infant, who was to be apprenticed to the plaintiff for seven years with a view to being taught stage dancing, agreed that she would not marry or accept any professional engagements during the period of her apprenticeship without the consent of the plaintiff. The contract also contained terms whereby the young woman was to be paid a certain small sum for such engagements as she should fulfil, but there was no stipulation that the plaintiff should provide engagements for the infant or maintain her while she was unemployed. In breach of this agreement she signed a contract to dance for the defendant and the plaintiff sought to enforce the provisions of the deed and claimed damages for breach of contract. *Held*, the claim must fail as the provisions of the deed were unreasonable and could not be enforced against the minor or her mother and no action would lie against the defendant for enticing her away from the plaintiff's employment. (But see *Clements v London & North Western Railway Co.*)

De La Bere v Pearson Ltd [1908] 1 KB 280   **[170]**

The defendants advertised in their newspaper that their city editor would advise readers on financial matters. The plaintiff wrote to ask for the name of a 'good stockbroker'. The editor recommended a broker whose honesty he had no reason to doubt but who was, in fact, an undischarged bankrupt. The plaintiff sent £1,400 to the broker who immediately misappropriated the money and the plaintiff sued the defendants for breach of contract. *Held*, the defendants were liable for breach of their contract (the defendants' advertisement was the offer and the plaintiff accepted it when he wrote to them) to use reasonable care that the person recommended should answer the description of a 'good stockbroker'. 'There was a contract as between the plaintiff and the defendants ... to take reasonable care in the nomination of a broker, and I think there was a clear breach of this contract ... the measure of damages would include all damage which would be sustained by the plaintiff through consequences arising in strict course of business with a stockbroker' *(per* VAUGHAN WILLIAMS LJ).

De Lassalle v Guildford [1901] 2 KB 215 (Court of Appeal)   **[171]**

The parties agreed terms for the lease of a house but the plaintiff refused to hand over the counterpart of the lease until he had received a verbal assurance that the drains were in order. The drains were not in good order and the plaintiff sought to recover damages for breach of warranty. *Held*, the plaintiff would succeed as the verbal assurance constituted a warranty which was collateral to the lease and for the breach of which an action could be maintained. (See also *Record v Bell*.)

De Mattos v Benjamin (1894) 63 LJQB 248   **[172]**

The plaintiff employed the defendant to make bets for him as his agent but the defendant failed to pay him the winnings. When sued for money had and received the defendant relied on s1 of the Gaming Act 1892. *Held*, the plaintiff could recover as the Act would not be allowed to enable a person who had received money on behalf of another to retain it for his own use. (See also *Bridger v Savage.*)

Dennant v Skinner [1948] 2 All ER 29   **[173]**

A van had been knocked down to the highest bidder and the auctioneer asked him his name. The bidder said that his name was King and that he was the son of the proprietor of King's Motors of Oxford, a firm of high repute, which he was representing. These representations were repeated and certain evidence as to his identity produced when the man offered to pay by cheque but it transpired, after his cheque had been dishonoured, that although his name was King he had no connection with the well-known firm of King's Motors. The plaintiff, the seller of the car, sued to recover the car or its value from the person to whom King had sold it. *Held,* the contract was made when the hammer fell and at that moment there was no mistake as to the identity of the bidder and the property in the car passed to him. He was therefore able to give the defendant a good title to the car and for this reason the action would fail. (But see *Hardman* v *Booth.*)

Derry v Peek (1889) 14 App Cas 337 (House of Lords) [174]

The Plymouth, Devonport and District Tramways Co was authorised to make certain tramways by special Act of Parliament which provided that the carriages might be moved by animal power and, with the consent of the Board of Trade, by steam or any mechanical power for fixed periods and subject to the regulations of the Board. The company issued a prospectus stating that 'one great feature of this undertaking, to which considerable importance should be attached, is, that by special Act of Parliament obtained, the company has the right to use steam or mechanical motive power, instead of horses'. The plaintiff bought shares on the faith of this statement but the Board of Trade afterwards refused their consent to the use of steam power and the company was wound up. At the time of issuing the prospectus the company honestly believed that consent would be granted as a matter of course. *Held,* the plaintiff's action in deceit must fail, as the statement contained in the prospectus was not a fraudulent misrepresentation as the company entertained an honest belief that it was true. (See also *Akerhielm* v *De Mare.*)

Diamond v Campbell-Jones [1960] 1 All ER 583 [175]

The defendants wrongly repudiated an agreement for the sale by the defendants to the plaintiff of a leasehold property in Mayfair and the question arose as to the amount of damages that the plaintiff was entitled to recover. The agreement was subject to and with the benefit of a contract for the grant of a new lease and this contract required the premises to be converted by the lessee into ground floor office accommodation and residential maisonettes. The plaintiff was a dealer in real property but it was not shown that the defendants were aware of this or that he intended to carry out a conversion of the premises. *Held,* the amount of damages should be limited to the difference between the purchase price and the market value at the date of the breach of contract as there were no special circumstances sufficient to impute to the defendants knowledge that the plaintiff intended to convert the property for profit. (See also *Ardennes (Cargo Owners)* v *Ardennes (Owners).*)

Dickinson v Dodds (1876) 2 Ch D 463 (Court of Appeal) [176]

The defendant signed a document which took the form of an agreement to sell certain property to the plaintiff but added a postscript 'This offer to be left over until Friday ...' The plaintiff decided to buy the property on the day before the offer (it was found that the document constituted an offer and not an agreement) expired but on the Thursday afternoon he heard from another person that the defendant had contracted to sell the property to a third party. On the Thursday evening the plaintiff delivered a formal acceptance at the house where the defendant was staying, and at about seven o'clock on the following morning a duplicate of this acceptance was handed to the defendant. The plaintiff sought a decree of specific performance. *Held,* the decree would not be awarded as retraction of an offer need not be express and in this case was implied by the sale of the property to the third party. 'If a man who makes an offer dies, the offer cannot be accepted after he is dead' (*per* MELLISH LJ). (See also *Cartwright* v *Hoogstoel.*)

Dies v British and International Mining and Finance Corp Ltd [1939] 1 KB 724   [177]

The purchaser ordered rifles and cartridges to the value of £270,000 and paid £100,000 by way of prepayment of part of the purchase price. The purchaser afterwards refused to take delivery of the goods and to pay the balance of the purchase price and the vendors elected to treat the contract as at an end. The purchaser sought to recover the amount of his prepayment. *Held,* he was entitled to succeed, subject to the payment of damages to the vendors in respect of his breach of contract. (But see *Stockloser* v *Johnson.*)

Diggle v Higgs (1877) 2 Ex D 422 (Court of Appeal)   [178]

Two men agreed to walk a match for £200 a side, the money to be deposited with a stakeholder, the defendant, and paid to the winner. The plaintiff lost the match but before the defendant had paid over the stakes to the winner gave notice to the defendant that he was not to pay the winner and demanded the £200 which he, the plaintiff, had deposited with the defendant. The defendant nevertheless paid £400 to the winner and the plaintiff sued to recover £200. *Held,* he was entitled to succeed. The proviso to s18 of the Gaming Act 1845, rendered the contract void but this did not prevent the plaintiff from recovering the amount of his own deposit from the stakeholder although the winner would not have been able to recover that of the plaintiff if the defendant had withheld payment. (See also *Varney* v *Hickman.*)

Doyle v White City Stadium Ltd [1935] 1 KB 110   [179]
(Court of Appeal)

The plaintiff, a minor, was a boxer and a term of the contract with the British Boxing Board of Control by which he was granted a licence to box provided that payment of the money due to a boxer might be withheld if he was disqualified for one of various reasons. The plaintiff took part in a contest for the heavyweight championship of Great Britain but was disqualified in the second round. The plaintiff sought to recover the amount due to him in respect of the fight and contended that he was not bound by the terms of the contract with the British Boxing Board of Control as he was an infant. *Held,* the plaintiff's action must fail as he was bound by the agreement, which was closely analogous to a contract of employment, because it was, on the whole, for his benefit. (See also *Slade* v *Metrodent Ltd* and *Chaplin* v *Leslie Frewin (Publishers) Ltd.*)

Dunk v George Waller & Son Ltd See Malik v Bank of Credit and Commerce International SA

Dunlop Pneumatic Tyre Co Ltd v New Garage and Motor Co Ltd [1915] AC 79 (House of Lords)   [180]

The appellants, manufacturers of motor tyres, supplied goods to the respondents under a contract which provided that the respondents would not sell tyres at less than the appellants' list price. It was further provided that if the respondents sold a tyre in breach of this agreement they would pay the appellants £5. *Held,* this sum would be regarded as liquidated damages and not as a penalty. (See also *Philips Hong Kong Ltd* v *A-G of Hong Kong*; but see *Ford Motor Co (England) Ltd* v *Armstrong.*)

Dunlop Pneumatic Tyre Co Ltd v Selfridge & Co Ltd [1915] AC 847 (House of Lords)   [181]

The defendants, who were large storekeepers and sold tyres retail to the public, ordered tyres made by the plaintiffs from Messrs A. J. Dew & Co, who were motor accessory factors. In accordance with the requirements of a contraet between the plaintiffs and Messrs A. J. Dew & Co, an agreement purporting to be made between the defendants and Messrs A. J. Dew & Co, provided that in consideration of Messrs A. J. Dew & Co allowing them certain discounts off the plaintiffs' list prices, the defendants would not sell or offer any tyres made by the plaintiffs at less than list prices. The plaintiffs sued the defendants for breach of this agreement. *Held,* their action could not succeed as 'only a person who is a party to a contract can sue on it' (*per* VISCOUNT HALDANE LC). (See also *Scruttons Ltd* v *Midland Silicones Ltd*; but see *Gregory and Parker* v *Williams.*)

Dutton v Poole (1678) Freem 471   [182]

The defendant's father intended to cut down some oak trees to make provision for his children, including the plaintiff, but the defendant promised his father that if he spared the trees he (the defendant) would give his sister (the plaintiff) £1,000. The plaintiff sought to enforce this promise. *Held,* she was entitled to do so. (But see *Crow* v *Rogers.*)

EP Finance Co Ltd v Dooley [1964] 1 All ER 527   [183]

Under the terms of a hire-purchase agreement in respect of a second-hand Bentley motor car, in the event of the termination of the agreement by the return of the vehicle the defendant hirer was liable to pay to the plaintiff hire-purchase company all arrears of rent calculated on a daily basis, the cost of repairs and replacement and 'by way of agreed depreciation ... a sum equal to fifty per cent of the total hire-purchase price ... plus a further five per cent of such total hire-purchase price for each month which has elapsed between the receipt of the [car] by the owners up to seventy-five per cent of the said total price less ... the total of the sum already paid and the moneys due to the owners for hire rentals at the date of the receipt of the [car] by them.' The defendant contended that this clause constituted a penalty and therefore could not be relied upon by the plaintiffs. *Held,* the formula used was not a genuine pre-estimate of the damage in this particular case and it followed that the clause was a penalty. However, the plaintiffs were entitled to recover damages for breach of the agreement as opposed to a sum under the terms of the agreement, in this case one month's arrears, with interest, and the cost of repairs. (But see *Dunlop Pneumatic Tyre Co Ltd* v *New Garage and Motor Co Ltd.*)

Eastes v Russ [1914] 1 Ch 468 (Court of Appeal)   [184]

The plaintiff, a pathologist, carried on the business of 'The Laboratories of Pathology and Public Health' in Queen Ann Street and there were only two or three similar institutions in London. At that time this work involved a new method of medical research. The defendant was engaged by the plaintiff as an assistant microscopist and a term of his contract of employment stipulated that he would not engage in any similar work within ten miles of the plaintiff's laboratory. The defendant left the plaintiffs employment and shortly afterwards established a pathological laboratory within half a mile of that of the plaintiff. The plaintiff sought to restrain him. *Held,* the restriction, which, in the absence of any provision to the contrary, lasted during the whole of the defendant's life, was wider than was reasonably necessary for the protection of the plaintiff and was therefore void. (But see *Fitch* v *Dewes.*)

Eastham v Newcastle United Football Club Ltd   **[185]**
[1963] 3 All ER 139

The plaintiff entered into a contract of employment with Newcastle United but later sought a transfer to another club. Newcastle United were unwilling to release him and placed him on their list of retained players, although his yearly contract with them had not been renewed. Under the rules of the Football Association and the regulations of the Football League while so retained the plaintiff was unable to play for another club in England, Scotland, Northern Ireland, Eire and most other countries where association football is played, provided Newcastle United offered him a 'reasonable' wage. *Held,* the plaintiff was entitled to declarations that his retention was not binding upon him as it was an unlawful restraint of trade. 'There may be players who have shown quite plainly that they are not going to continue with a particular club or to re-sign with it, and in their case, placing them on the retain list does substantially interfere with their right to seek other employment and – I emphasise this – does so at a time when they are not the employees of the retaining club. That seems to me to operate substantially in restraint of trade' *(per* WILBERFORCE J). (See also *Greig* v *Insole.*)

Eastwood v Kenyon (1840) 11 Ad & El 438   **[186]**

The plaintiff incurred expense in the maintenance and education of a child to whom he was guardian and in the management and improvement of her property. The plaintiff borrowed money to enable him to make this provision for the child and when she became of age she promised to repay this loan and the defendant, who became the girl's husband, made a similar promise. *Held,* the plaintiff could not recover as there was no consideration to support the defendant's promise to pay and mere moral obligation was not sufficient. (See also *Thomas* v *Thomas.*)

Edwards v Carter [1893] AC 360 (House of Lords)   **[187]**

The father of an intended husband, who was nearly of age, made a marriage settlement whereby the father promised to pay an annuity and the son agreed to vest in the trustees of the settlement upon certain trusts all property to which he should become entitled under the father's will. The father died nearly four years after the execution of the settlement and left certain property to his son. More than a year after the death of his father the son purported to repudiate the settlement. *Held,* he would have been able to do so within a reasonable time of his coming of age as the settlement as regards the son was voidable, not void, but as he had not repudiated the settlement within a reasonable time he was bound by its terms.

Edwards v Skyways Ltd [1964] 1 All ER 494   **[188]**

The plaintiff was told that it was necessary for the defendants, his employers, to declare a redundancy of approximately fifteen per cent of their pilot strength and, in accordance with the terms of his contract of service, he was given three months' notice of termination. In discussions between the defendants and the British Air Line Pilots Association (duly authorised agents of the plaintiff) it was agreed that pilots declared redundant would receive from the defendants an ex gratia payment approximating to the amount contributed by the defendants for each member of a pension fund. The plaintiff, a member of the pension fund, sought to recover a sum equal to the contributions made by the defendants to the pension fund on his behalf. *Held,* the plaintiff was entitled to succeed. The use of the words 'ex gratia' did not by itself warrant the conclusion that the promise was not intended by the parties to be enforceable in law, ie that there was no intention to enter into legal relations, and the fact that the agreed payment was to be of an amount 'approximating to' the amount of the defendants' contributions did not make the agreement unenforceable on the ground that its terms were too vague. 'In a case of this nature the onus is on the party who asserts that no legal effect was intended, and the onus is a heavy one' *(per* MEGAW J). (But see *Kleinwort Benson Ltd* v *Malaysia Mining Corpn Bhd.)*

Egerton v Earl Brownlow (1835) 4 HL Cas 1   [189]
(House of Lords)

A testator provided that if Lord Alford should die without having acquired the title of Duke or Marquis of Bridgwater certain gifts to him and his issue should fail. *Held,* this condition was void as it was contrary to public policy and the gifts in the will were not to be affected by it.

Eliason v Henshaw (1819) 4 Wheaton 225   [190]
(Supreme Court of the United States)

A offered to purchase flour from B and the letter which contained this offer stipulated the price to be paid and mode of transport and in a postscript A added: 'Please write by return of wagon whether you accept our offer.' B accepted the offer but in a letter sent by the first regular mail and A contended that it was not a valid acceptance as it was not sent 'by return of wagon'. *Held,* there was no contract as an offer creates no obligation unless it is accepted according to the terms on which the offer was made. Any departure from these terms invalidates the offer unless the different mode of acceptance is agreed by the person who made the offer. (See also *Tinn* v *Hoffmann & Co.)*

Ellen v Topp (1851) 6 Exch 424   [191]

Richard Topp, a minor, was an apprentice to an 'auctioneer, appraiser, and cornfactor'. Before Richard's apprenticeship was completed the master gave up the trade of corn-factor and Richard maintained that because of this he was no longer bound by the apprenticeship deed. *Held,* this argument would be upheld as the master had by his own choice disabled himself from acting as master in all three trades. (But see *Laws* v *London Chronicle (Indicator Newspapers) Ltd.)*

Ellesmere (Earl) v Wallace [1929] 2 Ch 1 (Court of Appeal)   [192]

The defendant nominated his horse 'Master Michael' for two races at Newmarket. The horse did not run and the plaintiffs, the Jockey Club, sued to recover the entrance fee. The defendant maintained that these sums could not be recovered as they were payable under a wagering contract. *Held,* the plaintiffs were entitled to succeed as they, one of the parties to the contract, did not stand to win or lose anything by the entry of the defendant's horse for these two races. The contract was not, therefore, a wagering contract. (See also *Thacker* v *Hardy.)*

Elpis Maritime Co Ltd v Marti Chartering Co Inc, The Maria D   [193]
[1991] 3 All ER 758 (House of Lords)

A charterparty of the appellants' ship was negotiated through brokers and, by telephone, the respondents, the charterers' agents, agreed to guarantee certain of the charterers' liabilities under the charterparty. The written charterparty was in standard form and it expressly incorporated six pages of additional clauses, by one of which (cl24) the respondents guaranteed the charterers' liabilities. The front sheet of the charterparty, together with the incorporation of the additional clauses, was signed by the respondents 'for and on behalf of charterers as brokers only': they simply signed the additional pages and the last page and above this latter signature the word 'charterers' was typed. The charterers having failed to pay, the appellants sued the respondents as guarantors. The respondents relied on s4 of the Statute of Frauds. *Held*, the appellants' claim would be successful as the oral agreement of guarantee had been subsumed into the written agreement containing cl24 which had been signed by the respondents on their own account. (Applied: *Re Hoyle, Hoyle* v *Hoyle*.)

Empire Meat Co Ltd v Patrick [1939] 2 All ER 85   [194]
(Court of Appeal)

The respondents were the owners of a butcher's business carried on in Mill Road, Cambridge, and the appellant was their manager. The appellant had contracted that he would not establish a rival business of butcher or meat seller within a distance of five miles of the respondents' shop, but he left their employment and shortly afterwards opened a butcher's shop a few doors away. There was evidence that the vast majority of the trade of the respondents' shop was done within a mile or even a half-mile of their premises. *Held,* the appellant's covenant could not be enforced as the area of restriction was, in the circumstances of the case, unnecessarily wide. (See also *M & S Drapers* v *Reynolds*.)

England v Davidson (1840) 11 Ad & El 856   [195]

The defendant offered a reward of £50 to anyone who gave information which led to the conviction of a certain felon and the plaintiff, a police constable, supplied the information. The defendant argued that the promise was of no effect as the plaintiff was bound to supply such information as part of his duty as a policeman. *Held,* the giving of the information was consideration for the defendant's promise to pay the reward and the plaintiff would succeed in his action to recover it. (See also *Glasbrook Brothers Ltd* v *Glamorgan County Council*.)

English Hop Growers Ltd v Dering [1928] 2 KB 174   [196]
(Court of Appeal)

The plaintiff society, English Hop Growers Ltd, was formed to organise the marketing and sale of home-grown hops. The defendant was a member and undertook to deliver to the society all hops grown or produced by him during 1926 on certain land consisting of 63 acres. It was provided that if any of his hops should not be delivered in accordance with the provisions of this agreement the defendant would pay to the society liquidated damages of £100 per acre. The defendant failed to deliver any hops and the plaintiff society sued to recover £6,300. *Held,* they were entitled to succeed as the agreement was not unreasonable as being in restraint of trade. The contract had been entered into from equal positions of bargaining and to their mutual advantage as it sought to avoid undue competition and excessive fluctuations of price. (See also *Hitchcock* v *Coker*; but see *McEllistrim* v *Ballymacelligott Co-operative etc, Society Ltd*.)

Entores Ltd v Miles Far East Corp   [197]
[1955] 2 All ER 493 (Court of Appeal)

The parties entered into an agreement by means of telex whereby each company had in its office (the plaintiffs were in London and the defendants in Amsterdam) a teleprinter which was connected by the Post Office to a teleprinter in the other office so that a message typed on one would be automatically typed out by the other. The contract was broken and the question arose as to where the contract had been concluded. *Held,* in cases where there was instantaneous communication, the contract was made when and where the acceptance was received; in this case, in London. (Approved in *Brinkibon Ltd v Stahag Stahl und Stahlwarenhandelsgesellschaft mbH.*)

Ertel Bieber & Co v Rio Tinto Co Ltd [1918] AC 260   [198]
(House of Lords)

An English company contracted to supply three German companies with cuperous sulphur ore. The agreement contained a provision that the contract was to be suspended in the event of war. War came and the English company sought declarations that the contracts were abrogated by that event. *Held,* notwithstanding the suspensory clause, the contracts had become illegal and void and the declarations asked for would be made.

Esso Petroleum Co Ltd v Harper's Garage   [199]
(Stourport) Ltd [1967] 1 All ER 699 (House of Lords)

The respondents, owners of Corner Garage, charged the same by way of legal mortgage to the appellants to secure the repayment of a principal sum of £7,000 and covenanted to repay that sum with interest by quarterly instalments over 21 years, and during the continuance of the mortgage to purchase exclusively from the appellants all motor fuels which they might require at Corner Garage. The mortgage further provided that the respondents were not entitled to redeem the security otherwise than in accordance with the covenant as to repayment. *Held,* the mortgage stipulation relating to the purchase of fuel was within the ambit of the legal doctrine relating to covenants in restraint of trade, and it was unenforceable as being in unreasonable restraint of trade, and the respondents were entitled to redeem the mortgage. (Applied in *Alec Lobb (Garages) Ltd v Total Oil GB Ltd*; but see *Cleveland Petroleum Co Ltd v Dartstone Ltd.*)

Esso Petroleum Co Ltd v Mardon   [200]
[1976] 2 All ER 5 (Court of Appeal)

The plaintiffs granted a tenancy of a new filling-station to the defendant. Before the tenancy was granted, the plaintiffs' representative told the defendant that they estimated an annual throughput of petrol of 200,000 gallons a year by a third year, although the defendant thought that a lower figure was more realistic. The defendant took the tenancy in reliance on the estimate. After three years the throughput was less than 100,000 gallons a year, largely because of the physical characteristics and lay-out of the site. The defendant was unable to make a profit, could not pay for the petrol, and the plaintiffs resumed possession. The issue was whether the defendant could recover on a counterclaim against the plaintiffs for breach of warranty and/or negligence in respect of the plaintiffs' estimate. *Held,* the counterclaim should succeed, and the plaintiffs were liable to the defendant for breach of warranty and also for negligence. The measure of damages was the loss the defendant has suffered by reason of having been induced to enter into the disastrous contract. (See also *Bentley (Dick) Productions Ltd v Harold Smith* and *Henderson v Merrett Syndicates Ltd.*)

Euro-Diam Ltd v Bathurst [1988] 2 All ER 23   **[201]**
(Court of Appeal)

The plaintiffs, an English company, supplied diamonds to wholesalers in England
and abroad. In a sale or return transaction, they sent diamonds worth over
US$223,000 to West Germany together with an invoice stating the value of the
diamonds to be US$131,411; the intention was to enable the customer to avoid
German customs duty. Some of the diamonds were stolen in Germany; their value
was agreed as being US$142,173.90 and the plaintiffs sued the insurers to recover
that sum. *Held,* they would succeed as, inter alia, the principle that, on grounds of
public policy, the courts would not assist a party who had been guilty of illegal
conduct of which the courts should take notice did not apply where – as here –
there was no direct, proximate connection between the plaintiffs' claim and the
illegality (the understated invoice). (Applied: *St John Shipping Corporation v Joseph
Rank Ltd.*)

Evans (J) & Son (Portsmouth) Ltd v Andrea   **[202]**
Merzario Ltd [1976] 2 All ER 930 (Court of Appeal)

The plaintiffs imported machines from Italy and, for many years, had contracted
with the defendant forwarding agents to make their transport arrangements. The
course of dealing between the parties was on the standard conditions of trade.
After some years, the defendants gave the plaintiffs an oral assurance that in future
shipments the machines would be transported in containers under deck. On faith
of this assurance, the plaintiffs agreed to change over to container transport. Due
to the defendant's oversight, a container was shipped on deck and the machine
was lost overboard. The standard conditions gave the defendants complete
freedom over the means and procedure to be followed in transportation of goods
subject to express written instructions. The plaintiffs claimed damages from the
defendants, alleging that the carriage of the container on deck had been a breach
of the contract for carriage. *Held,* the plaintiffs were entitled to damages. The
defendants' oral assurance amounted to an enforceable contractual promise and
the defendants were liable for breach of it unless they could rely on the standard
printed conditions. They could not do this so as to exempt them from liability for
breach of the oral promise, which was to be treated as overriding the printed
conditions. (See also *Mendelssohn v Normand Ltd.*)

Eyre v Measday [1986] 1 All ER 488 (Court of Appeal)   **[203]**

The plaintiff consulted the defendant gynaecologist regarding a sterilisation
operation. He told her that it 'must be regarded as a permanent procedure', but he
did not say that there was a small risk (less than 1%) of a subsequent pregnancy.
After the operation, the plaintiff gave birth to a child and she sought damages for
breach of contract. *Held,* her action could not succeed. On the facts, the
defendant's representations meant no more than that the operative procedure was
incapable of being reversed and a term or unqualified collateral warranty that the
expected result (the plaintiff's sterility) would actually be achieved would not be
implied. (But see *Thake v Maurice.*)

Faccenda Chicken Ltd v Fowler [1986] 1 All ER 617   **[204]**
(Court of Appeal)

The plaintiffs sold fresh chickens from refrigerated vans and the defendant was
their sales manager. Having left the plaintiffs' employment, he set up his own
similar business in the same area and eight of the plaintiffs' other employees
joined him. The plaintiffs sought, inter alia, damages for breach of their contracts

of employment in using the plaintiffs' sales information to the plaintiffs' disadvantage or detriment. *Held,* the plaintiffs would fail as the duty of fidelity owed by an employee to a former employer is not as great as the duty implied in a current contract of employment whereby use or disclosure of confidential information, even though not amounting to a trade secret, would be a breach of the duty of good faith. A former employer would only be protected if the confidential information could be classed as a trade secret (or was so confidential as to require such protection); here it could not. Furthermore, use or disclosure of confidential information could not be restricted by a covenant in a contract of employment unless the information was a trade secret or its equivalent. (See also *Herbert Morris Ltd* v *Saxelby*; but see *Robb* v *Green.*)

Fairline Shipping Corp v Adamson [1974] 2 All ER 967 [205]

The plaintiff's agent orally arranged to store some perishable goods in a cold store. The defendant was managing director of the cold storage company and, when writing to confirm the arrangements, used his private letterheading. Inter alia, the question arose as to whether the contract was between the plaintiff and the company or the plaintiff and the defendant. *Held,* in order to constitute a contract the acceptance of an offer had to be communicated to the offeror and the uncommunicated acceptance of the offer could not have the effect of binding the offeror. If the defendant's letter constituted an offer by him to take over the company's contract, the absence of any response from the plaintiff's agent could not be construed as an acceptance capable of binding the defendant. The claim in contract failed. (See also *Felthouse* v *Bindley.*)

Fawcett v Smethurst (1914) 84 LJKB 473 [206]

The defendant, who was a minor, hired the plaintiff's car in order to drive to a place six miles away to fetch his luggage and the plaintiff alleged that he had stipulated that the defendant was to be absolutely liable for such damage as was sustained by the car during the period of hire. The defendant drove to the place where his luggage was, but then drove a friend to a place 12 miles further on. In the course of this journey, without any negligence on the part of the defendant, the car caught fire and was damaged beyond repair. The plaintiff sought to recover damages in respect of his loss. *Held,* the action must fail. The defendant was not liable in tort as the extended journey was of the same nature as the original one. Although it might have been necessary for the defendant to hire the car to fetch his bags, it was not a necessary for him to enter into a contract of hire containing an onerous term, such as that which the plaintiff alleged was embodied in the contract in question, whereby the defendant was to be liable for all loss or damage to the car irrespective of negligence on his part. (But see *Burnard* v *Haggis.*)

Felthouse v Bindley (1862) 11 CB (NS) 869 [207]

The defendant was an auctioneer who had been instructed to sell the farming stock of John Felthouse. John's uncle was interested in one of the horses which was to be sold and after some verbal negotiations in which a misunderstanding arose as to whether the price was £30 or 30 guineas the uncle wrote to John, admitting that there might have been a mistake and offered to split the difference and pay £30 15s. He concluded: 'If I hear no more about him, I consider the horse mine at £30 15s.' John did not reply to this letter but instructed the defendant to withdraw the horse from the sale. By mistake it was put up with the rest of the stock and sold. *Held,* the uncle's action against the auctioneer for conversion must fail as the plaintiff had no property in the horse as the silence of John did not amount to acceptance of the plaintiff's offer to buy for £30 15s. (See also *Harvey* v *Facey*; but see *Carlill* v *Carbolic Smoke Ball Co* and *Vitol SA* v *Norelf Ltd*.)

Fenwick v Macdonald, Fraser & Co Ltd (1904) 6 F   [208]
(Ct of Sess) 850 (Scottish Court of Session)

At a sale by auction a bull was 'offered for unreserved sale'. The auctioneer withdrew the lot before the fall of the hammer and the person who had made the highest bid brought an action for delivery of the bull or for damages. *Held,* as the bidder is not bound until the fall of the hammer neither is the auctioneer and it makes no difference that the sale was said to be without reserve. (But see *Warlow* v *Harrison*.)

Fercometal SARL v Mediterranean Shipping Co SA,   [209]
The Simona [1988] 2 All ER 742 (House of Lords)

In June 1982 the charterers entered into a charterparty with shipowners for the carriage of steel coils from Durban to Bilbao on the owners' vessel: the charterers were entitled to cancel if the ship was not ready to load on or before 9 July. On 2 July the owners requested an extension to enable them to load other cargo first; in this case the vessel would not be able to load the steel coils until 13 July. The charterers cancelled the contract forthwith and engaged another vessel, but the owners did not accept this repudiation and on 5 July they told the charterers that the vessel would start loading on 8 July. The vessel arrived in Durban on 8 July and, although the owners tendered notice of readiness, they were not in fact ready to load the steel coils. The owners brought a claim for deadfreight for the charterers' wrongful repudiation. *Held,* they could not succeed. The owners, having affirmed the contract when they refused to accept the charterers' premature repudiation, could only avoid the cancellation provision by tendering the vessel ready to load on time (which they had not) or by establishing (which they could not) that their failure so to tender the vessel was the result of their acting on a representation by the charterers that they had given up their option to cancel. (See also *Startup* v *Macdonald*; but see *Vitol SA* v *Norelf Ltd*.)

Fibrosa Spolka Akcyjna v Fairbairn Lawson   [210]
Combe Barbour Ltd [1942] 2 All ER 122 (House of Lords)

In July 1939 the parties contracted for the delivery of certain machinery to Gdynia, in Poland. The appellants paid £1,000 on the signing of the contract and after it had been frustrated by the occupation of Gdynia by the Germans they argued that they were entitled to the return of this advance payment. *Held,* this view would prevail as the money had been paid upon a consideration (in these circumstances meaning the performance of a promise) which had wholly failed. (See also s1(2) of the Law Reform (Frustrated Contracts) Act 1943.)

Fielding and Platt Ltd v Najjar [1969] 2 All ER 150   [211]
(Court of Appeal)

The plaintiffs agreed to manufacture and sell an aluminium extrusion press to a foreign company of which the defendant was a director. Delivery was to be made in 10½ months and payment was to be made by two promissory notes. The defendant asked the plaintiffs to describe the goods misleadingly on the invoice so as to mislead the foreign customs authorities. The first promissory note was not paid on the due date, and subsequently the plaintiffs suspended work and obtained summary judgment against the defendant who, inter alia, pleaded illegality as a defence. *Held,* the defence of illegality could not succeed because the request to describe the goods misleadingly was not a term of the contract. Even had it been a term it would have been severable. The defendant had also failed to show that the plaintiffs knew of the illegal purpose of the false invoice and had agreed to participate in that purpose. (But see *Foster* v *Driscoll.*)

Financings Ltd v Baldock [1963] 1 All ER 443 [212]
(Court of Appeal)

The defendant entered into a hire-purchase agreement with the plaintiffs in respect of a Bedford truck. The cash price of the truck was £675, the interest charge £97 16s, and the defendant paid £100 as the first instalment of rent, the balance being payable over two years by 24 monthly instalments of £22 0s 8d 'unless determined by the hirer or the owner', and the agreement also provided for interest at ten per cent on all overdue instalments. The agreement could be determined by the plaintiffs for failure to pay any instalment or by the defendant by returning the truck. In either event, under clause 11 of the agreement there became payable to the plaintiffs such further sum as with the total amount of instalments previously paid would equal two-thirds of the total hiring cost as agreed compensation for depreciation or the amount of instalments and other moneys already due, whichever was the greater. The defendant defaulted in paying two instalments and the plaintiffs 'put an end to the hiring' and retook possession of the truck, at the same time telling the defendant that they would allow him seven days to pay the arrears. Nothing was heard from the defendant, so the truck was again offered for sale and some 18 months later was sold for £140. The plaintiffs sued to recover £538 1s but recovered judgment for damages to be assessed. *Held,* 'when an agreement of hiring is terminated by virtue of a power contained in it and the owner retakes the vehicle, he can recover damages for any breach up to the date of termination, but not for any breach thereafter, for the simple reason that there are no breaches thereafter' (*per* LORD DENNING MR). Clause 11 was a penalty clause and therefore unenforceable and it followed that the plaintiffs were entitled to recover only two months' instalments plus interest at ten per cent. In this case there had been no repudiation by the defendant of the obligation to pay future instalments, but only non-payment, and the plaintiffs, under an express stipulation in that behalf, had terminated the agreement. In these circumstances they could recover only unpaid instalments with interest by way of damages for breach of the agreement prior to its termination. (But see *Lombard North Central plc* v *Butterworth.*)

Financings Ltd v Stimson [1962] 3 All ER 386 [213]
(Court of Appeal)

The defendant saw an Austin motor car which he wished to buy on the premises of the Stanmore Motor Co and on 16 March 1961 he signed a hire-purchase agreement form produced to him by the dealer. This form was not in itself an agreement, but only an offer by the defendant to enter into a hire-purchase agreement with the plaintiff finance company. The plaintiffs signed an acceptance on 25 March 1961. On 18 March the defendant paid the first instalment of £70 and drove the car away but, because he was not satisfied with its condition and performance, returned it two days later and told the dealer that he no longer wished to purchase it. During the night of 24/25 March the car was stolen from the dealer's premises and was later recovered, badly scratched and damaged. The plaintiffs sold the car and sought damages from the defendant and the defendant counterclaimed for the return of the deposit of £70. *Held,* the defendant's counterclaim would succeed and the plaintiffs would fail as by returning the car to the dealer (the plaintiffs' agent, a person authorised to receive a revocation) the defendant had revoked his offer and there was no concluded contract between the parties. Further, on the facts of the case, the offer made by the defendant was conditional upon the car remaining in substantially the same condition until the moment of acceptance and, in view of the damage which occurred before the plaintiffs' acceptance was given, the plaintiffs were not in a position to accept the offer because the condition on which it was made had not been fulfilled. On this ground also there was no contract.

Finelvet AG v Vinava Shipping Co Ltd, The Chrysalis   [214]
[1983] 2 All ER 658

A vessel under charter docked at Basrah on 14 September 1980: eight days later war broke out between Iraq and Iran and the ship became trapped on the Shatt-al-Arab. The Iraqis prevented the ship leaving because of the risk of damage and injury and on 14 November the charterers purported to cancel the charterparty. By 24 November, most informed people in shipping circles believed that trapped vessels would be unable to leave safely for several months, probably much longer. *Held,* the contract had not been frustrated until 24 November: it had not been automatically frustrated by the outbreak of war as its performance remained legally possible. (But see *Bank Line Ltd v Arthur Capel & Co.*)

Firstpost Homes Ltd v Johnson [1995] 4 All ER 355   [215]
(Court of Appeal)

Having reached an oral agreement for the sale of some 15 acres of land, the purchaser typed a letter, addressed to the purchaser and setting out the agreement, for the vendor to sign. The letter contained the vendor's name and address and referred to an 'enclosed plan' identifying the land which was attached to the letter by paperclip. The vendor signed the letter and the plan: the purchaser signed only the plan. *Held,* the purchaser's claim for specific performance had been properly struck out. The letter and the plan were separate documents. Section 2(3) of the Law of Property (Miscellaneous Provisions) Act 1989 required the letter, the contractual document, to be signed by both parties. Neither the purchaser's signing of the plan nor the typing of his name on the letter satisfied this requirement. 'I am not prepared to construe the word "signed" in s2(3) of the ... 1989 [Act] by reference to the old learning on what amounted to a signature of a note or memorandum sufficient for the purposes of the Statute of Frauds (1677) or s40 of the Law of Property Act 1925. To do so would ... defeat the obvious intention of s2 of the 1989 Act ... I can see no justification for retaining the old law ... and every reason for consigning it to the limbo where it clearly belongs ...' (*per* BALCOMBE LJ). (See also *McCausland v Duncan Lawrie Ltd.*)

Fisher v Bell [1960] 3 All ER 731   [216]

A shopkeeper displayed in his shop window a knife behind which was a ticket 'Ejector knife—4s'. He was charged with offering for sale a flick knife, contrary to a now repealed statute. *Held,* no offence had been committed as the exhibition of goods in a shop window is not in itself an offer for sale. 'According to the ordinary law of contract, the display of an article with a price on it in a shop window is merely an invitation to treat. It is in no sense an offer for sale the acceptance of which constitutes a contract' (*per* LORD PARKER CJ). (See also *Payne v Cave.*)

Fisher & Co v Apollinaris Co (1875) 10 Ch App 297   **[217]**

The prosecutors in a trade-mark case offered no evidence against the offender when the matter was brought for trial. The accused was accordingly acquitted and it was agreed that he should write a letter of apology which the prosecutors were authorised to publish. The offender sought to avoid this agreement on the ground of duress. *Held,* this plea would fail and the agreement would be upheld as in the case of an offence of this nature where the offender may be proceeded against either civilly or criminally, there is nothing illegal or improper in a compromise of the criminal proceedings. (But see *Kearley* v *Thomson.*)

Fitch v Dewes [1921] 2 AC 158 (House of Lords)   **[218]**

A Tamworth solicitor entered into an agreement with his managing clerk whereby the managing clerk undertook to serve for three years and that he would not, on the expiration or sooner determination of his term of employment, 'be engaged or manage or concerned in the office, profession, or business of a solicitor, within a radius of seven miles of the Town Hall of Tamworth'. *Held,* although the covenant was unlimited in point of time, it would be enforced as it did not in the circumstances exceed what was reasonably required for the solicitor's protection and was not against the public interest. (See also *Deacons* v *Bridge*; but see *Wyatt* v *Kreglinger and Fernau.*)

Fitch v Snedaker (1868) 38 NY 248 (Court of Appeals of   **[219]** the State of New York)

A sheriff offered a reward of $200 to any person 'who will give such information as shall lead to the apprehension and conviction of the person or persons guilty of the murder' of an unknown woman. The plaintiff contended that as he had given the required information he was entitled to recover the amount of the reward although at the time of giving the information he did not know that the reward had been offered. *Held,* his action must fail as the plaintiff could not be said to have assented to the defendant's offer since he did not know of its existence, and unless the offer was accepted there was no contract between the parties. (But see *Gibbons* v *Proctor.*)

Fitzgerald v Dressler (1859) 7 CB (NS) 374   **[220]**

A parcel of linseed was sold by A to B who sold it to C. C orally promised to pay A (in the normal course of events he would have paid B, the person from whom he bought the goods) for the linseed if A would deliver the goods to C who at the time had a property in the seed subject to A's lien for the price. *Held,* A was entitled to enforce this promise, consideration for which could be found in A's surrender of his lien over the goods when delivery was made and it could not be maintained that C's promise was merely a guarantee to make payment if B should default so that the promise was brought within the protection afforded by s4 of the Statute of Frauds. (But see *Harburg India Rubber Comb Co* v *Martin.*)

Flavell, Re, Murray v Flavell (1883) 25 Ch D 89   **[221]** (Court of Appeal)

A partnership agreement between two solicitors provided that the personal representatives of a deceased partner should be entitled to receive out of the net profits of the partnership business a yearly sum to be paid to his widow for her own benefit. *Held,* the partnership agreement had created a trust, of which the personal representatives were trustees, in favour of the widow and she was entitled to receive the amount specified in the agreement. (But see *Gandy* v *Gandy.*)

Foakes v Beer (1884) 9 App Cas 605 (House of Lords) [222]

There was an agreement between a judgment debtor and creditor whereby, in consideration of the debtor paying part of the judgment debt and costs and the balance by instalments, the creditor would not proceed on the judgment. The debtor eventually paid the amount of the debt and costs and the creditor sought to recover interest on the original judgment debt. *Held,* she was entitled to recover such interest as payment of a smaller sum (ie the debt and costs) was not consideration for the promise to accept this amount in satisfaction of the judgment debt, costs and interest. (But see *British Russian Gazette, etc, Ltd* v *Associated Newspapers Ltd*; see also *Vanbergen* v *St Edmund's Properties Ltd, D & C Builders Ltd* v *Rees* and *Re Selectmove Ltd.*)

Foley v Classique Coaches Ltd [1934] 2 KB 1 [223]
(Court of Appeal)

The plaintiff, who was a retail dealer in petrol, contracted to supply the defendants, who were the owners of motor coaches, with all the petrol which they required for the purposes of their business 'at a price to be agreed by the parties in writing and from time to time'. No agreement in writing as to the price was ever concluded and after three years the defendants purported to repudiate the contract. *Held,* they were not entitled to do so as in the absence of an express agreement a term would be implied that the petrol supplied by the plaintiff should be of reasonable quality and sold at a reasonable price.

Ford Motor Co (England) Ltd v Armstrong (1915) [224]
31 TLR 267 (Court of Appeal)

A dealer, the defendant, agreed to sell the plaintiffs' motor-cars and, in the event of his selling any car or parts below list price, to pay £250 for every breach of such undertaking 'such sum being the agreed damages which the manufacturers will sustain'. *Held,* the sum of £250 was a penalty and not liquidated damages. (But see *Associated Distributors Ltd* v *Hall and Hall.*)

Fores v Johnes (1802) 4 Esp 97 [225]

The defendant placed an order 'for all the caricature prints that had ever been published' with the plaintiff, a printseller in Piccadilly, but refused to accept delivery as several were obscene and immoral. The plaintiff sued to recover the price of the prints. *Held,* the action must fail as the contract was illegal and void by reason of the fact that some of the prints were immoral and obscene. (See also *Berg* v *Sadler & Moore.*)

Forsikringsaktieselskapet Vesta v Butcher [226]
[1989] 1 All ER 402 (House of Lords)

The plaintiffs were awarded damages for breach of a reinsurance contract, but it was found that they had been guilty of contributory negligence. They contended, inter alia, that the Law Reform (Contributory Negligence) Act 1945 did not apply to a claim for breach of contract. *Held,* where – as here – liability in contract was the same as liability in the tort of negligence independently of the existence of any contract, blame could be apportioned under the 1945 Act, even though the claim was made in contract. (But see *Barclays Bank plc* v *Fairclough Building Ltd.*)

Foster v Driscoll [1929] 1 KB 470 (Court of Appeal)   [227]

Agreements were entered into the real object of which was to smuggle whiskey into the United States of America contrary to the prohibition laws of that country. *Held,* the object of the transaction constituted a breach of international comity and the agreements were therefore contrary to public policy and void. (See also *Regazzoni* v *K C Sethia (1944) Ltd* and *Fielding and Platt Ltd* v *Najjar.*)

Foster v Mackinnon (1869) LR 4 CP 704   [228]

The defendant, an old man of feeble sight, was induced to sign his name on the back of a bill of exchange by a fraudulent misrepresentation that he was signing a guarantee. *Held,* if the defendant signed without knowing that it was a bill of exchange under the belief that it was a guarantee, and if he had not been guilty of negligence in so signing, he was entitled to be released from liability under the bill. (See also *Lewis* v *Clay* and *Saunders* v *Anglia Building Society.*)

Francis v Municipal Councillors of Kuala Lumpur   [229]
[1962] 3 All ER 633 (Privy Council)

The appellant clerk was dismissed and he sought, inter alia, a declaration that the termination of his employment was wrongful and void and that he had the right to continue his employment with the respondents. *Held,* because of the general principle of law that the courts will not grant specific performance of contracts of service such a declaratory judgment would only be made in special circumstances. In this case there were no circumstances which would make it either just or proper to make such a declaration. (See also *Whitwood Chemical Co* v *Hardman.*)

Frost v Knight (1872) LR 7 Exch 111   [230]

The defendant promised to marry the plaintiff when his father died. Before his father passed away the defendant made it known that he no longer intended to marry the plaintiff who thereupon and in the lifetime of the defendant's father claimed damages for breach of promise of marriage. *Held,* the plaintiff would succeed as a breach of contract had been committed on which she could found her claim. She was entitled to proceed as if the death of the defendant's father had actually occurred. (NB – breach of promise of marriage is no longer actionable.)

Galloway v Galloway (1914) 30 TLR 531   [231]

The parties, who believed that they were lawfully married, entered into a deed of separation. It afterwards appeared that their marriage was void as the defendant's first wife was alive at the time of his marriage to the plaintiff. *Held,* there had been a mutual mistake of fact as to the relationship of the parties and in these circumstances the separation agreement was void. (But see *Bell* v *Lever Brothers Ltd.*)

Gandy v Gandy (1885) 30 Ch D 57 (Court of Appeal)   [232]

By a deed of separation the husband covenanted with the trustees to pay to them an annuity for the use of his wife and two eldest daughters and also, in some respects at the discretion of the trustees, all the expenses in connection with the maintenance and education of his two youngest daughters. When one of the two youngest daughters was 16 the husband refused to maintain her and she brought an action as beneficiary against the husband and the trustees to enforce the husband's covenant so far as she was concerned. *Held,* because the trustees were given a certain discretion, it was not possible to hold that the deed had created a trust in favour of the youngest daughters and for this reason the action failed. (But see *Affréteurs Réunis Société Anonyme, Les* v *Leopold Walford (London) Ltd.*)

Gardner v Coutts & Co [1967] 3 All ER 1064 [233]

In July 1948, J, a vendor of land who retained an adjoining smaller property, entered into a written agreement, on the day after the conveyance of the land he had sold, that the purchaser and her successors should have an option of purchasing the adjoining property should he, at any time during his life, wish to sell it. In 1958 the plaintiff became entitled to the land with the benefit of this right of pre-emption. In 1963 J conveyed the adjoining property by way of gift to F, without making offer of the first refusal. J having died, the plaintiff sued his executors for damages. *Held,* it was implicit in the grant of the first refusal that the person who had to offer the first refusal should not give the property away without offering it, and so defeat the right of pre-emption. Accordingly, the plaintiff was entitled to damages. (See also *Moorcock, The.*)

Garnham, Harris & Elton Ltd v Alfred W Ellis [234] (Transport) Ltd [1967] 2 All ER 940

The plaintiffs made an oral contract with the defendants for the carriage of some copper wire from London to Glasgow. The contract was subject to a trade association's standard terms, one of which excluded liability for 'non-delivery (howsoever arising)', unless non-delivery was reported to the carrier within 28 days of the receipt of the goods by him. The defendants decided to sub-contract the work, though no express power to do so was given, and they employed a rogue, without checking his identity or character. The load of wire disappeared and its loss was not discovered until the expiry of the time limit. *Held,* the defendants were not protected by the clause because the right to subcontract could not be implied, because of the valuable nature of the goods, and as carried out the sub-contracting amounted to the tort of conversion. (But see *Suisse Atlantique, etc* v *Rotterdamsche, etc.*)

General Billposting Co Ltd v Atkinson [1909] AC 118 [235]
(House of Lords)

The respondent was employed as the company's manager. His contract of service provided that the engagement should be subject to 12 months' notice by either side and also contained a covenant in restraint of trade. The appellants wrongfully dismissed the respondent without notice. *Held,* this action constituted a repudiation of the contract by the appellants and the respondent was not bound by the clause which restricted his right to engage in similar work. (See also *Briggs* v *Oates.*)

Gibbons v Proctor (1891) 64 LT 594 [236]

The defendant gave instructions for the printing of handbills to announce that a reward of £25 would be given to any person who gave information to the superintendent of police which led to the conviction of a certain criminal. The plaintiff, a police constable, communicated the information required to a fellow police officer some nine hours before the instructions for the printing of the handbills were given but the information reached the superintendent after the handbills had been printed and distributed. The plaintiff sought to recover the reward of £25. *Held,* he was entitled to do so as the condition (the communication of the information to the superintendent) was fulfilled after the publication of the handbills.

Gibbons v Westminster Bank Ltd [1939] 3 All ER 577   [237]

The defendant bank wrongfully dishonoured the plaintiff's cheque. *Held*, the plaintiff was entitled to recover only nominal damages unless special or actual damage could be proved, but this proof is not required where the plaintiff in a similar case is a trader.

Gibson v Manchester City Council [1979] 1 All ER 972   [238]
(House of Lords)

A council tenant who wished to purchase the freehold interest in his house filled in an application form supplied by the council. The council wrote him a letter which informed him that it might bc prepared to sell the house to him on terms stated and invited him to make a formal application on an attached form. He filled in the form and returned it with a letter stating that he wished to continue with the purchase. The council subsequently reversed its policy of selling houses to tenants. *Held,* the language of the council's letter stating that it might be prepared to sell the house was such that it could not be converted into a firm offer capable of acceptance. There was no legally enforceable contract of sale. (But see *Clarke* v *Dunraven, The Satanita.*)

Giles v Thompson [1994] 1 AC 142   [239]
(House of Lords)

The plaintiff's car was involved in an accident with the defendant's car and, while her car was being repaired, she obtained a replacement from Forward Hire Ltd under a written contract. Under that agreement, inter alia, the plaintiff was given credit for hire charges until damages were recovered from the defendant (whom the plaintiff alleged was liable) and the hire company was authorised to appoint its own solicitor to pursue the claim. Proceedings were duly brought and the defendant challenged only liability for the hire charges, contending that the hiring agreement was champertous (ie, that the hire company had, in effect, purchased a share in litigation) and was hence unlawful and that the plaintiff had suffered no loss under this head as she had enjoyed the use of a substitute vehicle free of charge. *Held*, on the facts, both contentions would be rejected. The hire company made its profits from the hire charges (which were reasonable), not from the litigation, and the plaintiff had not obtained the replacement vehicle free of charge but merely on credit. 'The hiring company has no direct right to the damages. The car hire company is not an assignee or chargee of the cause of action or its fruits, although it expects that the damages for loss of use will form part of the assets from which the motorist will in due course pay for the substitute. The liability for the car hire, although suspended as regards enforcement, rests upon the motorist throughout. It is a real liability, the incurring of which constitutes a real loss to the motorist ... the provision of the substitute ... was not "free"' (*per* LORD MUSTILL).

Glasbrook Brothers Ltd v Glamorgan County Council   [240]
[1925] AC 270 (House of Lords)

During a strike a colliery manager applied for police protection for his colliery and insisted that it could only be efficiently protected by the stationing of a police force on the colliery premises. The police superintendent thought that a mobile force would give sufficient protection and would only billet police officers at the colliery when the manager agreed to pay the force at a specified rate. *Held,* there was consideration for the manager's promise as the police superintendent was only under a duty to provide what protection he thought was reasonable and sufficient. As he had provided more than this the manager was bound by his promise to pay the amount agreed. (But see *Collins* v *Godefroy*.)

Goldsoll v Goldman [1915] 1 Ch 292 (Court of Appeal)   **[241]**

Both parties were dealers in imitation jewellery, one in Old Bond Street and the other in New Bond Street. In order to avoid competition the defendant sold his business to the plaintiff and covenanted that he would not for a period of two years carry on or be engaged, concerned or interested in the sale of real or imitation jewellery in any part of the United Kingdom, France, United States, Russia or Spain or within 25 miles of Berlin or Vienna. The defendant committed breaches of this covenant and the plaintiff sought an injunction. *Held,* unless the terms of the covenant could be severed it would be void as it was wider than was reasonably necessary for the plaintiff's protection. However, the injunction would be granted as the covenant not to carry on business in the United Kingdom, which was reasonable in the circumstances of the case, was severable from the rest as was the covenant which prevented the defendant from dealing in real jewellery, the provision restraining him from dealing in imitation jewellery being also reasonably necessary for the plaintiff's protection. (But see *Attwood* v *Lamont* and *British Reinforced Concrete Engineering Co Ltd* v *Scbelff*.)

Goldsworthy v Brickell [1987] 1 All ER 853 (Court of Appeal)   **[242]**

The plaintiff owned a large (and valuable) farm, but it was run down and losing money. From November 1976 the defendant, a neighbouring farmer, began to give the plaintiff advice and help: the plaintiff came to trust him implicitly and by early 1977 the defendant was effectively managing the farm. In April the 85 year old plaintiff granted the defendant a tenancy of the farm at an annual rent of £500 with an option to purchase at the 'prevailing value' on the plaintiff's death. The agreement provided that the plaintiff could remain in the farm house, prohibited rent increases and permitted (but did not oblige) the defendant to make improvements; the plaintiff did not receive independent advice. In 1983 the plaintiff sought rescission of the tenancy agreement on the ground of undue influence. *Held,* his action would be successful. On the facts, undue influence would be presumed and, as it could not be said that the plaintiff had affirmed the agreement, it was just and equitable that it be set aside. (But see *National Westminster Bank plc* v *Morgan*.)

Goodinson v Goodinson [1954] 2 All ER 255   **[243]**
(Court of Appeal)

A husband and wife entered into an agreement whereby the husband would pay to the wife a weekly sum for the support and maintenance of the wife and their child. The wife covenanted that so long as the husband made these weekly payments she would not 'commence or prosecute any matrimonial proceedings against the husband', that she 'would maintain herself and the child and indemnify the husband against all debts incurred by her' and would not 'in any way at any time hereafter pledge the husband's credit'. The wife claimed payment of arrears of maintenance under this agreement and the husband maintained that she should not succeed as the clause prohibiting the taking of matrimonial proceedings was illegal and for this reason that the agreement itself was void. *Held,* the wife was entitled to recover as the clause which purported to restrain the institution of matrimonial proceedings would be eliminated from the agreement. (Distinguished in *Sutton* v *Sutton;* see also *Ronbar Enterprises Ltd* v *Green*.)

Goodman v Chase (1818) 1 B & Ald 297 [244]

The defendant's son, having failed to satisfy a judgment of £686, had been arrested by the sheriff and was about to be taken to prison when the defendant obtained his release by orally promising to pay the amount of the judgment debt. *Held,* the defendant was not protected by s4 of the Statute of Frauds. The release of his son had discharged the son's debt and the promise by the defendant was an original promise and not one to answer for the debt, default or miscarriage of another which, to be enforceable, needed to be in writing.

Gore v Gibson (1845) 13 M & W 623 [245]

The defendant indorsed a bill of exchange when in a state of intoxication. *Held,* the defendant was not bound by this indorsement as no contract made by a person in this condition, when he does not know what he is doing, is binding upon him. (But see *Molton* v *Camroux.*)

Gore v Van der Lann (Liverpool Corp intervening) [246]
[1967] 1 All ER 360 (Court of Appeal)

The plaintiff was injured when boarding a Liverpool Corporation bus, and claimed damages against its conductor on grounds of his alleged negligence in failing to take proper precautions for her safety. She was travelling on an elderly person's free pass, issued on the following condition: 'In consideration of my being granted a free pass ... I undertake and agree that the use of such pass by me shall be subject to the conditions overleaf, which have been read to or by me before signing.' The conditions exempted the corporation and its servants and agents from liability to the holder for loss of life, injury or other loss or damage to property, however caused, and stated that the pass was a 'licence' only. The corporation sought to stay the proceedings on grounds that they constituted a fraud on them. *Held,* they were not entitled to a stay of proceedings because, (i) on the facts the issue and acceptance of the pass constituted a contract and not merely a licence, and the condition relied on by the corporation was made void by statute; and, (ii) even if this were not so, the corporation had no interest entitling them to relief as they were under no obligation to indemnify the conductor. (See also s29 of the Public Passenger Vehicles Act 1981; but see *Wilkie* v *LPTB.*)

Goss v Lord Nugent (1833) 5 B & Ad 58 [247]

The defendant agreed in writing to purchase 14 lots of freehold land from the plaintiff. As the plaintiff could not make a good title to one of the lots, the defendant orally agreed to waive the title to that lot. The defendant afterwards refused to pay the balance of the purchase money in view of the plaintiff's defective title to this one piece of land. *Held,* the plaintiff could not recover the purchase price as the original contract would not be enforced because of the bad title to one lot and it was not possible to vary a contract which was required to be evidenced in writing by means of an oral agreement. (But see *Morris* v *Baron & Co.*)

Gould v Gould [1969] 3 All ER 728 (Court of Appeal) [248]

The husband left the wife in May 1966 and then orally agreed to pay her £15 a week 'as long as I can manage it'. He kept the agreement until October 1967 when he fell behind with the payments. In February 1968 he informed the wife that he could not pay the full amount in future, and the wife then sued for arrears of maintenance under the terms of the agreement. *Held,* the wife's claim must fail. It had not been within the contemplation of the parties to make a legally binding agreement. The uncertainty of the terms and the absence of any quid pro quo from the wife precluded that result. (See also *Jones* v *Padavatton* and *Balfour* v *Balfour*.)

Graham v Pitkin [1992] 1 WLR (Privy Council) [249]

The parties contracted for the sale and purchase of a property in Kingston, Jamaica. After considerable delay, on 28 April the purchaser said she would try to find the balance of the purchase price and report back in about seven days. Without serving a notice to complete, as nothing more had been heard on 9 July the vendor purported to rescind the contract. *Held*, the purchaser was entitled to specific performance as her conduct had not been such as to entitle the vendor to rescind. 'It is common ground that time is not of the essence of a contract for the sale of land in the absence of an express term to that effect or in circumstances which imply that time is of the essence ... If a vendor serves a valid notice requiring completion within a reasonable time and the purchaser fails to complete in accordance with the notice, the failure can be treated by the vendor as a repudiatory breach which the vendor is entitled to accept by rescission ... In the absence of a valid notice to complete a purchaser is entitled to specific performance unless his conduct has been such as to render it inequitable for specific performance to be granted' (*per* LORD TEMPLEMAN).

Grainger & Son v Gough [1896] AC 325 (House of Lords) [250]

The appellants were agents for a French wine merchant and canvassed for orders and distributed price-lists on his behalf. *Held*, the canvassing by the agents was not an offer to sell the goods. The orders they received were offers to buy, made by the prospective customers, and no contract was created until something which amounted to acceptance of the customer's offer was done by the merchant or his agents. (See also *Pharmaceutical Society of Great Britain* v *Boots Cash Chemists (Southern) Ltd.*)

Great Northern Railway Co v Witham (1873) LR 9 CP 16 [251]

The plaintiffs invited tenders for the supply of goods, including iron, for a period of 12 months. The defendant submitted a tender to supply the goods over the period at a fixed price and in 'such quantities ... as the company's store-keeper may order from time to time'. The plaintiffs accepted this tender and the defendant made several deliveries of iron but before the period of 12 months expired he refused to supply any more. The plaintiffs sued for breach of contract. *Held*, although there was no binding contract on the part of the plaintiffs to order any goods during the year in question, the defendant was bound to supply such as were ordered. The defendant had made a standing offer which was accepted by the plaintiffs whenever they ordered goods.

Gregory v Ford [1951] 1 All ER 121 [252]

An employee drove his employer's lorry negligently and caused injury to the plaintiff. At the time of the accident the lorry was not covered by a policy of insurance against third party risks and driving the lorry without such a policy was a breach of a statutory duty. *Held*, there was an implied term in the contract of service that the employee should not be required to do an unlawful act and for this reason he was able to recover from his employer the amount of damages and costs which he was liable to pay to the plaintiff. (See also *Moorcock, The.*)

Gregory and Parker v Williams (1817) 3 Mer 582   [253]

Parker was indebted to Williams, his landlord, and also to Gregory. Williams promised Parker that if he would surrender his lease and assign all his property to him, he (Williams) would first pay off the debt to Gregory, then to himself and pay the balance (if any) to Parker. Parker acted in accordance with this suggestion but Williams failed to pay Gregory. *Held,* Gregory and Parker were able to compel the performance of this promise in equity as Parker was a trustee for Gregory. (See also *Flavell, Re.*)

Greig v Insole [1978] 1 WLR 302   [254]

Some English professional cricket players contracted with a promoter to play a series of winter matches in Australia. The International Cricket Conference and the Test and County Cricket Board made or proposed to make new rules which effectively banned the players from test and county cricket if they played for the promoter. It was claimed on the cricketers' behalf that the new rules were void as being in unreasonable restraint of trade. *Held,* the new rules were so void. The cricketing authorities had not shown that the ban was reasonable or justified. The new rules would substantially restrict the areas in which the cricketers could earn a living. As Australia was the only test playing country whose finances were threatened by the proposed series of matches, the new rules went further than was reasonably necessary for the protection of the game. The International Cricket Conference was found to have induced the players to breach their contract with the promoters. (See also *Eastham* v *Newcastle United Football Club Ltd.*)

Grist v Bailey [1966] 2 All ER 875   [255]

B agreed to sell a freehold house to G at a price of £850, in the belief that the house was subject to an existing statutory tenancy. In fact the house was not subject to a statutory tenancy, and on a vacant possession basis was worth £2,250. G sought specific performance of the agreement, and B pleaded the existence of a common mistake of fact, and counterclaimed for rescission of the sale agreement. *Held,* the sale agreement would be set aside for a fundamental common mistake of fact, on terms which gave G the option to buy the house at vacant possession price. (See also *Solle* v *Butcher*; but see *Bell* v *Lever Bros Ltd* and *Sindall (William) plc* v *Cambridgeshire County Council.*)

Guild & Co v Conrad [1894] 2 QB 885 (Court of Appeal)   [256]

The defendant orally promised the plaintiff that if he, the plaintiff, would accept certain bills for a firm in which the defendant's son was a partner he, the defendant, would provide the plaintiff with funds to meet the bills. *Held,* to be enforceable this promise need not be in writing as it was an indemnity and not a guarantee and therefore not within the provisions of s4 of the Statute of Frauds.

Guthing v Lynn (1831) 2 B & Ad 232   [257]

The plaintiff purchased a horse for £63 and promised to give the defendant an additional £5, or the buying of another horse, 'if the horse was lucky'. *Held,* this promise was too vague to be legally enforced. (See also *Scammell and Nephew Ltd* v *Ouston.*)

Hadley v Baxendale (1854) 9 Exch 341   [258]

The plaintiffs were millers and mealmen in Gloucester. The crankshaft of the steam engine which worked their mill was fractured and they ordered another from a firm in Greenwich who asked that the old shaft should be sent to them for use as a pattern. The plaintiffs gave the shaft to the defendants, who were common carriers, and the defendants promised to deliver the shaft on the following day. In fact they took a week to deliver it and because their mill was out of action for longer than would otherwise have been the case the plaintiffs claimed damages for loss of profit. *Held,* the plaintiffs would not succeed as the loss of profit could not reasonably be considered a consequence of the breach of contract which could have been fairly and reasonably contemplated by both parties when they entered into the contract of carriage. 'Where two parties have made a contract which one of them has broken, the damages which the other party ought to receive in respect of such breach of contract should be such as may fairly and reasonably be considered either arising naturally, ie, according to the usual course of things, from such breach of contract itself, or such as may reasonably be supposed to have been in the contemplation of both parties, at the time they made the contract, as the probable result of the breach of it. Now, if the special circumstances under which the contract was actually made were communicated by the plaintiffs to the defendants, and thus known to both parties, the damages resulting from the breach of such a contract, which they would reasonably contemplate, would be the amount of injury which would ordinarily follow from a breach of the contract under the special circumstances so known and communicated. But, on the other hand, if these special circumstances were wholly unknown to the party breaking the contract, he, at the most, could only be supposed to have had in his contemplation the amount of injury which would arise generally, and in the great multitude of cases not affected by any special circumstances, from such a breach of contract. For, had the special circumstances been known the parties might have specially provided for the breach of contract by special terms as to damages in that case; and of this advantage it would be very unjust to deprive them' (*per* ALDERSON B). (See also *Koufos v C Czarnikow Ltd, Victoria Laundry (Windsor) Ltd v Newman Industries Ltd, Seven Seas Properties Ltd v Al-Essa (No 2)* and *Parsons (H) (Livestock) Ltd v Uttley Ingham & Co Ltd.*)

Hancock v B W Brazier (Anerley) Ltd   [259]
[1966] 2 All ER 901 (Court of Appeal)

A builder sold a house, which was in the course of erection, it being an express term of the contract that the house would be completed in a proper manner. Before the contract was made, the foundations had been laid and, unknown to the builder, the hard-core used as a base contained soluble sulphates, which made it totally unsuitable. More than two years after the sale had been completed, the sulphates caused the concrete to expand and crack, causing substantial damage to the house. The plaintiff claimed damages for breach by the builder of implied warranty of fitness of materials. *Held,* the claim would succeed, for the express term of the contract dealt only with workmanship and not with fitness of materials. Where a purchaser buys a house from a builder who contracts to build it, a threefold warranty is implied: (a) that the builder will do the work in a good and workmanlike manner; (b) supplying good and proper materials; and, (c) that the house would be reasonably fit for human habitation. (But see *Lynch v Thorne*; see also *Gregory v Ford* and *Independent Broadcasting Authority v EMI Electronics Ltd.*)

Harburg India Rubber Comb Co v Martin   [260]
[1902] 1 KB 778 (Court of Appeal)

The plaintiffs were judgment creditors of a company of which the defendant was a director and in which he held a large number of shares. The plaintiffs agreed to withdraw a writ of execution against the company in consideration of an oral promise by the defendant to indorse two bills of exchange for the amount of the debt. The plaintiffs claimed damages for breach of this promise. *Held,* their action must fail as the defendant's promise was made to a person to whom another was already indebted which brought the promise within s4 of the Statute of Frauds. In these circumstances the defendant's oral promise constituted a guarantee and not an indemnity and for this reason it could not be enforced. (But see *Fitzgerald* v *Dressler.*)

Hardman v Booth (1863) 1 H & C 803 [261]

An agent for the plaintiffs, who were worsted manufacturers, called at the place of business of 'Gandell & Co' with a view to obtaining orders for goods. At that time the firm consisted of Thomas Gandell only and the business was managed by Edward Gandell who was his son and also his clerk. The agent had asked to be directed to the offices of 'Messrs Gandell' where he found Edward who led the agent to believe that he was a member of the firm of Gandell & Co. Business was transacted and when the goods, which were invoiced to 'Edward Gandell & Co', were delivered, Edward pledged them with the defendant who afterwards sold them under his power of sale. *Held,* the defendant was liable in conversion as there was no contract of sale between the plaintiffs and Edward as they had believed, to Edward's knowledge, that they were dealing with Gandell & Co and not Edward personally. In consequence Edward had no property in the goods to pledge to the defendant. (See also *Cundy* v *Lindsay.*)

Hare v Murphy Brothers Ltd [1974] 3 All ER 940 [262]
(Court of Appeal)

The claimant was a foreman of previous good character. He was sentenced to 12 months' imprisonment for an assault unconnected with his employment. The question arose as to whether the prison sentence automatically terminated his contract of employment. *Held,* the passing of the sentence automatically terminated the contract of employment as from the date of the sentence since it had rendered it impossible for the claimant to perform his part of the contract. (But see *Davis Contractors Ltd* v *Fareham Urban District Council.*)

Hare v Nicoll [1966] 1 All ER 285 (Court of Appeal) [263]

The plaintiff had an option to purchase 25,000 shares in a private company, so long as he gave notice of his intention to do so by 1 May 1963, and paid for them by 1 June 1963. He failed to pay for them by that date, and so the defendant sold the shares to a third party. The plaintiff sued for breach of contract. The defendant maintained that she was not liable because the time of payment was of the essence of the contract, that payment had not been made by the specified date, and that therefore the option had lapsed. *Held,* time was of the essence of the contract and strict compliance was required both as to the time for the giving of the notice to exercise the option and as to the time of payment. (Distinguished in *Millichamp* v *Jones*; see also *Rickards (Charles) Ltd* v *Oppenheim.*)

Harlington & Leinster Enterprises Ltd v Christopher Hull [264]
Fine Art Ltd [1990] 1 All ER 737 (Court of Appeal)

The defendant art dealers were asked to sell two oil paintings which had been described in a 1980 auction catalogue as being by Gabriele Münter of the German expressionist school. They contacted the plaintiffs, specialists in the German expressionist school, and told them that they had two Münter paintings for sale. When the plaintiffs' employee called to view the paintings, the defendants made it clear that they did not know much about them and that they were not expert in them. Without asking any questions, the employee bought one of the paintings for £6,000. The invoice described it as being by Münter. The painting turned out to be a forgery and the plaintiffs sought recovery of the purchase price, claiming, inter alia, that there had been a sale of goods by description (s13(1) of the Sale of Goods Act 1979) or that the painting was not of merchantable quality (s14(2), (6) of the 1979 Act). *Held,* the plaintiffs could not succeed. In making the purchase, they had not relied on the defendants' description and, therefore, there had not been a sale by description. Further, the painting was still capable of being appreciated and resold, even though it was not by Münter. 'If the plaintiffs fail to establish a breach of contract through the front door of s13(1), they cannot succeed through the back door of s14' (*per* SLADE LJ). (But see *Varley* v *Whipp.*)

Harris v Nickerson (1873) LR 8 QB 286 [265]

An auctioneer advertised that certain goods, including office furniture, would be sold at a certain place on certain days. The plaintiff went to the sale but all the lots of office furniture, in which he was interested, were withdrawn and he sued the auctioneer to recover damages for his loss of time and expenses. *Held,* the plaintiff's claim must fail as the advertising of the sale was a mere declaration of intention to hold a sale and not an offer which could be accepted to form a binding contract. If the sale was not held the auctioneer was not bound to indemnify those who attended. (But see *Warlow* v *Harrison.*)

Harris v Wyre Forest District Council See Smith v Eric S Bush

Harrison and Jones Ltd v Bunten and Lancaster Ltd [266]
[1953] 1 All ER 903

The appellants, who were manufacturers of articles made of kapok, and the respondents, who were importers of kapok, contracted for the sale of 300 bales of Calcutta kapok, Sree brand, which was to be equal to a standard sample in the respondents' possession. After the goods had been delivered it appeared that the kapok contained an admixture of cotton which rendered it unsuitable for use in the appellants' machines. At the date of the contract both parties believed that the agreement was in respect of pure kapok. *Held,* such a mutual mistake of fact would not render the contract a nullity although, from the point of view of the buyer, the mistake was of fundamental importance. (See also *Rose (Frederick E) (London) Ltd* v *William H Pim Jnr & Co Ltd.*)

Hart v O'Connor [1985] 2 All ER 880 (Privy Council) [267]

The appellant agreed to buy farmland in New Zealand from a sole trustee who, unknown to the appellant, was of unsound mind when he signed the agreement. The present trustees and beneficiaries sought to have the sale set aside. *Held,* they would not succeed. In cases such as this, where the affliction was not apparent and the consequent incapacity unknown to the other party, the validity of the contract would be judged by the same standards as a contract made by a person of sound mind and here there had been no unfairness amounting to equitable fraud. (See also *Molton* v *Camroux.*)

Hartley v Ponsonby (1857) 7 E & B 872 [268]

Some members of the crew deserted and a vessel was left short of hands. In order to induce the remainder of the crew to complete the voyage the master promised to pay each seaman an additional £40. It was found that it was dangerous and unreasonable for the ship to go to sea with the smaller crew. *Held,* the crew's original agreement did not require them to sail a ship which was unseaworthy due to lack of hands and their undertaking to continue the voyage with the reduced crew was consideration for the master's promise. (See also *Ward* v *Byham.*)

Hartog v Colin and Shields [1939] 3 All ER 566 [269]

The defendants offered to sell the plaintiff 30,000 Argentine hare skins at certain prices per pound but after the plaintiff had accepted this offer the defendants failed to deliver the skins, as they had intended, as was the usual practice, that they should be sold at the specified prices per piece. *Held,* the plaintiff's action for damages would not succeed as he must have realised that the offer made by the defendants contained a mistake. (But see *Scott* v *Littledale.*)

Harvela Investments Ltd v Royal Trust Co of Canada (CI) [270]
Ltd [1985] 2 All ER 966 (House of Lords)

The plaintiffs and the second defendants were rival offerors for a parcel of shares held by the first defendants who bound themselves to accept the highest offer. The plaintiffs offered $2,175,000 and the second defendants '$2,100,000 or ... $101,000 in excess of any other offer'. The second defendants' bid was accepted and the plaintiffs contended that the second defendants' bid had been invalid. *Held,* this was the case as a referential bid (such as the second defendants') was inconsistent with the purpose of a sale, such as that here, by fixed bidding. As to whether it was a fixed bidding sale or an auction sale depended on the presumed intention of the vendor as deduced from the express provisions of the invitation to bid. No fresh contract had been created by the acceptance of the second defendants' referential bid because, at the time, the first defendants had been acting under the misapprehension that the second defendants were entitled to the shares.

Harvey v Facey [1893] AC 552 (Privy Council) [271]

The appellants telegraphed 'Will you sell us Bumper Hall Pen? Telegraph lowest cash price' and the respondents replied 'Lowest price for Bumper Hall Pen £900'. The appellants then telegraphed 'We agree to buy Bumper Hall Pen for £900 asked by you. Please send us your title-deed in order that we may get early possession', to which they received no reply and thereupon brought an action for specific performance. *Held,* the action must fail as the respondents' telegram was not an offer to sell but a statement of the minimum price required for the property if they eventually decided to sell. The appellants' final telegram was itself an offer to buy the property for £900, acceptance of which could not be implied by the silence of the respondents. (See also *Clifton* v *Palumbo* and *Bigg* v *Boyd Gibbins Ltd.*)

Hayes v James and Charles Dodd [1990] 2 All ER 815
(Court of Appeal) [272]

The plaintiffs were negotiating for the purchase of a workshop for their motor repair business and their solicitors, the defendants, assured them – incorrectly – that they would have a right of way over adjoining land. This means of access was critical to the success of the business and, within two or three days of the plaintiffs' completion of the purchase, the owner of the land blocked it off. In the plaintiffs' action for breach of contract the judge awarded damages on the basis of capital expenditure thrown away in the purchase of the business and the expenses incurred, together with £3,000 for anguish and vexation. The defendants appealed. *Held*, in the circumstances the judge had been entitled to award damages on the basis of comparing the plaintiffs' actual situation with the position in which they would have been if they had never entered into the transaction at all. However, damages are not recoverable for anguish and vexation arising out of the breach of a purely commercial contract and to that extent the defendants' appeal would be allowed. (See also *Watts* v *Morrow*.)

Head v Tattersall (1871) LR 7 Exch 7   [273]

The plaintiff bought a horse from the defendant who said the horse had hunted with the Bicester hounds and promised that if the horse did not answer this description it was to be returned by the following Wednesday 'otherwise the purchaser shall be obliged to keep the lot with all faults'. The horse had not hunted with the Bicester hounds and the plaintiff returned the horse within the period specified and sued to recover the purchase price. *Held*, he would succeed as the option to return the horse was a condition subsequent and it made no difference that the horse had been injured, through no fault of the plaintiff, while in the plaintiff's possession.

Heilbut, Symons & Co v Buckleton [1913] AC 30   [274]
(House of Lords)

The appellants' manager had been instructed to obtain applications for shares in a rubber company. The respondent telephoned the appellants' manager and said 'I understand you are bringing out a rubber company' and the manager replied 'We are.' The respondent asked 'if it was all right' and was told 'We are bringing it out' to which the respondent rejoined 'That is good enough for me'. As a result of this conversation 6,000 shares were allotted to the respondent but they quickly fell in value. The respondent contended that as the company could not be properly described as a rubber company there was a breach of warranty that it was a rubber company whose main object was to produce rubber. *Held*, the words of the appellants' manager constituted a mere representation and not a warranty. (But see *Couchman* v *Hill* and *IBA Ltd* v *EMI Construction Ltd*.)

Henderson v Merrett Syndicates Ltd [1994] 3 All ER 506   [275]
(House of Lords)]

On appeal against a decision that underwriting agents owed various Lloyd's names a duty of care in tort, the question arose, inter alia, whether a claimant was automatically restricted to either a tortious or a contractual remedy. *Held*, a plaintiff who has available to him concurrent remedies in contract and tort may choose the remedy which appears to him to be the most advantageous unless his contract precludes him from doing so.

Henthorn v Fraser [1892] 2 Ch 27 (Court of Appeal)   [276]

The defendants handed the plaintiff an option to purchase some houses for £750, but on the following day between 12 and 1 o'clock posted a letter of withdrawal which did not reach the plaintiff until 5 pm on the same day. At 3.50 pm on that day the plaintiff posted a letter of acceptance which was delivered after the defendants' office had closed. The defendants refused to complete and the plaintiff brought an action for specific performance. *Held*, the decree would be made as where it is reasonably to be expected that the post might be used as a means of communicating the acceptance, although the offer was not sent by post, the acceptance is complete as soon as it is posted. A revocation of an offer is of no effect until brought to the notice of the person to whom the offer was made so that in the case of a withdrawal by post it takes effect when the letter of withdrawal is received and not when it is posted. (But see *Re London and Northern Bank.*)

Herbert Morris Ltd v Saxelby [1916] 1 AC 688 **[277]**
(House of Lords)

The appellants carried on business as engineers and were the leading manufacturers of hoisting machinery in the United Kingdom. The respondent had been employed by them for several years as a draughtsman and in various other capacities and had entered into a contract to serve for two years certain, and thereafter subject to four weeks' notice on either side, at a salary of £3 17s 6d per week. The respondent covenanted that he would 'not at any time during a period of seven years from the date of his ceasing to be employed by the company whether under this agreement or otherwise howsoever either in the United Kingdom of Great Britain or Ireland carry on either as principal, agent, servant or otherwise alone or jointly or in connection with any person firm or company' work similar to that undertaken by the appellants. In breach of this agreement the respondent became employed by competitors of the appellants, a company in Manchester engaged in the manufacture of lifting machinery. The appellants claimed to be entitled to an injunction to restrain the respondent from committing breaches of his contract. *Held,* the appellants would not succeed as the covenant was wider than that required for their protection. In circumstances such as this an injunction will only be granted to restrain a former servant from competing with his former master if the former employer has an exceptional proprietary right which requires protection, such as a trade connection or secret. (See also *Faccenda Chicken Ltd v Fowler.*)

Hermann v Charlesworth [1905] 2 KB 123 (Court of Appeal) **[278]**

The defendant was proprietor of *The Matrimonial Post and Fashionable Marriage Advertiser*. In consequence of an advertisement in this paper the plaintiff, who was seeking a husband, signed an agreement whereby she would pay the defendant £250 if a marriage took place as a result of an introduction made by the defendant. The plaintiff also paid a 'special client's fee' of £52, £47 of which was to be returned if the plaintiff had not become engaged or married within nine months. The defendant did not succeed in arranging a marriage for the plaintiff within nine months and the plaintiff sued to recover £52. *Held,* she was entitled to recover as the money was paid by her as the consideration for an illegal contract and the fact that the defendant had brought about introductions and incurred expense did nothing to defeat the plaintiff's claim.

Herne Bay Steam Boat Co v Hutton [1903] 2 KB 683 **[279]**
(Court of Appeal)

The parties entered into an agreement whereby the plaintiffs' ship was to be 'at the disposal' of the defendant on a certain date 'for the purpose of viewing the naval review and for a day's cruise round the fleet'. The Royal review was afterwards cancelled but the fleet was still at Spithead on the day in question. In view of the cancellation of the review the defendant did not use the ship and declined to pay the balance of the hire. The plaintiffs claimed damages for breach of contract. *Held,* the plaintiffs should succeed. The naval review was not the sole foundation of the contract as the object of the voyage was also to cruise round the fleet. (But see *Krell* v *Henry.*)

Heron II, The See **Koufos v C Czarnikow Ltd**

Heyman v Darwins Ltd [1942] 1 All ER 337 (House of Lords)   [280]

A contract between the parties contained a clause to the effect that all disputes which should arise under the contract should be referred for arbitration. A dispute arose and, in view of the repudiation of the contract by the respondents, the appellants maintained that they could not afterwards rely on the arbitration clause. *Held,* this view would not be upheld as the repudiation of the contract, although accepted by the appellants, did nothing to impair the validity of the arbitration clause. (See also *Woolf* v *Collis Removal Service.*)

Heywood v Wellers [1976] 1 All ER 300 (Court of Appeal)   [281]

The appellant went to the defendant solicitors as she wished to recover a £40 debt and to prevent the debtor from molesting her. She was given the wrong advice regarding the cost and length of proceedings. High Court proceedings were started instead of magistrates' court proceedings and finally, when an injunction was obtained ordering the debtor not to molest the appellant, he was not taken to court when he did molest her again. The appellant claimed £170 of the costs actually paid and £150 for 'damages and expenses'. *Held,* the solicitors were not entitled to recover any costs as they had failed completely to fulfil their part of the contract as their work had been useless. They were in breach of their duty to take reasonable care as they had not prevented the appellant from being molested. Consequently, the appellant was entitled to damages for the disappointment, upset and mental distress she had suffered as a result of their breach of contract. (See also *Jackson* v *Horizon Holidays Ltd* and *Jarvis* v *Swans Tours Ltd.*)

Hill v Hill (William) (Park Lane) Ltd [1949] 2 All ER 452   [282]
(House of Lords)

The appellant, a racehorse owner, was indebted to the respondents, who were bookmakers, in the sum of £3,635 12s 6d and was unable to pay this amount. The Committee of Tattersalls decided that the appellant should pay £635 12s 6d within 14 days and the balance by monthly instalments of £100. The respondents brought an action to recover the amount of the debt under this agreement although it was conceded that the original contracts, which resulted in the appellant's indebtedness, were wagers and therefore void. *Held,* the payments under the instalment agreement were payments of a 'sum of money ... alleged to have been won upon any wager' within s18 of the Gaming Act 1845, and could not therefore be recovered. (See also *Coral* v *Kleyman.*)

Hillas & Co Ltd v Arcos Ltd (1932) 38 Com Cas 23   [283]
(House of Lords)

There was an agreement in writing for the supply of wood during 1930 and it contained an option to buy more wood during the following year but the option clause did not specify the precise kind or size of timber to be supplied, the ports to which it was to be shipped or the manner of shipment. The suppliers argued that the option clause was not binding as it was intended merely to form the basis of a future agreement. *Held,* the agreement in respect of the supply of timber during 1930 was couched in similar terms and had been duly observed. The option clause showed a sufficient intention to be bound and could create a valid contract, as those points which were not specifically resolved in the option clause could be determined by reference to the previous dealings between the parties and normal business practice in the timber trade. (See also *Foley* v *Classique Coaches Ltd*; but see *Scammell and Nephew Ltd* v *Ouston* and *Walford* v *Miles*.)

Hillingdon Estates Co v Stonefield Estates Ltd [284]
[1952] 1 All ER 853

In 1938 the purchasers contracted in writing to buy certain land at South Ruislip for building purposes. The contract was not completed, partly because of the war, and in 1948 the Middlesex County Council made a compulsory purchase order in respect of the whole of the land. The purchasers contended that the basis of the agreement had thus been destroyed and that they were therefore discharged from their contract. The vendors counterclaimed for specific performance. *Held,* the vendors would succeed. The contract had not been frustrated as the making of the compulsory purchase order did nothing to preclude the performance of the contract, ie, the conveyance of the legal estate from the vendors to the purchasers. (See also *Paradine* v *Jane*.)

Hirachand Punamchand v Temple [1911] 2 KB 330 [285]
(Court of Appeal)

The debtor's father offered to pay Rs1,500 'in full settlement' of the debt and enclosed a draft for that amount. The creditor cashed the draft and afterwards brought an action against the debtor to recover the balance of the debt. *Held,* the action could not be maintained as the creditor must be taken to have accepted the draft on the terms on which it was sent, that is, 'in full settlement' of the debt. (See also *Welby* v *Drake*.)

Hivac Ltd v Park Royal Scientific Instruments Ltd [286]
[1946] 1 All ER 350 (Court of Appeal)

The plaintiff company, which engaged in the highly skilled work of the manufacture of midget valves for deaf aids, discovered that a number of their employees were doing spare time work for a competitor, the defendants. The plaintiffs sought an injunction to restrain the employment of their staff by the defendants and this relief would be given if it could be shown that by working for the defendants the employees were breaking their contracts of service. *Held,* an injunction would be granted as the employees were in breach of their obligation to render faithful service to the plaintiffs which was an implied term of their contract of service. (See also *Winter Garden Theatre (London) Ltd* v *Millennium Productions Ltd*; but see *Provident Financial Group plc* v *Hayward*.)

Hollier v Rambler Motors (AMC) Ltd [287]
[1972] 1 All ER 399 (Court of Appeal)

The plaintiff's car needed some repair work done to it. He telephoned the defendants' garage and asked if and when they could do the work. The defendants' manager replied that they could not do the work immediately but if the plaintiff could have the car brought to the garage they would attend to the defects in due course. The plaintiff agreed, and these were the only express terms agreed. On three or four occasions during the preceding five years the defendants had carried out work for the plaintiff and on each occasion he had signed an 'invoice' describing the work to be done and the price. Underneath the space for signature was a clause stating that 'The company is not responsible for damage caused by fire to customers' cars on the premises'. A fire occurred owing to the defendants' negligence and the defendants pleaded that, although on this occasion the plaintiff had not signed an 'invoice', the exemption clause had been incorporated in the oral contract by a course of dealing and its effect was to bar the plaintiff's claim. *Held,* the plaintiff's claim should succeed. There was insufficient previous course of dealing to justify the incorporation into the contract of the exemption clause. In any case, the clause could be read as being a mere warning that liability did not exist for loss caused by fire started without negligence. Ambiguous clauses are construed contra proferentem. (See also *McCutcheon* v *David MacBrayne Ltd.*)

Hollins v J Davy Ltd [1963] 1 All ER 370   **[288]**

The plaintiff garaged his Sunbeam Rapier with the defendants and terms of the contract excluded the defendants' liability for (a) loss or damage however caused, and (b) loss or misdelivery of any vehicle arising from any cause including negligence. The defendants' servant negligently allowed a stranger to drive away the plaintiff's car honestly but mistakenly believing that the plaintiff had sent him to collect it. The stranger stole the car and the plaintiff sought to recover, inter alia, damages for breach of contract. *Held,* his action would fail: the defendants' servant had acted honestly and it followed that there had not been such a deliberate disregard of contractual obligations as would disentitle the defendants from relying on the exemption clauses. (See also *Suisse Atlantique, etc* v *Rotterdamsche, etc.*)

Holwell Securities Ltd v Hughes   **[289]**
[1974] 1 All ER 161 (Court of Appeal)

The defendant granted the plaintiffs an option to purchase a dwelling-house, the option to be exercised within six months by notice in writing to the defendant. The plaintiffs posted a letter exercising the option and sent it by ordinary post. The letter was not delivered. *Held,* the option was not validly exercised since it could only be so exercised in the prescribed way. The rule that an acceptance of an offer could be effected, so as to constitute a binding contract, merely by posting a letter of acceptance, did not apply when the express terms of the offer stipulated that the acceptance had to reach the offeror. (But see *Henthorn* v *Fraser* and *Household Fire Insurance Co* v *Grant.*)

Hong Kong Fir Shipping Co Ltd v Kawasaki   **[290]**
Kisen Kaisha Ltd [1962] 1 All ER 474 (Court of Appeal)

On 26 December 1956, the defendants chartered the *Hong Kong Fir* from the plaintiffs, its owners, for a period of 24 months from the time at which it arrived at Liverpool. The charter period began on 13 February 1957 but it was necessary for the vessel to undergo repairs for about 20 of the first 24 weeks of the charter and in June 1957 the defendants repudiated it. It was found that the delays were attributable to breaches of the charter by the plaintiffs in failing to maintain the vessel in an efficient state and also that in June 1957 the defendants had no reasonable grounds for thinking that the plaintiffs would be unable to make the vessel seaworthy at the latest by mid-September. *Held,* the defendants were not entitled to repudiate the charter as the plaintiffs' obligation to maintain the vessel was a warranty (for the breach of which the remedy was damages) and not so fundamental a matter as to amount to a condition of the contract, the breach of which would have entitled the defendants to accept it as a repudiation and to withdraw from the charter. Further, the delays, serious though they were, were not such as to amount to a frustration of the contract, ie to make further commercial performance of the contract impossible. (Distinguished in *Bunge Corpn v Tradax SA*; but see *Barber v NWS Bank plc*.)

Hood v West End Motor Car Packing Co [1917] 2 KB 38   [291]

The plaintiff wished to ship a motor car from London to Messina and insured it against marine risks. He did not give notice of the fact that it was to be carried on deck and there was evidence that if such notice had been given many underwriters would have refused to insure altogether and that others would have charged a very high premium. The car was damaged by sea and rendered valueless. *Held,* the risk was not covered by the policy as the fact that the car was to be carried on deck had not been disclosed. (See also *Seaman v Fonereau, Simner v New India Assurance Co Ltd* and s18 of the Marine Insurance Act 1906.)

Hopkins v Norcross plc [1993] 1 All ER 565   [292]

The plaintiff was wrongfully dismissed when aged 58. Under the defendant employers' pension scheme he was entitled to a pension equal to his loss of salary from the date of his dismissal until his 60th birthday. In his action for wrongful dismissal (ie, breach of his contract of employment) should the amount of the pension be set off against the amount to be awarded by way of damages? *Held,* it should not as, in the absence of any provision to the contrary in the employment contract or the pension rules, there is no distinction in this regard between claims for breach of contract and claims in tort for lost earning capacity as a result of injury. (Applied: *Parry v Cleaver* [1969] 1 All ER 555 and *Smoker v London Fire and Civil Defence Authority* [1991] 2 All ER 449.)

Hopkins v Tanqueray (1854) 15 CB 130   [293]

The defendant sent his horse to Tattersall's for sale by auction and when he saw the plaintiff examining the horse's legs he said 'You need not examine his legs; you have nothing to look for; I assure you he is perfectly sound in every respect' and the plaintiff replied 'If you say so, I am perfectly satisfied'. The plaintiff attended the auction sale on the following day and bought the horse which was subsequently found to be unsound. *Held,* the plaintiff could not recover his loss as the defendant's assurance was a mere representation and not a warranty which formed part of the contract. (But see *Bannerman v White*.)

Horne v Midland Railway Co (1873) LR 8 CP 131   [294]

The plaintiffs, who were shoe manufacturers in Kettering, obtained a contract for the supply of a quantity of shoes to a London firm at 4s per pair, an exceptionally good price, and the shoes were to be delivered by a certain date. The plaintiffs delivered the shoes to the defendants, a railway company, for carriage to London, in time, in the normal course of events, for delivery in accordance with the terms of the contract, and told the station master that they, the plaintiffs, had undertaken to deliver the shoes by the date specified in the contract. The shoes arrived in London a day late and the purchasers of the shoes refused to accept delivery. The plaintiffs were forced to sell them at 2s 9d a pair and contended that the defendants were liable in damages for the difference between this price and that fixed by the contract. *Held,* the plaintiffs' claim must fail as this loss was not such as might reasonably be considered to have arisen naturally from the defendants' breach of contract and could not reasonably be supposed to have been contemplated by both parties when the contract of carriage was made. (But see *Simpson* v *London and North Western Railway Co.*)

Horsfall v Thomas (1862) 1 H & C 90   [295]

The defendant employed the plaintiff to make a steel gun. When the plaintiff delivered the gun it was defective in such a way as would have justified the defendant in refusing to accept delivery and this defect might have been apparent if the gun had been examined. The gun was fired by the defendant and after several shots it burst and became worthless. There was some evidence that the plaintiff had concealed the defect and when he sued to recover the cost of the gun the defendant maintained that he was entitled to rescind the contract as the plaintiff had induced him to accept delivery by fraud and misrepresentation. *Held*, the plaintiff would succeed as the defendant's contention as to fraud and misrepresentation was defeated by the fact that the defendant had not examined the gun so that the concealment of the defect had not influenced his acceptance. (See also *Smith* v *Chadwick*.)

Horton v Horton [1960] 3 All ER 649 (Court of Appeal)   [296]

The defendant husband executed a separation agreement under seal whereby he undertook to pay the plaintiff wife 'the monthly sum of £30'. Such payments continued for about ten months and they were made without deduction of tax, although tax should have been deducted by the husband who should have accounted for the tax to the Inland Revenue. The husband then executed a supplemental agreement not under seal and without any expressed consideration by which he undertook to pay a monthly amount 'which after deduction of tax shall amount to the clear sum of £30'. The parties originally intended that the husband should pay the monthly sums free of tax and they entered into the supplemental agreement to clarify the position. Was the supplemental agreement enforceable by the plaintiff or was she merely entitled to £30 a month less tax? *Held*, she was entitled to £30 a month free of tax. The original deed did not carry out the parties' intention and the wife could have made some claim to rectification and had some prospect of success. It followed that the supplemental agreement was made for consideration, viz, that the wife refrained from taking rectification proceedings. (See also *Pitt* v *PHH Asset Management Ltd.*)

Houghton Main Colliery Co Ltd, Re [1956] 3 All ER 300   [297]

A limited company went into voluntary liquidation at a time when it was under an obligation to pay pensions to two men. *Held*, in assessing the amount which should be paid to the two men by way of compensation for breach of contract, their income tax liability should be taken into account and the sums payable to them reduced accordingly. (See also *Parsons* v *BNM Laboratories Ltd.*)

Household Fire and Carriage Accident Insurance   [298]
Co Ltd v Grant (1879) 4 Ex D 216 (Court of Appeal)

The defendant applied for shares in the plaintiffs' company. The shares were allotted to the defendant and notice of the allotment was posted to him but never arrived. The question arose as to whether the defendant was a shareholder. *Held*, he was, as the contract was completed at the time of posting the letter of acceptance and this was the case although the letter was delayed or never delivered. (See also *Byrne & Co* v *Leon Van Tienhoven & Co.*)

Howard v Shirlstar Container Transport Ltd [1990] 3 All ER 366   **[299]**
(Court of Appeal)

The defendants engaged the plaintiff pilot to recover their two aircraft which had been hired out in Nigeria. After being told by a Nigerian government official that his life was in imminent danger, he flew one of the aircraft to the Ivory Coast without obtaining clearance from air traffic control, a breach of Nigerian law. When he sued to recover the balance of the agreed fee, the defendants contended, inter alia, that the contract had been performed illegally in Nigeria and was therefore unenforceable in England. *Held,* the plaintiff's claim would be successful. While the court would not normally enforce a contract so as to enable a plaintiff to benefit from his criminal conduct, here the public conscience would not be affronted by enforcement because the plaintiff's criminal conduct was designed to free himself and his wireless operator from pressing danger. (See also *St John Shipping Corporation* v *Joseph Rank Ltd.)*

Howard Marine & Dredging Co Ltd v   **[300]**
A Ogden & Sons (Excavations) Ltd [1978] 2 All ER 1134
(Court of Appeal)

An excavation and dredging company hired barges from the owners. During pre-contract negotiations, the owners substantially overstated the dead-weight capacity of the barges. They did so having consulted Lloyd's Register, but not the correct information which was contained in the barges' documents. On discovering the overstatement, the dredging company refused to pay the hire charges and claimed damages for misrepresentation under s2(1) of the Misrepresentation Act 1967. This provides that where a misrepresentation would have been actionable if fraudulent, the person making it is liable even though the misrepresentation is not fraudulent, unless he proves that he believed, on reasonable grounds, that the misrepresentation was true. *Held,* that as the misrepresentation would have been actionable if fraudulent, the onus was on the owners to prove their reasonable belief in its truth. The evidence did not establish that the owners had objectively reasonable grounds for disregarding the correct figures in the barges' documents and preferring the incorrect information in Lloyd's Register. Accordingly, the owners had not discharged the onus placed on them by s2(1) of the 1967 Act and were therefore liable.

Howatson v Webb [1908] 1 Ch 1 (Court of Appeal)   **[301]**

A solicitor was asked to execute a deed and did so on being told that it was a conveyance relating to property in which he had an interest. In fact it was a transfer by way of mortgage. *Held,* the solicitor was bound by the terms of the mortgage as the misrepresentation related to the contents and not to the character of the deed. (See also *Saunders* v *Anglia Building Society.)*

Hoyle, Re, Hoyle v Hoyle [1893] 1 Ch 84 (Court of Appeal)   **[302]**

A testator orally promised his partners in a firm of solicitors that he would guarantee them against loss from a certain debt due from the testator's son. In his will the testator stated that 'he had guaranteed' the firm in this respect and in a codicil he 'confirmed the guarantee mentioned in his will'. *Held,* these references in the will and codicil were a sufficient note or memorandum in writing for the purposes of s4 of the Statute of Frauds. (See also *Elpis Maritime Co Ltd* v *Marti Chartering Co Inc, The Maria D.)*

Huddersfield Banking Co Ltd v Henry Lister & Son Ltd   [303]
[1895] 2 Ch 273 (Court of Appeal)

The defendant company mortgaged their leasehold mills and all the fixed plant and machinery therein to the plaintiffs. An order was made for the winding-up of the defendant company and the plaintiffs, after inspecting the premises, agreed that certain looms were not affixed to the premises within the provisions of the mortgage and therefore consented to an order being made for the sale of certain machinery and plant, including these looms. The plaintiffs, who afterwards ascertained that the looms in question were originally affixed to the mills and had been wrongfully loosened and severed after the winding-up order had been made, claimed a declaration that the consent order should be set aside and that the looms were their property as mortgagees. *Held,* they were entitled to succeed as they had given their consent to the order while they were under a common mistake as to a material fact as to whether the looms were attached to the property so as to form part of it. (See also *Solle* v *Butcher.*)

Hughes v Asset Managers plc [1995] 3 All ER 669   [304]
(Court of Appeal)

The parties entered into five discretionary management agreements and, under these agreements, the respondents invested £3 million on the appellants' behalf. The market fell and the appellants directed the respondents to sell the shares. They did so, at a loss of nearly £1 million. While the respondents held a principal's licence, the director who actually made and signed the agreements on their behalf did not at the time hold a representative's licence and thus he had acted in contravention of s1(1)(b) of the Prevention of Fraud (Investments) Act 1958. The appellants contended that the management agreements were therefore void and that they were entitled to recover from the respondents the amount of the loss. *Held,* this was not the case since the agreements in question were neither expressly nor impliedly forbidden by the 1958 Act. 'I can see no basis in either the words the legislature has used or the type of prohibition under discussion, or in considerations of public policy (including the mischief against which this part of the 1958 Act was directed), for the assertion that Parliament must be taken to have intended that ... protection [of the investing public] required (over and above criminal sanctions) that any deals effected through the agency of unlicensed persons should automatically be struck down and rendered ineffective' (*per* SAVILLE LJ). (See also *Archbolds (Freightage) Ltd* v *S Spanglett Ltd.*)

Hughes v Metropolitan Railway Co   [305]
(1877) 2 App Cas 439 (House of Lords)

The appellant gave the respondents six months' notice to repair but before the notice expired opened negotiations for the purchase of their lease. These negotiations were broken off and when six months had passed from the service of the notice the appellant brought an action of ejection. *Held,* the respondents were entitled to relief in equity as the negotiations had the effect of suspending the notice, which would not expire until six months had passed from the time when the negotiations were discontinued. (See also *Central London Property Trust Ltd* v *High Trees House Ltd*; but see *Ajayi* v *Briscoe.*)

Hunt and Winterbotham (West of England) Ltd v   [306]
BRS (Parcels) Ltd [1962] 1 All ER 111 (Court of Appeal)

The plaintiffs contracted with the defendants for the carriage of 15 parcels of woollen goods to Manchester. Only 12 parcels arrived and the defendants relied upon a term of the special contract of carriage by which their liability was limited. If there had been a fundamental breach of the contract the defendants would not have been so protected. *Held,* on the facts of this particular case the defendants were not obliged to prove the absence of such a breach and as the plaintiffs had not alleged that a fundamental breach of the contract was the cause of the loss, their claim to the full value of the goods could not succeed. (See also *Hong Kong Fir Shipping Co Ltd* v *Kawasaki Kisen Kaisha Ltd.*)

Hutton v Warren (1836) 2 Gale 71 [307]

The lease of a farm was determined and the lessee claimed to be entitled to a reasonable sum in respect of tillage, sowing and cultivation. The lessee, as an off-going tenant, relied upon the custom of the country as the foundation of his claim, the lease itself making no provision for any such payment. *Held,* the lessee was entitled to recover as custom required a tenant to plough and to sow and a landlord to pay for this work. (But see *Affréteurs Réunis Société Anonyme, Les* v *Leopold Walford (London) Ltd.*)

Hyde v Wrench (1840) 3 Beav 334 [308]

The defendant offered to sell his farm for £1,000. The plaintiff at first made a counter-offer of £950 but two days later agreed to pay £1,000 and when the defendant refused to complete the sale brought an action for specific performance. *Held,* there was no binding contract between them as the counter-offer had destroyed that previously made and the original offer was not revived when the plaintiff purported to tender acceptance. (But see *Brogden* v *Metropolitan Railway Co.*)

Independent Broadcasting Authority v EMI Electronics Ltd [309] and BICC Construction Ltd (1980) 14 BLR 1 (House of Lords)

At the request of the appellants, IBA, BICC designed three cylindrical television masts. Thereafter, IBA engaged EMI as sub-contractors for the design, supply and erection of the masts and, on IBA's instructions, EMI engaged BICC as sub-contractors for the design, supply and erection of the masts. Faults appeared in the first mast erected and IBA wrote directly to BICC who gave a written assurance that they were 'well satisfied that the structures will not oscillate dangerously'. A mast erected subsequently collapsed and IBA brought proceedings against EMI claiming damages for breach of contract and negligence and also against BICC claiming damages for negligence, breach of warranty and negligent misstatement. As a result of the claims made against them, EMI claimed over against BICC. *Held,* (i) Although EMI took no part in the design of the mast, in light of the express terms of their accepted tender, EMI contractually accepted responsibility for the design of the mast. (ii) The written assurance by BICC was not a contractual warranty because there was no evidence that, at the time it was given, either party intended the creation of a contractual undertaking: see *Heilbut, Symons & Co* v *Buckleton.* (iii) BICC were negligent in the design of the mast and owed a duty of care to IBA in relation to the written assurance. Since the assurance had been given negligently and IBA had relied on it BICC were liable in damages. 'One who in the course of his business contracts to design, supply and erect a television aerial mast is under an obligation to ensure that it is reasonably fit for the purpose for which he knows it is intended to be used' (*per* LORD SCARMAN). (See also *Hancock* v *B W Brazier (Anerley) Ltd.*)

Interfoto Picture Library Ltd v Stiletto Visual [310]
Programmes Ltd [1988] 1 All ER 348

In response to the defendant advertising agency's enquiry, on 5 March the plaintiff library of photographic transparencies, with whom the defendants had not dealt before, sent them 47 transparencies packed in a bag with a delivery note which clearly specified that the transparencies were to be returned by 19 March. Under the heading 'Conditions', which was printed prominently in capitals, the delivery note set out nine printed conditions, one of which said that a holding fee of £5 plus VAT per day would be charged for each transparency retained longer than 14 days. It was unlikely that the defendants read these conditions and, having forgotten about the transparencies, they did not return them until 2 April. The plaintiffs sent the defendants an invoice for £3,783.50 and, when the defendants refused to pay, they sued to recover the amount of the invoice. *Held,* their claim would fail as the condition, an unreasonable and extortionate clause, had not been fairly and reasonably brought to the defendants' attention. However, the defendants were ordered to pay on a quantum meruit (£3.50 per week per transparency) for their retention beyond a reasonable period. (Applied: *Parker* v *South-Eastern Railway Co* and *Thornton* v *Shoe Lane Parking Ltd*.)

Interoffice Telephones Ltd v Robert Freeman Co Ltd [311]
[1957] 3 All ER 479 (Court of Appeal)

There was an agreement for the hiring of a telephone installation for a period of 12 years but, six years before the expiration of this term, the hirers repudiated the contract and the owners regained possession of the apparatus. The owners claimed damages for breach of contract. *Held,* as the owners had enough plant to satisfy all demands which might have been made upon them without recourse to the apparatus hired under the agreement in question and the owners' loss would not therefore be diminished by a re-hiring of such apparatus, they would be entitled to recover by way of damages the loss of rental for the unexpired term, less appropriate deductions, so that the owners should be placed so far as possible in the same position as if the contract had been performed by the hirers. (But see *Payzu Ltd* v *Saunders*.)

Jackson v Horizon Holidays Ltd [312]
[1975] 3 All ER 92 (Court of Appeal)

The plaintiff booked a holiday for himself and his family with the defendants. The defendants' brochure described the hotel as 'of the highest standard' and listed numerous facilities. None of these materialised and the plaintiff's holiday was spoilt. *Held,* the plaintiff was entitled to damages not only for his disappointment, but also for that of his family. Although he was not a trustee for his wife and children, he had entered into the contract for their benefit. (See also *Beswick* v *Beswick, Ruxley Electronics and Construction Ltd* v *Forsyth* and *Jarvis* v *Swans Tours Ltd*.)

Jackson v Union Marine Insurance Co Ltd [313]
(1874) LR 10 CP 125

The *Spirit of the Dawn* was chartered to sail from Liverpool to Newport with a view to taking a cargo of iron rails to San Francisco. The ship struck rocks in Carnarvon Bay and was forced to return to Liverpool for repairs which took about eight months to carry out. *Held,* the original adventure had been frustrated and both parties were discharged from the contract. (But see *Tamplin (FA) Steamship Co Ltd* v *Anglo-Mexican Petroleum Products Co Ltd*.)

Jaggard v Sawyer [1995] 2 All ER 189 (Court of Appeal)   **[314]**

The plaintiff owned a house in a private cul-de-sac and the defendants owned a property at the other end. Having bought land behind their house, the defendants sought and were granted planning permission for the erection of a house there which would have access over the garden of their existing property and the estate road. Such development would constitute trespass (over the plaintiff's part of the road) and a breach of the covenants which applied to all of the properties on the estate. The plaintiff threatened proceedings for an injunction, but did not institute proceedings until the building of the new house had reached an advanced stage. The judge refused to grant an injunction but awarded the plaintiff £694 by way of damages in lieu, being the sum that the defendants might reasonably have paid for a right of way and release of the covenants. *Held*, the judge's approach had been correct and his judgment would not be disturbed. 'Clearly a defendant who wished to build would pay for the release of the covenants, but only so long as the court could still protect it by the grant of an injunction. The proviso is important. It is the ability to claim an injunction which gives the benefit of the covenant much of its value. If the plaintiff delays proceedings until it is no longer possible for him to obtain an injunction, he destroys his own bargaining position and devalues his right. The unavailability of the remedy of injunction at one and the same time deprives the court of jurisdiction to award damages under [Lord Cairns'] Act and removes the basis for awarding substantial damages at common law ... In the present case the plaintiff brought proceedings at a time when her rights were still capable of being protected by injunction. She has accordingly been able to invoke the court's jurisdiction to award in substitution for an injunction damages which take account of the future as well as the past. In my view, there is no reason why compensatory damages for future trespasses and continuing breaches of covenant should not reflect the value of the rights which she has lost, or why such damages should not be measured by the amount which she could reasonably have expected to receive for their release' (*per* MILLETT LJ). (Applied: *Wrotham Park Estate Co Ltd* v *Parkside Homes Ltd*.)

Jarvis v Swans Tours Ltd   **[315]**
[1973] 1 All ER 71 (Court of Appeal)

The defendants' winter sports holidays brochure represented various facilities available at a ski-resort. On faith of these representations, the plaintiff booked a holiday. The advertised facilities were not available and the plaintiff was very disappointed. The plaintiff claimed damages for breach of contract to provide the holiday promised. *Held,* the plaintiff was entitled to compensation for loss of entertainment and enjoyment. Damages for mental distress can be recovered in an action for breach of contract in a proper case. This was such a case, since the parties contemplated that on breach there might be mental inconveniences, eg frustration, annoyance and disappointment. (See also *Heywood* v *Wellers* and *Jackson* v *Horizon Holidays Ltd*.)

Jennings v Broughton (1854) 5 De GM & G 126   **[316]**

The directors of a mining company sought and obtained expert advice as to the value of a certain mine and issued a prospectus and advertised 'in glowing and exaggerated colours' to invite applications for shares. The plaintiff purchased some shares but only after he had examined the mine itself and the reports of the experts upon which the prospectus and advertisements were founded. *Held,* the plaintiff's claim for rescission on the ground of misrepresentation in the prospectus and advertisements must fail as in making his application for shares he had not relied upon them but on his own observations and reading of the reports. (See also *Northumberland and Durham District Banking Co, Re.*)

Jennings v Rundall (1799) 8 Term Rep 335 [317]

The defendant, a minor, hired a mare from the plaintiff on the understanding that the animal was to be ridden with moderation. The defendant 'wrongfully and injuriously rode, used, and worked the said mare in so immoderate, excessive and improper a manner ... that ... the said mare became, and was greatly strained, damaged, etc' and the plaintiff claimed damages in tort. *Held,* the plaintiff could not succeed in tort as his action was founded on the contract of hire. (See also *Leslie (R) Ltd v Sheill*; but see *Burnard v Haggis.*)

Jobson v Johnson [1989] 1 All ER 621 (Court of Appeal) [318]

The defendant agreed to purchase the shares in Southend United Football Club Ltd for £351,688 and to make a first payment of £40,000 followed by six payments of £51,948. If he defaulted on any payment, the shares were to be transferred back for £40,000. After paying £140,000, the defendant defaulted: the plaintiff, the vendors' assignee, sought specific performance of the agreement for the retransfer of the shares. *Held,* the retransfer clause was a penalty and it would not be enforced beyond the amount of the plaintiff's actual loss. (See also *Bridge v Campbell Discount Co Ltd.*)

Jones v Padavatton [1969] 2 All ER 616 (Court of Appeal) [319]

The plaintiff, who lived in Trinidad, made an offer to the defendant (her daughter) to maintain her if she began to study for the Bar. The agreement was an informal one, and there was uncertainty as to its exact terms. The daughter came to London and began to read for the Bar, her fees and maintenance being paid by the plaintiff. Two years later the plaintiff offered to buy a large house in London, to be occupied partly by the defendant and partly by tenants, the rental income to go to the daughter in lieu of the maintenance previously paid to her. The house was bought in the mother's name. Three years later the plaintiff claimed possession of the house, and the daughter counterclaimed some £2,000, said to have been paid in respect of it. The daughter had not completed her studies at the time of the hearing. *Held,* the mother was entitled to possession, and the daughter had no legal interest in the property. The agreement was a family arrangement, not intended to be legally enforceable; and in any event it was too vague and uncertain to be enforceable as a contract. (See also *Balfour v Balfour*; but see *McGregor v McGregor.*)

Jones v Vernon's Pools Ltd [1938] 2 All ER 626 [320]

The plaintiff alleged that he had completed and posted a coupon by way of entry for the defendants' football pool but the defendants said that they had never received it. One of the conditions governing the competition provided that all arrangements relating to the pool and to the coupons and to 'any agreement or transaction entered into or payment made by or under it shall not be attended by or give rise to any legal relationships, rights, duties or consequences whatsoever or be legally enforceable ... but all such arrangements, agreements and transactions are binding in honour only'. *Held,* the plaintiff could not enforce payment as the parties had denied, by the conditions, that it was their intention to create legal relations.

Joscelyne v Nissen [1970] 1 All ER 1213 (Court of Appeal)   **[321]**

The plaintiff sought rectification of a written contract whereby he made over his car-hire business to the defendant, his daughter. It had been expressly agreed that, in return, she should pay certain coal, gas and electricity bills. This agreement was not incorporated into the written contract. The defendant failed to pay the bills and the plaintiff sought a declaration that she should so pay them and, alternatively, that the agreement should be rectified to that effect. *Held,* the agreement should be rectified. The rectification was based on antecedent expressed accord on a point adhered to in intention by the daughter and father as parties to the subsequent written contract and since both parties were in agreement up to the moment when they executed the written contract that the daughter should pay the bills, and the written contract did not conform to that agreement, the court had jurisdiction to rectify the written contract, although there may have been no concluded and binding contract between the parties until the written contract was executed.

Kaufman v Gerson [1904] 1 KB 591 (Court of Appeal)   **[322]**

The defendant, a married woman, was induced by the plaintiff to sign an agreement which provided that, in consideration of the plaintiff forbearing to prosecute the defendant's husband, which would have meant ruin for him and disgrace to his wife and children, the defendant would repay within three years the amount of the plaintiff's money which her husband had appropriated to his own use. *Held,* this contract would not be enforced. (See also *Lemenda Trading Co Ltd* v *African Middle East Petroleum Co Ltd.*)

Kearley v Thomson (1890) 24 QBD 742 (Court of Appeal)   **[323]**

A firm of solicitors acted for the petitioning creditor in certain bankruptcy proceedings and incurred costs which were to be paid out of the estate. One of the bankrupt's friends, the plaintiff, offered to pay the solicitors, the defendants, a certain sum of money in settlement of these costs if they would undertake not to appear at the public examination of the bankrupt or to oppose his discharge. The defendants agreed to this and were paid the agreed amount and observed the conditions imposed by the plaintiff in so far as they did not appear at the public examination, but before an application was made for the discharge of the bankrupt the plaintiff sued to recover the money he had paid. *Held,* the plaintiff's claim must fail. There had been a partial carrying into effect of an illegal purpose in a substantial manner and this prevented the plaintiff from recovering the money which he had paid under the illegal agreement. (See also *Cooper* v *Willis.*)

Keen v Holland [1984] 1 All ER 75 (Court of Appeal)   **[324]**

Although the defendant knew that the plaintiff landowners had not been willing to grant him a tenancy which would be protected by the Agricultural Holdings Act 1948 and both parties believed that the tenancies granted did not attract such protection, the defendant relied on that Act when the plaintiffs sued for possession. *Held,* he was entitled to do so as the provisions of the Act could not be overridden by estoppel (even if the conditions for an estoppel existed) and it was not unconscionable for the defendant to rely on the Act's protection. (See also *Peyman* v *Lanjani.*)

Keir v Leeman (1846) 9 QB 371   **[325]**

The plaintiff prosecuted several persons for riot and assault upon a constable who was engaged in levying execution upon the property of another on the plaintiff's behalf. The plaintiff said that he would not proceed with the indictment if the defendants would promise to pay the amount of the debt in respect of which the writ of execution had been issued together with the costs of the prosecution. The defendants accepted this offer and by leave of the court no evidence was given against them and they were therefore acquitted. The defendants did not honour their promise and the plaintiff sued to enforce it. *Held,* judgment would be entered for the defendants as the contract to withdraw the prosecution was void as it was founded upon an illegal consideration. The fact that the judge had consented to the arrangement did not render the compromise lawful. (See also *Clubb* v *Hutson*.)

Kelly v Solari (1841) 9 M & W 54 [326]

An insurance company, the plaintiffs, effected a policy on the life of the defendant's late husband. The policy was allowed to lapse, but the plaintiffs forgot this fact, and when the defendant's husband died the defendant applied for and received a large payment. *Held,* the plaintiffs were entitled to recover the amount which they paid. (See also *Norwich Union Fire Insurance Society Ltd* v *Wm H Price Ltd* and *Rover International Ltd* v *Cannon Film Sales Ltd (No 3)*.)

Kenyon, Son and Craven Ltd v Baxter Hoare & Co Ltd [327]
[1971] 2 All ER 708

The plaintiffs stored 250 tons of groundnuts in the defendants' warehouse, and when received there the nuts were apparently in good condition. The warehouse was structurally sound and suitable for storing nuts, but it was not rat-proof. The contract provided that the defendants should 'not be liable for loss of or damage to goods unless (it) occurs whilst the goods are in the actual custody of the company and under its actual control and unless such loss or damage is due to the wilful neglect or default of the company or its servants', and a further clause limited any liability to a specified amount. Rats badly damaged the groundnuts, and when sued the defendants pleaded the exemption clause. *Held,* the plaintiffs' claim must fail and the exemption clause was effective on its true construction. (See also *Photo Production Ltd* v *Securicor Transport Ltd*.)

Kerr v Morris [1986] 3 All ER 217 (Court of Appeal) [328]

A partnership agreement between doctors within the national health service provided that, if one of them was expelled from the partnership, he would not for two years practise within a radius of two miles. The defendant was so expelled and he proposed to set up in practice a few doors away. *Held,* an interlocutory injunction would be granted as the restrictive covenant was not contrary to public policy or the public interest. The remaining partners were entitled to protect the practice's goodwill by a reasonable restraint of trade even though, by statute, it was unsaleable. (See also *Michael (John) Design plc* v *Cooke*.)

King's Norton Metal Co Ltd v Edridge, Merrett & Co Ltd [329]
(1897) 14 TLR 98 (Court of Appeal)

Both parties were metal manufacturers and the plaintiffs had received a letter ordering certain goods which purported to come from Hallam & Co, Soho Hackle Pin and Wire Works, Sheffield. At the head of the paper on which the letter was written there was a representation of a large factory with a number of chimneys and a statement that the firm had depots and agencies in Belfast, Lille and Ghent. The plaintiffs supplied the goods but it afterwards appeared that they had been ordered by a man called Wallis who in turn had sold them to the defendants. The firm Hallam & Co did not exist but the plaintiffs had received payment in respect of previous orders made in the name of that firm. On the occasion in question Wallis did not pay for the goods and the plaintiffs brought an action for damages for conversion. *Held,* their action must fail as they were found to have contracted with the writer of the letter. The property in the goods had therefore passed to Wallis who was able to give the defendants a good title to the goods when they purchased them. (See also *Phillips* v *Brooks Ltd.*)

Kingsnorth Trust Ltd v Bell [1986] 1 All ER 423   [330]
(Court of Appeal)

A husband wished to expand by buying another business and he arranged to borrow £18,000 from the plaintiffs, security for the loan to include a second charge on the matrimonial home in which his wife had a beneficial interest. Unknown to the plaintiffs, it was arranged that the husband would obtain his wife's signature to the mortgage deed and the wife duly signed, induced by the husband's fraudulent misrepresentation that the loan was for the benefit of his existing business. The wife did not receive any independent advice. Following the husband's default, the plaintiffs obtained an order for possession. *Held,* the order would be set aside. The husband had been the plaintiffs' agent in obtaining the wife's execution of the deed and they were bound by his fraudulent misrepresentation made to her. (Distinguished in *Coldunell Ltd* v *Gallon.*)

Kiriri Cotton Co Ltd v Dewani [1960] 1 All ER 117   [331]
(Privy Council)

In order to obtain a sub-lease of a flat in Kampala, a tenant paid a premium to the landlord. The Uganda Rent Restriction Ordinance stipulated that any person who, in consideration of the sub-letting of a dwelling-house, asked for a premium was guilty of an offence, but neither the landlord nor the tenant thought that the payment of a premium was an illegal act. *Held,* as the duty of observing the law rested on the landlord, the parties were *not* in pari delicto and the tenant was entitled at common law to recover the premium.

Kleinwort Benson Ltd v Malaysia Mining Corp Bhd   [332]
[1989] 1 All ER 785 (Court of Appeal)

The plaintiff bank agreed with the defendants to make a loan facility of up to £10m available to the defendants' wholly-owned subsidiary. As part of this agreement, the defendants gave the plaintiffs two 'letters of comfort' stating that it was their policy to ensure that their (the defendants') subsidiary was at all times in a position to meet its liabilities under the agreement. The subsidiary went into liquidation and the plaintiffs sought payment of the amount owing from the defendants. *Held,* the plaintiffs would not succeed as there was nothing in the evidence to show that the parties intended the letters to be a contractual promise. (But see *Rose & Frank Co* v *J R Crompton & Bros Ltd* and *Edwards* v *Skyways Ltd.*)

Kores Manufacturing Co Ltd v Kolok Manufacturing   [333]
Co Ltd [1958] 2 All ER 65 (Court of Appeal)

The parties occupied adjoining premises and engaged in the manufacture of carbon papers, typewriter ribbons and similar products. They agreed that they would not without the written consent of the other 'at any time employ any person who during the then past five years shall have been a servant' of that other. The defendants proposed to employ a chemist in breach of this agreement and the plaintiffs sought an injunction to prevent such employment. *Held,* the injunction would not be granted as the agreement between the parties was void and unenforceable because the reciprocal restraints which it contained, which did not distinguish between employees possessing trade secrets and confidential information and those who did not and were not limited to the period for which the parties' factories were in close proximity to each other, were excessive and unreasonable in the interests of parties to it. (But see *English Hop Growers Ltd* v *Dering.*)

Koufos v C Czarnikow Ltd, The Heron II [1967]   [334]
3 All ER 686 (House of Lords)

A vessel was chartered for a voyage from Constanza to Basrah for the carriage of sugar. She deviated to Berbera to load livestock for the shipowners. If she had not deviated she would have arrived at Basrah 10 days earlier than she did in fact. The charterers claimed damages for the difference between the market value of the sugar at the due date of delivery and at the actual date of delivery. *Held,* their claim should succeed. Although the shipowners did not know what the charterers intended to do with the sugar, they knew that there was a market for sugar in Basrah. They must have realised that at least it was not unlikely that the sugar would be sold there on arrival, and that in any ordinary market, prices were apt to fluctuate daily. It was an even chance that the fluctuation would be downwards. The loss was of a kind which the shipowners, when they made the contract, ought to have realised was liable to result from a breach causing delay in delivery. (NB The Law Lords emphasised that the measure of damages in contract and the measure of damages in tort are not the same. In contract there is opportunity for the injured party to protect himself against risk by directing the other party's attention to it before the contract is made; in tort there is no such opportunity, and a tortfeasor cannot reasonably complain if he has to pay for unusual but foreseeable damage resulting from his wrongdoing.) (See also *Hadley* v *Baxendale* and *Victoria Laundry (Windsor) Ltd* v *Newman Industries Ltd.*)

Krell v Henry [1903] 3 KB 740 (Court of Appeal)   [335]

The processions in connection with the coronation of Edward VII were due to be held on 26 and 27 June 1902, and shortly before this the defendant agreed to hire from the plaintiff a flat in Pall Mall along which the processions were to pass. The contract made no mention of the purpose of the letting but when the processions were not held on the days originally appointed the defendant refused to pay the balance of the rent. *Held,* the plaintiff's claim to recover such amount would fail as, by a necessary inference drawn from the surrounding circumstances, the holding of the procession on the days planned was regarded by both parties as the foundation of the contract. (But see *Herne Bay Steam Boat Co* v *Hutton.*)

Lakeman v J P Mountstephen (1874) LR 7 HL 17   [336]
(House of Lords)

The appellant was chairman of a local board of health and the respondent was a builder and contractor who had often executed works for the board. A question arose in relation to the construction of certain drains and when the respondent was asked why he was not making the necessary connections he intimated that he would carry out the work if the board or the appellant would order the work and become responsible for the payment of his charges. The appellant replied 'Go on, Mountstephen, and do the work, and I will see you paid'. The respondent did the work but the board refused to pay and the respondent sued upon the appellant's promise 'I will see you paid'. The appellant contended that his promise could not be enforced as it did not satisfy the requirements of s4 of the Statute of Frauds as to writing. *Held,* the respondent would succeed as the appellant's promise did not constitute a promise to pay the debt of another as the local board were not indebted to the respondent; for this reason the appellant's promise would be enforced as the statutory requirement as to writing did not apply. (See also *Guild & Co* v *Conrad.*)

Lamare v Dixon (1873) LR 6 HL 414 (House of Lords)   [337]

Lamare, a wine merchant, signed an agreement for a lease in respect of some wine cellars owned by Dixon. Before Lamare took possession of the premises Dixon orally promised that they would be made dry. In fact they remained damp and, after occupying the cellars for two years and regularly paying the rent, Lamare refused to execute a lease and withdrew from the premises. Dixon sought an order for the specific performance of the agreement for a lease. *Held,* such an order would not be granted as Lamare's conduct did not prevent him from relying upon the non-performance of Dixon's oral promise, which had been an inducement to him to enter into the agreement, as a good defence to such a claim. (See also *Whittington* v *Seale-Hayne.*)

Lampleigh v Braithwait (1615) 80 ER 255   [338]

The defendant had feloniously slain another and, at his request, the plaintiff did all that he could to obtain the King's pardon for the defendant. This involved 'many days labour' and much 'riding and journeying at his own charges' and in consideration of this the defendant afterwards promised to pay the plaintiff £100. *Held,* there was a binding contract to make this payment as the promise to pay £100 'couples itself' with the request to obtain the King's pardon and the plaintiff's efforts on the defendant's behalf were executed in consideration for the defendant's promise. (See s15 of the Supply of Goods and Services Act 1982; see also *Re Casey's Patents* and *Pao On* v *Lau Yiu Long.*)

Lamson Pneumatic Tube Co v Phillips   [339]
(1904) 91 LT 363 (Court of Appeal)

The plaintiffs manufactured and sold pneumatic tube systems for use in shops and stores for the transmission of cash and documents from one part of the building to another. The defendant was employed as the plaintiffs' general agent and his contract of employment provided that he would not within five years of the cessation of his employment engage, in the Eastern Hemisphere, in any business similar to that of the plaintiffs. *Held,* this provision was valid and binding as it did not exceed what was reasonably necessary for the protection of the plaintiffs in their business, having regard to the nature of the business and the position held by the defendant. (But see *Leng (Sir W C) & Co Ltd* v *Andrews.*)

Lancashire Loans Ltd v Black [1934] 1 KB 380   [340]
(Court of Appeal)

A daughter married at 18 and after the marriage went to live with her husband. Some time after the daughter came of age her mother, who was very extravagant and a frequent borrower from moneylenders, requested her daughter to raise certain money to pay off her debts, sign promissory notes and give a second charge on a vested interest in remainder without which the moneylenders refused to make any further loans. The only advice which the daughter received was from a solicitor who acted for the mother and the moneylenders. The moneylenders sued to enforce a promissory note given by the daughter. *Held, so* far as the daughter was concerned, the transaction must be set aside. She had given the note under her mother's influence and as the moneylenders had notice of the fact that the mother had exercised undue influence they were in no stronger position than she was.

Lansing Linde Ltd v Kerr [1991] 1 All ER 418   [341]
(Court of Appeal)

The plaintiffs were the English subsidiary of an international fork-lift trucks company and the contract of employment of the defendant, the director of the plaintiffs' northern division, included a covenant against competition for 12 months after leaving their employment, effectively on a worldwide basis. The defendant resigned and a month or so later he was appointed managing director of one of the plaintiffs' competitors. The plaintiffs sought, inter alia, an interlocutory injunction but, because it seemed that the trial of the action could not take place for nearly a year and that the worldwide covenant would probably not be upheld, the judge refused to grant it. *Held*, the judge had been right to adopt this course as, in these circumstances, some assessment of the merits, more than merely whether there was a serious issue of be tried, was required. The likely effect of the granting of the injunction would have been finally to decide the dispute against the defendant. (But see *David (Lawrence) Ltd v Ashton.*)

Laurence v Lexcourt Holdings Ltd See Sindall (William) plc v Cambridgeshire County Council

Lavery v Pursell (1888) 39 Ch D 508   [342]

There was a contract for the sale of 'the building materials' of a house which was to be demolished. *Held,* such a contract was for the sale of an interest in land within s4 of the Statute of Frauds (which became s40 of the Law of Property Act 1925; see now s2 of the Law of Property (Miscellaneous Provisions) Act 1989) and in this case the contract could not be enforced as there was not a sufficient memorandum or note. (See also *Webber* v *Lee.*)

Law v Dearnley [1950] 1 All ER 124 (Court of Appeal)   [343]

The plaintiff sought to recover the sum alleged to have been paid by him to a bookmaker in respect of bets which he had made on behalf of the defendant as his agent. Although s1 of the Gaming Act 1892 would normally defeat the plaintiff's claim, it was argued that the plaintiff could recover on an account stated as the defendant had orally admitted that he was indebted to the plaintiff and agreed the amount of the debt. *Held,* the claim would not succeed. An action to recover the amount of the bets was not maintainable under s1, and the provision could not be circumvented by basing a claim on an account stated.

Laws v London Chronicle (Indicator Newspapers) Ltd   [344]
[1959] 2 All ER 285 (Court of Appeal)

An advertisement representative disobeyed an order by the managing director of the company by which she was employed and she was dismissed summarily for misconduct. *Held,* she was entitled to damages for wrongful dismissal as her single act of disobedience did not show that she was repudiating the contract of service or one of its essential conditions. (But see *Ellen* v *Topp.*)

Lazenby Garages Ltd v Wright   [345]
[1976] 2 All ER 770 (Court of Appeal)

The plaintiffs were second-hand car dealers from whom the defendant agreed to purchase a second-hand car for £1,670, to be delivered several weeks later. The defendant repudiated the contract. The plaintiffs resold the car for £1,770. They sued the defendant for breach of contract claiming £345, this sum being calculated as representing the difference between the amount the plaintiffs paid for the vehicle and what the defendant had agreed to pay. *Held*, second-hand cars were in their nature unique and there was no basis for any proper inference as to what the effect on the plaintiffs' trade would have been if the car had in fact been sold and delivered to the defendant. There was no 'available market' for second-hand cars and the appropriate test was what could reasonably be expected to have been in the contemplation of the parties as a natural consequence of the breach. The defendant could not possibly have contemplated that, as a result of his breach, the plaintiffs would sell one car less. As the plaintiffs had sold the car for more than the price agreed with the defendant they had suffered no loss and were not entitled to damages. (See also *Hadley* v *Baxendale*.)

Leaf v International Galleries [1950] 1 All ER 693   [346]
(Court of Appeal)

The plaintiff bought an oil painting of Salisbury Cathedral and accepted it as a genuine Constable on the representation of the sellers, the defendants. Five years after the sale the plaintiff discovered that the painting was not by Constable and he claimed rescission on the ground of innocent misrepresentation. *Held*, his claim must fail as the action had not been commenced within a reasonable time and, further, the mistake in question was not one which would entitle the plaintiff to avoid the contract. (See also *Harrison & Jones Ltd* v *Bunten & Lancaster Ltd*; but see *Peco Arts Inc* v *Hazlitt Gallery Ltd* and *Naughton* v *O'Callaghan*.)

Learoyd v Bracken [1894] 1 QB 114 (Court of Appeal)   [347]

A broker made certain dealings on the Stock Exchange for his principal and an attempt was made to recover the commission in respect of these transactions. The contract notes which the broker had sent to his principal had not been stamped in accordance with the statutory requirements and this omission on the part of the broker rendered him liable to certain penalties. *Held*, the fact that the contract notes had not been stamped did not affect the validity of the contract between the broker and his principal, who was therefore liable to pay the broker's commission. (But see *Anderson Ltd* v *Daniel*.)

Lee (John) & Son (Grantham) Ltd v Railway Executive   [348]
[1949] 2 All ER 581 (Court of Appeal)

A railway warehouse was let to the plaintiffs by the defendants and the plaintiffs sued to recover damages in respect of damage caused to their goods by a fire which resulted from the negligence of the defendants. The tenancy agreement provided that 'The tenant shall be responsible for and shall release and indemnify the [defendants] and their servants and agents from and against all liability for personal injury (whether fatal or otherwise), loss of or damage to property and any other loss, damage, costs and expenses however caused or incurred (whether by the act or neglect of the [defendants] or their servants or agents or not) *which but for the tenancy hereby created* or anything done pursuant to the provisions hereof *would not have arisen*'. *Held*, the plaintiffs could recover as the effect of the words which are here printed in italics was to confine the protection which the clause afforded to liability arising out of the relationship of landlord and tenant.

Lemenda Trading Co Ltd v African Middle East [349]
Petroleum Co Ltd [1988] 1 All ER 513

The defendants contracted with the Qatar national oil company for the supply of crude oil, at the same time signing a 'side letter' confirming that the contract had been negotiated without the involvement of agents or brokers on a commission basis. Under the law of Qatar, a commission contract for the supply of oil by the national oil company was void and unenforceable on grounds of Qatar public policy. The defendants later entered into an agreement with the plaintiffs whereby the plaintiffs, in return for a commission on any oil shipped, agreed to assist the defendants in procuring the renewal of the supply contract by exerting influence on the chairman or managing director of the national oil company. The supply contract was renewed and the plaintiffs sued for their commission. *Held*, their claim could not succeed as such an agreement for the use of personal influence was contrary to public policy in both England and Qatar and would not be enforced in England. (See also *Kaufman* v *Gerson* and *Parkinson* v *College of Ambulance Ltd.*)

Leng (Sir W C) & Co Ltd v Andrews [1909] 1 Ch 763 [350]
(Court of Appeal)

The plaintiffs sought an injunction to restrain the defendant from being connected with any newspaper business carried on in Sheffield or within a radius of 20 miles of the Town Hall. The defendant was employed by the plaintiffs as a junior reporter on their paper the *Sheffield Daily Telegraph*. A term of his contract of employment provided that he would not, after leaving the plaintiffs' service, 'be connected, as proprietor, employee, or otherwise, with any newspaper business carried on' in Sheffield or within a radius of 20 miles. The defendant entered the service of the Sheffield Independent Press Ltd, who were newspaper proprietors, as a reporter. *Held*, the plaintiffs would not succeed as the restriction was wider than was reasonably necessary for the protection of their interests and therefore could not be enforced. (See also *Mason* v *Provident Clothing and Supply Co Ltd.*)

Leslie (R) Ltd v Sheill [1914] 3 KB 607 (Court of Appeal) [351]

The plaintiffs were money-lenders and they sued the defendant, a minor, to whom they had advanced £400, to recover the amount of the loan plus £75 interest. The jury found that the plaintiffs had been induced to make the loan by the fraudulent misrepresentation of the defendant that he was of full age. *Held*, the plaintiffs could not recover in tort for deceit as the action was based on the contract of loan. (See also *Fawcett* v *Smethurst.*)

L'Estrange v F Graucob Ltd [1934] 2 KB 394 (Court of Appeal) [352]

The plaintiff ordered an automatic slot machine by signing a printed form supplied by the defendants for this purpose and on this form in very small print were certain special terms. One of these terms provided that 'any express or implied condition, statement or warranty … is hereby excluded'. The machine did not work satisfactorily and the plaintiff, who contended that she was not bound by the condition as she had not read it and knew nothing of its contents, claimed damages. *Held*, her action must fail as, having signed the contract, in the absence of misrepresentation, she was bound by its terms and the provision in the contract had successfully excluded the defendant's liability under the implied warranty that the machine was fit for the purpose for which it was sold. (But see *Curtis* v *Chemical Cleaning and Dyeing Co Ltd.*)

Levison v Patent Steam Carpet Cleaning Co Ltd   [353]
[1977] 3 All ER 498 (Court of Appeal)

When cleaners collected a carpet for cleaning from the plaintiff's house, the plaintiff signed a printed form which provided that goods were accepted at owner's risk and limited the maximum value of the carpet to £40 for the purposes of any claim. In fact, the carpet was worth £400. The carpet was never returned to the defendants. *Held,* there was inequality of bargaining power between the parties. Where this was so, in relation to a standard form contract, the party with superior bargaining power could not rely on an exclusion clause contained in the contract if it had been guilty of a breach going to the root of the contract. The contract in this case was one for bailment and the onus of proof was on the bailee (the defendants) to show what happened to the goods while they were in his possession. As the defendants could not explain what had happened to the carpet, they could not rely on the exclusion clause. Accordingly, the defendants were liable for the full value of the carpet. (See also *Alderslade* v *Hendon Laundry Ltd.*)

Lewis v Averay [1971] 3 All ER 907 (Court of Appeal)   [354]

The plaintiff advertised a car for sale. A man telephoned for an appointment to view the car, but did not give his name. He came along and tested the car and the plaintiff took him to a flat to discuss the details. At the flat the potential buyer stated that he was 'Richard Green', the well-known actor, and he agreed to buy the car at £450. He tendered a cheque in payment, signed 'R. A. Green' and on producing evidence of his identity he was allowed to take the car away. The cheque proved worthless. The buyer was a rogue, not Richard Green, and later sold the car to the defendant, who bought it in good faith. The plaintiff sued the defendant in conversion. *Held,* where a transaction takes place between people face to face there is a presumption that the offer by one person is made to the other and not to any person that other says he is, and there was nothing on the facts of the case to rebut this presumption. Thus, the plaintiff's offer was made to the rogue and not to 'Richard Green'. The rogue accordingly got a voidable title to the car, under which he sold the car to the defendant before the contract between the plaintiff and the rogue had been avoided. The plaintiff's claim therefore failed. (See also *Phillips* v *Brooks Ltd.*)

Lewis v Clay (1897) 67 LJQB 224   [355]

A document had been covered with blotting paper in which four holes had been cut and the defendant was asked to sign his name in these holes for the purpose, he was told, of witnessing a deed concerning a private matter. In fact the defendant signed certain promissory notes. *Held,* the notes would be cancelled so far as the defendant was concerned. He had been induced to sign them by a fraudulent representation which led him to believe that he was witnessing a deed. The defendant had no knowledge of the promissory notes and he had not been negligent and for these reasons he would not be bound by his signature in any way. (But see *Howatson* v *Webb*; see also *Saunders* v *Anglia Building Society.*)

Linden Gardens Trust Ltd v Lenesta Sludge Disposals Ltd   [356]
[1994] 1 AC 85 (House of Lords)

Arising out of building contracts in standard form, the questions were, first, as to the effect of a contractual provision which prohibits a party from assigning the benefit of the contract and, second, whether a building owner can recover substantial damages for breach of a building contract if he has parted with the property. *Held*, such a prohibition on assignment is not void on grounds of public policy or for any other reason and any purported assignment, without the consent of the other party to the original contract, is therefore invalid and ineffective. However, where, on the facts, the parties are to be treated as having entered into the contract on the footing that the building owner is entitled to enforce the contract for the benefit of those who suffer from defective performance, the building owner is entitled to substantial damages. 'The present case falls within the rationale of the exceptions to the general rule that a plaintiff can only recover damages for his own loss. The contract was for a large development of property which, to the knowledge of both [parties to the building contract], was gong to be occupied, and possibly purchased, by third parties ... Therefore it could be foreseen that damage caused by a breach would cause loss to a later owner and not merely to the original contracting party ... As in contracts for the carriage of goods by land, there would be no automatic vesting in the occupier or owners of the property for the time being who sustained the loss of any right of suit against [the contractor]. On the contrary, [the contractor] had specifically contracted that the rights of action under the building contract could *not* without [its] consent be transferred to third parties who became owners or occupiers and might suffer loss. In such a case, it seems to me proper, as in the case of the carriage of goods by land, to treat the parties as having entered into the contract on the footing that [the building owner] would be entitled to enforce contractual rights for the benefit of those who suffered from defective performance but who, under the terms of the contract, could not acquire any right to hold [the contractor] liable for breach' (*per* LORD BROWNE-WILKINSON). (Applied: *The Albazero*.)

Liverpool City Council v Irwin   [357]
[1976] 2 All ER 39 (House of Lords)

The conditions in a block of high-rise flats were such that there was no lighting on the stairs, the lifts were continually in disrepair, the rubbish chutes were blocked and the cisterns overflowed. This situation was due partly to vandalism, partly to non-cooperation by the tenants and partly to neglect by the landlords, the council. When the tenants refused to pay rent, the council claimed possession. The tenants counter-claimed for damages alleging that the council were in breach of their implied obligation to keep the common parts in repair. *Held,* the contract under which the tenants took possession contained no covenant by the landlord; as the contract did not state fully all the terms the court would complete it by taking into account the actions of the parties and the circumstances. The contract implied a grant of exclusive possession with implied easements for the tenants to use the stairs, lifts and rubbish chutes. As these were essentials without which the tenants could not live, using the test of necessity, the landlords were under an obligation to maintain the common parts in good repair and accordingly such an obligation was to be implied. This also placed a responsibility on the tenants to behave reasonably. Consequently, in the circumstances, there was no breach of the landlord's obligation. (Applied in *Wettern Electric Ltd* v *Welsh Development Agency*; see also *Scally* v *Southern Health and Social Services Board* and *Spring* v *Guardian Assurance plc*.)

Lloyd v Johnson (1798) 1 Bos & P 340 [358]

The plaintiff's wife washed clothes for the defendant, a prostitute, and sought to recover her charges for this work. There was evidence that to the knowledge of the plaintiff and his wife the clothes in question were used for the purposes of the defendant's trade. The defendant maintained that the contract was void on the ground of immorality. *Held,* the plaintiff would succeed as the court would not take into consideration the immoral purpose for which the clothes were worn. (But see *Pearce* v *Brooks.*)

Lloyds Bank Ltd v Bundy [1974] 3 All ER 757 [359]
(Court of Appeal)

The defendant was an elderly farmer who was not well-versed in business affairs. Both he and his son were customers of the same bank. His son's company was in financial difficulties, and the defendant guaranteed the company's overdraft, by way of a charge on his house, which was his only asset. At a subsequent meeting, the bank required the defendant to give a charge for the full value of his house as a condition of continued financial support for the company. The bank failed to advise the defendant to obtain independent advice on the company's affairs. The defendant signed the necessary documents produced by the bank manager. Subsequently, the bank enforced the charge and guarantee against the defendant. *Held,* the guarantee and charge would be set aside. The relationship between the bank and the defendant was one of trust and confidence. The confidential relationship imposed a duty of fiduciary care on the bank to advise the defendant to obtain independent advice. There was a breach of that duty and a presumption of undue influence, and the transaction was set aside on that ground. (Applied in *Avon Finance Co Ltd* v *Bridger* and *O'Sullivan* v *Management Agency and Music Ltd*; distinguished in *Alec Lobb (Garages) Ltd* v *Total Oil GB Ltd*; see also *Allcard* v *Skinner*; but see *National Westminster Bank plc* v *Morgan.*)

Lobb (Alec) (Garages) Ltd v Total Oil GB Ltd See Alec Lobb (Garages) Ltd v Total Oil GB Ltd

Locker and Woolf Ltd v Western Australian Insurance [360]
Co Ltd [1936] 1 KB 408 (Court of Appeal)

When proposing for fire insurance in respect of their premises the claimants failed to disclose that an insurance on their motor cars had been declined by another company on the grounds of misrepresentation and non-disclosure. *Held,* the non-disclosure of this previous refusal was a material fact in the proposal for fire insurance which entitled the respondents to avoid the policy. In all classes of insurance what constitutes a 'material fact' is decided by reference to s18 of the Marine Insurance Act 1906. (See also *Hood* v *West End Motor Car Packing Co.*)

Lombard North Central plc v Butterworth [361]
[1987] 1 All ER 267 (Court of Appeal)

The plaintiff finance company leased a computer to the defendant for a period of five years. Clause 2(a) of the hiring agreement made punctual payment of the quarterly instalments of the essence of the agreement; under cl 5 failure to make due and punctual payment entitled the plaintiffs to terminate the agreement; cl 6 provided that, on termination, the plaintiffs were entitled to all arrears and all future instalments. The defendant paid the first two instalments promptly; the next three were late and on four occasions payment made by direct debit was recalled by the bank. When the sixth instalment was six weeks overdue, the plaintiffs wrote to the defendant to terminate the agreement; subsequently they sold the computer for just £172.88. *Held,* cl 6 was unenforceable as, in the absence of a repudiatory breach, it created a penalty; the defendant's conduct in failing to make payments punctually had not amounted to a repudiation by him of the agreement. However, in the light of cl 2(a), prompt payment was a condition and, when read with cll 5 and 6, it had the effect of making default in punctual payment a breach of the agreement going to the root of the contract. Accordingly, the plaintiffs were entitled to terminate the contract, independently of cl 6, and to recover damages for the loss of the whole transaction. (But see *Financings Ltd* v *Baldock.*)

London and Northern Bank, Re [1900] 1 Ch 220　　　　　　　　**[362]**

J applied for shares in a bank. On 26 October he wrote to withdraw his application and on that afternoon the directors resolved to allot shares to J and the allotment notice was handed to a postman at 7am on the following day but was not actually posted, that is, received in a post office, until after the letter of withdrawal had been received by the bank. *Held,* the retraction was effective as the acceptance was not posted until after the receipt of the withdrawal. (But see *Adams* v *Lindsell.*)

London and Northern Estates Co v Schlesinger　　　　　　　**[363]**
[1916] 1 KB 20

The defendant, an Austrian, was lessee of a flat at Westcliffe-on-Sea. On the outbreak of war the defendant became an alien enemy and as such was prohibited from living in certain places, including Westcliffe-on-Sea. The defendant refused to pay his rent and his landlords, the plaintiffs, brought an action to recover it. *Held,* the plaintiffs were entitled to judgment as the defendant's residence in the flat was not the foundation of the contract between the parties. (See also *Matthey* v *Curling.*)

London Assurance v Mansel (1879) 11 Ch D 363　　　　　　　**[364]**

In answer to a question contained in a proposal to the plaintiffs for an assurance on his life the defendant did not disclose the fact that he had made application to several other offices and been declined. The plaintiffs accepted his proposal but the fact that he had been declined by other insurers was afterwards discovered. *Held,* the concealment of this fact was material and they were entitled to have the contract of insurance set aside. (See also *Locker & Woolf Ltd* v *Western Australian Insurance Co Ltd.*)

Long v Lloyd [1958] 2 All ER 402 (Court of Appeal)　　　　　**[365]**

The defendant advertised for sale a motor lorry which he described as being in 'exceptional condition' and told the plaintiff, who purchased it, that it was capable of 40mph and did 11 miles to the gallon. Two days later certain defects appeared and the plaintiff accepted the defendant's offer to pay half the cost of a reconditioned dynamo. On the following day the plaintiff's brother set out to drive the lorry to Middlesbrough but it broke down on the way and an expert found that it was not in a roadworthy condition. The defendant's representations concerning the vehicle were untrue, although honestly made, and the plaintiff sought to rescind the contract on the ground of the defendant's innocent misrepresentation. *Held,* the plaintiff had finally accepted the lorry and any right of rescission which he might otherwise have had was lost. (See also *Leaf* v *International Galleries.*)

Lord Strathcona Steamship Co Ltd v Dominion Coal [366]
Co Ltd [1926] AC 108 (Privy Council)

The respondents chartered the steamship *Lord Strathcona* for use for a number of years on the St Lawrence during the summer season. During the period of the charterparty the ship was sold to the appellants with notice of the charterparty but they refused to let the respondents use the ship in accordance with the terms of the charter. The respondents sought an injunction to restrain the appellants from using the ship in any way which was inconsistent with the charterparty. *Held,* the injunction would be granted as the appellants were in the position of constructive trustees. (See also *Sky Petroleum Ltd* v *VIP Petroleum Ltd*; but see *Port Line Ltd* v *Ben Line Steamers Ltd.*)

Lumley v Wagner (1852) 1 De GM & G 604 [367]

The defendant contracted to sing at the plaintiff's theatre for a certain period and promised that she would not sing elsewhere during that time without his written consent. *Held,* an injunction would be granted to restrain the defendant from singing for a third party in breach of this agreement. (See also *Warner Brothers Pictures Inc* v *Nelson*; but see *Whitwood Chemical Co* v *Hardman.*)

Lynch v Thorne [1956] 1 All ER 744 (Court of Appeal) [368]

The plaintiff agreed to purchase from the defendant, a builder, a plot of land with a building in the course of erection. The defendant agreed to and did complete the house in accordance with the specification annexed to the contract but, because the building was in an exposed position, damp penetrated into one of the bedrooms. The plaintiff claimed damages alleging that it was an implied term of the contract of sale that the house when completed should be reasonably fit for human habitation. *Held,* his action could not succeed as, in these circumstances, no such term would be implied. (Distinguished in *Basildon District Council* v *J E Lesser (Properties) Ltd*; but see *Gregory* v *Ford*; see also *Hancock* v *BW Brazier (Anerley) Ltd.*)

M and S Drapers v Reynolds [1956] 3 All ER 814 [369]
(Court of Appeal)

The defendant, a collector-salesman employed by the plaintiffs, a firm of credit drapers, promised that for a period of five years following the determination of his contract of service he would not sell or canvass or solicit orders by way of the business of a credit draper from any person whose name should have been inscribed on the books of his employers as a customer during the three years immediately preceding such determination upon whom he had called in the course of his duties for his employers. The defendant left the service of the plaintiffs and sold goods in breach of this provision of his contract of service. *Held,* in all the circumstances of the case, the restraint for as long as five years for a man in the defendant's position was an unreasonable restraint of trade and would not be enforced. (See also *Eastham* v *Newcastle United Football Club Ltd.*)

McArdle, Re [1951] 1 All ER 905 (Court of Appeal) [370]

The occupants carried out certain improvements and decorations in a house at a cost of £488 and after the work was completed those beneficially interested in the property executed a document by which they promised, in consideration of the execution of the work, to repay £488. *Held,* the consideration for the promise was past as the work had been completed when the promise was made and the claim to recover £488 must fail. (See also *Roscorla* v *Thomas*; but see *Nye* v *Moseley*.)

McCausland v Duncan Lawrie Ltd (1996) The Times 18 June   [371]
(Court of Appeal)

A written agreement for the sale of a certain property was signed by both parties: the completion date stated was 26 March 1995. By letter the plaintiffs' solicitors suggested that 'completion be re-arranged for … March 24': by letter the defendants' solicitors confirmed that completion could take place on that date. *Held*, the agreement could not be enforced since the contract as varied by the letters had not satisfied the requirements of s2 of the Law of Property (Miscellaneous Provisions) Act 1989. (See also *United Bank of Kuwait plc* v *Sahib*.)

McCutcheon v David MacBrayne Ltd   [372]
[1964] 1 All ER 430 (House of Lords)

The appellant asked his brother-in-law, Mr McSporran, to have his (the appellant's) car sent by the respondents to West Loch Tarbert. Mr McSporran took the car to Port Askaig where the respondents' purser quoted the freight which he (Mr McSporran) paid and for which he was given a receipt. The ship carrying the appellant's car sank owing to negligent navigation by the respondents' servants; the car was a total loss and the appellant sought to recover its value. The respondents' liability was excluded under the terms of their printed conditions if, as they maintained, those conditions had been incorporated in the contract of carriage. Reference was made to the conditions on the receipt given to Mr McSporran and the conditions were displayed on notices in the respondents' offices, but neither the appellant nor Mr McSporran had read these notices and Mr McSporran put the receipt in his pocket without looking at it. The purser omitted to ask Mr McSporran to sign a risk note, which included the conditions, although it had been prepared for his signature. Both Mr McSporran and the appellant had signed risk notes on some other occasions, but not always; they had never read them, but they knew that they contained conditions. *Held*, the appellant was entitled to succeed. The receipt given to Mr McSporran after he had paid the freight and the notices displayed in the offices did not form part of the oral contract (the receipt was given after the contract had been concluded and the appellant and Mr McSporran had not read the notices: the respondents had not done what was reasonably sufficient in bringing them to their attention) and there had been no consistent course of dealing by which the conditions could be imported as terms of the contract of carriage. 'The course of dealing on earlier occasions is often relevant in determining contractual relations, but does not assist when, as here, there was on the part of the respondents a departure from an earlier course in that they omitted to ask the appellant's agent to sign the document by which they would have obtained protection' (*per* LORD HODSON). (See also *Hollier* v *Rambler Motors (AMC) Ltd*; but see *Hillas & Co* v *Arcos Ltd*.)

Macdonald v Green [1950] 2 All ER 1240 (Court of Appeal)   [373]

The plaintiff was managing director of a bookmaking company to which the defendant was indebted in the sum of £4,020 in respect of betting transactions. The plaintiff agreed to lend the amount of the debt privately to the defendant who undertook to repay it to the plaintiff in weekly instalments. The plaintiff sued to recover the balance outstanding under this agreement. *Held*, the action must fail as there was a stipulation, to be inferred from the circumstances, that the loan of £4,020 was to be applied solely in payment of the defendant's betting debt to the company and the transaction therefore fell within s1 of the Gaming Act 1892, and was void. (See also *CHT Ltd* v *Ward.*)

McEllistrim v Ballymacelligott Co-operative Agricultural and Dairy Society Ltd [1919] AC (House of Lords) [374]

The respondents carried on the business of manufacturing for sale cheese and butter from milk supplied by members. The society bound itself to accept all the milk produced by members' cows kept on land within a defined area and the members agreed not to sell such milk to any other creamery unless the consent of the committee of the society had first been obtained. The rules also provided that members were not allowed to withdraw from the society unless their shares had been transferred or cancelled and the consent of the committee, which could be withheld without assigning any reason, was required before such transfer or cancellation could take effect. *Held,* such an agreement imposed upon members greater restrictions than were reasonably required for the protection of the society and was therefore illegal and void as in restraint of trade. (See also *Kores Manufacturing Co Ltd* v *Kolok Manufacturing Co Ltd.*)

McGregor v McGregor (1888) 21 QBD 424 [375]

A husband and wife took out cross-summonses against each other for assault but agreed to withdraw the summonses and live apart if the husband, on his part, would promise to pay the wife maintenance of £1 per week. *Held,* the wife's action for arrears of maintenance would succeed. The fact that the agreement was between husband and wife was not in itself sufficient to make it unenforceable and this was a case where the parties had intended to create legal relations. (See also *Carlill* v *Carbolic Smoke Ball Co*; but see *Jones* v *Padavatton.*)

M'Kinnell v Robinson (1838) 3 M & W 434 [376]

The defendant borrowed £30 from the plaintiff which, to the knowledge of the plaintiff, was to be used for the purpose of playing Hazard, an illegal game. *Held,* the plaintiff could not recover this sum as it was lent for the express purpose of a violation of the law and to enable the defendant to do a prohibited act. (See also *Tatam* v *Reeve.*)

McRae v Commonwealth Disposals Commission (1951) 84 CLR 377 (High Court of Australia) [377]

The defendants invited tenders 'for the purchase of an oil tanker lying on Journaund Reef'. The plaintiff's offer of £285 was accepted and at considerable expense he fitted out a salvage expedition. The tanker could not be found and it was established that no tanker had been in the locality of Journaund Reef at any material time. The plaintiff sought to recover, inter alia, damages for breach of contract. *Held,* he should succeed and recover the amount of the purchase price and the amount spent in reliance upon the promise that there was an oil tanker at the locality stated. 'The only proper construction of the contract is that it included a promise by the [defendants] that there was a tanker in the position specified. The [defendants] contracted that there was a tanker there ... If, on the other hand, the case of *Couturier* v *Hastie* and this case ought to be treated as cases raising a question of "mistake", then the [defendants] cannot in this case rely on any mistake as avoiding the contract, because any mistake was induced by the serious fault of their own servants, who asserted the existence of a tanker recklessly and without any reasonable ground. There *was* a contract, and the [defendants] contracted that a tanker existed in the position specified. Since there was no such tanker, there has been a breach of contract, and the [plaintiff is] entitled to damages for that breach' (*per* DIXON and FULLAGAR JJ). (But see *Couturier* v *Hastie*; see also s2(1) of the Misrepresentation Act 1967.)

Magee v Pennine Insurance Co Ltd   [378]
[1969] 2 All ER 891 (Court of Appeal)

In 1961, the plaintiff, who could not drive, bought a car for his son aged 18, who at that time had a provisional licence. The proposal form for the insurance policy was wrongly filled in by the manager of the garage where the car was bought, and stated, inter alia, that the plaintiff had a provisional licence. Four years later, the car was written off as a result of an accident which occurred while the son was driving. The plaintiff had claimed £600 but accepted the defendants' offer of £385 to settle, the agreement being repudiated by the defendants after making enquiries about the statements in the proposal. The county court judge found that the defendants were entitled to repudiate the policy because of the inaccuracy of the answers in the proposal but that there was a concluded agreement to settle at £385 and no fraud. The plaintiff was given judgment for £385. The defendants appealed. *Held,* by a majority, the settlement agreement should not in all the circumstances be held binding on the insurance company in equity. Both parties were under a mutual mistake with regard to the policy: they thought it was good and binding. The mistake was fundamental, and the parties did not think the policy was avoidable. (See also *Solle* v *Butcher* and *Bell* v *Lever Bros.*)

Malik v Bank of Credit and Commerce International SA   [379]
[1995] 3 All ER 545 (Court of Appeal)

Following the collapse of the respondent bank and the discovery that it had been involved in fraudulent activities, the appellants, who held senior posts at branch level, were made redundant by the bank's liquidators. The appellants were unable to obtain work in the financial services sector and they now sought 'stigma compensation' for breach of terms allegedly implied in their contracts of employment. *Held,* their claims, in reality for damages for injury to their previously existing reputations, could not succeed. '... damages are not recoverable in contract for damage to or loss of an existing reputation. This ... principle does not apply to cases where the damage is recoverable in accordance with other normal principles notwithstanding that it could be described as compensation for damage to an existing reputation. Such cases include those where the nature of the contract is one to provide for a status, for example apprenticeships, or the promotion or preservation of a reputation, for example advertising or the opportunity to appear in a prestigious place or part. Similarly, damage to goodwill, as legally recognised, is a recoverable head of loss as damage to property' (*per* MORRITT LJ). 'In my view, the reason why a theatrical artiste who is wrongly dismissed can receive damages for the loss of the opportunity to enhance his reputation, as in *Withers* v *General Theatre Corp Ltd* [1993] 2 KB 536, or an apprentice damages when wrongly dismissed for the loss of training and instruction, as in *Dunk* v *George Waller & Son Ltd* [1970] 2 QB 163, is that the theatre proprietor or the employer has, expressly or impliedly, promised to provide the artiste with that opportunity, the apprentice with the training. Those promises are part of the consideration for the contract ... Such a promise is not to be found, expressly or impliedly, in the majority of contracts of employment, and it was not suggested that such a term was incorporated in the contracts between the parties in this case' (*per* GLIDEWELL LJ). (See also *Addis* v *Gramophone Co Ltd.*)

Maritime National Fish Ltd v Ocean Trawlers Ltd   [380]
[1935] AC 524 (Privy Council)

The appellants chartered the St Cuthbert, a steam trawler, from the respondents to be used only for fishing. It was an offence to use an otter trawler without first obtaining a licence from the Canadian Minister of Fisheries and the St Cuthbert was fitted with this equipment and could not use any other. The appellants applied for five licences but were granted only three. They stipulated the three trawlers to which they were to apply and excluded the St Cuthbert. It was argued that the appellants' liability under the charterparty had been determined. *Held,* this argument would not succeed; the charterparty had not been frustrated, as the failure to obtain a licence for the St Cuthbert was due to the election of the appellants. (See also *Davis Contractors Ltd* v *Fareham Urban District Council* and *Ocean Tramp Tankers Corporation* v *V/O Sovfracht.*)

Marles v Philip Trant & Sons Ltd [1953] 1 All ER 651   [381]
(Court of Appeal)

The defendants were seed merchants and the plaintiff a farmer. The plaintiff ordered 29 cwt of dressed spring wheat seed which the defendants had described as Fylgia. The greater part of the seed delivered was not Fylgia nor was it suitable for spring sowing. It was Vilmorin, a winter wheat, and the plaintiff successfully claimed damages for breach of contract and breach of warranty. The defendants claimed to be indemnified by the third party from whom they had purchased the seed under the description of Fylgia. When the defendants delivered the seed to the plaintiff they omitted to comply with certain statutory requirements and the third party argued that the defendants could not recover from them as the contract between the defendants and the plaintiff was illegal. *Held,* the defendants would succeed against the third party as their contract with the plaintiff was not illegal and void but merely unenforceable due to its illegal performance. (See also *St John Shipping Corporation* v *Joseph Rank Ltd.*)

Marshall v Glanvill [1917] 2 KB 87   [382]

A representative for a firm of drapers joined the Royal Flying Corps. Four days later he would in any case have been conscripted. *Held,* the contract of service had been terminated and not merely suspended, as it had become unlawful for the representative to fulfill his part of the contract by serving his former master. (See also *Morgan* v *Manser, Metropolitan Water Board* v *Dick, Kerr and Co Ltd* and *Hare* v *Murphy Brothers Ltd.*)

Marshall v NM Financial Management Ltd [1995] 4 All ER 785   [383]

The plaintiff served the defendants for twelve years as a self-employed agent selling financial services, eg, life assurance. He was paid commission on business introduced. The contract also provided that entitlement to commission would cease upon its termination, although commission arising prior to termination would be paid after termination if, inter alia, within a year of the termination the plaintiff did not become employed by a competitor. The plaintiff terminated the contract and immediately joined a competitor and he now sued for prior commission. *Held,* his action would be successful. The contract was in restraint of trade and, since it could not be justified as being reasonably required to protect the defendants' legitimate interests (which lay largely with existing clients), it was unlawful. The unlawful restriction would be severed and excised since, on the facts, the plaintiff's real consideration for the payment of prior commission was his service under the contract, not his agreement not to compete. (Applied: *Wyatt* v *Kreglinger and Fernau*; see also *Re Prudential Assurance Co's Trust Deed*.)

Martin-Baker Aircraft Co Ltd v Canadian Flight Equipment Ltd [1955] 2 All ER 722 [384]

Manufacturers of aircraft ejection seats agreed 'to permit' a Canadian company 'to manufacture, sell and exploit' all their products on the American continent. Provision was also made for the payment, every six months, of royalties, but the agreement contained no provision for determination. *Held,* bearing in mind that the relationship created was essentially a commercial relationship of confidence and trust, the agreement was determinable on reasonable notice which, in this case, was 12 months. (See also *Staffordshire Area Health Authority* v *South Staffordshire Waterworks Co*; but see *Lynch* v *Thorne*.)

Mason v Provident Clothing and Supply Co Ltd [385]
[1913] AC 724 (House of Lords)

The defendant was employed by the plaintiffs, a clothing and supply company with branches all over England, as a canvasser and collector. His contract provided that the defendant would not within three years of the termination of his employment be employed by or assist any person, firm or company carrying on or engaged in a business similar to that of the plaintiffs 'within 25 miles of London'. The plaintiffs dismissed the defendant who thereupon entered the employment of the People's Supply Company, who carried on a similar business to that of the plaintiffs within 25 miles of London. The plaintiffs sought an injunction to restrain the defendant from violating his original contract of employment. *Held,* the plaintiffs' claim must fail as the restriction was wider than was reasonably necessary for the plaintiffs' protection. All covenants in restraint of trade are void unless it can be shown that they are reasonable and as a general rule a restraint imposed on the vendor of a business may be more severe than that imposed upon a servant by his master. (See also *Empire Meat Co Ltd* v *Patrick*.)

Matthews v Baxter (1873) LR 8 Exch 132 [386]

The defendant attended an auction and bought certain houses and land from the plaintiff. At the time of making his bid the defendant was so drunk as to be incapable of transacting business or knowing what he was doing but after he had become sober he ratified and confirmed his contract. The defendant refused to complete the purchase and the plaintiff claimed damages for breach of contract. *Held,* he was entitled to recover as the defendant's contract was voidable only, and not void, and therefore capable of ratification by him when he regained sobriety. (But see *Gore* v *Gibson;* see also s3 of the Sale of Goods Act 1979.)

Matthey v Curling [1922] 2 AC 180 (House of Lords) [387]

A house known as Offley Holes, which had been requisitioned by the military authorities, was destroyed by fire and the lessor claimed damages for breach of the lessee's covenant to repair and to rebuild on the occurrence of such an event. The lessee contended that the requisitioning of the house operated to determine the lease and free him from the covenants which it contained and that the lease had been frustrated by the destruction of the premises by fire. *Held,* the lessee remained bound by the terms of the lease. (See also *Cricklewood Property & Investment Trust Ltd* v *Leightons Investment Trust Ltd*.)

Mendelssohn v Normand Ltd [1969] 2 All ER 1215   **[388]**
(Court of Appeal)

The plaintiff left his car in the defendants' garage and was given a ticket which stated that the defendants 'will not accept responsibility for any loss sustained ... no variation of these conditions will bind the (defendants) unless made in writing signed by their duly authorised manager'. The plaintiff did not read the conditions. He had used the garage before and intended to lock the car, as was his practice, because he had a case containing valuables on the back seat. A garage attendant told him that the car must not be locked. The plaintiff gave the attendant the keys, and the attendant promised to lock the car later. The suitcase was stolen, and the plaintiff sued the defendants. *Held,* the plaintiff was entitled to damages. The defendants could not rely on the exemption clause, although the conditions printed on the ticket formed part of the contract, because the attendant's statement that he would lock the car took priority over the printed conditions. It was a representation having a decisive influence on the transaction. The attendant had apparent authority to make the representation and it was an inducing clause of the contract. (See also *Curtis* v *Chemical Cleaning & Dyeing Co.*)

Mersey Steel and Iron Co Ltd v Naylor, Benzon & Co   **[389]**
(1884) 9 App Cas 434 (House of Lords)

The respondents bought 5,000 tons of steel blooms from the appellants to be delivered at the rate of 1,000 tons monthly. In the first month the appellants delivered about half of the specified amount and in the next month made another delivery. Shortly before payment for these quantities became due a petition was presented for the winding-up of the appellants and the respondents, acting in good faith and in accordance with the erroneous advice of their solicitor, withheld payment. The liquidator of the appellants sued to recover the price of the steel actually delivered and the respondents counterclaimed for damages for breach of contract. *Held,* the respondents were entitled to succeed as their refusal to pay did not, in the circumstances of the case, constitute a repudiation of the contract so as to discharge the appellants from all further liability under it.

Metropolitan Water Board v Dick, Kerr & Co Ltd   **[390]**
[1918] AC 119 (House of Lords)

In July 1914 the appellants contracted to construct extensive reservoirs near Staines within six years. The agreement contained a proviso to the effect that if the work should be 'unduly delayed or impeded' an extension of the time for the completion of the work would be granted. War broke out and in February 1916 the Minister of Munitions ordered the work to stop and the plant to be sold. This prohibition was still in force in November 1917. The appellants claimed that the order had put an end to the contract. *Held,* this plea would be upheld as the interruption caused by the prohibition was of such a character and duration as to make the contract when resumed essentially different from that the performance of which was compulsorily brought to an end. (See also *Bank Line Ltd* v *Arthur Capel & Co.*)

Michael (John) Design plc v Cooke [1987] 2 All ER 332   **[391]**
(Court of Appeal)

The defendants, an associate director and a senior designer, left the plaintiffs' high-class shopfitting company and set up in business on their own. Their contracts with the plaintiffs provided, in effect, that they would not for two years do business with any of the plaintiffs' clients. The plaintiffs learned that a client of theirs was intending to place an order with the defendants and that they were not, in any event, going to do further business with the plaintiffs. The plaintiffs sought an interlocutory injunction. *Held,* they were entitled to succeed. The covenants were prima facie enforceable and the fact that this particular customer would not do any further business with the plaintiffs was not per se a reason for excluding that customer from the scope of the injunction. (See also *Fitch* v *Dewes* and *David (Lawrence) Ltd* v *Ashton.)*

Midland Bank plc v Shephard [1988] 3 All ER 17   [392]
(Court of Appeal)

A husband made arrangements with the bank to transfer his overdraft to a new joint account with his wife and the bank subsequently agreed a further overdraft for the husband's business purposes. Although the wife knew of the husband's intention to borrow the money, she did not know and was not told that it would be a liability on the joint account. The husband became bankrupt and the bank obtained summary judgment against the wife: she appealed. *Held,* the appeal would be dismissed. The confidential relationship between husband and wife did not by itself give rise to a presumption of undue influence and in this case there was no evidence that the husband had induced the wife to sign the joint account mandate by means of fraudulent misrepresentation or by some fraudulent concealment, or that he had induced the wife to sign by exercising undue influence over her. (See also *Bank of Baroda* v *Shah.*)

Miller v Karlinski (1945) 62 TLR 85 (Court of Appeal)   [393]

There was a contract of employment whereby the employee was to be paid a salary of £10 per week and to receive from his employer, in addition to expenses properly incurred, the amount payable out of his salary in respect of income-tax and this sum was to be included in his account for expenses. The employee sued to recover arrears of salary and expenses. *Held,* he would not succeed as the whole contract, an object of which was to defraud the revenue, was illegal and therefore void on the ground of public policy. (See also *Bigos* v *Bousted.*)

Miller's Agreement, Re, Uniacke v A-G [1947] 2 All ER 78   [394]

By deed Noad transferred his interest in a partnership to his fellow partners, Miller and Vos, who undertook to pay certain annuities to Noad's three daughters from the date of his death. The question arose as to whether the daughters were liable to pay estate duty and succession duty in respect of these annuities by reason of the fact that the agreement had conferred upon them 'beneficial interests'. *Held,* the daughters were not so liable as they were strangers to the covenant in the deed, under which they therefore had no rights either at common law or in equity as the deed would not be construed as having created a trust in their favour. (But see *Smith and Snipes Hall Farm Ltd* v *River Douglas Catchment Board.)*

Millichamp v Jones [1983] 1 All ER 267   [395]

By an agreement under seal, the defendant granted the plaintiffs an option to purchase a plot of land, the agreement providing for the serving of a notice of intention to purchase and payment of a deposit within a stated time. The plaintiffs duly served the notice but inadvertently failed to pay the deposit and they sought specific performance. *Held,* they were entitled to succeed. Although a requirement as to the payment of a deposit is a fundamental term breach of which entitles a vendor to treat the contract as at an end (and to sue for damages including the unpaid deposit), where, as here, the failure to pay the deposit was a mere oversight, the vendor should first give the purchaser an opportunity to pay. (Distinguished: *Hare* v *Nicoll*.)

Mistry Amar Singh v Kulubya [1963] 3 All ER 499   **[396]**
(Privy Council)

The plaintiff, an African and registered owner of certain Mailo land, purported to lease the land to the defendant, an Indian, and, as both parties were aware, the agreements contravened certain statutory enactments which prohibited the leasing of Mailo land to non-Africans. The plaintiff sought to recover possession. *Held,* he was entitled to succeed because his right to possession did not depend on the illegal agreements, but rested on his registered ownership of the land. The defendant could not rely on the illegal agreements and without doing so he could not defeat the plaintiff's claim. (See also *Bowmakers Ltd* v *Barnet Instruments Ltd;* but see *Shaw* v *Shaw*.)

Mitchell v Homfray (1881) 8 QBD 587 (Court of Appeal)   **[397]**

Without receiving independent advice Mrs Geldard gave her doctor, the defendant, £800 to enable him to buy a house. The jury found that the defendant had not exercised any undue influence and that after the relationship of doctor and patient had come to an end, three years before Mrs Geldard's death, she always stood by what she had done. *Held,* Mrs Geldard's executors were not entitled to recover the amount of the gift. (See also *Allcard* v *Skinner*; but see *Moody* v *Cox*.)

Mitchell (George) (Chesterhall) Ltd v Finney Lock   **[398]**
Seeds Ltd [1983] 2 All ER 737 (House of Lords)

Under an agreement made in December 1973 the appellant seed merchants supplied the respondent farmers with Dutch winter cabbage seed. The invoice, in standard form, limited liability for defective seed to its replacement or refund of the purchase price and further purported to exclude liability for loss or damage arising from the use of the seeds, for consequential loss or damage 'or for any other loss or damage whatsoever'. As a result of the negligence of the appellants' associate company, the seed supplied was of inferior quality and the respondents lost a year's production. The respondents sought damages for breach of contract. *Held,* they were entitled to succeed. Although the limitation clause was enforceable at common law, in the circumstances it would not have been fair or reasonable to permit the appellants to rely on it. (Applied: *Photo Production Ltd* v *Securicor Transport Ltd*; but see *Ailsa Craig Fishing Co Ltd* v *Malvern Fishing Co Ltd*.)

Molton v Camroux (1849) 18 LJ Ex 68, 356   **[399]**

The deceased purchased two annuities from the National Loan Fund Life Assurance Society. At the time of this transaction, unknown to the society, the deceased was a mentally disabled person. The personal representatives of the deceased sought to recover the purchase money from the society. *Held,* they were not entitled to do so as an executed contract entered into in good faith and in the normal course of business is not void by reason of the fact that at the time of making the contract one of the parties, unknown to the other, was of unsound mind. (See also *Matthews* v *Baxter* and *Hart* v *O'Connor*.)

Moody v Cox [1917] 2 Ch 71 (Court of Appeal) [400]

Cox, a solicitor, sold property of which he was trustee, to Moody, one of his clients. Moody alleged that the property was considerably overvalued, and sought to have the contract set aside on grounds of undue influence. *Held,* rescission would be granted. 'If a man who is in the position of solicitor to a client, so that the client has presumably confidence in him and the solicitor has presumably influence over the client, desires to contract with his client, he must make a full disclosure of every material fact that he knows, and must take upon himself the burden of satisfying the court that the contract is one of full advantage to his client' (*per* SCRUTTON LJ). (But see *Mitchell* v *Homfray.*)

Moorcock, The (1889) 14 PD 64 (Court of Appeal) [401]

The appellants made an agreement with the respondent for the use of their wharf and jetty for the purpose of loading and storing cargo from the *Moorcock.* The bed of the river adjoining the jetty was vested in a third party: it was beyond the control of the appellants and they had taken no steps to ascertain whether it was a safe place for the *Moorcock* to lie as was inevitable at low water on every tide. The vessel grounded and suffered damage because of the uneven condition of the river bed. *Held,* the appellants were liable as the jetty could not have been used without the *Moorcock* grounding and in these circumstances they would be deemed to have impliedly represented that they had taken reasonable care to ascertain that the river bed adjoining the jetty was in such a condition as not to cause injury to the vessel. (Applied in *Wettern Electric Ltd* v *Welsh Development Agency* and *Associated Japanese Bank (International) Ltd* v *Crédit du Nord SA.*)

Morgan v Manser [1947] 2 All ER 666 [402]

The defendant was a variety artiste (Charlie Chester) and, by an arrangement concluded in 1938, the plaintiff was to act as his manager for a period of 10 years. War came and the defendant was called up. The plaintiff claimed damages for breach of contract. *Held,* the plaintiff's action would be unsuccessful as the contract between the parties had been frustrated by the calling-up of the defendant. (See also *Boast* v *Firth*; but see *Mount* v *Oldham Corporation.*)

Morgan Grenfell & Co Ltd v Welwyn Hatfield [403]
District Council [1995] 1 All ER 1

In an action in which restitution was claimed of money paid under an interest rate swap contract, the court was asked to decide, inter alia, whether such a transaction fell within s18 of the Gaming Act 1845 and/or s1 of the Gaming Act 1892. *Held,* on the facts, it did not. While there was a potential for wagering, the normal inference would be that it was a commercial or financial transaction to which the law would give full recognition and effect. 'I now turn to the evidence regarding the purpose and interest of the respective parties to the relevant transaction to see whether the normal inference is to be rebutted. It will only be if the purpose and interest of both parties to the transaction was to wager that the consequence of legal invalidity and enforceability will follow. If either party was not wagering, the contract is not a wagering contract ... What Welwyn did in the present case was not to enter into any speculation. Welwyn wholly insulated itself from any speculative risk. Whatever the movement in interest rates, their element of profit would remain the same and they would not be exposed to any loss ... The purpose and interest of Welwyn was to realise a non-speculative profit and was in no way directed to or concerned with gaming or wagering' (*per* HOBHOUSE J). In any case, it was a transaction to which s63 of the Financial Services Act 1986 applied as the parties entered into it by way of business. (Section 63 of the 1986 Act provides that certain contracts for dealing in investments 'by way of business' are not void or unenforceable by reason of s18 of the 1845 Act or s1 of the 1892 Act). (See also *City Index Ltd* v *Leslie*.)

Morley v Loughnan [1893] 1 Ch 736 [404]

Loughnan was a member of a religious sect whose main tenet was to give everything to the Lord; he was employed as a travelling companion to one Morley, who was an epileptic who had inherited a large fortune. Loughnan converted Morley to that sect, received him into his family and in the course of six or seven years obtained from him most of his fortune amounting to about £140,000. Morley died and his executors sued to recover the money given to Loughnan. *Held, it* ought to be refunded as Loughnan had obtained the money by undue influence under the guise of religion. (See also *Powell* v *Powell*.)

Morley v United Friendly Insurance plc [1993] 1 WLR 996 [405]
(Court of Appeal)

A personal accident insurance policy excluded liability for death or injury resulting from 'wilful exposure to needless peril'. As the deceased approached a car driven by his fiancée, she drove slowly away; he jumped on the rear bumper; she increased speed and steered in a 'zig-zag' fashion; he fell off and sustained injuries from which he later died. *Held,* liability under the policy was not excluded as, at the moment of stepping onto the bumper, the deceased had not wilfully exposed himself to unnecessary peril but had merely engaged in a momentary act of stupidity.

Morris v Baron & Co [1918] AC 1 (House of Lords) [406]

By an agreement in writing the appellant contracted to sell to the respondent 500 pieces of moss blue serge. The appellant instituted proceedings to recover the value of 223 pieces of cloth which were delivered under the contract and the respondents counterclaimed in respect of their failure to deliver the remainder. The parties orally agreed terms of settlement in this action. *Held,* notwithstanding the then requirements as to writing, the original written contract had been impliedly rescinded by the conclusion of the oral settlement of the claims of both sides. The settlement itself constituted a new contract but as it did not satisfy the statutory requirements as to writing it could not be enforced. (But see *Bessler, Waechter, Glover & Co* v *South Derwent Coal Co Ltd*.)

Moschi v LEP Air Services Ltd [1972] 2 All ER 393 [407]
(House of Lords)

The defendants agreed to pay £40,000 to the plaintiffs, payment to be made in seven weekly instalments. The defendants' managing director personally guaranteed payment of the debt. After three weeks, the payments were in arrears, and this amounted to a repudiation of the contract by the defendants. The plaintiffs accepted the repudiation and then sued the guarantor for the recovery of the money. *Held,* the guarantor was liable. The plaintiffs' acceptance of the repudiation was not a variation of the contract so as to discharge the guarantor from his liability, and he was liable to make good in damages the whole loss which the plaintiffs had suffered.

Mount v Oldham Corporation [1973] 1 All ER 26   **[408]**
(Court of Appeal)

The plaintiff headmaster owned a special school for maladjusted children. As a result of pending criminal charges (of which he was subsequently cleared) he was away from school for six months. The running of the school was continued by the staff. The defendants withdrew children from the school without notice and, when sued for a term's fees in lieu of notice, pleaded that the contract was frustrated. *Held*, the plaintiff's claim should succeed. His temporary absence did not frustrate the contract. The claim was properly made for a term's fees rather than damages since the usage of the educational world was a term's notice or a term's fees in lieu. (But see *Morgan* v *Manser.*)

Mountstephen v Lakeman See Lakeman v J P Mountstephen

Museprime Properties Ltd v Adhill Properties Ltd   **[409]**
[1990] 36 EG 114

On the purchase by the plaintiffs from the defendants of a certain property at auction, inaccurate statements were made in the auction particulars and by the auctioneer in relation to rent reviews of three leases to which the property was subject. *Held*, the plaintiffs could rescind the contract and recover their deposit, conveyancing costs and interest. Any misrepresentation which induces a person to enter into a contract is a ground for rescission. Here, the plaintiffs had been induced to make their bid by the misrepresentation. (But see *Overbrooke Estates Ltd* v *Glencombe Properties Ltd.*)

Nash v Inman [1908] 2 KB 1 (Court of Appeal)   **[410]**

The plaintiff was a tailor in Savile Row and the defendant an undergraduate at Trinity College, Cambridge. While under age the defendant ordered certain clothes from the plaintiff, including 11 fancy waistcoats at two guineas each, and the plaintiff instituted proceedings to recover the cost of the clothes supplied. Evidence given by the defendant's father showed that the defendant already had an adequate supply of clothes suitable and necessary for his condition in life. *Held*, in view of this fact, the goods ordered from the plaintiff were not necessaries and the plaintiff's action must fail. (See also *Fawcett* v *Smethurst* and s1 of the Minors' Contracts Act 1987; but see *Chapple* v *Cooper.*)

National Carriers Ltd v Panalpina (Northern) Ltd   **[411]**
[1981] 1 All ER 161 (House of Lords)

The appellants leased a warehouse from the respondents for a term of 10 years. In May 1979, five years into the term, the local authority closed the street giving the only access to the warehouse because of the dangerous condition of a listed building on the opposite side of the road. After holding a local inquiry, in March 1980 the Secretary of State gave his consent for the demolition of the listed building and it was envisaged by the local authority that the demolition would be completed, and the street reopened, in January 1981. The appellants maintained that the closure of the street, denying them the use of the warehouse for the purpose contemplated by the lease, had frustrated the lease. *Held,* this contention would be rejected. Although in exceedingly rare circumstances the doctrine of frustration could apply to a lease of land, the loss of use for just two out of ten years was not sufficiently grave to amount to a frustrating event. (See also

Cricklewood Property and Investment Trust Ltd v *Leighton's Investment Trust Ltd* and *Universal Corporation* v *Five Ways Properties Ltd.*)

National Westminster Bank plc v Morgan [412]
[1985] 1 All ER 821 (House of Lords)

A husband was in financial difficulties and a mortgagee had commenced proceedings for possession of the house which he owned jointly with his wife. In response, the husband made a refinancing arrangement with a bank and the bank manager called to get the wife to execute a charge. During his brief visit the wife said she did not want the charge to cover her husband's business liabilities and the manager assured her in good faith—but incorrectly—that it would not do so. The wife did not receive independent legal advice before signing the charge. When the bank sought possession, the wife contended that the charge should be set aside because of the bank's undue influence. *Held,* the bank was entitled to succeed. The bank manager had not entered into a relationship with the wife in which he had a dominating influence over her, and furthermore the transaction was not unfair to the wife. The bank had not been under a duty to ensure that she received independent advice. 'It was ... conceded by counsel for the wife that the relationship between banker and customer is not one which ordinarily gives rise to a presumption of undue influence; and that in the ordinary course of banking business a banker can explain the nature of the proposed transaction without laying himself open to a charge of undue influence. This proposition has never been in doubt, though some, it would appear, have thought that the Court of Appeal held otherwise in *Lloyds Bank Ltd* v *Bundy.* If any such view has gained currency, let it be destroyed now once and for all time' (*per* LORD SCARMAN). (Followed in *Cornish* v *Midland Bank plc* and *O'Sullivan* v *Management Agency and Music Ltd*; see also *CTN Cash and Carry* v *Gallaher Ltd*; but see *Goldsworthy* v *Brickell* and *Cheese* v *Thomas.*)

Naughton v O'Callaghan [1990] 3 All ER 191 [413]

At Newmarket sales in September 1981 the plaintiffs bought Fondu, a chestnut colt, from the defendant for £27,300. For two seasons Fondu raced unsuccessfully and its value fell to £1,500. In mid 1983 the plaintiffs discovered that Fondu's pedigree had been incorrectly described in the sales catalogue. After a further year's training, they claimed damages for breach of contract and misrepresentation. *Held,* the plaintiffs were entitled to recover the difference between the colt's purchase price and its present value (£1,500) together with training fees and costs of upkeep until they discovered its true pedigree. (But see *Smith New Court Securities Ltd* v *Scrimgeour Vickers (Asset Management) Ltd.*)

New Zealand Shipping Co Ltd v A M Satterthwaite & Co Ltd, [414]
The Eurymedon [1974] 1 All ER 1015 (Privy Council)

Cargo was shipped to the respondents as consignees in New Zealand. Carriage was subject to a bill of lading issued by the carrier's agents. The bill of lading conferred various exemptions on the carrier and extended to independent contractors employed by them. The appellants acted as stevedores for the carrier as independent contractors. After the respondents had become the holders of the bill of lading, the cargo was damaged through the stevedores' negligence during unloading. The respondents sued for damages and claimed that the appellants could not rely on the exemption clause, since they were not a party to the contract. *Held,* the exemptions were designed to cover the whole operation from loading to discharge, irrespective of the fact of who performed it. The bill of lading was a bargain between the consignor and the appellants made through the carrier as agent. The contract in fact materialised when the appellants performed services by discharging the goods, Performance was sufficient consideration for the agreement by the consignor that the appellants should have the benefit of the exemptions and immunities conferred by the bill of lading. The performance of services by the appellants in discharging the cargo was adequate consideration to constitute a contract, even though they were already under an obligation because the respondents thereby obtained the benefit of a direct obligation which they could enforce. (But see *Scruttons Ltd* v *Midland Silicones Ltd*.)

Newbigging v Adam (1886) 34 Ch D 582   [415]

The plaintiff was induced by certain innocent misrepresentations to enter into a contract of partnership. It afterwards appeared that the business was not what it was represented to be, in fact it was insolvent. *Held,* the plaintiff could not claim damages but was entitled to rescission of the contract, repayment of the capital which he had paid and an indemnity against all claims and demands in respect of liability created by the partnership agreement. (See also *Whittington* v *Seale-Hayne* and the Misrepresentation Act 1967).

Nicolene Ltd v Simmonds [1953] 1 All ER 822   [416]
(Court of Appeal)

The plaintiffs offered to buy a specified quantity of reinforcing bars on certain terms and conditions and when the defendant wrote to accept the offer he said 'I assume that we are in agreement that the usual conditions of acceptance apply'. In fact there were no such usual conditions and the plaintiffs made no reference to this statement in a subsequent letter. When the defendant was sued for breach of contract for non-delivery of the bars he argued that as they had not agreed the exact form of 'the usual conditions' there was no contract between them. *Held,* this clause was meaningless and as it could be severed from the rest of the contract without impairing its sense or reasonableness it should be ignored and the correspondence between the parties had concluded a binding contract. (See also *Carney* v *Herbert*.)

Nicoll v Beere (1855) 53 LT 659   [417]

The defendant, who was employed by the plaintiff, a Regent Street tailor, as a cutter and fitter, agreed with the plaintiff that he would not, upon the termination of his employment, carry on business as a tailor within a radius of 10 miles of Charing Cross for the period of three years from the date of such termination. The defendant left the employment of the plaintiff and set up business in opposition about 200 yards along Regent Street from the plaintiff's premises. The plaintiff sought an injunction to restrain the defendant from continuing in business in breach of this agreement with him. *Held,* an injunction would be awarded as the agreement was valid and binding as the restraint which it imposed was not unreasonable either in point of space or time. (But see *Pearks Ltd* v *Cullen* and *Attwood* v *Lamont*.)

Nicholson and Venn v Smith Marriot (1947) 177 LT 189   [418]

The defendants auctioned some table linen, described in the sale catalogue as being seventeenth century. The plaintiffs, who were antique dealers, read the description, saw the linen, and bought it. It was in fact eighteenth century linen. *Held,* as the plaintiffs had relied upon the catalogue description, there was a breach of what is now s13 of the Sale of Goods Act 1979, which implies a condition that goods shall correspond with their description. (See also *Varley* v *Whipp.*)

Nordenfelt v Maxim Nordenfelt Guns and [419]
Ammunition Co Ltd [1894] AC 535 (House of Lords)

Nordenfelt, a manufacturer of quick-firing guns and ammunition, sold his business to the respondent company and covenanted that he would not, during the period of 25 years from the incorporation of the company, engage in the manufacture of guns, gun mountings or carriages, gunpowder explosives or ammunition or in any trade or business competing or liable to compete in any way with that carried on by the respondent company. Nordenfelt was made managing director of the respondent company for which he received £2,000 pa together with commission on the net profits. Nordenfelt entered into an agreement with other manufacturers of guns and ammunition and the respondent company sought an injunction to enforce Nordenfelt's covenant. *Held,* the injunction would be granted as the covenant was valid. Although it was unrestricted as to space it was not, having regard to the nature of the business and the limited number of customers (various governments), wider than was necessary for the protection of the company, nor injurious to the public interest. (See also *Goldsoll* v *Goldman.*)

North Ocean Shipping Co Ltd v Hyundai Construction [420]
Co Ltd, The Atlantic Baron [1978] 3 All ER 1170

Shipbuilders and shipowners entered into a contract to build a ship, the currency of the contract being US dollars. Under the contract, the builders undertook to open a letter of credit to provide security for repayment of instalments of the price if they defaulted in performing the contract. Following the devaluation of the US dollar the builders threatened to terminate the contract unless the owners agreed to a price increase. Because they were anxious to have the ship to fulfil a charter,the owners agreed on condition that the letter of credit was correspondingly increased. The builders agreed. The increased price was paid and the ship was delivered. Subsequently the owners claimed the return of the amount paid in excess of the original price. They contended that the agreement to increase the price was void for lack of consideration or alternatively that it was voidable as it had been made under economic duress. *Held,* a promise by one party to fulfil an existing contractual obligation was not good consideration and thus the builders' original contractual liability to build the ship did not constitute good consideration. By undertaking to increase the letter of credit the builders had, however, provided consideration because this was an additional obligation. The contract was thus not void. Although it was possible to avoid a contract on grounds of economic duress, by failing to make any protest the owners had affirmed the agreement and could not avoid it on this ground. They were not entitled to claim the return of the excess payment. (See also *Stilk* v *Myrick.*)

Northumberland and Durham District Banking Co, Re, [421]
ex parte Bigge (1858) 28 LJ Ch 50

A shareholder objected to his name being placed on the list of contributories on the ground that he had been induced to take the shares by fraudulent reports of the affairs of the company. It was proved that he had not become a shareholder because of the statements contained in the reports and there was considerable doubt as to whether he had read or even seen them. *Held,* the shareholder could not avoid his liability on the ground of misrepresentation. (See also *Horsfall* v *Thomas* and *Oakes* v *Turquand and Harding.*)

Norwich and Peterborough Building Society v Steed [422]
[1993] Ch 116 (Court of Appeal)

While the appellant was living in the United States, his sister and her husband persuaded him to execute a power of attorney in favour of his mother, although he did not tell her that she had been so appointed. The sister and her husband tricked her mother into signing a transfer of the appellant's home in their favour and they then charged the property to the respondents by way of security for a loan. When the sister and her husband defaulted on the mortgage repayments, the respondents sought possession of the house and the appellant pleaded, inter alia, non est factum on the ground that the mother had not known of her appointment and had not known that she was signing a transfer. *Held*, this plea could not succeed. As the appellant had not told his mother of her appointment he could not rely on her ignorance of the power and, as donor of the power, he could not rely on any lack of understanding on her part. (See also *Saunders v Anglia Building Society*.)

Norwich Union Fire Insurance Society Ltd v [423]
William H Price Ltd [1934] AC 455 (Privy Council)

An insurance company paid the insured value of a cargo of lemons acting on the false information that they had been damaged and sold. In fact they had been sold because they ripened too quickly, a contingency for which the insurers were not liable under the terms of the policy. *Held*, the insurers were entitled to recover the amount which they paid as it had been paid under a mistake of fact.

Nye v Moseley (1826) 6 B & C 133 [424]

Sophia Nye was first engaged in the household of John Moseley, a married man, in the capacity of cook but soon became her employer's mistress and bore him two children. When Moseley put an end to this relationship he promised by deed to pay her an annuity of £100 and to give the children £500 each on his death. Sophia sued to recover arrears of the annuity. *Held*, her claim would succeed as the deed was not made in contemplation of further immoral acts. If the promise had been made orally or under hand Sophia would not have succeeded as the consideration for Moseley's promise would have been past. (But see *Beaumont v Reeve* and *Roscorla v Thomas*.)

Oakes v Turquand and Harding (1867) LR 2 HL 325 [425]
(House of Lords)

Relying on certain statements in a prospectus, which amounted to fraudulent misrepresentations, Oakes contracted to purchase some shares. The shares were allotted and when after nine months the company was ordered to be wound up Oakes applied to the court to have his name removed from the list of shareholders. *Held*, Oakes' name should remain on the list as he was only entitled to repudiate his liability within a reasonable time and in any case he could not do so after winding-up proceedings had been commenced. (See also *Northumberland and Durham District Banking Co, Re, ex parte Bigge*.)

Ocean Tramp Tankers Corporation v V/O Sovfracht, [426]
The Eugenia [1964] 1 All ER 161 (Court of Appeal)

By a time charterparty (the voyage being the measure of the time) concluded on 9 September 1956, the *Eugenia* was chartered for a trip from Genoa 'out to India via Black Sea'. The Suez Canal had been nationalised by the Government of Egypt on

26 July 1956 and both parties to the contract realised that intervention by English and French forces might lead to the canal becoming impassable to traffic. Although the charterparty did not deal with this possibility (the matter was discussed, but no agreement was reached), it did provide that the Eugenia should not, unless the consent of the owners be first obtained, be used on any service which would bring her within a zone which was dangerous as the result of actual or threatened warlike operations; if the vessel should be brought within such a zone the owners could, inter alia, insure their interests in the vessel, the charterers to refund the premium on demand. The Eugenia proceeded towards the Suez Canal with a cargo of iron and steel and arrived off Port Said on 30 October to find that Egyptian anti-aircraft guns were already in action and on 31 October, after the Eugenia had entered the canal, bombing began and the Egyptian Government blocked the canal at both ends. The vessel was thus trapped in the canal until 8 January 1957, and on 4 January 1957, the charterers claimed that the charterparty had been frustrated by the blocking of the canal. The owners claimed hire for the period that the vessel was trapped in the canal. *Held,* the charterers were in breach of the war clause in entering the canal and could not rely upon a self-induced frustration: it followed that the owners were entitled to recover any damages they may have suffered. Their lordships also considered the hypothetical question whether, had the Eugenia not entered the canal, the contract would have been frustrated because the vessel's only course would have been via the Cape of Good Hope. In their lordships' view, it would not, because the blocking of the canal did not bring about a fundamentally different situation. 'The fact that it has become more onerous or more expensive for one party than he thought is not sufficient to bring about a frustration. It must be more than merely more onerous or more expensive. It must be positively unjust to hold the parties bound' (*per* LORD DENNING MR). (See also *Maritime National Fish Ltd* v *Ocean Trawlers Ltd*; but see *Tatem (WJ) Ltd* v *Gamboa*.)

O'Laoire v Jackel International Ltd   [427]
[1991] IRLR 170 (Court of Appeal)

The defendants had summarily dismissed the plaintiff and an industrial tribunal had awarded him the statutory maximum (£8,000) by way of compensation for unfair dismissal. In an action for wrongful dismissal, the plaintiff claimed, inter alia, damages for loss of reputation and injury to feelings and the question also arose as to whether the £8,000 should be deducted from any damages recoverable at common law. *Held,* applying *Addis* v *Gramophone Co Ltd*, damages were not recoverable for loss of reputation and injury to feelings, except in the case of contracts of apprenticeship. However, the £8,000 was not deductible: this sum had not been allocated by the tribunal to any one of the particular elements making up the plaintiff's total loss, as found by the court, so it could not be shown that there had been a double recovery. (See also *Malik* v *Bank of Credit and Commerce International SA*.)

Olley v Marlborough Court Ltd [1949] 1 All ER 127   [428]
(Court of Appeal)

The plaintiff was a guest at the defendants' hotel and during her stay some of her property was stolen. There was a notice in her room which stated that 'The proprietors will not hold themselves responsible for articles lost or stolen ...' *Held,* this notice could not be read into the contract between the parties as the contract was concluded before the plaintiff was shown to her room and therefore before she saw the notice which purported to exclude liability. (See also *Chapleton* v *Barry Urban District Council*.)

Oscar Chess Ltd v Williams [1957] 1 All ER 325   [429]
(Court of Appeal)

The defendant sold to the plaintiffs, who were motor dealers, a second hand Morris 10 hp saloon motor car. The defendant honestly believed that the car was a 1948 model and he showed the plaintiffs the registration book which confirmed that the vehicle was first registered in that year. Six months later the plaintiffs discovered that the vehicle was a 1939 model and they claimed damages for breach of warranty. *Held,* their action could not succeed as the true inference from all the facts was that the defendant did not intend to bind himself in contract that the car was a 1948 model, but made an innocent misrepresentation as to the date of its manufacture. (But see *Wells (Merstham) Ltd* v *Buckland Sand and Silica Co Ltd*.)

O'Shea, Re, ex parte Lancaster [1911] 2 KB 981   [430]
(Court of Appeal)

Lancaster lent money to O'Shea for the purpose of setting him up as a bookmaker. The business was not successful and Lancaster guaranteed an overdraft at O'Shea's bank to enable him to pay an amount which he owed to another bookmaker. *Held,* O'Shea was liable to make good to Lancaster the amount which he had to pay under this guarantee as there was no provision, express or implied, that the money was to be used for the payment of his betting losses. For this reason the money was not paid by Lancaster 'in respect of' a gaming contract within the meaning of s1 of the Gaming Act 1892. (But see *Carlton Hall Club Ltd* v *Laurence.*)

O'Sullivan v Management Agency and Music Ltd   [431]
[1985] 3 All ER 351 (Court of Appeal)

In 1970 the plaintiff, then a young unknown musician with no business experience, entered into a management contract with Mills whom he trusted implicitly. Between 1970 and 1976 the plaintiff concluded various contracts with Mills' companies; the plaintiff did not receive independent professional advice and Mills did not warn him that he ought to obtain it. The agreements, in effect, bound the plaintiff to Mills and his companies completely on terms less favourable to the plaintiff than they would have been had they been negotiated at arm's length with the benefit of independent advice. The plaintiff became enormously successful and in 1979 alleged that the agreements were void because, inter alia, they had been obtained by undue influence. *Held,* he was entitled to succeed and the contracts would be set aside even though restitutio in integrum was impossible because the contracts had been performed. However, Mills and the companies were entitled to reasonable remuneration for their significant contribution to the plaintiff's musical success. (Applied: *Lloyds Bank Ltd* v *Bundy* and *National Westminster Bank plc* v *Morgan.*)

Overbrooke Estates Ltd v Glencombe Properties Ltd   [432]
[1974] 3 All ER 511

The plaintiffs instructed auctioneers to sell a property. The auction catalogue contained a condition excluding the auctioneers' authority to make representations in relation to the property. In reply to an inquiry, the auctioneers gave the defendants information about the property, and the defendants bought the property. The information was inaccurate and the defendants refused to proceed. *Held,* the plaintiffs' claim for specific performance should succeed. The condition limited the auctioneers' ostensible authority, and so the representation was not binding on the plaintiffs. The Misrepresentation Act 1967 (s3) only applied to a provision excluding or restricting liability for a misrepresentation made by a party or his duly authorised agent and did not qualify a principal's right publicly to limit the otherwise ostensible authority of his agent. (But see *Museprime Properties Ltd* v *Adhill Properties Ltd.*)

Paget v Marshall (1884) 28 Ch D 255 [433]

The plaintiff wrote to the defendant to offer him a part of a block of three houses consisting of the first, second, third and fourth floors at a rent of £500 pa. The defendant wrote to convey his acceptance of this offer and a lease was executed whereby the floors mentioned in the exchange of letters were demised at the agreed rent. The plaintiff contended that he had always intended to keep the first floor of one of the houses as a shop. *Held,* the plaintiff was entitled to have the lease annulled on the ground of mistake or to have the lease rectified to exclude the floor which he had intended to retain for his own use. (But see *Solle* v *Butcher.*)

Pan Atlantic Insurance Co Ltd v Pine Top Insurance Co Ltd [434]
[1994] 3 All ER 581 (House of Lords)

The defendant reinsurer sought to avoid a contract of insurance with the plaintiff insurer on the ground of non-disclosure of the plaintiffs' loss record for previous years. *Held,* the defendants were entitled to judgment as they had shown that they had been induced by the non-disclosure to enter into the policy. Although the policy was non-marine, the common law, in relevant respects, for both marine and non-marine insurance was the same and the Marine Insurance Act 1906 embodied a partial codification of those principles. A 'material circumstance' in s18 of the 1906 Act was one that would have an effect, not necessarily a decisive influence, on the mind of the prudent insurer in deciding whether to accept the risk or as to the premium to be charged. (See also *St Paul Fire and Marine Insurance Co (UK) Ltd* v *McConnell Dowell Constructors Ltd*; but see *Simner* v *New India Assurance Co Ltd.*)

Pao On v Lau Yiu Long [1979] 3 All ER 65 [435]
(Privy Council)

The plaintiffs controlled a private company. The defendants were majority shareholders in a public company. The plaintiffs contracted with the public company to sell the shares in the private company in return for the issue of shares in the public company. To avoid depressing the market, the plaintiffs agreed not to sell a percentage of the shares for a year. A subsidiary agreement between the parties provided for the purchase by the defendants at a fixed price at the end of a year. Later the plaintiffs refused to carry out the main agreement unless the defendants cancelled the subsidiary agreement and replaced it with a guarantee by way of indemnity. The defendants, under pressure, did so. The share price dropped and the plaintiffs sought to rely on the guarantee. The defendants refused to indemnify them. *Held,* the plaintiffs' promise, under the main agreement, not to sell a percentage of the shares for a year was made at the defendants' request and it was recognised that the plaintiffs would be compensated by some form of guarantee against a fall in price. The agreed cancellation of the subsidiary agreement left the plaintiffs unprotected. The consideration for the guarantee included the plaintiffs' promise not to sell the shares for a year and, although antecedent to the guarantee, was good consideration for the defendants' promise of indemnity. It was not merely an invalid past consideration. To secure a party's promise by threat of repudiation of a pre-existing obligation was not an abuse of dominant bargaining position. There had been commercial pressure, but no coercion. (Applied: *Lampleigh* v *Braithwaite*; see also *Re Casey's Patents.*)

Paradine v Jane (1647) 82 ER 897   [436]

The defendant was lessee of certain land and when sued for arrears of rent he contended that he was not liable to pay as the land in question had been occupied by a German Prince who had 'invaded the realm with a hostile army of men' thus preventing the defendant from receiving the profits from the land. *Held,* the plaintiff was entitled to recover as the defendant had covenanted to pay the rent and if he had wished to be excused payment in circumstances such as this he should have inserted a term to that effect in the contract. (But see *Taylor* v *Caldwell.*)

Parker v South-Eastern Railway Co (1877) 2 CPD 416   [437]

The plaintiff deposited his bag in the defendants' cloak-room, paid 2d and was given a ticket on the front of which were the words 'See back': on the back there was a condition purporting to exclude the company's liability in respect of any package which was in excess of £10 in value. There was a notice in the cloak-room to the same effect. The plaintiff denied that he had seen the notice or read what was printed on the ticket. *Held,* it was a question of fact as to whether the defendants did all that was reasonably sufficient to give the plaintiff notice of the condition and in this instance the defendants had satisfied that requirement. (Applied in *Interfoto Picture Library Ltd* v *Stiletto Visual Programmes Ltd*; see also *Watkins* v *Rymill.*)

Parkinson v College of Ambulance Ltd [1925] 2 KB 1   [438]

The secretary of a charity fraudulently represented to Colonel Parkinson that he or the charity was in a position to ensure that Colonel Parkinson would receive a knighthood if he made a large donation to the funds of the charity, and undertook that the title would be conferred if the donation was made. Colonel Parkinson made a large donation as requested but as he did not receive a knighthood he sued the charity and its secretary to recover the amount of his gift. *Held,* the action must fail as a contract for the purchase of a title, however the money is to be expended, is improper and illegal, it being contrary to public policy, and as Colonel Parkinson knew that he was entering into an improper and illegal contract he could not recover the amount of his donation as damages for deceit or breach of contract nor could he repudiate the contract and recover the money on the ground that the contract was still executory. (See also *Lemenda Trading Co Ltd* v *African Middle East Petroleum Co Ltd.*)

(handwritten margin note: IMPROPER AND ILLEGAL Contract: Action fail to recover money could not expended on)

Parkinson (Sir Lindsay) & Co Ltd v Commissioners   [439]
of Works and Public Buildings
[1950] 1 All ER 208 (Court of Appeal)

The plaintiffs contracted with the defendants to erect an ordnance factory at a cost of £3¹/₂ million. Under the contract the defendants could require the plaintiffs to perform additional work and at the date of the contract it was thought that this would cost a further £500,000. In order to complete the work by the date originally fixed, the parties subsequently agreed that uneconomic methods should be employed which would add £1 million to the cost of the work and that the plaintiffs should be allowed a net profit between £150,000 and £300,000. The total cost of the work exceeded £6¹/₂ million and the plaintiffs claimed that their net profit should not be restricted to £300,000. *Held,* their action would succeed as when the maximum profit was agreed both parties believed that the work would cost approximately £5 million, but as the final figure was greatly in excess of this sum the additional work was not within the scope of the agreement and the plaintiffs were entitled to recover a reasonable net profit in respect of it. (But see *British Movietonews Ltd* v *London & District Cinemas Ltd.*)

Parsons v BNM Laboratories Ltd [1963] 2 All ER 658   **[440]**
(Court of Appeal)

The plaintiff chemist was employed by the defendants for a minimum period of three years at a salary of £2,000 per annum plus commission. The defendants wrongfully determined the contract of service within the three year period and the amount of damages due to him was disputed. *Held,* notwithstanding the provisions of ss37 and 38 of the Finance Act 1960 the common law principle applied and income tax at the standard rate should be taken into account by way of deduction from the amount of damages awarded in respect of the plaintiff's loss of annual earnings, the damages themselves being tax-free in his hands. An amount of £59 2s 6d should also be deducted in respect of the amount received by him by way of State unemployment benefit. 'The effect of the dismissal was not to deprive him of all income but to reduce his income by substituting unemployment benefit for his salary. It would be unrealistic to disregard the unemployment benefit, because to do so would confer on the plaintiff, to the extent of £59 2s 6d, a fortuitous windfall in addition to compensation' (*per* PEARSON LJ). (See also *Re Houghton Main Colliery Co Ltd.*)

Parsons (H) (Livestock) Ltd v Uttley Ingham   **[441]**
& Co Ltd [1978] 1 All ER 525 (Court of Appeal)

The plaintiffs were pig farmers and fed their stock on pig nuts. In 1968 they bought a bulk feed hopper from the defendants. They ordered a second one in 1971 and, when it was delivered, the ventilator on the hopper was closed. This was unnoticed because the ventilator was 28 feet above ground and the hopper was filled with nuts. A few nuts went mouldy, but they were fed to the pigs and they became ill with a serious illness called E Coli. More nuts subsequently went mouldy and the nuts were no longer fed to the pigs. It was then discovered that the hopper ventilator was closed. 254 pigs from the plaintiffs' total stock of 700 died. The defendants appealed against a decision that they were liable for all the damage of which their breach of what is now s14(3) of the Sale of Goods Act 1979 (fitness for purpose) was the cause. *Held,* the defendants were liable for the estimated loss directly and naturally resulting in the ordinary course of events from the breach. The unventilated hopper was a breach of a warranty that the hopper should be reasonably fit for storing pig nuts in a condition suitable for feeding to pigs. The plaintiffs' losses were caused by that breach. Although nobody could have expected E Coli to result from the mouldy nuts, it was reasonable to suppose that the parties would have contemplated at the time of the contract, in the event of the hopper being unfit for its purpose, the serious possibility of injury and even death among the pigs. Recovery was not limited because the specific consequence would not have been anticipated as long as the type of consequence was contemplated. (See also *Hadley* v *Baxendale;* but see *Slater* v *Finning Ltd*)

Partabmull Rameshwar v KC Sethia (1944) Ltd See **Sethia (KC)**
(1944) Ltd v Partabmull Rameshwar

Patel v Ali [1984] 1 All ER 978   **[442]**

The defendants contracted to sell their house to the plaintiffs: at that time (July 1979) the defendant wife, a Pakistani who spoke little English, had one child and she (the wife) was in good health. Due to the husband's bankruptcy, the wife could not have completed the sale before July 1980: by that time it had been discovered that she was suffering from bone cancer and she had a leg amputated. On 11 August the plaintiffs issued a writ seeking specific performance. At the end of that month the wife gave birth to her second child and in August 1983 she had her third. The following month the court made an order for specific performance and the wife appealed, contending that she would suffer hardship, in being deprived of daily assistance from friends and relations, if she had to move to another area. *Held,* inter alia, the order would be discharged. In view of unforeseeable changes the order would cause the wife hardship amounting to injustice and after the long delay (for which neither party was to blame) it would be just to leave the plaintiffs to their remedy in damages. (See s50 of the Supreme Court Act 1981; but see *Tamplin* v *James.*)

Payne v Cave (1789) 3 Term Rep 148 [443]

The defendant was last bidder at an auction sale but before the fall of the hammer he retracted his bid. Held, he was entitled to do so as it is the bid which is the offer and not the auctioneer's invitation to bid and the defendant's offer had not been accepted until the hammer fell. The defendant's offer could be revoked at any time before acceptance. (See also s57(2) of the Sale of Goods Act 1979.)

Payzu Ltd v Saunders [1919] 2 KB 581 (Court of Appeal) [444]

The defendant agreed to sell to the plaintiffs 200 pieces of crêpe de Chine. The goods were to be delivered during a period of nine months and payment was to be made for each instalment within one month of delivery. The plaintiffs did not pay for the first consignment punctually and the defendant thereupon stated that he would only deliver further supplies at the contract price if the plaintiffs would agreed to pay cash at the time of making each order. The plaintiffs did not agree to this and sued the defendant for breach of contract, claiming the difference between the contract price and the current market price. *Held,* the plaintiffs' failure to pay for the first instalment did not constitute repudiation of the contract and the defendant was therefore liable in damages for its breach. However, the plaintiffs should have mitigated their loss by accepting the defendant's subsequent offer and they were entitled to recover only the amount which they would have lost if they had done so. (But see *Pilkington* v *Wood.*)

Pearce v Brooks (1866) LR 1 Exch 213 [445]

The plaintiffs, who were coach-builders, supplied the defendant, who was to their knowledge a prostitute, with a brougham (a closed carriage). The jury found that the plaintiffs knew that the carriage would be used for the purposes of the defendant's trade. The plaintiffs sought to recover the amount due in respect of the hire of the brougham. *Held,* the plaintiffs' action must fail. The contract of hire was void as the plaintiffs had contributed to an immoral act by supplying the brougham with the knowledge that it was going to be used for the purposes of prostitution. (But see *Lloyd* v *Johnson.*)

Pearks Ltd v Cullen (1912) 28 TLR 371 [446]

The defendant, who was employed by the plaintiffs as a shop assistant on the grocery counter in a branch store at Southend, agreed that for a period of two years after leaving the plaintiffs' employment he would not 'establish, carry on, or be engaged in, or interested in ... a business of a similar character to the business of the company within the distance of two miles of any shop for the time being belonging to the company at which he has been employed within the twelve months prior to his leaving their employ'. The defendant left the plaintiffs' employment and went to work for a nearby rival in a similar capacity. The plaintiffs sought to enforce the agreement. *Held,* the plaintiffs' action must fail as the restrictive covenant was not reasonably necessary for the protection of the plaintiffs' business and could not therefore be enforced. It might have been held otherwise if the defendant had been the plaintiffs' manager, which position would have provided him with access to their trade secrets. (See also *Bowler* v *Lovegrove.*)

Peco Arts Inc v Hazlitt Gallery Ltd [1983] 3 All ER 193 [447]

In 1970, on the recommendation of a specialist, the plaintiffs bought from the defendants what both parties at the time believed to be an original drawing by Ingres. When, in 1981, the drawing was, for only the second time, professionally revalued for insurance purposes, it was discovered that it was a reproduction worth virtually nothing. In 1982 the plaintiffs commenced proceedings claiming on grounds of mistake of fact recovery of the purchase price and interest and rescission of the contract in equity. The defendants contended that the action was time-barred. *Held,* the plaintiffs would succeed as, on the facts, there had been no lack of diligence on their part. They were therefore protected by s32(1)(c) of the Limitation Act 1980. ' ... reasonable diligence means not the doing of everything possible, not necessarily the using of any means at the plaintiff's disposal, not even necessarily the doing of anything at all, but that it means the doing of that which an ordinarily prudent buyer and possessor of a valuable work of art would do having regard to all the circumstances, including the circumstances of the purchase' (*per* WEBSTER J). (Distinguished: *Leaf* v *International Galleries.*)

Pelly v Royal Exchange Assurance Co (1757) 1 Burr 341 [448]

The plaintiff insured his ship and its sails and furniture in respect of a return voyage to China. When the ship arrived in the River Canton for a clean and refit, according to custom, the sails and furniture were removed and placed in a storehouse. The sails and furniture were destroyed when the storehouse was burnt and the plaintiff claimed that the insurers were liable under the policy to make good his loss. *Held,* they were so liable as the custom of removing the sails and furniture would be recognised to the extent of bringing these acts within the scope of the policy. (See also *Hutton* v *Warren.*)

Petrofina (Great Britain) Ltd v Martin [449]
[1966] 1 All ER 126 (Court of Appeal)

The plaintiffs sought to enforce a solus agreement in gross whereby the defendants had agreed to sell only the plaintiffs' fuel oil products at their garage for a period of 12 years, although this period might be extended if sales did not come up to expectation. The restriction was limited to trading at particular garage premises. *Held,* a solus agreement in gross is in restraint of trade. While not automatically bad, it is invalid unless the person seeking to enforce it can show that it is reasonable as between the parties and is not injurious to the public interest. On the facts, the plaintiffs could not show that the restraint was no more than reasonable in the circumstances because it contained a restriction on the sale of the garage unless the purchaser would enter into a similar agreement, and the period of the tie was too long. The plaintiffs' action failed. (See also *Attwood* v *Lamont*; but see *Esso Petroleum Co Ltd* v *Harper's Garage (Stourport) Ltd.*)

Peyman v Lanjani [1984] 3 All ER 703 (Court of Appeal) [450]

In October 1978 the defendant agreed with the tenants to take an assignment of the lease of a restaurant and, in order to obtain the landlord's consent, the defendant arranged for his agent to impersonate him at an interview with the landlord's agent. After the assignment had been completed, the defendant agreed to assign the lease to the plaintiff, the plaintiff's house to be taken in part exchange and the balance in cash. Contracts were exchanged (the defendant's solicitor acting for both parties) and completion was set for April 1979. The agent again impersonated the defendant in seeking the landlord's consent and, although the plaintiff and the solicitor had become aware of the impersonation, urged so to do by the solicitor the plaintiff paid the defendant £10,000 and took possession pending the landlord's formal consent. A month later, before the landlord's consent had been given, the plaintiff consulted new solicitors who advised him of his right to rescind (in view of the original impersonation) and the plaintiff purported to follow this advice. *Held,* he was entitled to do so as, at the material time, he had not known that he had the right to rescind and he could not therefore be said, by his subsequent actions, to have elected to affirm the contract. The defence of estoppel also failed because the plaintiff had not, on the facts, unequivocally represented that he was affirming the contract, his actions had not been adverse to the defendant and the defendant had not acted on them to his detriment.

Pharmaceutical Society of Great Britain v Boots Cash Chemists (Southern) Ltd [451]
[1953] 1 All ER 482 (Court of Appeal)

Goods, which were wrapped and priced, were displayed in a 'self-service' shop. *Held,* when the customer took the goods from the shelf his action amounted to an offer to buy and this offer was accepted when the cashier received payment for the goods. The mere display of the goods did not constitute an offer by the shopkeeper to sell at the marked price. (See also *Fisher* v *Bell*.)

Philips Hong Kong Ltd v A-G of Hong Kong [452]
(1993) The Times 15 February (Privy Council)

A contract between Philips and the Hong Kong government for a highway construction project contained a number of provisions as to liquidated damages for delay in completion of the work. The company argued that the rigid application of these provisions could result in it having to pay more than the cost of the loss sustained and that the provisions were in consequence penal and void. *Held,* unless the parties were on very unequal terms, the desirability of achieving certainty in a commercial contract was paramount. Having regard to the range of possible losses, the terms that the parties had agreed were perfectly valid liquidated damages clauses. The company's contention that they were penal would therefore be dismissed. Their Lordships acknowledged, however, that difficulty could arise where the range of possible loss was broad. Where it should be obvious that, in relation to part of the range, the liquidated damages were totally out of proportion to certain of the losses which might be incurred, the failure to make special provisions for those losses might result in the 'liquidated damages' not being recoverable. (See also *Dunlop Pneumatic Tyre Co Ltd* v *New Garage and Motor Co Ltd*.)

Phillips v Brooks Ltd [1919] 2 KB 243 [453]

A man entered the plaintiff's shop and asked to inspect some jewellery. He selected some pearls and rings to the value of £3,000 and when he was signing a cheque for that amount stated: 'You see who I am, I am Sir George Bullough', and he gave an address in St James's Square. The plaintiff knew that there was such a man as Sir George Bullough and reference to a directory confirmed that Sir George lived at the address mentioned. The plaintiff asked the man in the shop if he would like to take the jewels with him but was told 'You had better have the cheque cleared first, but I should like to take the ring as it is my wife's birthday tomorrow'. The plaintiff let the man have the ring but his cheque was dishonoured and the man pledged the ring to the defendants from whom the plaintiff sought to recover either the ring or its value. *Held,* the plaintiff intended to contract with the man who came into the shop although he believed (mistakenly) that he was Sir George Bullough. The property in the ring had therefore passed to the actual purchaser who was able to give a good title to the defendants. For this reason the plaintiff's action failed. (See also *Lewis* v *Averay.)*

Phillips Products Ltd v Hyland (1984) [1987] 2 All ER 620   [454]
(Court of Appeal)

The second defendants, a plant hire company, hired an excavator to the plaintiffs together with a driver, the first defendant. The contract, in standard form, provided that the driver was to be regarded as the plaintiffs' servant or agent and that they alone would be responsible for any claims. In the course of his work for them, the driver negligently damaged the plaintiffs' factory. *Held,* both defendants were liable. The relevant clause as to liability was within s2(2) of the Unfair Contract Terms Act 1977 and, on the facts, it was not fair and reasonable and it did not therefore afford the defendants an answer to the plaintiffs' claim. (Distinguished in *Thompson* v *T Lohan (Plant Hire) Ltd*; see also *Smith* v *Eric S Bush.)*

Photo Production Ltd v Securicor Transport Ltd   [455]
[1980] 1 All ER 556 (House of Lords)

An employee of the defendant security company deliberately lit a fire which set alight the plaintiffs' factory, while on night patrol duty. The defendants denied liability on the basis of exemption clauses in their contract with the plaintiffs which excluded liability for injurious acts or defaults by employees. The Court of Appeal held that the defendants could not rely thereon because they had committed a fundamental breach of contract. *Held,* allowing the defendants' appeal, there was no rule of law by which exemption clauses were deprived of effect regardless of their terms, where there was a fundamental breach of contract. In deciding whether an exemption clause is to be applied, the question is one of construction of the contract as a whole. On its true construction, the exemption clause relied on by the defendants was clear and unambiguous and covered the deliberate acts of employees. The defendants were therefore protected by it. (Applied in *Mitchell (George) (Chesterhall) Ltd* v *Finney Lock Seeds Ltd*; see also *Suisse Atlantique Société d'Armement Maritime SA* v *NV Rotterdamsche Kolen Centrale.)*

Pilkington v Wood [1953] 2 All ER 810   [456]

When the plaintiff bought a house in Hampshire he employed the defendant, a solicitor, to act for him. Over a year later the plaintiff decided to sell the house and it was then that a defect in the plaintiff's title came to light. The defendant admitted that he had been guilty of negligence and the question arose as to the amount of damages which he should pay. In addition to the difference between the market value of the house with a good title and its value when the title was defective, the plaintiff claimed certain hotel, travelling and telephone expenses which he would not have incurred if he had been able to sell the house and move to Lancashire, his new place of employment, and interest on a bank overdraft which would have been paid off when the house was sold. The defendant maintained that it was the duty of the plaintiff to mitigate the damage which he had suffered by suing the vendor in respect of a breach of his implied covenant for title. *Held,* the plaintiff's duty to mitigate the damage did not go so far as to require him to undertake a difficult piece of litigation, but his claim for additional damages would fail as it arose out of facts which could not reasonably be supposed to have been in the contemplation of the parties at the time at which the plaintiff bought the house. (See also *Hadley* v *Baxendale* and *Interoffice Telephones Ltd* v *Robert Freeman Co Ltd.*)

Pinnel's Case (1602) 77 ER 237   [457]

The plaintiff brought an action to recover £8 10s and the defendant pleaded that he had, at the request of the plaintiff and before the amount was due, tendered £5 2s 2d which the defendant had accepted in full satisfaction of the debt. *Held,* the plaintiff would succeed on the ground of insufficient pleading, but if this had not been the case judgment would have been given in favour of the defendant as payment was made at an earlier date; this constituted satisfaction as early payment was beneficial to the plaintiff. (But see *Cumber* v *Wane*; see also *D & C Builders Ltd* v *Rees.*)

Pioneer Shipping Ltd v BTP Tioxide Ltd, The Nema   [458]
[1981] 2 All ER 1030 (House of Lords)

A vessel was chartered for six or seven consecutive voyages from Sorel in Canada to Europe between April and December. A strike broke out at Sorel while the vessel was away on the first voyage and was still in progress when she returned, thus preventing her from being loaded for the second voyage. The parties agreed that the vessel could be used for one intermediate voyage, but when she arrived back at Sorel the port was still strikebound. The owners claimed that the charterparty had been frustrated and the arbitrator shared this view, explaining that, at best, two further contractual voyages were likely and the performance of only three out of seven was something radically different from what had originally been agreed. *Held,* he had been justified on the facts and correct in law in arriving at this conclusion. 'I see no reason in principle why a strike should not be capable of causing frustration of an adventure by delay. It cannot be right to divide causes of delay into classes and then say that one class can and another class cannot bring about frustration of an adventure. It is not the nature of the cause of delay which matters so much as the effect of that cause on the performance of the obligations which the parties have assumed one towards the other' (*per* LORD ROSKILL).

Pitt v PHH Asset Management Ltd [1994] 1 WLR 327   [459]
(Court of Appeal)

The defendant, acting for mortgagees in possession of The Cottage, placed the property on the market at £205,000. Two people were intereseted in purchasing the property – the plaintiff and Miss Buckle. After various offers had been made and overtaken by the other party Miss Buckle offered £210,000 and the selling agent told the plaintiff that the acceptance, subject to contract, of his offer of £200,000 had been withdrawn. Next day the plaintiff told the agent by telephone that he would seek an injunction to prevent the sale to Miss Buckle, tell her that he was withdrawing and that she should therefore lower her offer and that he was able to exchange contracts as soon as the agent wanted. After discussion with the defendant, the agent told the plaintiff that the sale to him at £200,000 would proceed, subject to contract, and that no other offer would be considered provided contracts were exchanged within 14 days of submission of the draft. In breach of

123

this 'lock-out' agreement, the property was sold to Miss Buckle for £210,000. *Held,* the plaintiff was entitled to damages for breach of the lock-out agreement, even though it was not in writing and the sale was subject to contract. The plaintiff had given valuable consideration by withdrawing his threats to seek an injunction and to advise Miss Buckle to lower her offer and by committing himself to the exchange of contracts within 14 days. Section 2 of the Law Reform (Miscellaneous Provisions) Act 1989 did not apply: the agreement was not a contract for the sale of an interest in land, merely a contract not to negotiate for 14 days with anyone except the plaintiff for the sale of the property. (But see *Walford* v *Miles* and *Commission for the New Towns* v *Cooper (GB) Ltd*; see also *Horton* v *Horton*.)

Port Line Ltd v Ben Line Steamers Ltd [460]
[1958] 1 All ER 787

In November 1954, the plaintiffs entered into a time charter with the Silver Line Ltd, the owners of a certain vessel, for a period of 30 months from March 1955. In February 1956, the vessel was sold, with the plaintiffs' consent, to the defendants. The sale was subject to a bareboat charter to Silver Line Ltd, which enabled them to carry out the terms of their time charter with the plaintiffs and was for the balance of the period of the charterparty entered into in November 1954. The bareboat charter provided that 'if the ship be requisitioned, this charterparty shall thereupon expire' but there was no such clause in the charter between the plaintiffs and Silver Line Ltd. The defendants were unaware of this disparity and in August 1956, the ship was requisitioned by the Crown. The plaintiffs sued to recover the whole or part of the compensation received by the defendants from the Crown in respect of the period for which the vessel was requisitioned. *Held,* they could not succeed: '(1) Because the *Strathcona* case *[Lord Strathcona Steamship Co Ltd* v *Dominion Coal Co Ltd]* was wrongly decided; (2) because, even if it was rightly decided, the defendants do not come within its principles as they had no actual knowledge at the time of their purchase of the plaintiffs' rights under their charter; (3) because, even if it was rightly decided, and the defendants come within its principles (a) they were in breach of no duty to the plaintiffs since it was by no act of theirs that the vessel during the period of requisition was used inconsistently with the terms of the plaintiffs' charter ... and (b) the plaintiffs are not entitled to any remedy against the defendants except a right to restrain the defendants from using the vessel in a manner inconsistent with the terms of the charter' (*per* DIPLOCK J). (But see *Tulk* v *Moxhay*.)

Posner v Scott-Lewis [1986] 3 All ER 513 [461]

Leases of flats within a block provided that the defendant landlords would employ a resident porter: the porter employed became non-resident and the plaintiff tenants sought an order for specific performance. *Held,* the order would be made. The obligation was sufficiently defined, the order would not require protracted superintendence by the court and the plaintiffs (but not the defendants) could suffer hardship if a resident porter was not in post. (Distinguished: *Ryan* v *Mutual Tontine Westminster Chambers Association*.)

Poussard v Spiers and Pond (1876) 1 QBD 410 [462]

The plaintiff agreed with the defendants to sing the chief female part for a period of three months in a new opera which was about to be produced at the defendants' theatre. Owing to illness the plaintiff was not able to attend the final rehearsals or the first four performances and when she offered to take her part in the fifth performance the defendants refused to accept her services and the plaintiff bought an action for wrongful dismissal. *Held,* the plaintiff could not recover as her inability to perform on the opening day and early performances was a breach of a condition precedent which went to the root of the matter and justified the rescission of the contract by the defendants. (See also *Marshall* v *Glanvill;* but see *Bettini* v *Gye.*)

Powell v Braun [1954] 1 All ER 484 (Court of Appeal) [463]

An employer wrote to his secretary and told her that he was pleased with her past services and that he wished her to undertake added responsibility in the future. In view of this, instead of an increase in salary, he offered to pay her a yearly bonus on the net trading profits of the business. The secretary accepted this offer but the manner in which the bonus was to be assessed was never agreed. *Held,* the employer was bound to pay her a reasonable sum each year. (See also *British Bank for Foreign Trade Ltd* v *Novinex Ltd.*)

Powell v Lee (1908) 99 LT 284 [464]

The defendants resolved to appoint the plaintiff headmaster of a school of which they were the managers. The terms of the resolution were never communicated to the plaintiff. *Held,* there was no contract between the parties as the defendants' acceptance of the plaintiff's offer of his services had not been communicated to him. (See also *Felthouse* v *Bindley.*)

Powell v Powell [1900] 1 Ch 243 [465]

When Ellen was 21 she made a voluntary settlement in favour of her step-mother and she sought to have it set aside on the ground of undue influence. Ellen was advised by her step-mother's solicitor who himself prepared and became a trustee of the settlement. *Held,* the settlement would be set aside. (See also *Wright* v *Carter.*)

Price v Easton (1833) 4 B & Ad 433 [466]

Price owed the plaintiff £13 and agreed to work for the defendant who promised to pay the amount of Price's wages to the plaintiff in settlement of the debt. Price worked for the defendant but the defendant did not pay his wages to the plaintiff. *Held,* the plaintiff could not recover £13 from the defendant as no consideration moved from the plaintiff to the defendant. (See also *Tweddle* v *Atkinson.*)

Provident Financial Group plc v Hayward [467]
[1989] 3 All ER 298 (Court of Appeal)

The defendant was financial director of the plaintiffs' estate agency business. His contract prohibited him from working for anyone else during the period of his employment. He resigned on 1 July and it was mutually agreed that the period of notice would be six instead of the contractual 12 months. He worked until 5 September from when, at the plaintiffs' request, he stayed home on full pay. On 13 October the defendant announced his intention to work for a supermarket chain as financial controller of their estate agency offices. The plaintiffs sought an injunction to restrain the defendant from working for anyone else before 31 December. *Held,* the injunction would not be granted as, on the facts, there was no real prospect of serious or significant damage to the plaintiffs from the defendant working as proposed for the rival company before the end of the year. (But see *Hivac Ltd* v *Park Royal Scientific Instruments Ltd.*)

Prudential Assurance Co's Trust Deed, Re   [468]
[1934] Ch 338

A contributory pension scheme for the benefit of the employees of the Prudential Assurance Co contained a clause to the effect that the pension should cease if the pensioner engaged in or became connected with any business which competed with that of his former employers and in such a case the pensioner was to have the amount of his contributions returned to him, less the sum already received by him as pension. *Held,* whether or not that particular clause was invalid or unenforceable, its inclusion did not invalidate the remainder of the pension scheme. (See also *Goodinson* v *Goodinson* and *Marshall* v *NM Financial Management Ltd.*)

Pym v Campbell (1856) 6 E & B 370   [469]

The parties negotiated for the sale of a 3/8th share in a certain invention and drew up and signed a memorandum of agreement which was not to be binding until a third party had approved the invention. *Held,* parol evidence of the fact that the agreement depended upon the approval of another for its validity was rightly admitted as it was evidence to show that no agreement had been concluded.

Quinn v Burch Brothers (Builders) Ltd [1966] 2 All ER 283   [470]
(Court of Appeal)

Quinn was engaged in carrying out certain building work as a sub-contractor of the defendants. It was an implied term of the contract between them that the defendants should supply any equipment reasonably necessary for the work within a reasonable time of being requested to do so. The defendants were in breach of that term in that they failed to provide a step-ladder which the plaintiff requested. To save time, Quinn used a trestle, which he knew to be unsuitable unless it was footed by another workman. The trestle was not so footed, it slipped, and Quinn suffered injury. He claimed damages in respect of this injury, framing his action in contract. *Held,* although the defendants' breach of contract provided the occasion for the plaintiff to injure himself, it was not the cause of his injury, which was his own voluntary act in using the trestle. Accordingly, the defendants were not liable to pay damages for the plaintiff's injury, for the damage he had suffered was not a natural and probable consequence of the breach of contract. (See also *Victoria Laundry (Windsor) Ltd* v *Newman Industries Ltd.*)

R v Clarke (1927) 40 CLR 227 (High Court of Australia)   [471]

Two police officers had been murdered and the Government of Western Australia offered a reward of £1,000 'for such information as shall lead to the arrest and conviction of the murderers'. Clarke, who knew of the reward, gave the information required, but it was found that he did so in order to clear himself of a false charge of murder and not in answer to the appeal which had been made for information. *Held,* when he gave the information, Clarke had not addressed his mind to the reward but to his release and therefore he could not be said to have accepted the offer contained in the announcement of the reward which he was unable to recover. (But see *Williams* v *Carwardine.*)

R & B Customs Brokers Co Ltd v United Dominions   [472]
Trust Ltd [1988] 1 All ER 847 (Court of Appeal)

The plaintiffs purchased a Colt Shogun car from the defendant finance company and it was supplied to them by the third party motor dealer. A clause of the conditional sale agreement purported to exclude any implied conditions as to the car's condition or fitness in relation to business transactions. The car was the second or third vehicle which the plaintiffs had acquired on credit terms and the contract was not executed until some weeks after the plaintiffs had taken delivery. Before signing the contract the plaintiffs discovered that the car's roof leaked; two days after signing they returned it to the dealer for repair. The dealer failed to rectify the leak so the plaintiffs rejected the car and sued to recover the amount paid under the sale agreement. The defendants in turn claimed an indemnity from the dealer. *Held,* the plaintiffs were entitled to judgment. The sale of the car was subject to an implied condition as to fitness under s14(3) of the Sale of Goods Act 1979 and, as the transaction was only incidental to a business activity, it was a consumer as opposed to a business transaction and the exclusion clause did not provide an answer to the claim (See also *Parsons (H) (Livestock) Ltd v Uttley Ingham & Co Ltd.)*

Raffles v Wichelhaus (1864) 33 LN (NS) 160 [473]

The defendants agreed to buy '125 bales of Surat cotton ... to arrive ex *Peerless* from Bombay ...' It appeared that the ship mentioned in the agreement was intended by the defendants to be the *Peerless* which sailed from Bombay in October, whereas the plaintiff offered 125 bales of Surat cotton from another ship called the *Peerless* which sailed from Bombay in December. *Held,* there was no binding contract between the parties as the defendants meant one ship and the plaintiff another. (But see *Smith v Hughes.)*

Ramsage Victoria Hotel Co Ltd v Montefiore [474]
(1866) LR 1 Exch 109

The defendant applied for shares on 8 June but no allotment was made until 23 November. *Held,* the allotment must be made within a reasonable time, the interval from June to November was not reasonable and the defendant's offer to take shares in the company had lapsed.

Rann v Hughes (1778) 7 Term Rep 350n (House of Lords) [475]

An administratrix personally undertook and promised to pay certain moneys which were due from the estate. *Held,* there was no consideration for the promise and for this reason the undertaking would not be enforced. SKYNNER LCB said 'the law of this country supplies no means, nor affords any remedy, to compel the performance of an agreement made without sufficient consideration.' (See also *Eastwood v Kenyon.)*

Reardon Smith Line Ltd v Hansen-Tangen [476]
[1976] 3 All ER 570 (House of Lords)

The appellants chartered a ship which was described in the charterparty as to be built by a named Japanese shipbuilding company and having a particular hull number. When delivered, the ship had been built by sub-contractors under the supervision of the named company, many of whose personnel had been seconded to work on the vessel. The hull number was also different. The appellants appealed against a decision that the ship in fact complied with the description having regard to Japanese custom. They contended that the words specifying the builders and the number were contractual terms forming part of the description and that because of the departure from the description they were entitled to reject the vessel. *Held,* dismissing the appeal, in reaching its decision the court had to place itself in the same factual position as that in which the parties had been when contracting. The relevant words were only intended as a means of identification. The strict rule of compliance with description which applied in sale of goods cases did not apply to a contract like the present, which came under the general law of contract. Even if it did apply, the description had been complied with in the strict sense. The words fulfilled their function of providing a means of identifying the vessel. They could not be read as essential terms of the contract which must be complied with literally. (But see *Wallis, Son and Wells* v *Pratt and Haynes*.)

Record v Bell [1991] 4 All ER 471 [477]

On 1 June 1990, the day before contracts were exchanged for the sale of a house in Smith Square, the vendor's solicitor wrote to the purchaser's solicitor informing him that he was awaiting original office copy entries from the Land Registry confirming his client's title. The purchaser's solicitor replied stating that the contract was conditional on, inter alia, delivery to the purchaser of the office copy entries and that the letter setting out this condition was to be attached to the contract. This letter was attached to the purchaser's part of the contract, but no letter was attached to the other part. Contemporaneously with this contract, the parties entered into a separate contract for the sale of certain chattels in the house. The office copy entries having been duly delivered, the vendor sought specific performance of both contracts. *Held*, he was entitled to succeed. Although the letter did not satisfy the requirements of s2 of the Law of Property (Miscellaneous Provisions) Act 1989 (it was not referred to in the contract and no letter was attached to one part of it), there was a contract collateral to the main contract which was not caught by s2 of the 1989 Act. The vendor's solicitor's letter had been an offer of a warranty as to the state of the title and this offer had been accepted by exchanging contracts. The circumstances were such that the court could and would also grant specific performance of the sale of the accompanying chattels. (Applied: *De Lassalle* v *Guildford*; see also *Pitt* v *PHH Asset Management Ltd*.)

Redgrave v Hurd (1881) 20 Ch D 1 (Court of Appeal) [478]

A solicitor inserted an advertisement in the *Law Times* stating that he had a moderate practice with extensive connections in a populous town and that he would like to take an efficient lawyer into partnership with him. Another solicitor answered the advertisement and at an interview the advertiser said that his business was worth about £300 pa. No accounts had been kept but the prospective partner inspected various papers which showed that the business produced a gross income of £200 pa and an agreement was concluded. In fact the practice was worthless. *Held*, the new partner was entitled to rescission as he had been induced to enter into a contract by representations which turned out to be untrue. It was no answer to his claim to say that if he had exercised due diligence he would have discovered the real situation. (See also *Central Railway Company of Venezuela* v *Kisch, Newbigging* v *Adam* and *Archer* v *Brown*.)

Reese River Silver Mining Co Ltd v Smith [479]
(1869) LR 4 HL 64 (House of Lords)

The directors of a company issued a prospectus stating that they proposed to carry on the business of mining and that they had acquired a valuable mine in America. On the faith of these representations a person applied for shares but it afterwards appeared that the mine in question was valueless. *Held*, the man who applied for shares was entitled to have his contract rescinded on the ground of misrepresentation. (See also *Redgrave* v *Hurd* and *Car and Universal Finance Co Ltd* v *Caldwell.*)

Regazzoni v K C Sethia (1944) Ltd [1957] 3 All ER 286   **[480]**
(House of Lords)

In protest against the racial policy of the Government of the Union of South Africa, the Indian Government prohibited the taking out of India of goods which were either destined for or intended to be taken to the Union. The parties contracted for the sale and delivery of some jute bags cif Genoa but the court found that they contemplated and intended that the goods should be shipped from India and made available in Genoa so that the buyer might make a re-sale or fulfil a bargain of re-sale to the South African buying agency. The seller failed to deliver the jute bags and the buyer sought damages for breach of contract. *Held,* as a matter of public policy, the action would fail as the performance of the contract would have involved doing in a foreign and friendly country (India) an act which would have violated a law (which was not a revenue or penal law) of that state. (See also *Foster* v *Driscoll.*)

Resolute Maritime Inc v Nippon Kaiji Kyokai, The Skopas   **[481]**
[1983] 2 All ER 1

The plaintiffs alleged that they had been misled into making the purchase of the vessel Skopas by incorrect representations and the question arose whether an agent (one of the defendants), acting in his express or ostensible authority, could be liable under s2(1) of the Misrepresentation Act 1967. *Held,* he could not, nor could the person who actually made the statement for him: such liability attached to the principal alone, although the agent could be liable in fraud and negligence.

Rhone v Stephens [1994] 2 WLR 429   **[482]**
(House of Lords)

Walford House and Walford Cottage, adjoining properties covered by the same roof, were in common ownership until 1960 when the cottage was sold. The conveyance contained a covenant by the vendor for himself and his successors to maintain such part of the roof of the house as lay above the cottage in wind and watertight condition. Both properties were subsequently sold and the present owners of the cottage sought damages for breach of this covenant. *Held,* their action could not succeed. Successors in title could not enforce a positive covenant at common law as they were not parties to the contract and the burden of positive covenants does not run with the freehold and is not enforceable in equity. (But see *Tulk* v *Moxhay.*)

Richards and Bartlet's Case (1584) 74 ER 17   **[483]**

There was a contract for the sale of two weights of corn for £10. The corn was subsequently 'drowned by tempest' and, in view of this, the plaintiff said that he would accept 33s 4d in satisfaction of the full price of the corn. *Held,* there was no consideration for this promise as no advantage accrued to the plaintiff who was not, therefore, bound to accept the smaller amount. (But see *Pinnel's Case.*)

Richardson, Spence & Co v Rowntree [1894] AC 217   **[484]**
(House of Lords)

The respondent paid the appellants passage money for a voyage on their steamer and was handed a folded ticket which purported to exclude liability in respect of loss or injury exceeding $100. No writing was visible unless the respondent unfolded the ticket. The jury found that the respondent knew there was writing or printing on the ticket, but did not know that it related to the terms of the contract of carriage. *Held,* the appellants did not do what was reasonably sufficient to give the respondent notice of the conditions and for this reason she was not bound by them. (But see *Thompson* v *London, Midland and Scottish Railway Co.*)

Rickards (Charles) Ltd v Oppenheim [1950] 1 All ER 429   [485]
(Court of Appeal)

The defendant placed an order with the plaintiffs for the building of a new body on a Rolls Royce chassis. The work was not completed within the period specified in the contract and the defendant waived this condition, but some months later, when the work was still not completed, he said that if the car was not delivered within four weeks he would refuse to accept it. The car was not delivered within that period. *Held,* the defendant could refuse delivery and recover the chassis or its value as he was entitled to give reasonable notice again making time of the essence of the contract and in the circumstances of the case four weeks' notice was reasonable. (See also *Hare* v *Nicoll* and *Scandinavian Trading Tanker Co AB* v *Flota Petrolera Ecuatoriana, The Scaptrade*; but see *Behzadi* v *Shaftesbury Hotels Ltd.*)

Riverplate Properties Ltd v Paul   [486]
[1974] 2 All ER 656 (Court of Appeal)

A lessor made a unilateral mistake in drafting a lease, the effect of which was that it threw the entire burden of repairing the building on the lessor. The lessor's intention was that the lessee should contribute to the cost of repairs. The lessee was unaware of the mistake. The lessor claimed rescission subject to rectification at the option of the lessee. *Held,* mere unilateral mistake in a lease is not a ground for rescission. Since the lessee had not known of the mistake which was in no way attributable to anything said or done by her, the lessor was not entitled to rescission.

Robb v Green [1895] 2 QB 315 (Court of Appeal)   [487]

During his employment as manager of the plaintiff's business the defendant made a list of the names and addresses of the customers with a view to using it for the purpose of soliciting orders after he had left the plaintiff's service and had established a similar business on his own account. *Held,* it was an implied term of the defendant's contract of service that he would show good faith towards his master and the compilation of the list of customers was a breach of that implied term which entitled the plaintiff to damages and an injunction. (But see *Faccenda Chicken Ltd* v *Fowler.*)

Roberts v Gray [1913] 1 KB 520 (Court of Appeal)   [488]

The plaintiff, who was a leading professional billiard player, agreed to take the defendant, who was a minor and also a billiard player, on a world tour during which they would compete with one another in matches. A dispute arose as to the type of billiard balls to be used and the defendant repudiated the contract. The plaintiff claimed damages for breach of contract. *Held,* he should succeed as the contract, which was in effect for the teaching and education of the defendant and was reasonable and for his benefit, was a contract for necessaries. (See also *Chaplin* v *Leslie Frewin (Publishers) Ltd.*)

Roberts (A) & Co Ltd v Leicestershire County Council   [489]
[1961] 2 All ER 545

The plaintiffs submitted a tender for work on a school stating that they would complete the work within 78 weeks of the date of instructions to proceed. The plaintiffs' tender was accepted, but the period for completion inserted in the contract by the defendants was 30 months. The period for completion was altered for the benefit of the defendants and if the plaintiffs had tendered on this basis their price would have been higher. The defendants did not call the attention of the plaintiffs to the fact that the period for completion included in the contract differed from the period specified in the tender and the contract was executed by the plaintiffs under the belief that the period for completion stated in the contract was 18 months. *Held,* at the time at which the contract was executed the defendants were aware of the plaintiffs' mistaken belief that the 18 month completion period was included therein and the contract would be rectified to make provision for completion within this period. (See also *Torrance* v *Bolton.*)

Robertson v Minister of Pensions [1948] 2 All ER 767   [490]

The plaintiff was injured during the war and the War Office assured him that his disability had been accepted as attributable to military service. In reliance upon this statement he did not obtain independent medical opinion and took no steps to retain X-ray plates, and the question arose as to whether the assurance given by the War Office was binding on the Minister of Pensions. *Held,* the Minister was bound as the assurance was one which was intended to be binding and to be acted on by the plaintiff and which became binding when the plaintiff acted on it by forbearing to obtain medical evidence of the consequences of his injury. (But see *Combe* v *Combe.*)

Rogers v Parish (Scarborough) Ltd [1987] 2 All ER 232   [491]
(Court of Appeal)

The plaintiffs bought from the defendants a new Range Rover; after a few weeks' use it proved unsatisfactory and it was replaced with another. The replacement was no more satisfactory; attempts were made to repair the faults but some of them persisted. After five months and about 5,500 miles the plaintiffs purported to reject the vehicle on the ground that it was not of merchantable quality within s14(6) of the Sale of Goods Act 1979. *Held,* they were entitled to succeed as, on the facts and bearing in mind that the expectations of the purchaser of a new Range Rover were higher than those of a purchaser of an ordinary family car, the vehicle had not been of merchantable quality. (Applied in *Shine* v *General Guarantee Corp Ltd* ; but see *Bernstein* v *Pamson Motors (Golders Green) Ltd.* See now s14 of the 1979 Act, as amended.)

Ronbar Enterprises Ltd v Green [1954] 2 All ER 266   [492]
(Court of Appeal)

The plaintiff company and the defendant entered into partnership to publish the *Weekly Sporting Review and Show Business.* The partnership agreement conferred on both partners the right to determine the partnership and the agreement stipulated that the outgoing partner should not 'for five years ... directly or indirectly carry on or be engaged or interested in any business similar to or competing with the business of the partnership'. The plaintiff company determined the partnership under the terms of the agreement and the defendant entered into the employment of another company to write articles for *Sport and Show News,* a similar periodical which was also published in London. The plaintiff company sought an injunction to restrain this activity. *Held,* the injunction would be granted. As it stood, the covenant, being unlimited in point of area, was unreasonably wide, but the words 'similar to or' would be struck out and the covenant was not then wider than was reasonably necessary for the protection of the plaintiff company. (See also *Goldsoll* v *Goldman.*)

Rooke v Dawson [1895] 1 Ch 480 [493]

A trust deed provided for the award of a scholarship and the trustees duly announced and held an examination in which the plaintiff obtained the highest marks. *Held,* the announcement was nothing more than a proclamation that the examination would be held and the trustees were not bound to award the scholarship to the candidate who gained the highest marks in the examination. (See also *Grainger & Son* v *Gough.*)

Roscorla v Thomas (1842) 3 QB 234 [494]

The plaintiff bought the defendant's horse and after the sale the defendant promised that the horse was sound and free from vice whereas it proved to be 'very vicious, restive, ungovernable and ferocious'. *Held,* the consideration for this promise was past and the plaintiff had no remedy. (See also *Re McArdle.*)

Rose and Frank Co v J R Crompton & Brothers Ltd [495]
[1925] AC 445 (House of Lords)

The appellants carried on business in New York as dealers in carbon paper and contracted to buy certain quantities from the respondents who manufactured that commodity in England. The contract stated that 'This arrangement is not entered into ... as a formal or legal agreement, and shall not be subject to legal jurisdiction in the Law Courts ... but it is only a definite expression and record of the purpose and intention of the ... parties concerned, to which they each honourably pledge themselves, with the fullest confidence ... that it will be carried through ... with mutual loyalty and friendly co-operation.' The appellants sued for breach of contract and non-delivery of goods. *Held,* their action must fail as legal relations had been expressly excluded, but this did not apply to instances where orders had been given and accepted as separate contracts of sale had been constituted in every case. (But see *Kleinwort Benson Ltd* v *Malaysia Mining Corpn Bhd*; see also *Jones* v *Vernon's Pools Ltd.*)

Rose (Frederick E) (London) Ltd v William H Pim [496]
Jnr & Co Ltd [1953] 2 All ER 739 (Court of Appeal)

The parties contracted for the sale of a quantity of horsebeans known in Egypt as 'feveroles'. At the time of making the contract both parties believed that 'feveroles' was simply another word for horsebeans but in fact they were another type of bean altogether. *Held,* the contract was not a nullity although both parties were under a fundamental mistake as to the nature of the subject matter, and the contract would not be rectified as it accurately expressed their erroneous intention to deal in 'feveroles'. (See also *Long* v *Lloyd.*)

Routh v Jones [1947] 1 All ER 758 (Court of Appeal) [497]

Two general medical practitioners in Okehampton engaged an assistant who covenanted that he would not for five years after leaving their practice engage in 'practice in any department of medicine, surgery or midwifery nor accept ... any professional appointment' within 10 miles of that town. *Held,* in so far as this restraint forbade the assistant from becoming, for example, a consultant or medical officer of health, it was wider than was necessary for the protection of his employers' practice and amounted to an illegal restraint of trade. (But see *Clarke* v *Newland.*)

Routledge v Grant (1828) 4 Bing 653   [498]

The defendant offered to purchase the plaintiff's house and gave him six weeks to decide whether to accept the offer. The defendant purported to withdraw his offer before the six weeks had passed. *Held,* he was entitled to do so at any time before the offer was accepted.

Routledge v McKay [1954] 1 All ER 855 (Court of Appeal)   [499]

A Douglas motor cycle combination was first registered in 1930, but when a new registration book was issued the date of original registration was given as '9.9.41'. In October 1949 the seller, who was not responsible for the incorrect entry in the registration book, in answer to a question by the buyer as to the date of the machine, said that it was a late 1941 or 1942 model and seven days later the buyer and seller entered into a contract of sale. The memorandum of agreement made no mention of the date of the machine. The buyer claimed damages for breach of warranty. *Held,* the incorrect statement in the registration book was a false representation and not a warranty and, in the absence of fraud, the buyer could not succeed. (See also *Oscar Chess Ltd* v *Williams.*)

Rover International Ltd v Cannon Film Sales Ltd (No 3)   [500]
[1989] 3 All ER 423 (Court of Appeal)

The parties contracted for the dubbing and distribution in Italy of certain films. Under the contract, the plaintiffs made five monthly advances by way of royalties. Unbeknown to both parties the contract was void ab initio because it ante-dated the plaintiffs' incorporation by about a month. The plaintiffs claimed repayment of the five instalments. *Held,* they were entitled to succeed as the money had been paid under a mistake of fact, ie, that the contract was valid. They could also recover on the ground that the money had been paid for a consideration that had wholly failed. (See also *Kelly* v *Solari* and *Rowland* v *Divall.*)

Rowland v Divall [1923] 2 KB 500 (Court of Appeal)   [501]

The plaintiff bought a car from the defendant. The car was delivered to him, and he used it for four months. He then discovered that the defendant had no title to the car, which belonged to a third party, to whom he returned it. The plaintiff then sued the defendant to recover the price. *Held,* the plaintiff was entitled to treat the contract as discharged; there had been a total failure of consideration, and he did not need to rest his case on the condition as to title implied by what is now s12 of the Sale of Goods Act 1979. 'There has been a total failure of consideration, that is to say the buyer has not got any part of that for which he paid the purchase money. He paid the money in order that he might get the property and he has not got it' (*per* ATKIN LJ). (See also *Rover International Ltd* v *Cannon Film Sales Ltd (No 3).*)

Royal Exchange Assurance v Hope [1928] Ch 179   [502]
(Court of Appeal)

By an insurance policy an assurance company, the plaintiffs, agreed to pay the assured, his executors, administrators or assigns the sum of £1,000 if he died before 31 July 1926. The assured assigned the benefit of the policy to the defendant and subsequently arranged to extend the period of insurance to 31 October 1926. The benefit of this extension was never assigned and the assured died on 1 October 1926. *Held,* the extension of the policy was not a new contract of insurance but a variation of the original policy, the benefit of which had been vested in the defendant who was therefore entitled to recover £1,000 by virtue of the assignment. The defendant was also entitled to the money as the assured would be regarded as having contracted for the extension of the policy for the benefit of and as trustee for the defendant. (But see *Vandepitte* v *Preferred Accident Insurance Corporation of New York.*)

Royscot Trust Ltd v Rogerson [503]
[1991] 3 All ER 294 (Court of Appeal)

The court had to decide whether the measure of damages for innocent misrepresentation giving rise to an action under s2(1) of the Misrepresentation Act 1967 was the measure of damages in tort or the measure of damages in contract. *Held,* it was the measure of damages in tort for fraudulent misrepresentation, so the innocent party is entitled to recover any loss which flows from the misrepresentation, even if the loss could not have been foreseen. (See also *Watts* v *Spence.*)

Rust v Abbey Life Assurance Co Ltd See Vitol SA v Norelf Ltd

Ruxley Electronics and Construction Ltd v Forsyth [504]
[1995] 3 All ER 268 (House of Lords)

The plaintiffs undertook to build a swimming pool in the defendant's garden and the contract specified a maximum depth of 7ft 6in: after completion its maximum depth was 6ft 9in and, at the point where people would dive, only 6ft. The plaintiffs claimed the balance of the contract price and the defendant counter-claimed for damages for breach of contract. Although there had been a breach of contract, the judge found that the shortfall in depth had not decreased the pool's value: he gave judgment for the plaintiffs but awarded the defendant £2,500 by way of general damages for loss of pleasure and amenity. The Court of Appeal awarded the defendant (in place of general damages) the cost of replacing the pool. *Held,* the plaintiffs' appeal would be allowed and the judge's judgment restored. 'Damages are designed to compensate for an established loss and not to provide a gratuitous benefit to the aggrieved party, from which it follows that the reasonableness of an award of damages is to be linked directly to the loss sustained ... Thus in the present appeal the respondent has acquired a perfectly serviceable swimming pool, albeit one lacking the specified depth. His loss is thus not the lack of a usable pool with consequent need to construct a new one. Indeed were he to receive the cost of building a new one and retain the existing one he would have recovered not compensation for loss but a very substantial gratuitous benefit, something which damages are not intended to provide' (per LORD JAUNCEY OF TULLICHETTLE). '... if, as the judge found, [the defendant] had no intention of rebuilding the pool, he has lost nothing except the difference in value, if any ... The basic rule of damages, to which exemplary damages are the only exception, is that they are compensatory not punitive ... *Addis* v *Gramophone Co Ltd* established the general rule that in claims for breach of contract, the plaintiff cannot recover damages for his injured feelings. But the rule, like most rules, is subject to exceptions. One of the well-established exceptions is when the object of the contract is to afford pleasure, as, for example, where the plaintiff has booked a holiday with a tour operator ... see *Jarvis* v *Swans Tours Ltd* and *Jackson* v

Horizon Holidays Ltd. This was, as I understand it, the principle which [the judge] applied in the present case. He took the view that the contract was one "for the provision of a pleasurable amenity". In the event, [the defendant's] pleasure was not so great as it would have been if the swimming pool had been 7 ft 6 in deep. This was a view which the judge was entitled to take. If it involves a further inroad on the rule in *Addis* v *Gramophone Co Ltd* then so be it. But I prefer to regard it as a logical application or adaptation of the existing exception to a new situation ...' (*per* LORD LLOYD OF BERWICK).

Ryan v Mutual Tontine Westminster Chambers Association [505]
[1893] 1 Ch 116 (Court of Appeal)

By the terms of a lease of a residential flat the landlords covenanted to provide a porter, who was to be constantly in attendance, or, during his temporary absence, a trustworthy assistant. The landlords appointed one Benton to be porter but, while he spent much of his time acting as chef at a neighbouring club, boys and charwomen performed his duties as porter. *Held,* the landlords were in breach of their covenant but the court would not grant an injunction to restrain the continuance of the breach or order the covenant to be specifically enforced. (Distinguished in *Posner* v *Scott-Lewis.*)

Said v Butt [1920] 3 KB 497 [506]

The proprietors of a theatre, the defendants, had good reason for excluding the plaintiff from their theatre and refused to sell him a ticket for the first performance of a play. The plaintiff asked a friend to buy a ticket in his own name on the plaintiff's behalf, which he did, but when the plaintiff attempted to gain admission his way was barred. The plaintiff claimed damages. *Held,* the identity of the plaintiff was a material factor in the formation of a contract as a result of the sale of the ticket; as the plaintiff's identity had not been disclosed, no contract had come into existence and his claim would not be successful. (See also *Sowler* v *Potter.*)

St Albans City and District Council v International [507]
Computers Ltd (1994) The Times 11 November

Owing to an error in the software supplied by the defendants, the plaintiffs' community charge rate was set too low and they suffered a total loss of £1,314,846. A term of the contract (on the defendants' standard terms and conditions) between the parties limited the defendants' liability to £100,000. *Held,* the plaintiffs were entitled to recover their total loss. It was immaterial that the shortfall had been made up by borrowing from the plaintiffs' general fund and that the deficit was passed on to the chargepayers the following year. Further, in the light of ss3, 6, 7 and 11(4) of and Schedule 2 to the Unfair Contract Terms Act 1977, the defendants had failed, on the facts, to establish that the exclusion clause was fair and reasonable. (See also *Walker* v *Boyle.*)

St John Shipping Corporation v Joseph Rank Ltd [508]
[1956] 3 All ER 683

A ship was overloaded and the master was prosecuted for a statutory criminal offence. The holders of a bill of lading in respect of part of the cargo carried by the ship paid most of the freight due, but withheld a sum equivalent to the overall additional cargo by which it was found that the ship was overloaded. *Held,* they were not entitled to do so as the consideration and the matter to be performed were both legal and the right to claim freight had not been brought into existence by a crime. (Applied in *Euro-Diam Ltd* v *Bathurst*; see also *Hughes* v *Asset Managers plc* and *Howard* v *Shirlstar Container Transport Ltd*; but see *Allen* v *Rescous*.)

St Paul Fire and Marine Insurance Co (UK) Ltd v [509]
McConnell Dowell Constructors Ltd [1996] 1 All ER 96
(Court of Appeal)

The appellants contracted to build new parliament buildings for the Marshall Islands and the respondent underwriters provided construction works insurance. The insurance risk was undertaken on the basis that the building would have piled foundations: without telling the respondents, the appellants used spread foundations, which were shallower and less expensive. The building suffered subsidence damage in the course of construction and the respondents sought a declaration that they were entitled to avoid the policy on grounds of material misrepresentation and non-disclosure. *Held,* the declaration sought would be made. The type of foundations was a matter which would have affected a prudent insurer's estimate of the risk and it was, therefore, a material fact. On the evidence, the actual insurers would not have effected the cover on the same terms had they been aware of the change in the type of foundations. 'The right of an insurer to avoid the contract of insurance in the event of material misrepresentation made to him is no different from the law of contract generally. There is a difference in relation to non-disclosure, because there is no general obligation upon a contracting party to disclose even material facts to the other party (provided the non-disclosure does not make any positive representations misleading) whereas contracts of insurance, being of the utmost good faith (s17 of the 1906 [Marine Insurance] Act), do give rise to such a duty. The House of Lords decided unanimously in the *Pan Atlantic Insurance Co Ltd* v *Pine Top Insurance Co Ltd* case that the insurer's right of avoidance arises only when the misrepresentation, or non-disclosure, induced him to make the contract. This is part of the general law of contract and although not stated expressly must be regarded as an implied qualification of the right to avoid the contract under the Act ...' (*per* EVANS LJ).

Sajan Singh v Sardara Ali [1960] 1 All ER 269 (Privy Council) [510]

A, who wanted to acquire a lorry but to whom a haulier's permit would not be granted, entered into an arrangement whereby the lorry would be bought by and registered in the name of S, who would obtain the permit. This was done, and the lorry was used and operated by A, to whom it was ultimately sold, he having paid for it. These transactions were contrary to Malayan statutory ordinances. After some time, S took possession of the lorry without A's consent and refused to return it to A, denying that it had been sold to him. A sought a declaration that the lorry was his and for the return of the vehicle or its value, the action being framed in detinue. *Held,* although the transaction whereby A obtained the lorry was illegal, yet A acquired title to the lorry notwithstanding that it was not registered in his name. Accordingly, A was entitled to the relief he claimed. (See also *Bowmakers Ltd* v *Barnet Instruments Ltd* and *Belvoir Finance Co Ltd* v *Stapleton*.)

Satanita, The See Clarke v Dunraven

Saunders v Anglia Building Society [1970] 3 All ER 961 [511]
(House of Lords)

An elderly widow signed without reading a document which X told her was a deed of gift of her house in favour of her nephew. In fact, it was a purported assignment of the leasehold to X, and the old lady would not have signed had she known the facts. X mortgaged the house to the building society, and on his defaulting on the repayments due under the mortgage, they sought possession. *Held,* the plaintiff could not rely on a plea of non est factum as against the building society, because on the facts the transaction she intended and what she actually carried out were the same character, and she was bound by what she had signed. (Applied in *Avon Finance Co Ltd* v *Bridger;* see also *Norwich and Peterborough Building Society* v *Steed.*)

Scally v Southern Health and Social Services Board   **[512]**
[1991] 4 All ER 563 (House of Lords)

The contracts of service of the plaintiffs, doctors employed by the defendants, incorporated statutory regulations regarding superannuation rights and liabilities. These regulations were amended so as to give, for a time, employees the right to purchase 'added years', but these amendments were not brought to the plaintiffs' attention. *Held,* the defendants were in breach of an implied term of the plaintiffs' contracts of employment that they (the defendants) would take reasonable steps to bring the relevant amendment to the plaintiffs' attention in order that they might be in a position to enjoy its benefit. (See also *Liverpool City Council* v *Irwin.*)

Scammell and Nephew Ltd v Ouston [1941] 1 All ER 14   **[513]**
(House of Lords)

The respondents agreed to purchase a motor van from the appellants but their order was given on the understanding 'that the balance of the purchase price can be had on hire purchase terms over a period of two years'. *Held,* no precise meaning could be attributed to this clause as hire-purchase agreements varied widely and consequently there was no enforceable contract. There were no previous dealings between the parties or an accepted trade practice to which the court could refer to determine the hire-purchase terms and, in any case, their lordships found that the matter had not passed the stage of negotiation. (See also *McCutcheon* v *David MacBrayne Ltd;* but see *Nicolene Ltd* v *Simmonds.*)

Scandinavian Trading Tanker Co AB v Flota Petrolera   **[514]**
Ecuatoriana, The Scaptrade [1983] 2 All ER 763
(House of Lords)

Payments of hire under a charterparty were to be made monthly in advance and the charter also provided that if the charterers defaulted in paying by the due date the owners could withdraw the vessel from hire. As a payment due on 8 July had not been made, on 12 July, the sum due still being unpaid, the owners gave notice to the charterers withdrawing the vessel. Tender of the overdue hire was made on the following day, but it was refused. *Held,* time had been made of the essence of the contract, there had been a breach of that condition and the owners had been entitled to elect to treat the breach as putting an end to all primary obligations under the contract which had not already been performed. The court had no discretion in such a case to grant an injunction to restrain the owners from exercising their right of withdrawal as it was juristically indistinguishable from a decree for specific performance of a contract to render services. (See also *Whitwood Chemical Co* v *Hardman* and *Rickards (Charles) Ltd* v *Oppenheim.*)

Schebsman, Re, ex parte Official Receiver [1943]   **[515]**
2 All ER 768 (Court of Appeal)

Schebsman was for many years employed by a Swiss company and its English subsidiary. His employment was terminated and an agreement entered into whereby the English company would pay him £2,000 immediately and a further sum of £5,500 by instalments or, if he should die, such amount was to be paid to his widow and daughter. Schebsman was adjudicated bankrupt on 5 March 1942 and died a week later; his trustee in bankruptcy claimed the sums payable under the agreement to Schebsman's widow and daughter. *Held,* the trustee's claim would fail as the contract did not create a trust in favour of the widow and daughter. 'It appears to me that the provisions for the widow and daughter are the result of the mutual agreement and that the debtor had, in conjunction with the English company and the Swiss company, done all that was necessary to complete the title of the widow and daughter to whatever might be payable to them or either of them under the agreement. On payment to the widow or daughter the legal title to each payment was complete and I can see no equity to support the contention that there is any resulting trust in favour of the trustee in bankruptcy, for the payments result from the mutual agreement and not from a purchase or quasi-purchase by the debtor' (*per* LUXMOORE LJ). (See also *Re Miller's Agreement.*)

Schroeder (A) Music Publishing Co Ltd v Macaulay   **[516]**
[1974] 3 All ER 616 (House of Lords)

The plaintiff, an unknown song-writer, entered into an exclusive services agreement with the defendants in their standard form. Under it, he assigned copyright in existing works and works to be composed for a five year period. The defendants were under no obligation to publish the plaintiff's works. The plaintiff was entitled to £50 advance on royalties and further advances of £50 on recoupment of previous advances from royalties received. Only the defendants could terminate the agreement by notice. *Held,* the restraints in the agreement were not fair and reasonable. The contract was in unreasonable restraint of trade. (See also *Watson v Prager.*)

Scotson v Pegg (1861) 6 H & N 295   **[517]**

The plaintiffs entered into a contract to deliver a cargo of coal to another or to his order. That other directed the plaintiffs to deliver it to the defendant, who promised to discharge it at the rate of 49 tons per day, but this undertaking was not observed. *Held,* although the plaintiffs were already bound to deliver the coal in accordance with the order of another, there was sufficient consideration for the defendant's promise to unload the coal at the specified rate in that he received the benefit of the delivery of the coal. (See also *Chichester and Wife v Cobb.*)

Scott v Avery (1856) 5 HL Cas 811 (House of Lords)   **[518]**

An insurance policy in respect of a ship Alexander provided that the amount to be paid in respect of any loss was, in the first instance, to be ascertained by a certain committee but if the finding of that committee was unacceptable the matter was to be referred to arbitration. It was provided that the insurer was not entitled to maintain an action at law in respect of the policy until the arbitrators had given their decision. *Held,* this provision was lawful. It did not oust the jurisdiction of the court but imposed a valid condition that no action was maintainable until the arbitrators had made their award.

Scott v Coulson [1903] 2 Ch 249 (Court of Appeal)   **[519]**

The parties entered into a contract for the sale of a life policy in the belief that the assured was alive and the contract was completed by assignment. The assured was dead at the date on which the contract was made. *Held*, there had been a common mistake and the purchaser was entitled to have the assignment set aside. (See also *Galloway* v *Galloway*.)

Scott v Hanson (1829) 1 Russ & M 128   **[520]**

The defendant agreed to purchase land which was described in the particulars of sale as 'uncommonly rich water meadow'. In fact the land was very imperfectly watered. *Held*, this misrepresentation was not such as would enable the defendant to avoid performance of his contract. (But see *Brooke (Lord)* v *Rounthwaite*.)

Scott v Littledale (1858) 8 E & B 815   **[521]**

'The parties contracted for the sale of 100 chests of Congou tea then lying in bond 'ex the ship Star of the East'. The sale was by sample which the defendants, the sellers, believed to be a sample of the tea referred to in the agreement but in fact and by mistake the sample was of a totally different tea. *Held*, this mistake did not entitle the defendants to avoid the contract. (But see *Raffles* v *Wichelhaus*.)

Scriven Brothers & Co v Hindley & Co   **[522]**
[1913] 3 KB 564

An auctioneer, acting on the instructions of the plaintiffs, offered for sale a number of bales of hemp and tow, samples of which were on view before the sale. The catalogue did not disclose the difference in the nature of the commodities and although the samples were marked with the number of the lots it was not specified which was hemp and which was tow. When the tow was offered for sale the goods were knocked down to the defendants who thought they had been bidding for hemp. The auctioneer realised that the defendants had made a mistake, but he thought that they were mistaken only as to the value of tow. The plaintiffs sued to recover the amount of the defendants' bid. *Held*, their action must fail as there was no binding contract of sale. The parties had never been ad idem as the plaintiffs had intended to sell tow while the defendants thought they were buying hemp. (See also *Hartog* v *Colin & Shields*.)

Scruttons Ltd v Midland Silicones Ltd [1962] 1 All ER 1   **[523]**
(House of Lords)

The respondents were the consignees and owners of a drum of chemicals shipped in New York for carriage to London on the terms of the shipowners' standard bill of lading one clause of which had the effect of limiting the carrier's (ie, the shipowners') liability for damage to the drum to $500. For some years the shipowners had engaged the appellant stevedores to discharge their vessels at the Port of London and the agreement between them provided that the appellants should have 'such protection as is afforded by the terms ... of ... bills of lading'. While lowering the drum into a lorry the appellants negligently dropped it causing damage to it amounting to £593. The act of lowering the drum into the lorry was one which, by the terms of their agreement with the shipowners, the appellants had contracted with the shipowners to do and which, by the terms of the bill of lading, the shipowners had contracted with the respondents to do. The appellants admitted negligence but contended that they were entitled to rely on the provisions in the bill of lading limiting liability to $500 (£179). *Held*, they were not so entitled as they were strangers to the bill of lading and it is a general principle (to which this case was not an exception) that a stranger cannot rely for his protection on provisions in a contract (ie the bill of lading) to which he is not a party. (See also *Adler* v *Dickson*.)

Seaman v Fonereau (1743) 2 Stra 1183   [524]

The plaintiff insured his ship with the defendant in respect of a journey from Carolina to Holland and it afterwards appeared that at the time of making the contract he knew that his ship was leaky but this fact had not been disclosed to the defendant. The ship overcame these difficulties but was later taken by the Spaniards. *Held,* the defendant was not liable for this loss as a material circumstance had been concealed. It mattered not that the loss did not occur as a result of a weakness which had not been disclosed. (See also *London Assurance* v *Mansel*.)

Selectmove Ltd, Re [1995] 2 All ER 531 (Court of Appeal)   [525]

In talks with a collector of taxes the company had offered to pay by instalments its debts to the Inland Revenue and it was agreed for the purposes of the appeal that the inspector had said he would come back to the company if the arrangement was not acceptable. The company had begun paying the instalments and had not heard from the Revenue until October, when it had threatened that the company would be wound up if the arrears were not paid forthwith. Was the agreement legally binding? Counsel for the company relied on a passage in *Williams* v *Roffey Bros & Nicholls (Contractors) Ltd* for the proposition that a promise to perform an existing obligation could amount to good consideration provided there were practical benefits to the promisee. Although in that case the obligation was to supply goods and services, counsel argued that the same principle applied to an obligation to pay. *Held,* this was not the position: if that argument was accepted the principle in *Foakes* v *Beer* that an agreement to pay an existing debt by instalments was not enforceable would have no application. The fact that a creditor might derive practical benefit from agreeing with a debtor to take payment by instalments does not constitute consideration such as to make the arrangement legally binding on the creditor.

Sethia (KC) (1944) Ltd v Partabmull Rameshwar   [526]
[1950] 1 All ER 51 (Court of Appeal); affd [1951] 2 All ER 352

The sellers contracted to ship certain quantities of jute to Genoa but, because of export restrictions imposed by the Indian Government, less than one-third of the amount ordered was actually delivered. When sued for breach of contract the sellers contended that, in order to give the contract business efficacy, a term should be implied that delivery was 'subject to quota'. *Held,* such a term would not be read into the contract as the buyers could not have known whether the quota system would prevent the sellers, who had some choice in determining the extent of their quota, from supplying the jute and as similar contracts had been entered into 'subject to quota' it would not be implied that the parties had intended such a provision to be included on this occasion. (But see *Martin-Baker Aircraft Co Ltd* v *Canadian Flight Equipment Ltd*.)

Seven Seas Properties Ltd v Al-Essa (No 2)   [527]
[1993] 1 WLR 1083

The defendants offered two properties for sale and, the plaintiffs having found sub-purchasers, they contracted for the purchase and resale. The defendants were not aware of the resale contract (at a profit to the plaintiffs) until after both contracts had been signed. After discovering the resale contract, the defendants refused to complete the sale. As the resale could not be completed the sub-purchasers considered that they were discharged from their contract, but the plaintiffs obtained an order for specific performance against the defendants and the properties were then sold (at a loss to the plaintiffs) to the sub-purchasers. By way of damages, the plaintiffs claimed, inter alia, their loss of profit on the first resale contract. *Held,* their claim could not succeed as the defendants had not been on notice, at the date of the contract, of the plaintiffs' intention to enter into the resale contract. In other words, this loss had not been within the parties' contemplation. (Applied: *Hadley* v *Baxendale.*)

Shadwell v Shadwell (1860) 9 CBNS 159 [528]

The plaintiff's uncle wrote to offer him congratulations on his engagement and promised to pay him £150 pa until such time as he was earning £600 pa as a Chancery barrister. The plaintiff married, and sued his uncle's executors upon this promise. *Held,* although the plaintiff was already bound by his promise to marry, consideration for the uncle's promise could be found in the fact that the plaintiff had incurred financial liabilities in reliance upon the uncle's promise, which would therefore be enforced. (See also *Scotson* v *Pegg.*)

Shanklin Pier Ltd v Detel Products Ltd [1951] 2 All ER 471 [529]

The plaintiffs entered into a contract with a certain company for the repair of their pier and, in accordance with the terms of the contract, specified that the defendants' paint should be used for the work. The defendants had told the plaintiffs that their paint had a life of from seven to ten years but in fact it had a very short life and the plaintiffs were put to much extra expense. The plaintiffs claimed damages for breach of warranty. *Held,* they were entitled to succeed. (See also *Wells (Merstham) Ltd* v *Buckland Sand and Silica Co Ltd.*)

Shaw v Shaw [1965] 1 All ER 638 (Court of Appeal) [530]

The plaintiff alleged that by an oral agreement made in London he had agreed to pay the defendant £4,000 for a flat in Majorca and had in fact paid him that sum. He also alleged that in the agreement there was an implied term that the agreement was made subject to the giving of Treasury consent to the payment under statute, and that such consent had not been received. The plaintiff sought the recovery of £4,000. *Held,* his claim would fail. 'There was an agreement: there was an implied term; that was not fulfilled, and therefore under the [statute] the payment was an illegal payment, and it follows, under the ordinary principles of law, that, in the absence of any exemption being established, the unlawful payment cannot be recovered back by the person who made it and thereby committed an unlawful act' (*per* PEARSON LJ). (See also *Bostel Brothers Ltd* v *Hurlock.*)

Shine v General Guarantee Corp Ltd [1988] 1 All ER 911 [531]
(Court of Appeal)

The defendant finance company purchased an enthusiast's Fiat X19 from the third party which it then let to the plaintiff under a hire-purchase agreement, having described the car as being in good condition. The plaintiff subsequently discovered that the car had been written off by an insurance company after having been submerged in water for 24 hours. The plaintiff sued the defendants alleging breach of condition of merchantable quality implied by s14(2) of the Sale of

Goods Act 1979. *Held,* he was entitled to succeed: he had thought he was buying a secondhand enthusiast's car in good condition at a fair price when in fact he was buying, at the same price, a car which no one, knowing its history, would have bought at other than a substantially reduced price. (Applied: *Rogers v Parish (Scarborough) Ltd.* See now s14 of the 1979 Act, as amended.)

Shipton v Cardiff Corporation (1917) 87 LJKB 51   [532]

The Cardiff corporation passed a resolution to the effect that any officer or servant of the corporation who volunteered for military service would have his pay made up to the amount of salary or wages he was receiving while in their employment. The plaintiff enlisted contrary to the wishes and without the consent of the managers of his department and he sued to recover the difference between his past and present income. *Held,* he was entitled to succeed as the resolution was an offer which was accepted by the plaintiff when he volunteered. (See also *Carlill* v *Carbolic Smoke Ball Co.*)

Shove v Downs Surgical plc [1984] 1 All ER 7   [533]

The plaintiff's contract of employment was wrongfully terminated and questions arose as to the assessment of damages, particularly in relation to taxation. *Held,* the plaintiff's tax liability was not too remote to be taken into account when determining his actual loss. Accordingly, the court would estimate the net amount which would have been received by the plaintiff after deduction of tax and add an amount equivalent to his estimated tax liability so that the net amount represents as realistically as possible his actual loss. However, damages could not be awarded for the plaintiff's distress. (See also *Addis v Gramophone Co Ltd.*)

Simner v New India Assurance Co Ltd   [534]
(1994) The Times 21 July

In an action to recover sums due under a stop loss reinsurance policy, the question arose whether a potential assured was under a duty to make enquiries or investigations as to facts outside his knowledge for the purpose of complying with his duty of disclosure to an insurer. *Held,* this was not the case. In the light of ss17 to 19 of the Marine Insurance Act 1906 which codified the pre-existing common law and were generally as applicable to non-marine as to marine insurance, the duty on the assured was essentially to make a fair presentation of the risk to the insurer. The duty however was limited to circumstances which were known to the assured, with the proviso that the assured, like the insurer, was presumed to know every circumstance which, in the ordinary course of business, ought to be known by him. (But see *Pan Atlantic Insurance Co Ltd* v *Pine Top Insurance Co Ltd.*)

Simpkins v Pays [1955] 3 All ER 10   [535]

The defendant, her grand-daughter and the plaintiff, a lodger, submitted forecasts in a fashion competition organised by a Sunday newspaper but all the entries were made out in the defendant's name. The grand-daughter's entry was successful and the prize of £750 was paid to the defendant. The plaintiff attempted to enforce the defendant's promise that they would share the prize if one of their entries should succeed. *Held,* he was entitled to recover £250 as a sufficient intention to create legal relations could be found in this mutual arrangement. (See also *Edwards* v *Skyways Ltd.*)

Simpson v London and North Western Railway Co [536]
(1876) 1 QBD 274

'The plaintiff was in the habit of sending cattle spice, which he manufactured, for exhibition at cattle-shows in the hope of attracting customers. The defendants, a railway company, collected some of his samples from a show ground in Bedford for carriage to another show ground in Newcastle and the plaintiff told the defendants that the goods 'must be at Newcastle on Monday certain'. 'The samples were not delivered until the show was over. The plaintiff, who had journeyed to Newcastle to display the goods at the show, claimed damages for loss of profit and loss of time. *Held*, the plaintiff was entitled to succeed as it would be inferred, from the circumstances of the case, that the object of the contract of carriage was within the contemplation of the parties and the plaintiff's loss flowed naturally and probably from the failure of the object. 'The principle is now settled that, whenever either the object of the sender is specially brought to the notice of the carrier, or circumstances are known to the carrier from which the object ought in reason to be inferred, so that the object may be taken to have been within the contemplation of both parties, damages may be recovered for the natural consequences of the failure of that object' (*per* COCKBURN CJ). (But see *Horne* v *Midland Railway Co*.)

Sindall (William) plc v Cambridgeshire County Council [537]
[1994] 3 All ER 932 (Court of Appeal)

The plaintiff builders purchased from the defendants a potential building site for some £5m. Nineteen months later, after the plaintiffs had obtained planning permission for residential development (and the value of the land had more than halved), they discovered a private foul sewer buried in the land. The contract had provided that the purchasers took subject to any easements, etc, without prejudice to the vendor's duty to disclose all latent incumbrances, etc, known to them. In answer to a pre-contractual inquiry the defendants had said that they were not aware of any easements, etc. The presence of the sewer had not been known to either party at the time of the sale, but it subsequently appeared that it was recorded in documents held by the defendants' planning department although it had not been noted against the title deeds. The judge decided that the plaintiffs had been entitled to rescind the contract on grounds of misrepresentation and common mistake and, in exercise of his discretion under s2(2) of the Misrepresentation Act 1967, ordered the defendants to pay to them the full purchase price with interest. *Held*, the defendants' appeal would be allowed as, on the facts, there were no grounds for rescission for misrepresentation (the defendants had not been negligent) or mistake. Even if there had been misrepresentation, the presence of the sewer was not in practice a serious problem and damages rather than rescission should have been awarded. 'I should say that neither in *Grist* v *Bailey* nor in *Laurence* v *Lexcourt Holdings Ltd* [1978] 2 All ER 810 did the judges who decided those cases at first instance advert to the question of contractual allocation of risk. I am not sure that the decisions would have been the same if they had. In this case the contract says in express terms that it is subject to all easements other than those of which the vendor knows or has the means of knowledge. This allocates the risk of such incumbrances to the buyer and leaves no room for rescission on the grounds of mistake' (*per* HOFFMANN LJ).

Sky Petroleum Ltd v VIP Petroleum Ltd [538]
[1974] 1 All ER 954

The plaintiffs agreed with the defendants that, for a minimum period of ten years, they would buy all petrol for their filling stations from the defendants. Some three years later the defendants purported to terminate the agreement for an alleged breach of its terms by the plaintiffs, who brought an action and sought an interlocutory injunction to restrain the defendants from withholding petrol supplies from them. There was evidence that the plaintiffs had little prospect of finding alternative sources of supply at that time. *Held,* the injunction would be granted because the court could order specific performance of a contract to sell and purchase chattels which were not specific or ascertained in cases where damages would not provide a sufficient remedy, as was the case here. (See also *Lord Strathcona Steamship Co Ltd* v *Dominion Coal Co Ltd.*)

Slade v Metrodent Ltd [1953] 2 All ER 336   [539]

The plaintiff, a minor, was bound to the defendant as an apprentice dental mechanic. The agreement contained a clause to the effect that such disputes as should arise between the parties should be referred to arbitration. The plaintiff issued a writ claiming damages in respect of the alleged failure of the defendant to teach him the craft in question in accordance with the provisions of the apprenticeship deed. *Held,* assuming that the clause providing for arbitration was not for the plaintiff's benefit, the proceedings would nevertheless be stayed as the plaintiff was bound by the terms of the deed which, taken as a whole, was beneficial to him. (But see *De Francesco* v *Barnum.*)

Slater v Finning Ltd [1996] 3 All ER 398 (House of Lords)   [540]

The appellants engaged the respondent marine engine suppliers to repair the engine of their fishing vessel. The respondents fitted a new type of camshaft but it (and two replacements of the same type) failed at sea. The appellants claimed damages for breach of the implied condition as to reasonable fitness for purpose contained in s14(3) of the Sale of Goods Act 1979. The trial judge found that the trouble had not lain in the camshafts themselves but in some external feature peculiar to the ship of which the respondents had not been made aware. *Held,* the appellants' claim could not succeed. 'Where a buyer purchases goods from a seller who deals in goods of that description there is no breach of the implied condition of fitness where the failure of the goods to meet the intended purpose arises from an abnormal feature or idiosyncrasy, not made known to the seller, in the buyer or in the circumstances of the use of the goods by the buyer. That is the case whether or not the buyer is himself aware of the abnormal feature or idiosyncrasy ... Lord Griffiths put the illustration of a new front wheel tyre being purchased for a car which, unknown to the buyer or the seller, had a defect in the steering mechanism as a result of which the tyre wore out after a few hundred miles of use, instead of the many thousands which would normally be expected. In these circumstances it would be totally unreasonable that the seller should be liable for breach of s14(3). The present case is closely analogous' (*per* LORD KEITH OF KINKEL). (But see *R & B Customs Brokers Co Ltd* v *United Dominions Trust Ltd.*)

Smith v Eric S Bush, Harris v Wyre Forest District Council   [541]
[1989] 2 All ER 514 (House of Lords)

In the first of these two similar cases, having found a terraced property at the lower end of the housing market, the plaintiff applied to the Abbey National for a mortgage to enable her to buy it. The application form stated that she would be given a copy of the survey report and mortgage valuation obtained by the society; it also disclaimed responsibility for the contents of the report and valuation. The defendant surveyors inspected the property and their report contained a disclaimer in similar terms. On the strength of the report the plaintiff purchased the property, but after 18 months flues collapsed because chimney breasts had been removed, a fact the defendants had failed to notice. The plaintiff sought damages for negligence and the defendants relied on their disclaimer. *Held,* she was entitled to succeed. In the circumstances, it would not be 'fair and reasonable', within ss2(2) and 11(3) of the Unfair Contract Terms Act 1977, for the defendants to rely on the disclaimer. 'I expressly reserve my position in respect of valuations of quite different types of property ... such as industrial property, large blocks of flats or very expensive houses. In such cases ... it may be reasonable for the surveyors valuing on behalf of those who are providing the finance either to exclude or limit their liability to the purchaser' (*per* LORD GRIFFITHS). (See also *Phillips Products Ltd* v *Hyland.*)

Smith v Chadwick (1884) 9 App Cas 187 (House of Lords) [542]

A prospectus contained a statement that 'the present value of the turnover or output of the entire works is over £1,000,000 sterling per annum'. This statement was ambiguous in that it could mean that in one year the works produced goods worth £1,000,000, in which case it was untrue, or that the works were capable of this output, in which case it was correct. *Held,* in order to succeed in an action of deceit for fraudulent misrepresentation, the plaintiff had to prove that he had interpreted the statement in the sense in which it was false and that he had in fact been influenced by it in making his decision to take shares. The plaintiff failed to satisfy the court on these points. (But see *Edgington* v *Fitzmaurice.*)

Smith v Hughes (1871) LR 6 QB 597 [543]

The plaintiff, who was a farmer, offered to sell oats to the defendant, who was an owner and trainer of race-horses. The defendant's manager, who had taken a sample of the oats, wrote to the plaintiff on the following day to say that the defendant would buy them at a certain price but afterwards refused to accept delivery on the ground that the oats were new whereas he thought he was buying old oats. It was found that the plaintiff had not asserted that the oats were 'old' but that the defendant's manager believed that they were and the plaintiff knew that he entertained this mistaken belief. *Held,* the passive acquiescence of the plaintiff in the self-deception of the defendant's manager would not entitle the defendant to avoid the contract. 'It ... was pressed upon us that the defendant ... intended to buy old oats, and the plaintiff to sell new, so the two minds were not ad idem; and that consequently there was no contract. This argument proceeds on the fallacy of confounding what was merely a motive operating on the buyer to induce him to buy with one of the essential conditions of the contract ... All that can be said is, that the two minds were not ad idem as to the age of the oats; they certainly were ad idem as to the sale and purchase of them' (*per* COCKBURN CJ). (But see *Scriven Brothers & Co* v *Hindley & Co.*)

Smith v Land and House Property Corp (1884) [544]
38 Ch D 7 (Court of Appeal)

In the particulars of sale the plaintiffs said that their hotel was 'now held by a very desirable tenant ... for an unexpired term of twenty-eight years, at a rent of £400 pa.' The defendants resisted the plaintiffs' claim for specific performance on the ground of misdescription in that it afterwards appeared that the rent was in arrear at the time of the sale and the tenant shortly afterwards filed his petition for liquidation. *Held,* the contract should be rescinded as the description of the tenant as 'very desirable' was not an expression of opinion but a misrepresentation on the faith of which the defendants contracted to purchase the hotel. (But see *Bisset* v *Wilkinson.*)

Smith v South Wales Switchgear Ltd   [545]
[1978] 1 All ER 18 (House of Lords)

The respondents employed the appellants to carry out the annual overhaul of the electrical equipment in their factory. The contract stated that it was 'subject to our General Conditions of Contract 24001 obtainable on request'. The appellants did not ask for a copy but a copy of the second version of the conditions was sent to them. There was also an earlier and a later version, all with the number 24001. Each version contained an indemnity clause providing that the appellants would keep the respondents indemnified against any liability, loss, claim or proceedings whatsoever in respect of personal injury arising out of or in the course of execution of the work. While the work was being done, one of the appellants' electrical fitters was injured and was successful in his claim for damages against the respondents, whose negligence and/or breach of statutory duty caused the accident. It was further held that the respondents were entitled to be indemnified by the appellants under the indemnity clause. The appellants appealed arguing, amongst other things, that it was uncertain which of the three versions of the conditions applied. *Held,* the reference to the general conditions must be taken to refer to the edition current at the date of contract, ie, the last edition. Therefore that edition must be taken to have been incorporated. However, on its wording the indemnity clause was not wide enough to cover negligence and the appeal was allowed. (But see *Alderslade* v *Hendon Laundry Ltd.*)

Smith and Snipes Hall Farm Ltd v River Douglas   [546]
Catchment Board [1949] 2 All ER 179 (Court of Appeal)

In 1938 a catchment board, the defendants, covenanted with a Mrs Smith and ten other owners of land through which a river ran that they, the defendants, would 'widen and deepen and make good the banks of the river ... and maintain for all time the work when completed'. In 1940 the first plaintiff, one Smith, took a conveyance of Mrs Smith's land with the benefit of the agreement of 1938 and in 1944 Smith let the land to the second plaintiffs, Snipes Hill Farm Ltd. Two years later, owing to faulty work by the board, the banks burst and flooded the plaintiffs' land. The plaintiffs claimed damages for breach of contract and the defendants maintained that, if there was a breach, there was no privity of contract between the parties. *Held,* the defendants were liable as the covenant affected the use and value of the land and the benefit of the covenant was obviously intended to attach to the land and extend to any subsequent owners. (See also *Gregory and Parker* v *Williams* and s56(1) of the Law of Property Act 1925; but see *Beswick* v *Beswick.*)

Smith New Court Securities Ltd v Scrimgeour Vickers   [547]
(Asset Management) Ltd [1994] 4 All ER 225 (Court of Appeal)

On 21 July 1989 the plaintiffs purchased Ferranti shares from the first defendants, brokers for the second defendants (Citibank), at 82.25p per share. In September 1989 the value of Ferranti shares fell sharply following the discovery of fraud unrelated to the present proceedings. The plaintiffs sold the shares in November and the months following at prices ranging from 49p down to 30p. The judge found that the plaintiffs had been induced to buy the shares by fraudulent misrepresentations made on behalf of Citibank and that the value of the shares on 21 July, had the unrelated fraud then been discovered, was 44p. Absent the misrepresentations, on 21 July the plaintiffs had been willing to pay 78p per share. On what basis should the plaintiffs' damages be assessed? *Held,* they were entitled to the difference between the price paid (82.25p and the price, absent the misrepresentations, which the shares would have fetched on the open market on the day of purchase (78p). 'The remedies available to a party who has been induced to enter into a contract by a fraudulent misrepresentation are rescission and damages. Rescission is a restitutionary remedy ... It is however a necessary condition of this remedy ... that the plaintiff should be able to make substantial restitution in specie of the property which he has received. If [the plaintiffs] had retained the shares, [they] would have been able to return them and claim repayment of the full price, even though the value of the shares had fallen ... [they] accepted that [they] could not pursue the claim to restitution ... the date upon which the loss must be ascertained is the date of acquisition. The measure of damages is, in Lord Atkin's words, "the actual damage directly flowing from the fraudulent inducement" (see *Clark* v *Urquhart* [1930] AC 28). Depreciation of the value of the shares by market forces operating after the date of acquisition does not flow directly from the fraudulent inducement ... 78p was the market price on the date in question. The loss flowing from the misrepresentation was therefore 4.25p a share ...' *(per* NOURSE LJ). (But see *Naughton* v *O'Callaghan.)*

Snell v Unity Finance Ltd [1963] 3 All ER 50   [548]
(Court of Appeal)

The plaintiff as hirer sued the defendants, a finance company, in respect of the hire-purchase of a Hillman motor car. Although the point was not taken in the county court, in the course of evidence it became clear that there had been a contravention of the terms of the relevant statutory instrument, because a deposit of twenty per cent of the cash price had not been paid before entering into the hire-purchase agreement. *Held,* it was the court's duty, as it had been the duty of the county court judge, once the facts which made the hire-purchase agreement illegal had been brought to the court's attention, to refuse to lend the plaintiff the court's aid in enforcing the contract. (See also *Anderson Ltd* v *Daniel.)*

Snelling v John G Snelling Ltd [1972] 1 All ER 79   [549]

Three brothers were directors of the defendant company, which was financed by loans from them. In order to borrow money from a finance house, the three of them made a contract not to demand repayment of their loans to the company while the finance house loan was current. The company was not a party to the contract. It was a further term of the contract that if any of the brothers resigned his directorship, the money owed to him on loan would be forfeited. The plaintiff resigned his directorship and then sued the company for repayment of the loan. *Held,* although the company was not entitled to rely directly on the contract since it was not a party to it, the co-defendant brothers were entitled to a stay of proceedings and, since all the parties were before the court, the reality of the situation was that the plaintiff's claim had failed, and his action was dismissed. The co-defendant brothers, having proved a breach of the contract by the plaintiff, or an intention on his part to repudiate it, were entitled to a declaration that its provisions were binding on him. (See also *Beswick* v *Beswick.)*

Société Commerciale de Reassurance v ERAS   [550]
(International) Ltd [1992] 2 All ER 82n
(Court of Appeal)

Arising out of a claim to contribution in an insurance dispute, the question was whether s14A of the Limitation Act 1980 (which postpones in certain circumstances the starting of the limitation period) extends to actions in contract as well as applying to actions arising solely in tort. *Held,* it does not as the words 'any action for damages in negligence' denote an action asserting that the defendant has committed the tort of negligence and are not wide enough to comprise so-called 'contractual negligence'.

Solle v Butcher [1949] 2 All ER 1107 (Court of Appeal) **[551]**

The parties negotiated for the lease of a flat and, on the mistaken assumption that the rent was unaffected by the provisions of the Rent Acts, it was agreed that the rent should be £250 pa. It later appeared that the controlled rent was £140 pa, and the plaintiff sued to recover the rent which he alleged had been overpaid. *Held,* the plaintiff's claim to recover the amount of the rent overpaid should be dismissed but the lease would be set aside on the ground of a common mistake of fact and the plaintiff would have the option of surrendering the lease or remaining in possession and paying the full controlled rent. (See also *Cooper* v *Phibbs*; but see *Paget* v *Marshall.*)

Sowler v Potter [1939] 4 All ER 478 **[552]**

The defendant, whose name at the time was Ann Robinson, had been convicted for permitting disorderly conduct in a tea-room. Nearly two months after this conviction she changed her name to Ann Potter by deed poll but before this date she made an offer in the name which she was later to assume to take a lease of certain of the plaintiff's premises. The lease, which provided that the premises should be used for a restaurant or tea-room, was entered into after the defendant had legally changed her name. *Held,* the plaintiff was entitled to a declaration that the lease was void ab initio as she had granted the lease under the mistaken impression that the lessee was someone other than Ann Robinson whom she would have regarded as an undesirable tenant. (But see *Dennant* v *Skinner.*)

Spellman v Spellman [1961] 2 All ER 498 **[553]**
(Court of Appeal)

The parties were husband and wife, and when the relationship between them became less happy, it was thought that the purchase of a motor car might bring them together. To this end the husband entered into a hire-purchase agreement in respect of an Austin Healy Sprite and he told his wife that he had bought it for her. The wife's name was entered in the registration book, but shortly afterwards the husband left his wife and took the car with him. The wife claimed the car as a gift from her husband. *Held,* the wife should deliver up to her husband the registration book: she had no rights or ownership in respect of the car because, inter alia, 'there was not any intention to create legal situations, but merely an informal dealing with the matter between the husband and wife which is common in daily life and which does not result in some legal transaction, but is merely a matter of convenience' *(per* DANCKWERTS LJ). (See also *Simpkins* v *Pays.*)

Spencer v Harding (1870) LR 5 CP 561 **[554]**

The defendants issued a circular offering for sale certain stock-in-trade for which they invited tenders and the tender which the plaintiffs submitted turned out to be the highest. *Held,* there was no contract as the circular was a mere attempt to ascertain whether an offer could be obtained and was not a promise to sell to the person who made the highest tender. (See also *Rooke* v *Dawson*; but see *Blackpool and Fylde Aero Club Ltd* v *Blackpool Borough Council.*)

Spiro v Glencrown Properties Ltd [1991] 1 All ER 600 **[555]**

The plaintiff granted the first defendants an option to purchase a property in Finchley: this option satisfied the requirements of s2 of the Law of Property (Miscellaneous Provisions) Act 1989. They gave notice to exercise the option, but failed to complete the purchase. When the plaintiff sued, the first defendants and the second defendant (their guarantor) maintained that the notice was unenforceable as it had not complied with s2 of the 1989 Act. *Held*, the plaintiff was entitled to judgment as the notice, a unilateral act, was not caught by s2 of the Act of 1989. (See also *Record* v *Bell*.)

Spring v Guardian Assurance plc [1994] 3 All ER 129 **[556]**
(House of Lords)

'The plaintiff was dismissed by the defendants who gave such a bad reference to a prospective employer that it refused to have anything to do with him. In the plaintiff's action for damages the trial judge found, inter alia, that the defendants had been negligent in preparing the reference. *Held*, the plaintiff's action would be successful as, inter alia, an employer's duty to take reasonable care in preparing a reference could in appropriate circumstances be expressed as arising from an implied term of the contract of employment, ie that if a reference was supplied by the employer in respect of the employee, due care and skill would be exercised in its preparation. However, the duty arising under such an implied term did not add anything to the duty of care which their Lordships found had arisen in negligence.

Spurling (J) Ltd v Bradshaw [1956] 2 All ER 121 **[557]**
(Court of Appeal)

'The defendant, who had had previous business dealings with the plaintiffs, who were warehousemen, delivered to them eight barrels of orange juice for storage. A few days later he received a 'landing account' on which was printed a condition which exempted the plaintiffs from liability for any loss, damage or detention in respect of goods entrusted to them occasioned by the negligence, wrongful act or default of themselves, their servants or agents. When collected, the barrels were found to be either empty or so damaged as to be useless. The plaintiffs sought to recover their charges for storage and the defendant counter-claimed for damages for the alleged breach of an implied term of the contract of bailment to take reasonable care of the barrels. *Held*, assuming that the plaintiffs had been negligent, the defendant's counter-claim should fail as the plaintiffs were protected by the exemption clause.

Staffordshire Area Health Authority v **[558]**
South Staffordshire Water Works
[1978] 3 All ER 769 (Court of Appeal)

Under a 1929 agreement between a water company and a health authority, the company agreed to supply a specified number of gallons of water a day free of cost to a hospital 'at all times hereafter'. The cost of supplying water rose sharply over the years. The Water Act 1973 placed a statutory duty on the company to ensure that by 1981 its charges would not show preference to or discriminate against any class of persons. Because of this, and the increased costs of supplying water, the company sought to terminate the 1929 agreement. There was no express provision in the agreement for its termination by notice. *Held*, in the absence of any express provision, the agreement was impliedly terminable on reasonable notice. (See also *Martin-Baker Aircraft Co Ltd* v *Canadian Flight Equipment Ltd*.)

Startup v Macdonald (1843) 6 Man & G 593 **[559]**

The parties contracted for the sale of 10 tons of linseed oil to be delivered 'within the last fourteen days of March'. The plaintiffs delivered the oil at 8.30 pm on

31 March, a Saturday, and the defendant refused to accept delivery because of the lateness of the hour. *Held,* the plaintiffs were entitled to recover damages in respect of the defendant's non-acceptance of the oil. (See also *Fercometal SARL v Mediterranean Shipping Co SA, The Simona.*)

Steinberg v Scala (Leeds) Ltd [1923] 2 Ch 452 [560]
(Court of Appeal)

An infant applied for and was allotted certain shares. She paid the amount due on allotment and also the first call. Eighteen months later, while still an infant, she purported to repudiate the contract and sought repayment of the money she had paid. *Held,* her claim must fail as there had not been a total failure of consideration, the ground on which she could have succeeded.

Stenhouse Australia Ltd v Phillips [1974] 1 All ER 117 [561]
(Privy Council)

The defendant's contract of employment contained a clause whereby he undertook not, for a period of five years after termination of the contract, to engage in the business of insurance broking or solicit the clients of his employers. This restraint was to extend over a geographical area of 25 miles from Sydney. *Held,* the clause was valid, being reasonable and necessary for the protection of the plaintiff's business. The prohibition on soliciting was a narrow restraint which left open a wide field of unrestrained competitive activity by the employee, and the covenant extended only to a small number of clients, who were narrowly defined. (See also *Attwood* v *Lamont.*)

Stevenson, Jaques & Co v McLean (1880) 5 QBD 346 [562]

The defendant offered to sell iron to the plaintiffs at 40s per ton. The plaintiffs telegraphed to the defendant: 'Please wire whether you would accept forty for delivery over two months, or if not, longest limit you could give.' Later in the day a further telegram was sent to the defendant in which the plaintiffs accepted the original offer and when the plaintiffs sought to recover damages for breach of contract the defendant maintained that the first telegram was a counter-offer which had destroyed the offer which he originally made. *Held,* the plaintiffs' first telegram was not a rejection of the defendant's offer but an inquiry as to whether he would be prepared to modify its terms. (But see *Hyde* v *Wrench.*)

Stilk v Myrick (1809) 2 Camp 317 [563]

In the course of a voyage two seamen deserted and the captain, having tried in vain to replace them, entered into an agreement with the rest of the crew whereby, if they completed the voyage, they would have divided equally amongst them the wages of the deserters, in addition to their own wages. *Held,* the captain's promise was not binding. There was no consideration for the agreement as by their original contract the crew were bound to do all they could to complete the voyage. (But see *Hartley* v *Ponsonby* and *Williams* v *Roffey Bros & Nicholls (Contractors) Ltd.*)

Stockloser v Johnson [1954] 1 All ER 630 (Court of Appeal) [564]

The defendant agreed to sell to the plaintiff certain plant and machinery in two quarries and the agreement provided that payment was to be made by instalments. The agreement further provided that if the plaintiff made default in payment of an instalment for a period exceeding 28 days the defendant was entitled to retake possession of the plant and machinery and that in such event all instalments paid should be forfeited to the defendant. Two years later the plaintiff failed to pay the instalments due from him and the defendant rescinded the agreement. *Held,* the plaintiff was not entitled to recover the instalments which he had paid as the forfeiture clause did not operate to exact a penalty and it was not unconscionable for the defendant to retain them. 'In my judgment, there is no sufficient ground for interfering with the contractual rights of a vendor under forfeiture clauses of the nature which are now under consideration, while the contract is still subsisting, beyond giving a purchaser who is in default, but who is able and willing to proceed with the contract, a further opportunity of doing so; and no relief of any other nature can properly be given, in the absence of some special circumstances such as fraud, sharp practice, or other unconscionable conduct of the vendor, to a purchaser after the vendor has rescinded the contract' (*per* ROMER LJ). (See also *English Hop Growers Ltd* v *Dering*; but see *Workers Trust and Merchant Bank Ltd* v *Dojap Investments Ltd* and *Dies* v *British and International Mining and Finance Corp Ltd.*)

Stocks v Wilson [1913] 2 KB 235   [565]

By fraudulently representing that he was of full age, the defendant induced the plaintiff to sell and deliver to him certain of her furniture and effects for £300. The defendant sold some of the goods for £30 and gave a bill of sale of the residue by way of security for an advance of £100. The defendant failed to pay the purchase money and the plaintiff claimed the reasonable value of the goods by way of equitable relief. *Held,* the defendant was liable to pay the plaintiff the £130 which he had actually received. (But see *Leslie (R) Ltd* v *Sheill.*)

Strange (SW) Ltd v Mann [1965] 1 All ER 1069   [566]

The defendant was appointed manager of the plaintiff bookmakers in Cheltenham. His contract provided that he would not for a period of three years after the cessation of his employment 'be in any way directly or indirectly engaged or interested in the business of commission agents either on his own account or in partnership with any person or persons or as manager agent or director of any other person or persons' firm or company in the town of Cheltenham or at any place within 12 miles thereof'. Although nearly three times as many of the plaintiffs' customers lived within 12 miles of Cheltenham as outside that area, some 93 per cent of bets placed with the plaintiffs were placed over the telephone, and the rest by telegram or letter. When the defendant was dismissed from the plaintiffs' service he set up as a bookmaker in Gloucester (which is nine miles from Cheltenham). The plaintiffs sought to enforce the agreement. *Held,* they would fail because the service agreement was in unlawful restraint of trade and therefore void. There was nothing to show that the defendant has established such a personal relationship or confidence with customers living outside Cheltenham as would make it likely that such customers would seek him out after he had left the plaintiffs' employment and for this reason the relevant term of the agreement was not reasonably necessary in order to protect the plaintiffs' trade connexion' (*per* STAMP J). (But see *Fitch* v *Dewes.*)

Strickland v Turner (1852) 7 Exch 208   [567]

The plaintiff purchased an annuity in ignorance of the fact that the annuitant was already dead. *Held,* the plaintiff was entitled to recover the purchase money as it had been paid wholly without consideration, ie he had 'purchased' something which no longer existed. (See also *Couturier* v *Hastie.*)

Strongman (1945) Ltd v Sincock [1955] 3 All ER 90   **[568]**
(Court of Appeal)

An architect contracted with builders to supply materials and carry out work at his premises and, in accordance with the universal practice, promised orally that he would obtain all the necessary licences. Work considerably in excess of the licence granted was carried out. *Held,* the builders were entitled to damages for breach of the warranty or collateral contract to obtain the licences. (See also *Townsend (Builders) Ltd* v *Cinema News & Property Management Ltd.*)

Sudbrook Trading Estate Ltd v Eggleton [1982] 3 All ER 1   **[569]**
(House of Lords)

A clause in a lease gave the lessees an option to purchase the reversion at a price to be agreed by two valuers, one to be nominated by the lessors and the other by the lessees and, in default of agreement, by an umpire appointed by the valuers. The lessees sought to exercise the option, but the lessors refused to appoint a valuer, claiming that the option clause was void for uncertainty. *Held,* the option would be ordered to be specifically performed. The machinery by which the value of the property was to be ascertained was subsidiary and non-essential to the main part of the agreement and, the lessors having been in breach of contract in refusing to appoint a valuer, there was no reason why the court should not substitute its own machinery and this it would do by ordering an inquiry into the reversion's fair value.

Sugar v London Midland & Scottish Railway Co   **[570]**
[1941] 1 All ER 172

The plaintiff had purchased a ticket from the defendants in respect of a journey on their railway and received injuries as a result of their negligence. On the front of the ticket were the words 'For conditions see back. Day Excursion' and on the back the passenger was referred to conditions contained in railway time-tables and bills which protected the defendants against claims for damages for negligence. On the plaintiff's ticket the words 'For conditions see back' had been obliterated by the date stamp. *Held,* the plaintiff could recover damages in respect of her injuries as the defendants had not taken reasonable steps to bring the conditions excluding liability to her notice. (See also *McCutcheon* v *David MacBrayne Ltd.*)

Suisse Atlantique Société d'Armement Maritime SA   **[571]**
v NV Rotterdamsche Kolen Centrale [1966] 2 All ER 61
(House of Lords)

The parties entered into a consecutive voyage charterparty, which was to remain in force for two years, for the carriage of coal from the United Kingdom to Europe. It was agreed that if the vessel was delayed beyond her lay days, demurrage would be payable at the rate of $1,000 a day. Over the two year period the vessel only performed eight voyages. The shipowners maintained that she ought to have performed a further six voyages at least if the charterers had loaded and discharged the cargo more rapidly. They alleged that they were not limited to claiming the sum payable under the demurrage clause, but were entitled to recover the full loss of freight which they would have obtained had these other voyages been performed. *Held,* only demurrage was payable. No term could be implied into the contract that there was no obligation to pay for the greatest number of voyages which could have been made if no delays had been experienced. The charterparty might have provided for this, but had not done so. Moreover, although the shipowners might have been able to treat the delays occurring during the period of the charterparty as a repudiation of the contract, they had not done so, and had elected to treat all its provisions as still binding. NB The House of Lords laid down that there is no rule of law that an exemption clause is nullified by a 'fundamental breach of contract' or breach of a 'fundamental term'; in each case the question is one of construction of the contract. (See also *Photo Production Ltd* v *Securicor Transport Ltd.*)

Sumpter v Hedges [1898] 1 QB 673 (Court of Appeal)   [572]

The plaintiff, a builder, contracted to build two houses and stables upon the defendant's land for the sum of £565. The plaintiff did part of the work, amounting in value to about £333, and then abandoned the contract. The defendant completed the buildings and the plaintiff claimed payment in respect of that part of the work which he had carried out. *Held,* the defendant was not liable to pay on a quantum meruit as there was no inference of a fresh contract to do so. (But see *Dakin (H) & Co Ltd* v *Lee.*)

Surrey County Council v Bredero Homes Ltd [1993]   [573]
1 WLR 1361 (Court of Appeal)

In breach of covenant, the defendants built more houses on land transferred to them by the plaintiffs than had been agreed at the time of the transfer. Although they had been aware of the breach, the plaintiffs had not sought an injunction. However, after all the houses had been sold, by way of damages they claimed an amount equal to the sum which might have been obtained from the defendants for modification of the covenant so as to allow the more profitable development of the site. *Held,* since, on the facts, there had been no possibility of the court granting an injunction to restrain the development and the plaintiffs had not suffered any loss, they could recover only nominal damages. 'Every student is taught that the basis of assessing damages for breach of contract is the rule in *Hadley* v *Baxendale*, which is wholly concerned with the losses which can be compensated by damages. Such damages may, in an appropriate case, cover profit which the injured plaintiff has lost, but they do not cover an award to a plaintiff who has himself suffered no loss, of the profit which the defendant has gained for himself by his breach of contract' (*per* DILLON LJ). (But see *Jaggard* v *Sawyer.*)

Sutton v Sutton [1984] 1 All ER 168   [574]

A husband and wife bought the matrimonial home with the aid of a mortgage for which the husband alone was responsible: the wife contributed to the purchase but the house was conveyed into the husband's name alone. Some years later they separated, the husband sought a divorce and they orally agreed (i) that the wife would consent to a divorce, take over responsibility for the mortgage and not apply for maintenance and (ii) that the husband would let the wife keep her savings and transfer the house to her. This agreement was not made subject to the court's approval. The wife consented to the petition, paid off the mortgage and did not apply for maintenance: after the decree absolute, the husband refused to transfer the house and the wife sought an order for specific performance. *Held,* she could not succeed. Although, inter alia, there had been a sufficient act of part performance to overcome the lack of a memorandum or note of the agreement as required by s40 of the Law of Property Act 1925, the court's jurisdiction under the Matrimonial Causes Act 1973 to order maintenance and property adjustment could not be ousted by a private agreement between the parties and, accordingly, it would be contrary to public policy to enforce the contract. (Distinguished: *Goodinson* v *Goodinson* and *Williams* v *Williams.*)

Sutton & Co v Grey [1894] 1 QB 285 (Court of Appeal)   **[575]**

The plaintiffs, who were stockbrokers, entered into an oral agreement with the defendant that he should introduce clients to them on the understanding that he would be paid half of the commission resulting from such transactions as proved to be profitable and pay half of any loss which might be incurred. The plaintiffs claimed payment in respect of a transaction which had been unprofitable and the defendant relied on s4 of the Statute of Frauds. *Held,* the plaintiffs could recover as the defendant had an interest in the transaction independently of his promise by way of guarantee to pay half the loss on business which he introduced. The contract was entered into to regulate the terms of the defendant's employment by the plaintiffs and was not merely a promise to answer for the debt or default of another within the meaning of the statute. (See also *Couturier* v *Hastie*.)

Sybron Corp v Rochem Ltd [1983] 2 All ER 707   **[576]**
(Court of Appeal)

Opting for early retirement, the appellant employee, a manager, was entitled, at the respondent employers' discretion, to certain benefits under the company's pension scheme. The company exercised its discretion in the appellant's favour, but subsequently discovered that, during his employment, the appellant had been a party to fraudulent misconduct with subordinates. Accordingly, the respondents sought to recover the discretionary benefits. *Held,* they should succeed as payment of the benefits had been made under a mistake of fact induced by the appellant's breach of duty to disclose the fraudulent misconduct of the subordinate employees with whom he had acted. (But see *Bell* v *Lever Brothers Ltd*.)

Taddy & Co v Sterious & Co [1904] 1 Ch 354   **[577]**

The plaintiffs, Taddy & Co, were manufacturers of 'Myrtle Grove' tobacco and they stipulated that this tobacco should not be sold under a fixed minimum price. Taddy & Co sold some of this tobacco to a wholesaler and a term of this contract was that: 'Acceptance of the goods will be deemed a contract between the purchaser and Taddy & Co that he will observe these stipulations. In the case of a purchase by a retail dealer through a wholesale dealer, the latter shall be deemed to be the agent of Taddy & Co.' The wholesaler re-sold the tobacco to the defendants, Sterious & Co, who had notice of this condition but nevertheless sold to the public below the prescribed minimum price. *Held,* there was no contract between the parties which the plaintiffs could enforce as conditions cannot be attached to goods so as to bind all subsequent purchasers, even if they have notice of those conditions. (But see *Lord Strathcona Steamship Co Ltd* v *Dominion Coal Co Ltd*.)

Tamplin v James (1880) 15 Ch D 215 (Court of Appeal)   **[578]**

'The Ship Inn' and a saddler's shop adjoining were put up for sale by auction and the extent of the property to be sold was clearly marked on plans which were on view in the auction room. At the back of the property were two pieces of garden which originally belonged to the vendors, the plaintiffs, but which were now let to them by the present owners. The tenants of the inn and shop used and enjoyed these gardens and the defendant, who purchased the inn and shop at the auction, refused to complete his purchase on the ground that he believed that he was buying the freehold of all that was in the occupation of the plaintiffs' tenants. The defendant said that he had not seen the plans which correctly delineated the property to be sold. *Held,* the plaintiffs were entitled to specific performance as the fact that the purchaser had made this mistake without any excuse ought not to enable him to escape from his bargain. (But see *Paget* v *Marshall* and *Patel* v *Ali*.)

Tamplin (FA) Steamship Co Ltd v Anglo-Mexican [579]
Petroleum Products Co Ltd [1916] 2 AC 397 (House of Lords)

The respondents chartered a ship for five years from December 1912 for the purpose of carrying oil. The ship was requisitioned by the Government in December 1914 and the appellants maintained that this had the effect of determining the charterparty. The respondents were willing to continue to pay the agreed freight and, of course, to receive the larger sum paid by the Government by way of compensation which would be payable to the appellants if it could be shown that the contract had been frustrated. *Held*, the requisitioning of the ship did not have the effect of determining or suspending the charterparty. (But see *Marshall* v *Glanvill*.)

Tatam v Reeve [1893] 1 QB 44 [580]

The plaintiff received a letter from the defendant asking him to settle four accounts on his behalf. The plaintiff paid the money to the persons named in the letter and sued to recover £148 as money paid to the use of the defendant at the defendant's request. It afterwards appeared that the money was due from the defendant in respect of losing bets on horse-races but this fact was not known to the plaintiff at the time of complying with the defendant's request. *Held*, the plaintiff's action would be unsuccessful as its purpose was to recover money paid 'in respect of ' a gaming contract within s1 of the Gaming Act 1892. (But see *Re O'Shea*.)

Tatem (W J) Ltd v Gamboa [1938] 3 All ER 135 [581]
(Court of Appeal)

The defendants hired a ship from the plaintiffs during the Spanish Civil War for the purpose of evacuating refugees. 'The ship was seized by a nationalist cruiser and the plaintiffs sued to recover the amount of hire which they alleged was due in respect of the period for which the ship was in nationalist hands. *Held*, the plaintiffs' claim must fail as the seizure of the ship had destroyed the foundation of the contract which would therefore be regarded as having been frustrated. (See also *Constantine (Joseph) Steamship Line Ltd* v *Imperial Smelting Corporation Ltd*.)

Taylor v Bowers (1876) 1 QBD 291 (Court of Appeal) [582]

The plaintiff, who was financially embarrassed, made over all his stock-in-trade, including a portable steam engine and threshing machine, to one Alcock, and fictitious bills of exchange were given in the plaintiff's favour as the pretended consideration for the assignment. The stock was removed by Alcock and later charged to the defendant, who knew of the unlawful assignment, without the knowledge of the plaintiff. The plaintiff sued to recover the goods. *Held*, he was entitled to succeed. Nothing had been done to carry out the fraudulent or illegal object of the transaction beyond the delivery of the goods to Alcock. The charge would be set aside and as the plaintiff had repudiated the whole transaction he could recover his property from the defendant. (But see *Bigos* v *Bousted*.)

Taylor v Caldwell (1863) 3 B & S 826 [583]

The plaintiffs entered into an agreement with the defendants for the hire of a certain music hall for the purpose of giving a series of concerts. Before the series was due to begin the hall was destroyed by accidental fire. *Held,* the plaintiffs could not recover damages as the destruction of the hall excused both parties from the performance of their promises. (But see *London and Northern Estates Co* v *Schlesinger.*)

Taylor v Chester (1869) LR 4 QB 309 [584]

The plaintiff, at the request of the defendant, delivered to the defendant half a promissory note for £50 as a pledge or security for the payment of £20. The money was due in respect of wine and suppers supplied to the plaintiff and divers prostitutes in the defendant's brothel. The plaintiff sued for the re-delivery of the note. *Held,* the plaintiff's claim would fail as he had to base his claim upon an immoral transaction to which he was himself a party. (Applied in *Tinsley* v *Milligan*; but see *Bowmakers Ltd* v *Barnet Instruments Ltd.*)

Thacker v Hardy (1878) 4 QBD 685 (Court of Appeal) [585]

The plaintiff, a stockbroker, was employed by the defendant to speculate on his behalf on the Stock Exchange and to pay him the 'differences' between the cost of the stock and the amount for which it was sold. The plaintiff knew that the defendant was a mere speculator and quite unable to pay for stocks bought or to deliver those sold. The defendant sued to recover his commission on these transactions and also claimed an indemnity against such liability as he might incur. *Held,* the action would succeed as the agreement between the parties was not a wagering contract which was rendered void (See also *Ellesmere (Earl)* v *Wallace*; but see *Universal Stock Exchange Ltd* v *David Strachan.*)

Thake v Maurice [1986] 1 All ER 497 (Court of Appeal) [586]

The defendant surgeon carried out a vasectomy on the plaintiff husband but the plaintiff wife subsequently became pregnant and gave birth to a baby girl. *Held,* the defendant had not been in breach of contract because his obligation was to carry out the operation with reasonable skill and care rather than to sterilise the plaintiff husband. However, the defendant had been guilty of negligence in failing to give his usual warning that there was a slight risk that the first plaintiff might become fertile again. Damages were awarded for the birth and upkeep of the child and for distress, pain and suffering which were not cancelled out by the relief and joy felt after the birth of a healthy baby. (But see *Eyre* v *Measday.*)

Thomas v Thomas (1842) 2 QB 851 [587]

Before his death the plaintiff's husband said that he wished the plaintiff to have the use of a certain house. In deference to his wish the defendant and his co-executor entered into an agreement, the effect of which was to allow the plaintiff to occupy the house in consideration of the express desire of her husband and the payment of £1 pa towards the ground rent. *Held,* the husband's desire was not consideration but the agreement was binding as the undertaking to pay £1 pa was valuable consideration although by no means adequate. (See also *Rann* v *Hughes.*)

Thompson v Lohan (T) (Plant Hire) Ltd [588]
[1987] 2 All ER 631 (Court of Appeal)

The first defendants, a plant hire company, hired an excavator with a driver to the third party for use at the third party's quarry. Condition 8 of certain standard conditions provided that drivers were to be regarded as the hirers' servants or agents and that they (the hirers) alone were responsible for all claims. Condition 13 stipulated that hirers would 'fully and completely' indemnify the owners. The plaintiff's husband was killed as a result of the driver's negligence and, having had damages awarded against them, the first defendants sought to be indemnified by the third party. *Held,* they were entitled to succeed. Section 2(1) of the Unfair Contract Terms Act 1977 did not apply to strike down condition 8 as that provision was not concerned with arrangements made by a wrongdoer with others for sharing or transferring the burden of compensating the victim. That condition was therefore effective and, under condition 13, the first defendants were entitled to their indemnity. (Distinguished: *Phillips Products Ltd* v *Hyland.*)

Thompson v London, Midland and Scottish Railway Co   [589]
[1930] 1 KB 41 (Court of Appeal)

The plaintiff, who could not read, was handed an excursion ticket on the face of which were printed the words: 'Excursion. For conditions see back'. On the back was a notice that the ticket was issued subject to the conditions in the defendant company's timetables and excursion bills, and the excursion bills stated that excursion tickets were issued subject to the conditions in the company's timetables. The timetables, which cost 6d each, excluded liability 'in respect of ... injury (fatal or otherwise)'. The plaintiff received injuries on the journey and claimed damages. *Held,* her action must fail. The fact that she could not read did not alter the legal position and she was bound by the contract which she made when she accepted the excursion ticket; the reference to the company's timetables was sufficient notice of the terms of that contract. (But see *Sugar* v *London, Midland & Scottish Railway Co.*)

Thornton v Shoe Lane Parking Ltd [1971] 1 All ER 686   [590]
(Court of Appeal)

The plaintiff parked his car at the defendants' automatic car-park. On entering the car-park he passed through an automatic barrier, taking a ticket from the machine at the barrier. On the ticket, in small print, it was stated that the ticket was issued subject to conditions displayed on the premises. To find where the conditions were displayed the plaintiff would have had to drive the car into the garage and walk around. The conditions were lengthy but included one exempting the defendants not only from liability for damage to cars but also from liability for any injury to a customer, howsoever caused, whilst his car was in the carpark. The plaintiff later returned to collect his car and there was an accident in which he was severely injured. *Held,* the defendants were not protected by the exemption clause. In order to show that the plaintiff was bound by it, it was necessary to show either that he knew of it or that the defendants had done what was reasonably necessary to draw it to his attention. For this purpose, where the clause was exceptionally wide and was one which was not usual in that class of contract, it was not enough to show that the plaintiff had been given notice that the ticket was issued subject to conditions. It must be shown that adequate steps had been taken to draw his attention in the most explicit way to the particular exempting condition relied on. Here the defendants had failed to show that the plaintiff knew of the condition or that they had taken sufficient steps to draw his attention to it. (Applied in *Interfoto Picture Library Ltd* v *Stiletto Visual Programmes Ltd*; see also *Parker* v *South Eastern Rail Co* and *Mendelssohn* v *Normand Ltd.*)

Thoroughgood's Case (1584) 2 Co Rep 9   [591]

A deed releasing all claims was read to an illiterate woman and she executed it on being told that it concerned arrears of rent. *Held,* the deed was null and void.

Tinn v Hoffmann & Co (1873) 29 LT 271 [592]

The plaintiff wrote to the defendant and asked him to quote his lowest price for 800 tons of iron. In reply to his inquiry the defendant offered the iron at 69s per ton and concluded the letter 'waiting your reply by return'. It was conceded that as the offer was not accepted by return there was no contract and the view was expressed that the requirement that acceptance should be by return of post would be satisfied if the reply was sent by any other method, such as a telegram or messenger, provided it reached its destination not later than a letter sent by return of post would have been delivered. (See also *Compagnie de Commerce, etc* v *Parkinson Stove Co Ltd.*)

Tinsley v Milligan [1993] 3 WLR 126 (House of Lords) [593]

The parties, women and lovers, using money which came ultimately from their joint business, bought a house which they agreed would be put into the name of one of them (the plaintiff) in order to facilitate fraudulent claims by the other (the defendant) for housing benefit. Shortly thereafter they quarrelled and the plaintiff moved out, but she now claimed possession and ownership of the whole of the house, contending that the defendant's counterclaim to joint ownership was tainted by illegality and therefore could not succeed. *Held*, the house was held by the plaintiff on trust for the parties in equal shares as, in establishing her equitable proprietary interest, the defendant had not needed to rely on the illegal arrangement. 'In my judgment the time has come to decide clearly that the rule is the same whether a plaintiff founds himself on a legal or equitable title: he is entitled to recover if he is not forced to plead or rely on the illegality, even if it emerges that the title on which he relied was acquired in the course of carrying through an illegal transaction. As applied in the present case, that principle would operate as follows. The [defendant] established a resulting trust by showing that she had contributed to the purchase price of the house and that there was a common understanding between her and the [plaintiff] that they owned the house equally. She had no need to allege or prove *why* the house was conveyed into the name of the [plaintiff] alone, since that fact was irrelevant to her claim: it was enough to show that the house was in fact vested in the [plaintiff] alone. The illegality only emerged at all because the [plaintiff] sought to raise it. Having proved these facts, the [defendant] had raised a presumption of resulting trust. There was no evidence to rebut that presumption. Therefore the [defendant] should succeed' (*per* LORD BROWNE-WILKINSON). (But see *Alexander* v *Rayson* and *Taylor* v *Chester.*)

Tool Metal Manufacturing Co Ltd v Tungsten [594]
Electric Co Ltd [1955] 2 All ER 657 (House of Lords)

The appellants granted the respondents a licence to import certain hard metal alloys for a period of 10 years from 1937 and thereafter until determined on six months' notice. The respondents agreed to pay a royalty in respect of such alloy as they used and an additional sum by way of 'compensation' if they used more than a specified amount, but payment of 'compensation' was suspended shortly after the outbreak of war in 1939. The appellants claimed compensation under the original agreement from 1 January 1947. *Held*, they were entitled to recover. Their promise to suspend payment of 'compensation' was binding upon them as it raised an equitable estoppel but they could resume their legal rights on giving reasonable notice to the respondents and this they had done when they delivered a counterclaim for 'compensation' from June 1945, in March 1946, in an action commenced by the respondents.

Torrance v Bolton (1872) 8 Ch App 118   **[595]**

Certain property was put up for sale by auction and in the advertised particulars it was described as an immediate absolute reversion of a freehold estate which would fall into possession on the death of a lady who was then in her 70th year. Before the property was sold the auctioneer's clerk read aloud the particulars and conditions of sale, which were not printed or circulated among those present, and one of these conditions stated that the property was sold subject to three mortgages. The land was bought by the plaintiff who said that he was deaf and did not understand that he was buying an equity of redemption. *Held*, the plaintiff was entitled to have the contract rescinded and his deposit returned as the vendor had not discharged the burden of showing that the purchaser was not actually misled. (But see *Tamplin v James.*)

Trollope and Colls Ltd v North West Metropolitan Regional   **[596]** Hospital Board [1973] 2 All ER 260 (House of Lords)

The respondents engaged the appellants to build a hospital and research centre, the work to be carried out in phases. The contract provided for the date of commencement of Phase III to be fixed by reference to the completion date of Phase I. The third phase was to be completed by a specified date. As a result of delays on Phase I for which the contract provided extensions of time, an unreasonably short time was left to complete the final phase. *Held*, no term for extending the date for completion of Phase III could be implied. The express terms were clear and unambiguous. A term could only be implied if the court found that the parties must have intended it to form part of their contract, and it must be one necessary to give business efficacy to the contract.

Tsakiroglou & Co Ltd v Noblee and Thorl GmbH   **[597]**
[1961] 2 All ER 179 (House of Lords)

By a contract dated 4 October 1956 the appellants agreed to sell to the respondents 300 tons of Sudanese groundnuts cif Hamburg, shipment during November/December 1956. As a result of the invasion of Egypt by Israel the Suez Canal was blocked to shipping from 2 November 1956 to April 1957. *Held*, the contract had not been frustrated as a term that the groundnuts were to be shipped via the Suez Canal would not be implied and shipping via the Cape of Good Hope did not render the contract fundamentally or radically different. 'An increase of expense is not a ground of frustration' (*per* VISCOUNT SIMONDS). (See also *Ocean Tramp Tankers Corporation v V/O Soufracht*; but see *Pioneer Shipping Ltd v BTP Tioxide Ltd, The Nema.*)

Tulk v Moxhay (1848) 2 Ph 774   **[598]**

The plaintiff, who owned several houses in Leicester Square, sold the gardens in the centre of the square to one Elms who covenanted, for himself, his heirs, and assigns, that he would keep the gardens and railings around them in their present condition and continue to allow the inhabitants of the square to have the use and enjoyment of the gardens. The land in question was sold to the defendant and the conveyance to him did not contain a covenant in similar terms although he knew of the restriction contained in the deed to which the plaintiff and Elms were parties. The defendant announced that he intended to build on the land and the plaintiff, who still remained the owner of several adjacent houses, sought an injunction to restrain him from doing so. *Held*, the injunction would be granted as the covenant would be enforced in equity against all subsequent purchasers with notice. (But see *Taddy & Co v Sterious & Co* and *Rhone v Stephens.*)

Turner v Green [1895] 2 Ch 205 [599]

Shortly before an interview between the parties' solicitors at which an action was compromised, the plaintiff's solicitor received a telegram informing him of the outcome of certain proceedings in the action which was favourable to the defendant. The plaintiff's solicitor did not disclose this information until the terms of the settlement had been agreed. *Held,* the defendant was bound by the terms of the settlement as there was no obligation on the plaintiff's solicitor to disclose all he knew. Mere silence as regards a material fact, which the solicitor was not bound to disclose, was not a ground for rescission of the compromise or a defence to specific performance.

Tweddle v Atkinson (1861) 1 B & S 393 [600]

The plaintiff's father and father-in-law agreed with each other to pay the plaintiff £100 and £200 respectively in consideration of his then intended marriage and after the marriage had taken place they confirmed their agreement in writing. The £200 was not paid and the plaintiff sued his father-in-law's executor to recover this sum. *Held,* his action must fail as no stranger to the consideration can take advantage of a contract, although made for his benefit. A promisee cannot bring a successful action unless the consideration for the promise moved from him. (See also *Dunlop Pneumatic Tyre Co Ltd* v *Selfridge & Co Ltd.*)

UBAF Ltd v European American Banking Corp [601]
[1984] 2 All ER 226 (Court of Appeal)

The defendant New York bank invited the plaintiff English bank to participate in a syndicate loan to a Panamanian shipping group, the defendants' assistant secretary supplying the plaintiffs with information about the group. The plaintiffs duly participated, but the group encountered financial difficulties and defaulted on the loans. The plaintiffs sued, inter alia, for damages under s2(1) of the Misrepresentation Act 1967 and the defendants relied, inter alia, on s6 of the Statute of Frauds Amendment Act 1828, arguing that any representations had not been signed by 'the party to be charged'. *Held,* the defendants' contention would be rejected as the assistant secretary had been acting in the course of his duties. Further, any failure by the defendants to inform the plaintiffs that security for the loan was insufficient was a continuing breach of their fiduciary duty which would, for the purposes of s32(1)(b) of the Limitation Act 1980, prevent time from running until the plaintiffs discovered the concealment or could with reasonable diligence have done so.

United Bank of Kuwait plc v Sahib [1996] 3 All ER 215 [602]
(Court of Appeal)

The main question was whether the rule that a deposit of a property's title deeds by way of security created an equitable mortgage of that property without any writing had survived the coming into force of s2 of the Law of Property (Miscellaneous Provisions) Act 1989. *Held,* it had not. Such a deposit took effect as a contract to create a mortgage and, as such, it came within s2 of the 1989 Act. (But see *Spiro* v *Glencrown Properties Ltd.*)

United Dominions Trust Ltd v Western [603]
[1975] 3 All ER 1017 (Court of Appeal)

The defendant agreed to buy a car for £550 from dealers on hire-purchase. He paid £34 deposit and signed the plaintiffs' standard form in blank, leaving the dealers to fill in the figures. The form sent to the plaintiffs was in fact for a loan agreement and the figures inserted were £730 for the purchase price and £185 for the deposit. The plaintiffs accepted the document as containing figures agreed between the defendant and the dealers and as constituting a contract between them and the defendant. When the defendant received the copy document he realised that it was not in accordance with the agreement between himself and the dealers but he did nothing to rectify the mistake and paid no instalments. The plaintiffs claimed £750. *Held,* for the purposes of the doctrine of non est factum, to distinguish between the careless signing of a completed document and a document in blank was neither right on the authorities nor acceptable to common sense. In permitting the dealer to complete the intended contractual document the onus was on the defendant to show that he had acted carefully, and that onus had not been discharged. The transaction which the document purported to effect was not essentially different in substance or in kind from the transaction intended and therefore could not be considered void. (See also *Saunders* v *Anglia Building Society.*)

Universal Corporation v Five Ways Properties Ltd   [604]
[1979] 1 All ER 552 (Court of Appeal)

Prospective purchasers of property paid a 10 per cent deposit of the purchase price. Due to a change in the exchange control regulations, the purchasers were unable to transfer funds from abroad. The vendors rescinded the contract and claimed to forfeit the deposit. The purchasers claimed repayment of the deposit on grounds, inter alia, of frustration. *Held,* although the purchasers had been unable to complete, the contract itself was not incapable of performance and had therefore not been frustrated. Even if the doctrine of frustration applies to sales of land, the mere inability of a purchaser to pay the purchase price on the completion date is not sufficient to frustrate the contract. (See also *National Carriers Ltd* v *Panalpina (Northern) Ltd.*)

Universal Stock Exchange Ltd v David Strachan   [605]
[1896] AC 166 (House of Lords)

The parties contracted for the sale and purchase of stocks on the secret understanding that the stock should never be called for or delivered although the contract between them provided that either party could require completion of the purchase and delivery or receipt of the stocks. *Held,* such a contract was nevertheless void by reason of s18 of the Gaming Act 1845 as it was really a gambling transaction, but securities deposited to secure the payment of these 'differences' could be recovered. (But see *Morgan Grenfell & Co Ltd* v *Welwyn Hatfield District Council.*)

Vanbergen v St Edmund's Properties Ltd   [606]
[1933] 2 KB 223 (Court of Appeal)

The plaintiff owed £208 to the defendants whose solicitors agreed that if this amount was paid into a bank at Eastbourne to their account they would withhold service of a bankruptcy notice. The plaintiff paid the money as arranged but the bankruptcy notice was served; the plaintiff contended that this was a breach of contract and that consideration for the defendants' solicitors' promise not to serve the bankruptcy notice was to be found in his payment into a bank at Eastbourne to the solicitors' account, whereas in the normal course of events it would have been paid to the defendants directly. *Held,* the action must fail as the agreement as to the place and method of payment was to oblige the plaintiff and of no benefit to the defendants and therefore was not sufficient consideration to support the promise to withhold service of the bankruptcy notice.

Vancouver Malt and Sake Brewing Co Ltd v   [607]
Vancouver Breweries Ltd [1934] AC 181 (Privy Council)

The appellants held a brewer's licence which entitled them to brew beer, but they had never brewed any liquor other than sake, a Japanese drink made from rice. The respondents, who held a similar licence but confined their activities to the brewing of beer, purported to purchase the goodwill of the appellants' brewer's licence for $15,000 and the appellants covenanted that they would not for 15 years engage in the manufacture or sale of beer. *Held,* the agreement was void as it was an agreement in restraint of trade. As the appellants did not in fact brew beer the contract contained in effect a bare covenant against competition which was not linked with any proprietary interest which would have justified the imposition of the restraint. (But see *Alec Lobb (Garages) Ltd* v *Total Oil GB Ltd.*)

Vandepitte v Preferred Accident Insurance   [608]
Corporation of New York [1933] AC 70 (Privy Council)

Mrs Vandepitte, the plaintiff, was being driven by her husband when their car was in collision with one driven by Jean Berry. Jean was driving her father's car with his permission and the plaintiff obtained a judgment, which was not satisfied, against her in respect of injuries which she received in the accident. Jean's father was insured with the defendants against third-party risks and the policy covered accidents which might occur while Jean was driving. The plaintiff sought to recover the amount of the judgment which she had previously obtained against Jean from the defendants and founded her claim on a local statute which enabled an injured person to avail himself of any rights possessed by the driver of the vehicle against the insurance company where an action against the negligent motorist had been unfruitful. *Held,* the plaintiff's action would fail as Jean was not a party to the contract of insurance and there was no evidence that her father had intended to create a trust in her favour. (See also *Re Schebsman.*)

Varley v Whipp [1900] 1 QB 513   [609]

The plaintiff agreed to sell a reaping machine to the defendant, stating that it was nearly new, and had been used only to cut 50 or 60 acres. The defendant had not seen the machine. On delivery, he returned it to the plaintiff as not answering to description, as it was extremely old. The plaintiff sued for the price, and the defendant pleaded that there had been a breach of the condition that goods will correspond with description, implied by what is now s13 of the Sale of Goods Act 1979. *Held,* this was a sale by description, and the defendant's argument prevailed. (See also *Beale* v *Taylor*; but see *Harlington & Leinster Enterprises Ltd* v *Christopher Hull Fine Art Ltd.*)

Varney v Hickman (1847) 5 CB 271   [610]

The action was brought to recover the sum of £20 deposited by the plaintiff with the defendant, as stakeholder, pending the outcome of a trotting match. Before the race was run, the plaintiff gave notice to the defendant that he repudiated the wager and demanded the return of his £20. *Held,* the plaintiff was entitled to recover the amount of the wager as at the time at which he asked for it to be refunded it was still in the hands of the defendant. (See also *Diggle* v *Higgs.*)

Victoria Laundry (Windsor) Ltd v Newman **[611]**
Industries Ltd [1949] 1 All ER 997 (Court of Appeal)

The plaintiffs, who were launderers and dyers, agreed to buy a boiler from the defendants. The defendants knew that the boiler was wanted for immediate use but, as a result of an accident which occurred while the boiler was being dismantled for removal to the plaintiffs' premises, delivery actually took place five months after the date specified in the contract. The plaintiffs claimed damages for breach of contract. *Held,* the plaintiffs were entitled to recover the profit which might reasonably have been expected to result from the normal use of the boiler during the five months in question but no account could be taken of the exceptionally profitable character of some of the contracts which they lost. (See also *Hadley* v *Baxendale* and *Koufos* v *C Czarnikow Ltd.*)

Vitol SA v Norelf Ltd [1996] 3 All ER 193 (House of Lords) **[612]**

The respondents contracted to buy from the appellants a cargo of propane with loading between 1 and 7 March 1991. The contract also required the appellants to tender a bill of lading promptly after the cargo was loaded on to the *Santa Clara*. By telex on 8 March the respondents told the appellants that they (the respondents) had been advised that loading would not be completed until 9 March and therefore that they would have to reject the cargo and repudiate the contract. The telex came to the appellants' notice on 11 March: loading had been completed on 9 March, a Saturday. The appellants failed to tender a bill of lading or to do anything else to affirm or perform the contract. Indeed, from 12 March they attempted to resell the cargo and succeeded in doing so – at a substantially lower price – on 15 March. The central issue was whether, as a matter of law, an aggrieved party can ever accept a repudiation of a contract merely by himself failing to perform the contract. *Held,* he could, depending on the particular contractual relationship and the particular circumstances of the case. The arbitrator's award in favour of the appellants would be restored. 'I am satisfied that a failure to perform may sometimes signify to a repudiating party an election by the aggrieved party to treat the contract as at an end ... Taking the present case as illustrative, it is important to bear in mind that the tender of a bill of lading is the pre-condition to payment of the price. Why should an arbitrator not be able to infer that when, in the days and weeks following loading and the sailing of the vessel, the seller failed to tender a bill of lading to the buyer, he clearly conveyed to a trader that he was treating the contract as at an end? ... Sometimes in the practical world of businessmen an omission to act may be as pregnant with meaning as a positive declaration. While the analogy of offer and acceptance is imperfect, it is not without significance that while the general principle is that there can be no acceptance of an offer by silence [see, eg, *Felthouse* v *Bindley*], our law does in exceptional cases recognise acceptance of an offer by silence. Thus in *Rust* v *Abbey Life Assurance Co Ltd* [1979] 2 Lloyd's Rep 334 the Court of Appeal held that a failure by a proposed insured to reject a proffered insurance policy for seven months justified on its own an inference of acceptance ... [Here] the arbitrator inferred an election, and communication of it, from the tenor of the rejection telex and the failure inter alia to tender the bill of lading. That was an issue of fact within the exclusive jurisdiction of the arbitrator' (*per* LORD STEYN). (But see *Fercometal SARL* v *Mediterranean Shipping Co SA*.)

Walford v Miles [1992] 1 All ER 453 (House of Lords) **[613]**

The respondents decided to sell their photographic processing business and received an offer of £1.9m from a third party. They had also negotiated with the appellants and had agreed in principle to sell the business to them for £2m. They further agreed with the appellants that, provided the appellants supplied a comfort letter from their bank, they 'would terminate negotiations with any third party'. The comfort letter was duly supplied and the respondents confirmed, subject to contract, the sale to the appellants for £2m. However, they sold the business to the third party and the appellants claimed damages for breach of the collateral 'lock-out' agreement alleging that it contained an implied term that, so long as the respondents desired to sell the business, they would continue to negotiate with the appellants in good faith. *Held,* while a lock-out agreement for good consideration could constitute an enforceable contract, here it did not as it was for an unspecified period and the court could not be expected to decide whether, subjectively, a proper reason had existed for the termination of the negotiations. It followed that the appellants' claim could not succeed. (But see *Hillas & Co v Arcos Ltd* and *Pitt v PHH Asset Management Ltd.*)

Walker v Boyle [1982] 1 All ER 634   **[614]**

When dealing with the sale of his wife's property, in answer to a preliminary inquiry a husband stated that to the vendor's knowledge there were no boundary disputes. He genuinely believed, but without reasonable grounds, that this was the case: in fact there was a dispute with a neighbour and his statement therefore amounted to an innocent misrepresentation. Contracts were exchanged and one clause of the standard form provided that 'no error, mis-statement or omission in any preliminary answer concerning the property ... shall annul the sale'. The purchaser sought rescission of the contract and the return of his deposit. *Held,* he was entitled to succeed as the vendor could not rely on the special condition, the true facts being within her knowledge. Even if the special condition had applied, it did not satisfy the requirements as to reasonableness set out in s11(1) of the Unfair Contract Terms Act 1977 and it was an exclusion clause within s3 of the Misrepresentation Act 1967. Further, s2(1) of the 1967 Act entitled the purchaser to loss of interest on his deposit. (See also *St Albans City and District Council v International Computers Ltd.*)

Wallis, Son and Wells v Pratt and Haynes   **[615]**
[1911] AC 394 (House of Lords)

The defendants sold a quantity of seed to the plaintiffs, describing it as 'common English sainfoin'. The plaintiffs re-sold it to X, by whom it was sown. It was later discovered to be 'giant sainfoin'. In seed, the two plants were indistinguishable, but 'common English sainfoin' was more valuable than 'giant sainfoin'. The plaintiffs claimed damages for breach of the condition as to description implied by what is now s13 of the Sale of Goods Act 1979, while the defendants relied on an exemption clause excluding all 'warranties, express or implied, as to growth or description'. *Held,* the exemption clause was inadequate to protect the defendants, who were liable. (But see *Reardon Smith Line Ltd v Hansen-Tangen.*)

Ward v Byham [1956] 2 All ER 318 (Court of Appeal)   **[616]**

The parents of an illegitimate child lived together for some years but the father then turned the mother out and later offered to let her have the child and to pay her an allowance of £1 per week, provided that the child was well looked after and happy. The mother took the child away and maintained it according to her promise but when, some months later, she married, the father discontinued the payments. When the mother sought to enforce the continuance of the payments the father contended that there was no consideration for his promise to pay £1 per week as the mother, in looking after the child, was only doing something that she was legally bound to do. *Held,* the agreement would be enforced as the mother, by undertaking that the child should be happy, had promised to do more than was required of her by statute. (See also *Williams* v *Williams.*)

Warlow v Harrison (1859) 29 LJQB 14   **[617]**

The defendant offered a horse for sale without reserve and the plaintiff made a bid for it which was the highest received apart from one from the owner upon whose instructions the horse was then withdrawn from the sale. *Held,* the plaintiff could not recover, but three of the judges took the view that if the plaintiff had argued that the highest bona fide bidder at an auction sale may sue the auctioneer upon his promise that the sale shall be without reserve, he would have been successful. (But see *Fenwick* v *Macdonald, Fraser & Co Ltd.*)

Warner Brothers Pictures Inc v Nelson   **[618]**
[1936] 3 All ER 160

Bette Davis entered into a contract with the plaintiffs, initially for a term of one year, but giving the plaintiffs the option of extending it, whereby she agreed that she would not undertake other film work without obtaining their written consent. The plaintiffs sought an injunction to restrain her from doing film work for another in breach of this agreement. *Held,* the injunction would be granted for the period of the continuance of the contract or for three years, whichever was the shorter. (See also *Lumley* v *Wagner.*)

Warren v Mendy [1989] 3 All ER 103 (Court of Appeal)   **[619]**

The plaintiff contracted to manage exclusively a professional boxer for three years. Within a few months the boxer agreed that the defendant should be his 'agent'. The plaintiff sought, inter alia, an injunction to restrain the defendant from inducing the boxer to breach his contract with him. *Held,* the injunction would not be granted as it would have the effect of compelling the boxer to perform his positive obligations under the contract, if he was to maintain his skill as a boxer, when he had lost confidence in the plaintiff's ability to act as his manager. (See also *Whitwood Chemical Co* v *Hardman.*)

Watson v Prager [1991] 3 All ER 487   **[620]**

The plaintiff professional boxer entered into an agreement with the defendant whereby the defendant would be his manager and promoter for three years. If, during that time, the plaintiff became a champion, the defendant could extend the agreement for a further three years. The plaintiff won the Commonwealth championship and the defendant exercised his extension option. The plaintiff contended that he was no longer bound by the agreement as it was in unreasonable restraint of trade. The agreement was in a form prescribed by the British Boxing Board of Control. *Held,* nevertheless, it was subject to the restraint of trade doctrine and it was unreasonable, particularly because the defendant's financial interests as promoter conflicted with his fiduciary duty as manager to obtain for the plaintiff the most advantageous financial terms possible. As the plaintiff had decided not to abide by the agreement it no longer had legal effect. (See also *M & S Drapers* v *Reynolds.*)

Watts v Morrow [1991] 4 All ER 937 (Court of Appeal)   **[621]**

Relying on the defendant surveyor's survey to the effect that the property's overall condition was sound, the plaintiffs bought Nutford Farm House for £177,500. After taking possession the plaintiffs discovered substantial defects in need of urgent attention and they had the necessary work carried out at a cost of £33,961. They sought to recover the cost of these repairs from the defendant and it was common ground that, in its true condition, the value of the house at the date of purchase had been £162,500. The judge awarded the plaintiffs the cost of the repairs and £8,000 for distress and inconvenience. The defendant appealed. *Held*, applying the principle of restitution, the plaintiffs were entitled to the amount required to put them in the position in which they would have been if the defendant had carried out the contract of survey properly, ie, £15,000, the amount they were caused to pay more than the property's value in its true condition. Further, the plaintiffs were not entitled to damages for mental distress not caused by physical discomfort or inconvenience resulting from the breach and damages under this head would therefore be reduced to £1,500 for physical discomfort. (See also *Hayes* v *James & Charles Dodd*.)

Watts v Spence [1975] 2 All ER 528 [622]

A husband and wife were joint owners of a house. The husband represented to the plaintiff that *he* owned the house and was in a position to sell. As a result, the plaintiff entered into a contract with the husband to buy the house. The wife, who had no knowledge of the discussions, refused to consent to the sale. The plaintiff claimed against the husband damages for misrepresentation under s2(1) of the Misrepresentation Act 1967. *Held*, the plaintiff's claim should succeed. The purchaser was not limited to damages measured by expenses incurred in consequence of the misrepresentation, but was entitled to damages for loss of bargain. (See also *Royscot Trust Ltd* v *Rogerson*.)

Webber v Lee (1882) 9 QBD 315 [623]

There was an agreement by which the defendant orally promised to pay £100 for certain shooting rights and in return he was to receive one-quarter of the game killed. *Held*, the agreement came within the provisions of what became s40 of the Law of Property Act 1925 (see now s2 of the Law of Property (Miscellaneous Provisions) Act 1989) in that the shooting rights were an interest in land and the plaintiff could not enforce payment of the amount promised unless the agreement complied with the requirements of that section. (See also *Lavery* v *Pursell*.)

Webster v Cecil (1861) 30 Beav 62 [624]

The defendant wrote to offer to sell some property to the plaintiff for £1,250. Although the defendant had already refused to sell this land to the plaintiff for £2,000, the plaintiff, who therefore had knowledge of the mistake, wrote to accept the offer contained in the defendant's letter. The defendant had intended that the price should be £2,250 and he immediately gave notice of the error. *Held*, a decree of specific performance would not be granted. (See also *Roberts (A) & Co Ltd* v *Leicestershire County Council*.)

Welby v Drake (1825) 1 C & P 557 [625]

The defendant drew a bill for £18 odd which was returned unaccepted. The plaintiff agreed that if the defendant's father would pay him £9 he would accept that amount in full satisfaction of the debt. The £9 was duly paid. *Held*, the plaintiff could not recover the balance from the defendant because by suing the son he committed a fraud on the father, who paid £9 on the understanding that his son would be discharged from further liability. (See also *Hirachand Punamchand* v *Temple*.)

Wells (Merstham) Ltd v Buckland Sand and   [626]
Silica Co Ltd [1964] 1 All ER 41

The plaintiffs were chrysanthemum growers and the defendants sellers of sand. The defendants produced a sample of their BW sand, and also a detailed analysis, and it appeared that this sand was of the quality required by the plaintiffs for use in their nursery. Upon being assured by the defendants that the sand delivered would conform to the analysis (as it later appeared, a misrepresentation which was made innocently), the plaintiffs decided to purchase some but, in order to reduce transport costs, placed the order through another firm. Thus the contract of sale was not between the plaintiffs and the defendants but between the plaintiffs and the other firm. The sand delivered purported to be BW sand but it contained an excess of iron oxide (ie it did not conform to the analysis) and, when it was used, it had a disastrous effect upon the plaintiffs' young chrysanthemums. The plaintiffs sued the defendants for damages for breach of warranty. *Held,* the plaintiffs were entitled to succeed as the warranty or collateral contract was enforceable notwithstanding the fact that the main contract was subsequently entered into between the plaintiffs and a third party. 'As between A (a potential seller of goods) and B (a potential buyer), two ingredients, and two only, are in my judgment required in order to bring about a collateral contract containing a warranty: (1) a promise or assertion by A as to the nature, quality or quantity of the goods which B may reasonably regard as being made animo contrahendi, and (2) acquisition by B of the goods in reliance on that promise or assertion' (*per* EDMUND DAVIES J). (See also *Shanklin Pier Ltd v Detel Products Ltd.*)

Wettern Electric Ltd v Welsh Development Agency   [627]
[1983] 2 All ER 629

In a letter dated 21 June 1979 the defendants offered the plaintiffs a licence to occupy a factory unit for 12 months from 25 June 1979. Without completing the acceptance portion of the letter, the plaintiffs moved in on 25 June. Structural defects appeared and, by 18 December, the plaintiffs were forced to evacuate the premises and on that day they commenced proceedings claiming damages for breach of an implied term that the unit was of sound construction and would be reasonably suitable for their purposes. On the following day they returned the acceptance portion of the letter, duly completed. *Held,* the plaintiffs' action would succeed. They had become occupants under a contract on the terms contained in the letter as, inter alia, by occupying the unit they had offered to enter into a contractual licence on the letter's terms and, by permitting them to occupy, the defendants had accepted their offer. A term would be implied as the plaintiffs claimed because it was necessary to give the contract business efficacy. Although such terms would not be implied into contracts for the sale of land or the grant of a lease, this was merely a contract granting a licence to occupy the land. (Applied: *The Moorcock* and *Liverpool City Council v Irwin.*)

White v John Warrick & Co Ltd [1953] 2 All ER 1021   [628]
(Court of Appeal)

The plaintiff contracted for the hire of a trademen's tricycle for use in the delivery of newspapers. The contract provided that 'Nothing in this agreement shall render the owners liable for any personal injuries to the riders of the machines hired' and another clause stipulated that the defendants agreed 'to maintain the machines in working order and condition'. *Held,* the clause which purported to exclude the defendants' liability would protect them from breach of their contractual obligation to maintain the machines but was not wide enough to exclude their liability in tort apart from contract should actual negligence be established. (See also *Alderslade v Hendon Laundry Ltd.*)

White and Carter (Councils) Ltd v McGregor [629]
[1961] 3 All ER 1178 (House of Lords)

The respondent's sales manager, acting within his authority, entered into a contract with the appellants for the fixing to litter bins of plates advertising the respondent's business. On the same day upon hearing of the contract, the respondent wrote to the appellants to cancel the agreement, but the appellants refused to accept this cancellation. The contract was for a period of 156 weeks and, under the terms of the contract, if any instalment was unpaid for four weeks, the whole of the amount due for the 156 weeks, or the remainder of that period, became due and payable. The respondent did not pay the first instalment within the time allowed and the appellants sought to recover the whole price. *Held,* they were entitled to succeed. 'If one party to a contract repudiates it ... the other party, the innocent party, has an option. He may accept that repudiation and sue for damages for breach of contract whether or not the time for performance has come; or he may if he chooses disregard or refuse to accept it and then the contract remains in full effect ... It is ... impossible to say that the appellants should be deprived of their right to claim the contract price merely because the benefit to them as against claiming damages and reletting their advertising space might be small in comparison with the loss to the respondent' (*per* LORD REID).

Whittington v Seale-Hayne (1900) 82 LT 49 [630]

The plaintiffs, who were lessees of certain premises which they used for breeding prize poultry, alleged that they had been induced to take up the lease by the representations of the defendant's agents, made during oral negotiations for the lease, that the premises were in a sanitary condition and in a good state of repair. The plaintiffs further alleged that in consequence of the insanitary condition of the premises their manager and his family became very ill and the poultry either died or became valueless for the purpose of breeding. The local authority declared that because of defective drainage the premises were unfit for human habitation. The plaintiffs contended that they were entitled to an indemnity against the consequences of entering into the contract which included losses in respect of stock and medical expenses. *Held,* their claim would fail as it was really a claim for damages which could not be awarded at that time in a case of innocent misrepresentation, but they were entitled to an indemnity in respect of those things which were required to be performed by the terms of the lease and this included rent, rates and repairs. (See also *Lamare* v *Dixon.*)

Whitwood Chemical Co v Hardman [1891] 2 Ch 416 [631]
(Court of Appeal)

The defendant, a manufacturing chemist, contracted to serve the plaintiffs for a period of 10 years and to give his whole time to their business. The defendant took steps to form a rival company and the plaintiffs wished to restrain him. *Held,* an injunction would not be granted and the plaintiffs should seek their remedy in damages. 'What injunction can be granted in this particular case which will not be, in substance, and effect, a decree for specific performance of this agreement?' (*per* LINDLEY LJ). (See also *Francis* v *Municipal Councillors of Kuala Lumpur, Scandinavian Trading Tanker Co AB* v *Flota Petrolera Ecuatoriana, The Scaptrade* and *Warren* v *Mendy.*)

Wilkie v London Passenger Transport Board [1947] [632]
1 All ER 258 (Court of Appeal)

The plaintiff was injured when attempting to board a bus. The accident was caused through the conductor's negligence. The plaintiff was himself a bus driver, and at the time of the accident was travelling on a free pass, issued and accepted on condition that neither the defendants nor their servants were liable to the holder for 'loss of life, injury or delay or other loss of or damage to property however caused'. *Held,* the pass was a mere licence and not a document conferring a contractual right, and the condition exempting liability prevailed. (But see *Gore* v *Van der Lann*.)

Williams v Bayley (1866) LR 1 HL 200 (House of Lords)   [633]

A son forged his father's signature on certain promissory notes. When the forgery, which the son did not deny, was discovered the bankers arranged a meeting with his father and issued veiled threats to the effect that if some settlement was not made the son would be prosecuted. The father thereupon executed an agreement to make an equitable mortgage of his property and the forged promissory notes were returned to him. *Held,* the agreement was invalid as in these circumstances the father could not be said to have entered into it freely and voluntarily. (See also *Davies* v *London and Provincial Marine Insurance Co.*)

Williams v Carwardine (1833) 5 C & P 566   [634]

The defendant had advertised that he would pay a reward of £20 to the person who gave information which led to the conviction of a certain murderer. The plaintiff knew of the reward but confessed that she gave the information required 'in consequence of her miserable and unhappy situation, and believing that she had not long to live ... to ease her conscience, and in hopes of forgiveness hereafter.' *Held,* she was entitled to the reward although she did not give the information for the sake of £20 or because she had seen the advertisement, 'but from stings of conscience'. (But see *Fitch* v *Snedaker*.)

Williams v Roffey Bros & Nicholls (Contractors) Ltd   [635]
[1990] 1 All ER 512 (Court of Appeal)

Having contracted to refurbish a block of flats, the defendants sub-contracted the carpentry work to the plaintiff and it was an implied term that the plaintiff would receive interim payments. After completing and being paid for some of the work, the plaintiff found himself in financial difficulty, largely because his price had been too low. Aware of these things, and facing themselves a penalty clause on the main contract, the defendants agreed to pay the plaintiff extra money to continue with the work and complete it on time. When sued, the defendants maintained that the agreement to pay extra money was unenforceable as it was not supported by any consideration. *Held,* the plaintiff was entitled to the extra money as the advantages which the defendant hoped to obtain (avoidance of a penalty or need to engage another sub-contractor) amounted to consideration. (Approved: *Stilk* v *Myrick*; but see *Re Selectmove Ltd*.)

Williams v Williams [1957] 1 All ER 305   [636]
(Court of Appeal)

A wife deserted her husband and they later entered into an agreement whereby the husband undertook to pay the wife £1 10s per week during their joint lives 'so long as the wife shall lead a chaste life'. The wife agreed that out of the weekly sum she would support and maintain herself; that she would indemnify the husband against all debts which she incurred, that she would not pledge her husband's credit and that she would not so long as the husband made the payments punctually bring any matrimonial proceedings other than proceedings for divorce. The wife sued to recover arrears of maintenance but the husband contended that there was no consideration for his promise to pay and that for this reason the agreement could not be enforced against him. *Held,* the husband was liable to pay the arrears as the wife's promise to maintain herself and indemnify the husband and not to pledge his credit was consideration for the husband's promise to pay her maintenance. The clause relating to the bringing of matrimonial proceedings was void and was not therefore a bar to these proceedings. (Distinguished in *Sutton* v *Sutton*; but see *Stilk* v *Myrick*.)

Wilson v Best Travel Ltd [1993] 1 All ER 353   [637]

The plaintiff booked a holiday on Kos through the defendant tour operator. While there, she fell through glass patio doors at the hotel and sustained serious injuries. The doors satisfied the requirements of Greek, but not British, safety standards and the plaintiff claimed damages, alleging that the defendants were in breach of the duty of care implied by s13 of the Supply of Goods and Services Act 1982. *Held,* her action could not succeed as, on the facts, the defendants had not failed to exercise reasonable care to exclude from their brochure accommodation in which guests could not stay with reasonable safety. (But see *Wong Mee Wan* v *Kwan Kin Travel Services Ltd*.)

Wilson v Wilson (1848) 1 HL Cas 538 (House of Lords)   [638]

Differences arose between a husband and wife and the wife left the matrimonial home. A deed of separation was entered into and when the wife sued to enforce the agreement the husband contended that it was contrary to public policy for the courts to entertain such a suit. *Held,* the deed would be enforced as it was not contrary to public policy to make provision for the wife in the event of a present separation. (But see *Brodie* v *Brodie*.)

Winter Garden Theatre (London) Ltd v Millennium   [639]
Productions Ltd [1947] 2 All ER 331 (House of Lords)

The appellants granted the respondents a licence for the use of their theatre for two periods of six months and thereafter the appellants agreed that the respondents were 'to have the option of further continuing the licence of the theatre on the payment each week of a flat rental of £300 per week and you will give us one month's notice of your intention of then terminating the licence'. The licence made no provision for its termination by the appellants but after more than three years from the date of the original licence they purported to give the respondents one month's notice to withdraw from the premises. *Held,* the notice was valid and effectual as the licence was not perpetual and could be determined by the appellants by giving sufficient notice, and in these circumstances notice of one month was sufficient. (But see *Sethia (KC) (1944) Ltd* v *Partabmull Rameshwar*.)

Withers v General Theatre Corp Ltd See Malik v Bank of Credit and Commerce International SA

Wong Mee Wan v Kwan Kin Travel Services Ltd   [640]
[1995] 4 All ER 745 (Privy Council)

A Hong Kong resident (Miss Ho Shui Yee) contracted with the defendant Hong Kong travel company to take a package guided tour to Pak Tang Lake, China. The tour included a crossing of the lake. The group missed the ferry and the guide said that the crossing would have to be made by speedboat. Neither the guide nor the inexperienced driver was an employee of the defendants. The speedboat hit a junk: Miss Ho Shui Yee drowned. Her mother, the plaintiff, claimed damages for, inter alia, breach of contract. It was accepted that the guide and the driver had both been negligent, the guide because he had not ensured that the speedboat was driven by a person of reasonable competence. Had the defendants undertaken no more than that they would arrange for services to be provided by others as their agents (where the law would imply a term into the contract that they would use reasonable care and skill in selecting those other persons) or had they themselves undertaken to supply the services when, subject to any exemption clause, there would be implied into the contract a term that they would as suppliers carry out the services with reasonable care and skill? *Held*, on a true construction of the contract (as contained in the tour brochure), the latter was the case, even though some of the services were to be supplied by others. Since the crossing of the lake had not been undertaken with reasonable care and skill, the defendants were liable. (But see *Wilson* v *Best Travel Ltd*.)

Workers Trust and Merchant Bank Ltd v Dojap [641]
Investments Ltd [1993] AC 573 (Privy Council)

A contract for the sale of certain premises in Jamaica at auction provided for payment of a deposit of 25 per cent which was to be forfeited if completion did not take place within 14 days, time being of the essence. The purchaser failed to complete on time and the vendor purported to forfeit the deposit. *Held*, the deposit should be repaid with interest, less an amount by way of damages for the loss suffered by the vendor by virtue of the purchaser's failure to complete. 'The question ... is whether or not the deposit of 25 per cent in this case was reasonable as being in line with the traditional concept of earnest money or was in truth a penalty intended to act in terrorem ... Since a true deposit may take effect as a penalty, albeit one permitted by law, it is hard to draw a line between a reasonable, permissible amount of penalty and an unreasonable, impermissible penalty. In their Lordships' view the correct approach is to start from the position that, without logic but by long continued usage both in the United Kingdom and formerly in Jamaica, the customary deposit has been 10 per cent. A vendor who seeks to obtain a larger amount by way of forfeitable deposit must show special circumstances which justify such a deposit ... [The] evidence falls far short of showing that it was reasonable to stipulate for a forfeitable deposit of 25 per cent of the purchase price or indeed any deposit in excess of 10 per cent' (*per* LORD BROWNE-WILKINSON). (But see *Stockloser* v *Johnson*.)

Wright v Carter [1903] 1 Ch 27 (Court of Appeal) [642]

Colonel Wright executed a trust in favour of his solicitor. The solicitor advised him to obtain independent advice from another solicitor but this solicitor was not fully informed of the actual circumstances of the matter. *Held,* the deed was void as Colonel Wright had not received advice from an independent solicitor who was fully aware of all the facts.

Wrotham Park Estate Co v Parkside Homes Ltd [643]
[1974] 1 WLR 798

In breach of covenant, the defendants started to build houses on certian land and the plaintiffs, who had the benefit of the covenant, sought an injunction (but not an interlocutory injunction) to restrain the building operations and the demolition of anything built in breach. By the time of the trial the houses had been completed and sold. *Held*, for social and economic reasons a mandatory injunction would not be granted but, in substitution for an injunction, although they had not suffered any financial loss, the plaintiffs would be awarded by way of damages such sum as might reasonably have been demanded by them as a quid pro quo for relaxing the covenant. (Applied in *Jaggard* v *Sawyer*; but see *Surrey County Council* v *Bredero Homes Ltd.*)

Wyatt v Kreglinger and Fernau [1933] 1 KB 793   [644]
(Court of Appeal)

When the plaintiff was 60 years of age and about to retire from the defendants' business they wrote to inform him that they would grant him a pension of £200 pa and that he would be at liberty to undertake any other employment, or enter into any business on his own account, except in the wool trade; the only other stipulation they attached to the continuance of the pension was that he did nothing at any time to their detriment (fair business competition excepted). The plaintiff acknowledged the receipt of this letter. Some nine years later the defendants purported to discontinue the payment of the pension and the plaintiff brought an action for damages for breach of contract. *Held*, assuming that there was a contract between the parties, it was a contract unreasonably in restraint of trade as it provided that if the plaintiff entered the wool trade at any time and in any place his pension would be lost. It was against public policy for the country to be deprived of the services of a man who was quite competent to enter into business and for this reason the contract was void and the plaintiff could not found a successful action upon it. Applied in *Marshall* v *NM Financial Management Ltd.*)

Zamet v Hyman [1961] 3 All ER 933 (Court of Appeal)   [645]

Mr Zamet, a widower aged 79 with assets of at least £10,000, became engaged to marry a widow aged 71. Three days before the marriage the widow went to a solicitor employed by her fiancé and executed a deed whereby, contingent on the proposed marriage being solemnised, in consideration of the payment of £600 on the death of Zamet she agreed to relinquish 'all rights that she may have under ... the Inheritance (Family Provision) Act 1938, or the Intestates' Estates Act 1952'. Although the terms of the deed were explained to her the solicitor did not make her aware of its full implications. Zamet died intestate and the widow maintained that the deed was not binding. *Held*, it was not and it should be delivered up for cancellation. On the facts of the case the widow had imposed on Zamet a duty of candour and protection and those claiming the estate on intestacy had not shown that the widow had executed the deed fully understanding its significance and after 'full, free and informed (and, particularly, informed) thought about it' (*per* LORD EVERSHED MR). (See also *Wright* v *Carter*.)

Statutes

STATUTE OF FRAUDS 1677
(29 Car 2 c 3)

4 No action upon a special promise unless agreement, [646] etc, be in writing, and signed

No action shall be brought whereby to charge the defendant upon any special promise to answer for the debt default or miscarriages of another person unless the agreement upon which such action shall be brought or some memorandum or note thereof shall be in writing and signed by the party to be charged therewith or some other person thereunto by him lawfully authorised.

[As amended by the Statute Law Revision Act 1883; Law of Property Act 1925, s207, Schedule 7; Statute Law Revision Act 1948; the Law Reform (Enforcement of Contracts) Act 1954, s1.]

GAMING ACT 1710
(9 Anne c 19)

1 Security given for money, etc, won by gaming or for [647] repayment of money lent for gaming void

All notes bills bonds judgments mortgages or other securities or conveyances whatsoever given granted drawn or entered into or executed by any person or persons whatsoever where the whole or any part of the consideration of such conveyances or securities shall be for any money or other valuable thing whatsoever won by gaming or playing at cards dice tables tennis bowles or other game or games whatsoever or by betting on the sides or hands of such as do game at any of the games aforesaid or for the reimbursing or repaying any money knowingly lent or advanced for such gaming or betting as aforesaid or lent or advanced at the time and place of such play to any person or persons so gaming or betting as aforesaid or that shall during such play, so play or bett shall be utterly void frustrate and of none effect to all intents and purposes whatsoever any statute law or usage to the contrary thereof in any wise notwithstanding.

[As amended by the Gaming Act 1835, s3.]

STATUTE OF FRAUDS AMENDMENT ACT 1828
(9 Geo 4 c 14)

6 Action not maintainable on representations of character, etc, unless they be in writing signed by the party chargeable   [648]

No action shall be brought whereby to charge any person upon or by reason of any representation or assurance made or given concerning or relating to the character, conduct, credit, ability, trade, or dealings of any other person, to the intent or purpose that such other person may obtain credit, money, or goods upon, unless such representation or assurance be made in writing, signed by the party to be charged therewith.

GAMING ACT 1835
(5 & 6 Will 4 c 41)

1 Securities given for considerations arising out of illegal transactions not to be void, but to be deemed to have been given for an illegal consideration   [649]

Every note bill or mortgage which if this Act had not been passed would, by virtue of the said several lastly herein-before mentioned Acts [including the Gaming Act 1710] or any of them, have been absolutely void, shall be deemed and taken to have been made, drawn, accepted, given or executed for an illegal consideration; and the said several Acts shall have the same force and effect which they would respectively have had, if, instead of enacting that any such note, bill, or mortgage should be absolutely void, such Acts had respectively provided that every such note, bill or mortgage should be deemed and taken to have been made, drawn, accepted, given, or executed for an illegal consideration: Provided always, that nothing herein contained shall prejudice or affect any note, bill, or mortgage which would have been good and valid if this Act had not been passed.

[As amended by the Statute Law Revision Act 1874; Statute Law Revision (No 2) Act 1890.]

GAMING ACT 1845
(8 & 9 Vict c 109)

18 Contracts by way of gaming to be void, and wagers or sums deposited with stakeholders not to be recoverable at law – Saving for subscriptions for prizes   [650]

All contracts or agreements, whether by parole or in writing, by way of gaming or wagering, shall be null and void; and no suit shall be brought or maintained in any court of law and equity for recovering any sum of money or valuable thing alleged to have been won upon any wager, or which shall have been deposited in the hands of any person to abide the event on which any wager shall have been made: Provided always, that this enactment shall not be deemed to apply to any subscription or contribution, or agreement to subscribe or contribute, for or towards any plate, prize, or sum of money to be awarded to the winner or winners of any lawful game, sport, pastime, or exercise.

[As amended by the Statute Law Revision Act 1891.]

BILLS OF EXCHANGE ACT 1882
(45 & 46 Vict c 61)

3 Bills of exchange defined [651]

(1) A bill of exchange is an unconditional order in writing, addressed by one person to another, signed by the person giving it, requiring the person to whom it is addressed to pay on demand or at a fixed or determinable future time a sum certain in money to or to the order of a specified person, or to bearer.

(2) An instrument which does not comply with these conditions, or which orders any act to be done in addition to the payment of money, is not a bill of exchange.

(3) An order to pay out of a particular fund is not unconditional within the meaning of this section; but an unqualified order to pay, coupled with (a) an indication of a particular fund out of which the drawee is to re-imburse himself or a particular account to be debited with the amount, or (b) a statement of the transaction which gives rise to the bill, is unconditional.

(4) A bill is not invalid by reason –

(a) That it is not dated;
(b) That it does not specify the value given, or that any value has been given therefor;
(c) That it does not specify the place where it is drawn or the place where it is payable.

17 Definition and requisites of acceptance [652]

(1) The acceptance of a bill is the signification by the drawee of his assent to the order of the drawer.

(2) An acceptance is invalid unless it complies with the following conditions, namely:

(a) It must be written on the bill and be signed by the drawee. The mere signature of the drawee without additional works is sufficient.
(b) It must not express that the drawee will perform his promise by any other means than the payment of money.

26 Person signing as agent or in representative capacity [653]

(1) Where a person signs a bill as a drawer, indorser, or acceptor, and adds words to his signature, indicating that he signs for or on behalf of a principal, or in a representative character, he is not personally liable thereon; but the mere addition to his signature of words describing him as an agent, or as filling a representative character, does not exempt him from personal liability.

(2) In determining whether a signature on a bill is that of the principal or that of the agent by whose hand it is written, the construction most favourable to the validity of the instrument shall be adopted.

27 Value and holder for value [654]

(1) Valuable consideration for a bill may be constituted by, –

(a) Any consideration sufficient to support a simple contract;
(b) An antecedent debt or liability. Such a debt or liability is deemed valuable consideration whether the bill is payable on demand or at a future time.

(2) Where value has at any time been given for a bill the holder is deemed to be a holder for value as regards the acceptor and all parties to the bill who became parties prior to such time.

73 Cheque defined [655]

A cheque is a bill of exchange drawn on a banker payable on demand.

Except as otherwise provided in this Part, the provisions of this Act applicable to a bill of exchange payable on demand apply to a cheque.

83 Promissory note defined [656]

(1) A promissory note is an unconditional promise in writing made by one person to another signed by the maker, engaging to pay, on demand or at a fixed or determinable future time, a sum certain in money, to, or to the order of, a specified person or to bearer.

(2) An instrument in the form of a note payable to maker's order is not a note within the meaning of this section unless and until it is indorsed by the maker.

(3) A note is not invalid by reason only that it contains also a pledge of collateral security with authority to sell or dispose thereof.

(4) A note which is, or on the face of it purports to be, both made and payable within the British Islands is an inland note. Any other note is a foreign one.

FACTORS ACT 1889
(52 & 53 Vict c 45)

1 Definitions [657]

For the purposes of this Act:

(1) The expression 'mercantile agent' shall mean a mercantile agent having in the customary course of his business as such agent authority either to sell goods, or to consign goods for the purpose of sale, or to buy goods, or to raise money on the security of goods;

(2) A person shall be deemed to be in possession of goods or of the documents of title to goods, where the goods or documents are in his actual custody or are held by any other person subject to his control or for him or on his behalf;

(3) The expression 'goods' shall include wares and merchandise;

(4) The expression 'document of title' shall include any bill of lading, dock warrant, warehouse-keeper's certificate, and warrant or order for the delivery of goods, and any other document used in the ordinary course of business as proof of the possession or control of goods, or authorising or purporting to authorise, either by endorsement or by delivery, the possessor of the document to transfer or receive goods thereby represented;

(5) The expression 'pledge' shall include any contract pledging, or giving a lien or security on, goods, whether in consideration of an original advance or of any further or continuing advance or of any pecuniary liability;

(6) The expression 'person' shall include any body of persons corporate or unincorporate.

2 Powers of mercantile agent with respect to disposition of goods **[658]**

(1) Where a mercantile agent is, with the consent of the owner, in possession of goods or of the document of title to goods, any sale, pledge, or other disposition of the goods, made by him when acting in the ordinary course of business of a mercantile agent, shall, subject to the provisions of this Act, be as valid as if he were expressly authorised by the owner of the goods to make the same; provided that the person taking under the disposition acts in good faith, and has not at the time of the disposition notice that the person making the disposition has not authority to make the same.

(2) Where a mercantile agent has, with the consent of the owner, been in possession of goods or of the documents of title to goods, any sale, pledge, or other disposition, which would have been valid if the consent had continued, shall be valid notwithstanding the determination of the consent: provided that the person taking under the disposition has not at the time thereof notice that the consent has been determined.

(3) Where a mercantile agent has obtained possession of any documents of title to goods by reason of his being or having been, with the consent of the owner, in possession of the goods represented thereby, or of any other documents of title to the goods, his possession of the first-mentioned documents shall, for the purposes of this Act, be deemed to be with the consent of the owner.

(4) For the purposes of this Act the consent of the owner shall be presumed in the absence of evidence to the contrary.

6 Agreements through clerks, etc **[659]**

For the purposes of this Act an agreement made with a mercantile agent through a clerk or other person authorised in the ordinary course of business to make contracts of sale or pledge on his behalf shall be deemed to be an agreement with the agent.

GAMING ACT 1892
(55 & 56 Vict c 9)

1 Promises to repay sums paid under contracts void by the Gaming Act 1845 to be null and void **[660]**

Any promise, express or implied, to pay any person any sum of money paid by him under or in respect of any contract or agreement rendered null and void by the Gaming Act 1845, or to pay any sum of money by way of commission, fee, reward, or otherwise in respect of any such contract, or of any services in relation thereto or in connexion therewith, shall be null and void, and no action shall be brought or maintained to recover any such sum of money.

MARINE INSURANCE ACT 1906
(6 Edw 7 c 41)

17 Insurance is uberrimae fidei **[661]**

A contract of marine insurance is a contract based upon the utmost good faith, and, if the utmost good faith be not observed by either party, the contract may be avoided by the other party.

18 Disclosure by assured   [662]

(1) Subject to the provisions of this section, the assured must disclose to the insurer, before the contract is concluded, every material circumstance which is known to the assured, and the assured is deemed to know every circumstance which, in the ordinary course of business, ought to be known by him. If the assured fails to make such disclosure, the insurer may avoid the contract.

(2) Every circumstance is material which would influence the judgment of a prudent insurer in fixing the premium, or determining whether he will take the risk.

(3) In the absence of inquiry the following circumstances need not be disclosed, namely: –

(a) Any circumstance which diminishes the risk;
(b) Any circumstance which is known or presumed to be known to the insurer. The insurer is presumed to know matters of common notoriety or knowledge, and matters which an insurer in the ordinary course of his business, as such, ought to know;
(c) Any circumstance as to which information is waived by the insurer;
(d) Any circumstance which it is superfluous to disclose by reason of any express or implied warranty.

(4) Whether any particular circumstance, which is not disclosed, be material or not is, in each case, a question of fact.

(5) The term 'circumstance' includes any communication made to, or information received by, the assured.

20 Representations pending negotiation of contract   [663]

(1) Every material representation made by the assured or his agent to the insurer during the negotiations for the contract, and before the contract is concluded, must be true. If it be untrue the insurer may avoid the contract.

(2) A representation is material which would influence the judgment of a prudent insurer in fixing the premium, or determining whether he will take the risk.

(3) A representation may be either a representation as to a matter of fact, or as to a matter of expectation or belief.

(4) A representation as to a matter of fact is true, if it be substantially correct, that is to say, if the difference between what is represented and what is actually correct would not be considered material by a prudent insurer.

(5) A representation as to a matter of expectation or belief is true if it be made in good faith.

(6) A representation may be withdrawn or corrected before the contract is concluded.

(7) Whether a particular representation be material or not is, in each case, a question of fact.

33 Nature of warranty   [664]

(1) A warranty, in the following sections relating to warranties, means a promissory warranty, that is to say, a warranty by which the assured undertakes that some particular thing shall or shall not be done, or that some condition shall be fulfilled, or whereby he affirms or negatives the existence of a particular state of facts.

(2) A warranty may be express or implied.

(3) A warranty, as above defined, is a condition which must be exactly complied with, whether it be material to the risk or not. If it be not so complied with, then, subject to any express provision in the policy, the insurer is discharged from liability as from the date of the breach of warranty, but without prejudice to any liability incurred by him before that date.

34 When breach of warranty excused [665]

(1) Non-compliance with a warranty is excused when, by reason of a change of circumstances, the warranty ceases to be applicable to the circumstances of the contract, or when compliance with the warranty is rendered unlawful by any subsequent law.

(2) Where a warranty is broken, the assured cannot avail himself of the defence that the breach has been remedied, and the warranty complied with, before loss.

(3) A breach of warranty may be waived by the insurer.

35 Express warranties [666]

(1) An express warranty may be in any form of words from which the intention to warrant is to be inferred.

(2) An express warranty must be included in, or written upon, the policy, or must be contained in some document incorporated by reference into the policy.

(3) An express warranty does not exclude an implied warranty, unless it be inconsistent therewith.

36 Warranty of neutrality [667]

(1) Where insurable property, whether ship or goods, is expressly warranted neutral, there is an implied condition that the property shall have a neutral character at the commencement of the risk, and that, so far as the assured can control the matter, its neutral character shall be preserved during the risk.

(2) Where a ship is expressly warranted 'neutral' there is also an implied condition that, so far as the assured can control the matter, she shall be properly documented, that is to say, that she shall carry the necessary papers to establish her neutrality, and that she shall not falsify or suppress her papers, or use simulated papers. If any loss occurs through breach of this condition, the insurer may avoid the contract.

37 No implied warranty of nationality [668]

There is no implied warranty as to the nationality of a ship, or that her nationality shall not be changed during the risk.

38 Warranty of good safety [669]

Where the subject-matter insured is warranted 'well' or 'in good safety' on a particular day, it is sufficient if it be safe at any time during that day.

39 Warranty of seaworthiness of ship [670]

(1) In a voyage policy there is an implied warranty that at the commencement of the voyage the ship shall be seaworthy for the purpose of the particular adventure insured.

(2) Where the policy attaches while the ship is in port, there is also an implied warranty that she shall, at the commencement of the risk, be reasonably fit to encounter the ordinary perils of the port.

(3) Where the policy relates to a voyage which is performed in different stages, during which the ship requires different kinds of or further preparation or equipment, there is an implied warranty that at the commencement of each stage the ship is seaworthy in respect of such preparation or equipment for the purposes of that stage.

(4) A ship is deemed to be seaworthy when she is reasonably fit in all respects to encounter the ordinary perils of the seas of the adventure insured.

(5) In a time policy there is no implied warranty that the ship shall be seaworthy at any stage of the adventure, but where, with the privity of the assured, the ship is sent to sea in an unseaworthy state, the insurer is not liable for any loss attributable to unseaworthiness.

40 No implied warranty that goods are seaworthy [671]

(1) In a policy on goods or other moveables there is no implied warranty that the goods or moveables are seaworthy.

(2) In a voyage policy on goods or other moveables there is an implied warranty that at the commencement of the voyage the ship is not only seaworthy as a ship, but also that she is reasonably fit to carry the goods or other moveables to the destination contemplated by the policy.

41 Warranty of legality [672]

There is an implied warranty that the adventure insured is a lawful one, and that, so far as the assured can control the matter, the adventure shall be carried out in a lawful manner.

42 Implied condition as to the commencement of risk [673]

(1) Where the subject-matter is insured by a voyage policy 'at and from' or 'from' a particular place, it is not necessary that the ship should be at that place when the contract is concluded, but there is an implied condition that the adventure shall be commenced within a reasonable time, and that if the adventure be not so commenced the insurer may avoid the contract.

(2) The implied condition may be negatived by showing that the delay was caused by circumstances known to the insurer before the contract was concluded, or by showing that he waived the condition.

LAW OF PROPERTY ACT 1925
(15 & 16 Geo 5 c 20)

41 Stipulations not of the essence of a contract [674]

Stipulations in a contract, as to time or otherwise, which according to rules of equity are not deemed to be or to have become of the essence of the contract, are also construed and have effect at law in accordance with the same rules.

52 Conveyances to be by deed   [675]

(1) All conveyances of land or of any interest therein are void for the purpose of conveying or creating a legal estate unless made by deed.

(2) This section does not apply to –

(a) assents by a personal representative;

(b) disclaimers made in accordance with sections 178 to 180 or sections 315 to 319 of the Insolvency Act 1986, or not required to be evidenced in writing;

(c) surrenders by operation of law, including surrenders which may, by law, be effected without writing;

(d) leases or tenancies or other assurances not required by law to be made in writing;

(e) receipts other than those falling within section 115 below;

(f) vesting orders of the court or other competent authority;

(g) conveyances taking effect by operation of law.

53 Instruments required to be in writing   [676]

(1) Subject to the provisions hereinafter contained with respect to the creation of interests in land by parol –

(a) no interest in land can be created or disposed of except by writing signed by the person creating or conveying the same, or by his agent thereunto lawfully authorised in writing, or by will, or by operation of law;

(b) a declaration of trust respecting any land or any interest therein must be manifested and proved by some writing signed by some person who is able to declare such trust or by his will;

(c) a disposition of an equitable interest or trust subsisting at the time of the disposition, must be in writing signed by the person disposing of the same, or by his agent, thereunto lawfully authorised in writing or by will.

(2) This section does not affect the creation or operation of resulting, implied or constructive trusts.

54 Creation of interests in land by parol   [677]

(2) Nothing in the foregoing provisions of this Part of this Act shall affect the creation by parol of leases taking effect in possession for a term not exceeding three years (whether or not the lessee is given power to extend the term) at the best rent which can be reasonably obtained without taking a fine.

55 Savings in regard to last two sections   [678]

Nothing in the last two foregoing sections shall –

(a) invalidate dispositions by will; or

(b) affect any interest validly created before the commencement of this Act; or

(c) affect the right to acquire an interest in land by virtue of taking possession; or

(d) affect the operation of the law relating to part performance.

56 Persons taking who are not parties   [679]

(1) A person may take an immediate or other interest in land or other property, or the benefit of any condition, right of entry, covenant or agreement over or respecting land or other property, although he may not be named as a party to the conveyance or other instrument.

205 General definitions   [680]

(1) In this Act unless the context otherwise requires, the following expressions have the meanings hereby assigned to them respectively, that is to say:

(ii) 'Conveyance' includes a mortgage, charge, lease, assent, vesting declaration, vesting instrument, disclaimer, release and every other assurance of property or of an instrument therein by any instrument, except a will; 'convey' has a corresponding meaning; and 'disposition' includes a conveyance and also a devise, bequest, or an appointment of property contained in a will; and 'dispose of' has a corresponding meaning; ...

(ix) 'Land' includes land of any tenure, and mines and minerals, whether or not held apart from the surface, buildings or parts of buildings (whether the division is horizontal, vertical or made in any other way) and other corporeal hereditaments; also a manor, an advowson, and a rent and other incorporeal hereditaments, and an easement, right, privilege, or benefit in, over, or derived from land; but not an undivided share in land; and 'mines and minerals' include any strata or seam of minerals or substances in or under any land, and powers of working and getting the same but not an undivided share thereof; and 'manor' includes a lordship, and reputed manor or lordship; and 'hereditament' means any real property which on an intestacy occurring before the commencement of this Act might have devolved upon an heir; ...

[As amended by the Insolvency Act 1986, s439(2), Schedule 14; Law of Property (Miscellaneous Provisions) Act 1989, s1(8), Schedule 1, para 2.]

LAW REFORM (FRUSTRATED CONTRACTS) ACT 1943
(6 & 7 Geo 6 c 40)

1 Adjustment of rights and liabilities of parties to   [681]
frustrated contracts

(1) Where a contract governed by English law has become impossible of performance or been otherwise frustrated, and the parties thereto have for that reason been discharged from the further performance of the contract, the following provisions of this section shall, subject to the provisions of section two of this Act, have effect in relation thereto.

(2) All sums paid or payable to any party in pursuance of the contract before the time when the parties were so discharged (in this Act referred to as 'the time of discharge') shall, in the case of sums so paid, be recoverable from him as money received by him for the use of the party by whom the sums were paid, and, in the case of sums so payable, cease to be so payable:

Provided that, if the party to whom the sums were so paid or payable incurred expenses before the time of discharge in, or for the purpose of, the performance of the contract, the court may, if it considers it just to do so having regard to all the circumstances of the case, allow him to retain or, as the case may be, recover the whole or any part of the sums so paid or payable, not being an amount in excess of the expenses so incurred.

(3) Where any party to the contract has, by reason of anything done by any other party thereto in, or for the purpose of, the performance of the contract, obtained a valuable benefit (other than a payment of money to which the last foregoing subsection applies) before the time of discharge, there shall be recoverable from him by the said other party such sum (if any), not exceeding the value of the said benefit to the party obtaining it, as the court considers just, having regard to all the circumstances of the case and, in particular, –

(a) the amount of any expenses incurred before the time of discharge by the benefited party in, or for the purpose of, the performance of the contract, including any sums paid or payable by him to any other party in pursuance of the contract and retained or recoverable by that party under the last foregoing subsection, and

(b) the effect, in relation to the said benefit, of the circumstances giving rise to the frustration of the contract.

(4) In estimating, for the purposes of the foregoing provisions of this section, the amount of any expenses incurred by any party to the contract, the court may, without prejudice to the generality of the said provisions, include such sum as appears to be reasonable in respect of overhead expenses and in respect of any work or services performed personally by the said party.

(5) In considering whether any sum ought to be recovered or retained under the foregoing provisions of this section by any party to the contract, the court shall not take into account any sums which have, by reason of the circumstances giving rise to the frustration of the contract, become payable to that party under any contract of insurance unless there was an obligation to insure imposed by an express term of the frustrated contract or by or under any enactment.

(6) Where any person has assumed obligations under the contract in consideration of the conferring of a benefit by any other party to the contract upon any other person, whether a party to the contract or not, the court may, if in all the circumstances of the case it considers it just to do so, treat for the purposes of subsection (3) of this section any benefit so conferred as a benefit obtained by the person who has assumed the obligations as aforesaid.

2 Provision as to application of this Act [682]

(1) This Act shall apply to contracts, whether made before or after the commencement of this Act, as respects which the time of discharge is on or after the first day of July, nineteen hundred and forty-three, but not to contracts as respects which the time of discharge is before the said date.

(2) This Act shall apply to contracts to which the Crown is a party in like manner as to contracts between subjects.

(3) Where any contract to which this Act applies contains any provision which, upon the true construction of the contract, is intended to have effect in the event of circumstances arising which operate, or would but for the said provision operate, to frustrate the contract, or is intended to have effect whether such circumstances arise or not, the court shall give effect to the said provision and shall only give effect to the foregoing section of this Act to such extent, if any, as appears to the court to be consistent with the said provision.

(4) Where it appears to the court that a part of any contract to which this Act applies can properly be severed from the remainder of the contract, being a part wholly performed before the time of discharge, or so performed except for the payment in respect of that part of the contract of sums which are or can be ascertained under the contract, the court shall treat that part of the contract as if it were a separate contract and had not been frustrated and shall treat the foregoing section of this Act as only applicable to the remainder of that contract.

(5) This Act shall not apply –

(a) to any charterparty, except a time charterparty or a charterparty by way of demise, or to any contract (other than a charterparty) for the carriage of goods by sea; or

(b) to any contract of insurance, save as is provided by subsection (5) of the foregoing section; or

(c) to any contract to which section 7 of the Sale of Goods Act 1979 (which avoids contracts for the sale of specific goods which perish before the risk has passed to the buyer) applies, or to any other contract for the sale, or for the sale and delivery, of specific goods, where the contract is frustrated by reason of the fact that the goods have perished.

3 Interpretation   [683]

(2) In this Act the expression 'court' means, in relation to any matter, the court or arbitrator by or before whom the matter falls to be determined.

[As amended by the Sale of Goods Act 1979, s63, Schedule 2, para 2.]

CORPORATE BODIES' CONTRACTS ACT 1960
(8 & 9 Eliz 2 c 46)

1 Cases where contracts need not be under seal   [684]

(1) Contracts may be made on behalf of any body corporate, wherever incorporated, as follows:—

(a) a contract which if made between private persons would be by law required to be in writing, signed by the parties to be charged therewith, may be made on behalf of the body corporate in writing signed by any person acting under its authority, express or implied, and
(b) a contract which if made between private persons would by law be valid although made by parol only, and not reduced into writing, may be made by parol on behalf of the body corporate by any person acting under its authority, express or implied.

(2) A contract made according to this section shall be effectual in law, and shall bind the body corporate and its successors and all other parties thereto.

(3) A contract made according to this section may be varied or discharged in the same manner in which it is authorised by this section to be made.

(4) Nothing in this section shall be taken as preventing a contract under seal from being made by or on behalf of a body corporate.

(5) This section shall not apply to the making, variation or discharge of a contract before the commencement of this Act but shall apply whether the body corporate gave its authority before or after the commencement of this Act.

2 Exclusion of companies under Companies Acts   [685]

This Act shall not apply to any company formed and registered under the Companies Act, 1985, or an existing company as defined in that Act.

[As amended by the Companies (Consequential Provisions) Act 1985, s30, Schedule 2.]

HIRE-PURCHASE ACT 1964
(1964 c 53)

27 Protection of purchasers of motor vehicles   [686]

(1) This section applies where a motor vehicle has been bailed or (in Scotland) hired under a hire-purchase agreement, or has been agreed to be sold under a

conditional sale agreement, and, before the property in the vehicle has become vested in the debtor, he disposes of the vehicle to another person.

(2) Where the disposition referred to in subsection (1) above is to a private purchaser, and he is a purchaser of the motor vehicle in good faith, without notice of the hire-purchaser or conditional sale agreement (the 'relevant agreement') that disposition shall have effect as if the creditor's title to the vehicle has been vested in the debtor immediately before that disposition.

(3) Where the person to whom the disposition referred to in subsection (1) above is made (the 'original purchaser') is a trade or finance purchaser, then if the person who is the first private purchaser of the motor vehicle after that disposition (the 'first private purchaser') is a purchaser of the vehicle in good faith without notice of the relevant agreement, the disposition of the vehicle to the first private purchaser shall have effect as if the title of the creditor to the vehicle had been vested in the debtor immediately before he disposed of it to the original purchaser.

(4) Where, in a case within subsection (3) above –

(a) the disposition by which the first private purchaser becomes a purchaser of the motor vehicle in good faith without notice of the relevant agreement is itself a bailment or hiring under a hire-purchase agreement, and
(b) the person who is the creditor in relation to that agreement disposes of the vehicle to the first private purchaser, or a person claiming under him, by transferring to him the property in the vehicle in pursuance of a provision in the agreement in that behalf.

the disposition referred to in paragraph (b) above (whether or not the person to whom it is made is a purchaser in good faith without notice of the relevant agreement) shall as well as the disposition referred to in paragraph (a) above, have effect as mentioned in subsection (3) above.

(5) The preceding provisions of this section apply –

(a) notwithstanding anything in section 21 of the Sale of Goods Act 1979 (sale of goods by a person not the owner), but
(b) without prejudice to the provisions of the Factors Act (as defined by section 61(1) of the said Act of 1979) or of any other enactment enabling the apparent owner of goods to dispose of them as if he were the true owner.

(6) Nothing in this section shall exonerate the debtor from any liability (whether criminal or civil) to which he would be subject apart from this section; and, in a case where the debtor disposes of the motor vehicle to a trade or finance purchaser, nothing in this section shall exonerate –

(a) that trade or finance purchaser; or
(b) any other trade or finance purchaser who becomes a purchaser of the vehicle and is not a person claiming under the first private purchaser,

from any liability (whether criminal or civil) to which he would be subject apart from this section.

28 Presumptions relating to dealings with motor vehicles   [687]

(1) Where in any proceedings (whether criminal or civil) relating to a motor vehicle it is proved –

(a) that the vehicle was bailed or (in Scotland) hired under a hire-purchase agreement, or was agreed to be sold under a conditional sale agreement and
(b) that a person (whether a party to the proceedings or not) became a private purchaser of the vehicle in good faith without notice of the hire-purchase or conditional sale agreement (the 'relevant agreement'),

this section shall have effect for the purposes of the operation of section 27 of this Act in relation to those proceedings.

(2) It shall be presumed for those purposes, unless the contrary is proved, that the disposition of the vehicle to the person referred to in subsection (1)(b) above (the 'relevant purchaser') was made by the debtor.

(3) If it is proved that that disposition was not made by the debtor, then it shall be presumed for those purposes, unless the contrary is proved –

(a) that the debtor disposed of the vehicle to a private purchaser purchasing in good faith without notice of the relevant agreement, and
(b) that the relevant purchaser is or was a person claiming under the person to whom the debtor so disposed of the vehicle.

(4) If it is proved that the disposition of the vehicle to the relevant purchaser was not made by the debtor, and that the person to whom the debtor disposed of the vehicle (the 'original purchaser') was a trade or finance purchaser, then it shall be presumed for those purposes, unless the contrary is proved, –

(a) that the person who, after the disposition of the vehicle to the original purchaser, first became a private purchaser of the vehicle was a purchaser in good faith without notice of the relevant agreement, and
(b) that the relevant purchaser is or was a person claiming under the original purchaser.

(5) Without prejudice to any other method of proof, where in any proceedings a party thereto admits a fact, that fact shall, for the purposes of this section, be taken as against him to be proved in relation to those proceedings.

29 Interpretation of Part III [688]

(1) In this Part of this Act –

'conditional sale agreement' means an agreement for the sale of goods under which the purchase price or part of it is payable by instalments, and the property in the goods is to remain in the seller (notwithstanding that the buyer is to be in possession of the goods) until such conditions as to the payment of instalments or otherwise as may be specified in the agreement are fulfilled;

'creditor' means the person by whom goods are bailed or (in Scotland) hired under a hire-purchase agreement or as the case may be, the seller under a conditional sale agreement, or the person to whom his rights and duties have passed by assignment or operation of law;

'disposition' means any sale or contract of sale (including a conditional sale agreement), any bailment or (in Scotland) hiring under a hire-purchase agreement and any transfer of the property in goods in pursuance of a provision in that behalf contained in a hire-purchase agreement, and includes any transaction purporting to be a disposition (as so defined), and 'dispose of' shall be construed accordingly.

'hire-purchase agreement' means an agreement, other than a conditional sale agreement, under which –

(a) goods are bailed or (in Scotland) hired in return for periodical payments by the person to whom they are bailed or hired, and
(b) the property in the goods will pass to that person if the terms of the agreement are complied with and one or more of the following occurs –

(i) the exercise of an option to purchase by that person,
(ii) the doing of any other specified act by any party to the agreement,
(iii) the happening of any other specified events; and

'motor vehicle' means a mechanically propelled vehicle intended or adapted for use on roads to which the public has access.

(2) In this Part of this Act, 'trade or finance purchaser' means a purchaser who, at the time of the disposition made to him, carries on a business which consists, wholly or partly, –

(a) of purchasing motor vehicles for the purpose of offering or exposing them for sale, or

(b) of providing finance by purchasing motor vehicles for the purpose of bailing or (in Scotland) hiring them under hire-purchase agreements or agreeing to sell them under conditional sale agreements,

and 'private purchaser' means a purchaser who, at the time of the disposition made to him, does not carry on any such business.

(3) For the purposes of this Part of this Act a person becomes a purchaser of a motor vehicle if, and at the time when, a disposition of the vehicle is made to him; and a person shall be taken to be a purchaser of a motor vehicle without notice of a hire-purchase agreement or conditional sale agreement if, at the time of the disposition made to him, he has no actual notice that the vehicle is or was the subject of any such agreement.

(4) In this Part of this Act the 'debtor' in relation to a motor vehicle which has been bailed or hired under a hire-purchase agreement, or, as the case may be, agreed to be sold under a conditional sale agreement, means the person who at the material time (whether the agreement has before that time been terminated or not) is either –

(a) the person to whom the vehicle is bailed or hired under that agreement, or

(b) is, in relation to the agreement, the buyer,

including a person who at the time is, by virtue of section 130(4) of the Consumer Credit Act 1974 treated as a bailee or (in Scotland) a custodier of the vehicle.

(5) In this Part of this Act any reference to the title of the creditor to a motor vehicle which has been bailed or (in Scotland) hired under a hire-purchase agreement, or agreed to be sold under a conditional sale agreement, and is disposed of by the debtor, is a reference to such title (if any) to the vehicle as, immediately before that disposition, was vested in the person who then was the creditor in relation to the agreement.

[As substituted by the Consumer Credit Act 1974, s192(3)(a), Schedule 4, para 22 and amended by the Sale of Goods Act 1979, s63, Schedule 2, para 4.]

MISREPRESENTATION ACT 1967
(1967 c 7)

1 Removal of certain bars to rescission for innocent   [689]
misrepresentation

Where a person has entered into a contract after a misrepresentation has been made to him, and –

(a) the misrepresentation has become a term of the contract; or

(b) the contract has been performed;

or both, then, if otherwise he would be entitled to rescind the contract without alleging fraud, he shall be so entitled, subject to the provisions of this Act, notwithstanding the matters mentioned in paragraphs (a) and (b) of this section.

2 Damages for misrepresentation [690]

(1) Where a person has entered into a contract after a misrepresentation has been made to him by another party thereto and as a result thereof he has suffered loss, then, if the person making the misrepresentation would be liable to damages in respect thereof had the misrepresentation been made fraudulently, that person shall be so liable notwithstanding that the misrepresentation was not made fraudulently, unless he proves that he had reasonable ground to believe and did believe up to the time the contract was made that the facts represented were true.

(2) Where a person has entered into a contract after a misrepresentation has been made to him otherwise than fraudulently, and he would be entitled, by reason of the misrepresentation, to rescind the contract, then, if it is claimed, in any proceedings arising out of the contract, that the contract ought to be or has been rescinded the court or arbitrator may declare the contract subsisting and award damages in lieu of rescission, if of opinion that it would be equitable to do so, having regard to the nature of the misrepresentation and the loss that would be caused by it if the contract were upheld, as well as to the loss that rescission would cause to the other party.

(3) Damages may be awarded against a person under subsection (2) of this section whether or not he is liable to damages under subsection (1) thereof, but where he is so liable any award under the said subsection (2) shall be taken into account in assessing his liability under the said subsection (1).

3 Avoidance of provision excluding liability [691]
for misrepresentation

If a contract contains a term which would exclude or restrict –

(a) any liability to which a party to a contract may be subject by reason of any misrepresentation made by him before the contract was made; or
(b) any remedy available to another party to the contract by reason of such misrepresentation,

that term shall be of no effect except in so far as it satisfies the requirement of reasonableness stated in section 11(1) of the Unfair Contract Terms Act 1977; and it is for those claiming that the term satisfies that requirement to show that it does.

[As amended by the Unfair Contract Terms Act 1977, s8(1).]

GAMING ACT 1968
(1968 c 65)

1 Gaming to which Part I applies [692]

(1) Except as provided by the next following subsection, this part of this Act applies to all gaming which takes place elsewhere than on premises in respect of which either –

(a) a licence under this Act is for the time being in force, or
(b) a club or miners' welfare institute is for the time being registered under Part II of this Act.

(2) This Part of this Act does not apply to –

(a) gaming by means of any machine to which Part III of this Act applies, or
(b) gaming to which section 41 of this Act applies [gaming at entertainments not held for private gain], or
(c) gaming which constitutes the provision of amusements with prizes as mentioned in sectiion 15(1) or 16(1) of the Lotteries and Amusements Act 1976.

2 Nature of game [693]

(1) Subject to the following provisions of this section, no gaming to which this Part of this Act applies shall take place where any one or more of the following conditions are fulfilled, that is to say –

(a) the game involves playing or staking against a bank, whether the bank is held by one of the players or not;

(b) the nature of the game is such that the chances in the game are not equally favourable to all the players;

(c) the nature of the game is such that the chances in it lie between the player and some other person, or (if there are two or more players) lie wholly or partly between the players and some other person, and those chances are not as favourable to the player or players as they are to that other person.

(2) The preceding subsection shall not have effect in relation to gaming which takes place on a domestic occasion in a private dwelling, and shall not have effect in relation to any gaming where the gaming takes place in a hostel, hall of residence or similar establishment which is not carried on by way of a trade or business and the players consist exclusively or mainly of persons who are residents or inmates in that establishment.

16 Provision of credit for gaming [694]

(1) Subject to subsections (2) and (2A) of this section, where gaming to which this Part of this Act applies takes place on premises in respect of which a licence under this Act is for the time being in force, neither the holder of the licence nor any person acting on his behalf or under any arrangement with him shall make any loan or otherwise provide or allow to any person any credit, or release, or discharge on another person's behalf, the whole or part of any debt, –

(a) for enabling any person to take part in the gaming, or

(b) in respect of any losses incurred by any person in the gaming.

(2) Neither the holder of the licence nor any person acting on his behalf or under any arrangement with him shall accept a cheque and give in exchange for it cash or tokens for enabling any person to take part in the gaming unless the following conditions are fulfilled, that is to say –

(a) the cheque is not a post-dated cheque, and

(b) it is exchanged for cash to an amount equal to the amount for which it is drawn, or is exchanged for tokens at the same rate as would apply if cash, to the amount for which the cheque is drawn, were given in exchange for them;

but, where those conditions are fulfilled, the giving of cash or tokens in exchange for a cheque shall not be taken to contravene subsection (1) of this section.

(2A) Neither the holder of a licence under this Act nor any person acting on his behalf or under any arrangement with him shall permit to be redeemed any cheque (not being a cheque which has been dishonoured) accepted in exchange for cash or tokens for enabling any person to take part in gaming to which this Part of this Act applies unless the following conditions are fulfilled, that is to say –

(a) the cheque is redeemed by the person from whom it was accepted giving in exchange for it cash, or tokens, or a substitute cheque, or any combination of these, to an amount equal to the amount of the redeemed cheque or (where two or more cheques are redeemed) the aggregate amount of the redeemed cheques;

(b) it is redeemed during the playing session in which it was accepted, or within 30 minutes after the end of the session;

(c) where a substitute cheque is given in whole or in part exchange for the redeemed cheque the substitute cheque is not a post-dated cheque; and

(d) where tokens are given in whole or in part exchange for the redeemed cheque, the value of each token is equal to the amount originally given in exchange for it or, if the token was won in the gaming, the value it represented when won;

but, where those conditions are fulfilled, the return of a redeemed cheque in exchange for cash, or tokens, or a substitute cheque, or any combination of these, shall not be taken to contravene subsection (1) of this section.

(3) Where the holder of a licence under this Act, or a person acting on behalf of or under any arrangement with the holder of such a licence, accepts a cheque in exchange for cash or tokens to be used by a player in gaming to which this Part of this Act applies or a substitute cheque, he shall not more than two banking days later cause the cheque to be delivered to a bank for payment or collection.

(3A) Subsection (3) of this section shall not apply to a redeemed cheque.

(4) Nothing in the Gaming Act 1710, the Gaming Act 1835, the Gaming Act 1845, or the Gaming Act 1892, shall affect the validity of, or any remedy in respect of any cheque which is accepted in exchange for cash or tokens to be used by a player in gaming to which this Part of this Act applies or any substitute cheque.

(5) In this section 'banking day' means a day which is a business day in accordance with section 92 of the Bills of Exchange Act 1882.

'playing session' means a continuous period during one day, or two consecutive days, throughout which gaming is permitted by or under this Act to take place on premises in respect of which a licence under this Act is for the time being in force; 'redeemed cheque' means a cheque accepted in fulfilment of the conditions specified in subsection (2) of this section and returned to the person from whom it was accepted in fulfilment of the conditions specified in subsection (2A) of this section; 'substitute cheque' means a cheque accepted in accordance with subsection (2A) of this section by either the holder of a licence under this Act or a person acting on behalf of or under any arrangement with the holder of such a licence.

52 Interpretation   [695]

(1) 'Gaming' means (subject to subsections (3) to (5) of this section) [which exclude certain lotteries (including the National Lottery), pool betting and certain games played by machines] the playing of a game of chance for winnings in money or money's worth, whether any person playing the game is at risk of losing any money or money's worth or not.

[As amended by the Lotteries and Amusements Act 1976, s25(2), Schedule 4, para 1; Gaming (Amendment) Act 1986, s1.]

FAMILY LAW REFORM ACT 1969
(1969 c 46)

1 Reduction of age of majority from 21 to 18   [696]

(1) As from the date on which this section comes into force a person shall attain full age on attaining the age of eighteen instead of on attaining the age of twenty-one; and a person shall attain full age on that date if he has then already attained the age of eighteen but not the age of twenty-one.

(2) The foregoing subsection applies for the purposes of any rule of law, and, in the absence of a definition or of any indication of a contrary intention, for the

construction of 'full age', 'infant', 'infancy', 'minor', 'minority' and similar expressions in –

(a) any statutory provision, whether passed or made before, on or after the date on which this section comes into force; and

(b) any deed, will or other instrument of whatever nature (not being a statutory provision) made on or after that date.

(6) In this section 'statutory provision' means any enactment (including, except where the context otherwise requires, this Act) and any order, rule, regulation, byelaw or other instrument made in the exercise of a power conferred by any enactment.

9 Time at which a person attains a particular age [697]

(1) The time at which a person attains a particular age expressed in years shall be the commencement of the relevant anniversary of the date of his birth.

(2) This section applies only where the relevant anniversary falls on a date after that on which this section comes into force, and, in relation to any enactment, deed, will or other instrument, has effect subject to any provision therein.

POWERS OF ATTORNEY ACT 1971
(1971 c 27)

4 Powers of attorney given as security [698]

(1) Where a power of attorney is expressed to be irrevocable and is given to secure –

(a) a proprietary interest of the donee of the power; or

(b) the performance of an obligation owed to the donee,

then, so long as the donee has that interest or the obligation remains undischarged, the power shall not be revoked –

(a) by the donor without the consent of the donee; or

(b) by the death, incapacity or bankruptcy of the donor or, if the donor is a body corporate, by its winding up or dissolution.

(2) A power of attorney given to secure a proprietary interest may be given to the person entitled to the interest and persons deriving title under him to that interest, and those persons shall be duly constituted donees of the power for all purposes of the power but without prejudice to any right to appoint substitutes given by the power.

(3) This section applies to powers of attorney whenever created.

SUPPLY OF GOODS (IMPLIED TERMS) ACT 1973
(1973 c 13)

8 Implied terms as to title [699]

(1) In every hire-purchase agreement, other than one to which subsection (2) below applies, there is –

(a) an implied term on the part of the creditor that he will have a right to sell the goods at the time when the property is to pass; and

(b) an implied term that –

(i) the goods are free, and will remain free until the time when the property is to pass, from any charge or encumbrance not disclosed or known to the person to whom the goods are bailed or (in Scotland) hired before the agreement is made, and

(ii) that person will enjoy quiet possession of the goods except so far as it may be disturbed by any person entitled to the benefit of any charge or encumbrance so disclosed or known.

(2) In a hire-purchase agreement, in the case of which there appears from the agreement or is to be inferred from the circumstances of the agreement an intention that the creditor should transfer only such title as he or a third person may have, there is –

(a) an implied term that all charges or encumbrances known to the creditor and not known to the person to whom the goods are bailed or hired have been disclosed to that person before the agreement is made, and

(b) an implied term that neither –

(i) the creditor; nor

(ii) in a case where the parties to the agreement intend that any title which may be transferred shall be only such title as a third person may have, that person; nor

(iii) anyone claiming through or under the creditor or that third person otherwise than under a charge or encumbrance disclosed or known to the person to whom the goods are bailed or hired, before the agreement is made;

will disturb the quiet possession of the person to whom the goods are bailed or hired.

(3) As regards England and Wales and Northern Ireland, the term implied by subsection (1)(a) above is a condition and the terms implied by subsections (1)(b), (2)(a) and (2)(b) above are warranties.

9 Bailing or hiring by description   [700]

(1) Where under a hire-purchase agreement goods are bailed or (in Scotland) hired by description, there is an implied term that the goods will correspond with the description, and if under the agreement the goods are bailed or hired by reference to a sample as well as a description, it is not sufficient that the bulk of the goods corresponds with the sample if the goods do not also correspond with the description.

(1A) As regards England and Wales and Northern Ireland, the term implied by subsection (1) above is a condition.

(2) Goods shall not be prevented from being bailed or hired by description by reason only that, being exposed for sale, bailment or hire, they are selected by the person to whom they are bailed or hired.

10 Implied undertakings as to quality or fitness   [701]

(1) Except as provided by this section and section 11 below and subject to the provisions of any other enactment, including any enactment of the Parliament of Northern Ireland or the Northern Ireland Assembly, there is no implied term as to the quality or fitness for any particular purpose of goods bailed or (in Scotland) hired under a hire-purchase agreement.

(2) Where the creditor bails or hires goods under a hire-purchase agreement in the course of a business, there is an implied term that the goods supplied under the agreement are of satisfactory quality.

(2A) For the purposes of this Act, goods are of satisfactory quality if they meet the standard that a reasonable person would regard as satisfactory, taking account of any description of the goods, the price (if relevant) and all the other relevant circumstances.

(2B) For the purposes of this Act, the quality of goods includes their state and condition and the following (among others) are in appropriate cases aspects of the quality of goods –

(a) fitness for all the purposes for which goods of the kind in question are commonly supplied,
(b) appearance and finish,
(c) freedom from minor defects,
(d) safety, and
(e) durability.

(2C) The term implied by subsection (2) above does not extend to any matter making the quality of goods unsatisfactory –

(a) which is specifically drawn to the attention of the person to whom the goods are bailed or hired before the agreement is made,
(b) where that person examines the goods before the agreement is made, which that examination ought to reveal, or
(c) where the goods are bailed or hired by reference to a sample, which would have been apparent on a reasonable examination of the sample.

(3) Where the creditor bails or hires goods under a hire-purchase agreement in the course of a business and the person to whom the goods are bailed or hired, expressly or by implication, makes known –

(a) to the creditor in the course of negotiations conducted by the creditor in relation to the making of the hire-purchase agreement, or
(b) to a credit-broker in the course of negotiations conducted by that broker in relation to goods sold by him to the creditor before forming the subject matter of the hire-purchase agreement,

any particular purpose for which the goods are being bailed or hired, there is an implied term that the goods supplied under the agreement are reasonably fit for that purpose, whether or not that is a purpose for which such goods are commonly supplied, except where the circumstances show that the person to whom the goods are bailed or hired does not rely, or that it is unreasonable for him to rely, on the skill or judgment of the creditor or credit-broker.

(4) An implied term as to quality or fitness for a particular purpose may be annexed to a hire-purchase agreement by usage.

(5) The preceding provisions of this section apply to a hire-purchase agreement made by a person who in the course of a business is acting as agent for the creditor as they apply to an agreement made by the creditor in the course of a business, except where the creditor is not bailing or hiring in the course of a business and either the person to whom the goods are bailed or hired knows that fact or reasonable steps are taken to bring it to the notice of that person before the agreement is made.

(6) In subsection (3) above and this subsection –

(a) 'credit-broker' means a person acting in the course of a business of credit brokerage.
(b) 'credit brokerage' means the effecting of introductions of individuals desiring to obtain credit –

(i) to persons carrying on any business so far as it relates to the provision of credit, or

(ii) to other persons engaged in credit brokerage.

(7) As regards England and Wales and Northern Ireland, the terms implied by subsections (2) and (3) above are conditions.

11 Samples   [702]

(1) Where under a hire-purchase agreement goods are bailed or (in Scotland) hired by reference to a sample, there is an implied term –

(a) that the bulk will correspond with the sample in quality; and
(b) that the person to whom the goods are bailed or hired will have a reasonable opportunity of comparing the bulk with the sample; and
(c) that the goods will be free from any defect, making their quality unsatisfactory, which would not be apparent on reasonable examination of the sample.

(2) As regards England and Wales and Northern Ireland, the term implied by subsection (1) above is a condition.

11A Modification of remedies for breach of statutory   [703]
condition in non-consumer cases

(1) Where in the case of a hire-purchase agreement –

(a) the person to whom goods are bailed would, apart from this subsection, have the right to reject them by reason of a breach on the part of the creditor of a term implied by sections 9, 10, or 11(1)(a) or (c) above, but
(b) the breach is so slight that it would be unreasonable for him to reject them,

then, if the person to whom the goods are bailed does not deal as a consumer, the breach is not to be treated as a breach of condition but may be treated as a breach of warranty.

(2) This section applies unless a contrary intention appears in, or is to be implied from, the agreement.

(3) It is for the creditor to show –

(a) that a breach fell within subsection (1)(b) above, and
(b) that the person to whom the goods were bailed did not deal as consumer.

(4) The references in this section to dealing as consumer are to be construed in accordance with Part I of the Unfair Contract Terms Act 1977. ...

12 Exclusion of implied terms   [704]

An express term does not negative a term implied by this Act unless inconsistent with it.

14 Special provisions as to conditional sale agreements   [705]

(1) Section 11(4) of the Sale of Goods Act 1979 (whereby in certain circumstances a breach of a condition in a contract of sale is treated only as a breach of warranty) shall not apply to a conditional sale agreement where the buyer deals as consumer within Part I of the Unfair Contract Terms Act 1977.

(2) In England and Wales and Northern Ireland a breach of a condition (whether express or implied) to be fulfilled by the seller under any such agreement shall be treated as a breach of warranty, and not as grounds for rejecting the goods and treating the agreement as repudiated, if (but only if) it would have fallen to be so

treated had the condition been contained or implied in a corresponding hire-purchase agreement as a condition to be fulfilled by the creditor.

15 Supplementary [706]

(1) In sections 8 to 14 above and this section –

'business' includes a profession and the activities of any government department (including a Northern Ireland department), [or local or public authority];

'buyer' and 'seller' includes a person to whom rights and duties under a conditional sale agreement have passed by assignment or operation of law;

'conditional sale agreement' means an agreement for the sale of goods under which the purchase price or part of it is payable by instalments, and the property in the goods is to remain in the seller (notwithstanding that the buyer is to be in possession of the goods) until such conditions as to the payment of instalments or otherwise as may be specified in the agreement are fulfilled;

'creditor' means the person by whom the goods are bailed or (in Scotland) hired under a hire-purchase agreement or the person to whom his rights and duties under the agreement have passed by assignment or operation of law; and

'hire-purchase agreement' means an agreement, other than a conditional sale agreement, under which –

(a) goods are bailed or (in Scotland) hired in return for periodical payments by the person to whom they are bailed or hired, and
(b) the property in the goods will pass to that person if the terms of the agreement are complied with and one or more of the following occurs –

(i) the exercise of an option to purchase by that person,
(ii) the doing of any other specified act by any party to the agreement,
(iii) the happening of any other specified event.

(3) In section 14(2) above 'corresponding hire-purchase agreement' means, in relation to a conditional sale agreement, a hire-purchase agreement relating to the same goods as the conditional sale agreement and made between the same parties and at the same time and in the same circumstances and, as nearly as may be, in the same terms as the conditional sale agreement.

(4) Nothing in sections 8 to 13 above shall prejudice the operation of any other enactment including any enactment of the Parliament of Northern Ireland or the Northern Ireland Assembly or any rule of law whereby any term, other than one relating to quality or fitness, is to be implied in any hire-purchase agreement.

[As amended by the Consumer Credit Act 1974, s192(3)(a), Schedule 4, paras 35 and 36; Unfair Contract Terms Act 1977, s31(3), Schedule 3; Sale of Goods Act 1979, s63, Schedule 2, para 16; Statute Law (Repeals) Act 1981, Schedule 1, Part XII; Sale and Supply of Goods Act 1994, s7(1), Schedule 2, para 4, Schedule 3 (with effect from 3 January 1995).]

MATRIMONIAL CAUSES ACT 1973
(1973 c 18)

34 Validity of maintenance agreements [707]

(1) If a maintenance agreement includes a provision purporting to restrict any right to apply to a court for an order containing financial arrangements, then –

(a) that provision shall be void; but

(b) any other financial arrangements contained in the agreement shall not thereby be rendered void or unenforceable and shall, unless they are void or unenforceable for any other reason (and subject to sections 35 and 36 below [which apply to the alteration of agreements by the court during the lives of parties and after the death of one party]), be binding on the parties to the agreement.

(2) In this section and in section 35 below –

'maintenance agreement' means any agreement in writing made, whether before or after the commencement of this Act, between the parties to a marriage, being –

(a) an agreement containing financial arrangements, whether made during the continuance or after the dissolution or annulment of the marriage; or
(b) a separation agreement which contains no financial arrangements in a case where no other agreement in writing between the same parties contains such arrangements

'financial arrangements' means provisions governing the rights and liabilities towards one another when living separately of the parties to a marriage (including a marriage which has been dissolved or annulled) in respect of the making or securing of payments or the disposition or use of any property, including such rights and liabilities with respect to the maintenance or education of any child, whether or not a child of the family.

CONSUMER CREDIT ACT 1974
(1974 c 39)

56 Antecedent negotiations [708]

(1) In this Act 'antecedent negotiations' means any negotiations with the debtor or hirer –

(a) conducted by the creditor or owner in relation to the making of any regulated agreement, or
(b) conducted by a credit-broker in relation to goods sold or proposed to be sold by the credit-broker to the creditor before forming the subject-matter of a debtor-creditor-supplier agreement within section 12(a), or
(c) conducted by the supplier in relation to a transaction financed or proposed to be financed by a debtor-creditor-supplier agreement within section 12(b) or (c).

and 'negotiator' means the person by whom negotiations are so conducted with the debtor or hirer.

(2) Negotiations with the debtor in a case falling within subsection (1)(b) or (c) shall be deemed to be conducted by the negotiator in the capacity of agent of the creditor as well as in his actual capacity.

(3) An agreement is void if, and to the extent that, it purports in relation to an actual or prospective regulated agreement –

(a) to provide that a person acting as, or on behalf of, a negotiator is to be treated as the agent of the debtor or hirer, or
(b) to relieve a person from liability for acts or omissions of any person acting as, or on behalf of, a negotiator.

(4) For the purposes of this Act, antecedent negotiations shall be taken to begin when the negotiator and the debtor or hirer first enter into communication (including communication by advertisement), and to include any representations made by the negotiator to the debtor or hirer and any other dealings between them.

137 Extortionate credit bargains [709]

(1) If the court finds a credit bargain extortionate it may reopen the credit agreement so as to do justice between the parties.

(2) In this section and sections 138 to 140 –

(a) 'credit agreement' means any agreement between an individual (the 'debtor') and any other person (the 'creditor') by which the creditor provides the debtor with credit of any amount, and

(b) 'credit bargain' –

(i) where no transaction other than the credit agreement is to be taken into account in computing the total charge for credit, means the credit agreement, or

(ii) where one or more other transactions are to be so taken into account, means the credit agreement and those other transactions, taken together.

138 When bargains are extortionate [710]

(1) A credit bargain is extortionate if it –

(a) requires the debtor or a relative of his to make payments (whether unconditionally, or on certain contingencies) which are grossly exorbitant, or

(b) otherwise grossly contravenes ordinary principles of fair dealing.

(2) In determining whether a credit bargain is extortionate, regard shall be had to such evidence as is adduced concerning –

(a) interest rates prevailing at the time it was made,

(b) the factors mentioned in subsections (3) to (5), and

(c) any other relevant considerations.

(3) Factors applicable under subsection (2) in relation to the debtor include –

(a) his age, experience, business capacity and state of health; and

(b) the degree to which, at the time of making the credit bargain, he was under financial pressure, and the nature of that pressure.

(4) Factors applicable under subsection (2) in relation to the creditor include –

(a) the degree of risk accepted by him, having regard to the value of any security provided;

(b) his relationship to the debtor; and

(c) whether or not a colourable cash price was quoted for any goods or services included in the credit bargain.

(5) Factors applicable under subsection (2) in relation to a linked transaction include the question how far the transaction was reasonably required for the protection of debtor or creditor, or was in the interest of the debtor.

139 Reopening of extortionate agreements [711]

(1) A credit agreement may, if the court thinks just, be reopened on the ground that the credit bargain is extortionate –

(a) on an application for the purpose made by the debtor or any surety to the High Court, county court or sheriff court; or

(b) at the instance of the debtor or a surety in any proceedings to which the debtor and creditor are parties, being proceedings to enforce the agreement, any security relating to it, or any linked transactioin; or

(c) at the instance of the debtor or a surety in other proceedings in any court where the amount paid or payable under the credit agreement is relevant.

(2) In reopening the agreement, the court may, for the purpose of relieving the debtor or a surety from payment of any sum in excess of that fairly due and reasonable, by order –

(a) direct accounts to be taken, or (in Scotland) an accounting to be made, between any persons,

(b) set aside the whole or part of any obligation imposed on the debtor or a surety by the credit bargain or any related agreement,

(c) require the creditor to repay the whole or part of any sum paid under the credit bargain or any related agreement by the debtor or a surety, whether paid to the creditor or any other person,

(d) direct the return to the surety of any property provided for the purposes of the security, or

(e) alter the terms of the credit agreement or any security instrument.

(3) An order may be made under subsection (2) notwithstanding that its effect is to place a burden on the creditor in respect of an advantage unfairly enjoyed by another person who is a party to a linked transaction.

(4) An order under subsection (2) shall not alter the effect of any judgment.

(5) In England and Wales an application under subsection (1)(a) shall be brought only in the county court in the case of –

(a) a regulated agreement, or

(b) an agreement (not being a regulated agreement) under which the creditor provides the debtor with a fixed-sum credit or running-account credit. ...

[As amended by the High Court and County Courts Jurisdiction Order 1991.]

RENT ACT 1977
(1977 c 42)

125 Recovery of premiums and loans unlawfully required or received   [712]

(1) Where under any agreement (whether made before or after the commencement of this Act) any premium is paid after the commencement of this Act and the whole or any part of the premium could not lawfully be required or received under the preceding provisions of this Part of this Act, the amount of the premium, or, as the case may be, so much of it as could not lawfully be required or received, shall be recoverable by the person by whom it was paid.

(2) Nothing in section 119 or 120 of this Act shall invalidate any agreement for the making of a loan or any security issued in pursuance of such an agreement but, notwithstanding anything in the agreement for the loan, any sum lent in circumstances involving a contravention of either of those sections shall be repayable to the lender on demand.

UNFAIR CONTRACT TERMS ACT 1977
(1977 c 50)

PART I

AMENDMENT OF LAW FOR ENGLAND AND WALES
AND NORTHERN IRELAND

1 Scope of Part I [713]

(1) For the purposes of this Part of this Act, 'negligence' means the breach –

(a) of any obligation, arising from the express or implied terms of a contract, to take reasonable care or exercise reasonable skill in the performance of the contract;

(b) of any common law duty to take reasonable care or exercise reasonable skill (but not any stricter duty);

(c) of the common duty of care imposed by the Occupiers' Liability Act 1957 or the Occupiers' Liability Act (Northern Ireland) 1957.

(2) This Part of this Act is subject to Part III; and in relation to contracts, the operation of sections 2 to 4 and 7 is subject to the exceptions made by Schedule 1.

(3) In the case of both contract and tort, sections 2 to 7 apply except where the contrary is stated in section 6 (4) only to business liability, that is liability for breach of obligations or duties arising –

(a) from things done or to be done by a person in the course of a business (whether his own business or another's);

(b) from the occupation of premises used for business purposes of the occupier;

and references to liability are to be read accordingly but liability of an occupier of premises for breach of an obligation or duty towards a person obtaining access to the premises for recreational or educational purposes, being liability for loss or damage suffered by reason of the dangerous state of the premises, is not a business liability of the occupier unless granting that person such access for the purposes concerned falls within the business purposes of the occupier.

(4) In relation to any breach of duty or obligation, it is immaterial for any purpose of this part of this Act whether the breach was inadvertent or intentional, or whether liability for it arises directly or vicariously.

2 Negligence liability [714]

(1) A person cannot by reference to any contract term or to a notice given to persons generally or to particular persons exclude or restrict his liability for death or personal injury resulting from negligence.

(2) In the case of other loss or damage, a person cannot so exclude or restrict his liability for negligence except in so far as the term or notice satisfies the requirement of reasonableness.

(3) Where a contract term or notice purports to exclude or restrict liability for negligence a person's agreement to or awareness of it is not of itself to be taken as indicating his voluntary acceptance of any risk.

3 Liability arising in contract [715]

(1) This section applies as between contracting parties where one of them deals as consumer or on the other's written standard terms of business.

(2) As against that party, the other cannot by reference to any contract term –

(a) when himself in breach of contract, exclude or restrict any liability of his in respect of the breach; or

(b) claim to be entitled –

(i) to render a contractual performance substantially different from that which was reasonably expected of him, or

(ii) in respect of the whole or any part of his contractual obligation, to render no performance at all,

except in so far as (in any of the cases mentioned above in this subsection) the contract term satisfies the requirement of reasonableness.

4 Unreasonable indemnity clauses   [716]

(1) A person dealing as consumer cannot by reference to any contract term be made to indemnify another person (whether a party to the contract or not) in respect of liability that may be incurred by the other for negligence or breach of contract, except in so far as the contract term satisfies the requirement of reasonableness.

(2) This section applies whether the liability in question –

(a) is directly that of the person to be indemnified or is incurred by him vicariously;

(b) is to the person dealing as consumer or to someone else.

5 'Guarantee' of consumer goods   [717]

(1) In the case of goods of a type ordinarily supplied for private use or consumption, where loss or damage

(a) arises from the goods proving defective while in consumer use; and

(b) results from the negligence of a person concerned in the manufacture or distribution of the goods,

liability for the loss or damage cannot be excluded or restricted by reference to any contract term or notice contained in or operating by reference to a guarantee of the goods.

(2) For these purposes –

(a) goods are to be regarded as 'in consumer use' when a person is using them, or has them in his possession for use, otherwise than exclusively for the purposes of a business; and

(b) anything in writing is a guarantee if it contains or purports to contain some promise or assurance (however worded or presented) that defects will be made good by complete or partial replacement, or by repair, monetary compensation or otherwise.

(3) This section does not apply as between the parties to a contract under or in pursuance of which possession or ownership of the goods passed.

6 Sale and hire-purchase   [718]

(1) Liability for breach of the obligations arising from –

(a) section 12 of the Sale of Goods Act 1979 (seller's implied undertakings as to title, etc);

(b) section 8 of the Supply of Goods (Implied Terms) Act 1973 (the corresponding thing in relation to hire-purchase);

cannot be excluded or restricted by reference to any contract term.

(2) As against a person dealing as consumer, liability for breach of the obligations arising from –

   (a) section 13, 14 and 15 of the 1979 Act (seller's implied undertakings as to conformity of goods with description or sample, or as to their quality or fitness for a particular purpose);
   (b) section 9, 10 or 11 of the 1973 Act (the corresponding things in relation to hire-purchase),

cannot be excluded or restricted by reference to any contract term.

(3) As against a person dealing otherwise than as consumer, the liability specified in subsection (2) above can be excluded or restricted by reference to a contract term, but only in so far as the term satisfies the requirement of reasonableness.

(4) The liabilities referred to in this section are not only the business liabilities defined by section 1(3), but include those arising under any contract of sale of goods or hire-purchase agreement.

7 Miscellaneous contracts under which goods pass [719]

(1) Where the possession or ownership of goods passes under or in pursuance of a contract not governed by the law of sale of goods or hire-purchase, subsections (2) to (4) below apply as regards the effect (if any) to be given to contract terms excluding or restricting liability for breach of obligation arising by implication of law from the nature of the contract.

(2) As against a person dealing as consumer, liability in respect of the goods' correspondence with description or sample, or their quality or fitness for any particular purpose, cannot be excluded or restricted by reference to any such term.

(3) As against a person dealing otherwise than as consumer, that liability can be excluded or restricted by reference to such a term, but only in so far as the term satisfies the requirement of reasonableness.

(3A) Liability for breach of the obligations arising under section 2 of the Supply of Goods and Services Act 1982 (implied terms about title etc in certain contracts for the transfer of the property in goods) cannot be excluded or restricted by references to any such term.

(4) Liability in respect of –

   (a) the right to transfer ownership of the goods, or give possession; or
   (b) the assurance of quiet possession to a person taking goods in pursuance of the contract,

cannot (in a case to which subsection (3A) above does not apply) be excluded or restricted by reference to any such term except in so far as the term satisfies the requirement of reasonableness.

(5) This section does not apply in the case of goods passing on a redemption of trading stamps within the Trading Stamps Act 1964 or the Trading Stamps Act (Northern Ireland) 1965.

9 Effect of breach [720]

(1) Where for reliance upon it a contract term has to satisfy the requirement of reasonableness, it may be found to do so and be given effect accordingly notwithstanding that the contract has been terminated either by breach or by a party electing to treat it as repudiated .

(2) Where on a breach the contract is nevertheless affirmed by a party entitled to treat it as repudiated, this does not of itself exclude the requirement of reasonableness in relation to any contract term.

10 Evasion by means of secondary contract [721]

A person is not bound by any contract term prejudicing or taking away rights of his which arise under, or in connection with the performance of, another contract, so far as those rights extend to the enforcement of another's liability which this Part of this Act prevents that other from excluding or restricting.

11 The 'reasonableness' test [722]

(1) In relation to a contract term, the requirement of reasonableness for the purposes of this Part of this Act, section 3 of the Misrepresentation Act 1967 and section 3 of the Misrepresentation Act (Northern Ireland) 1967 is that the term shall have been a fair and reasonable one to be included having regard to the circumstances which were, or ought reasonably to have been, known to or in the contemplation of the parties when the contract was made.

(2) In determining for the purposes of section 6 or 7 above whether a contract term satisfies the requirement of reasonableness, regard shall be had in particular to the matters specified in Schedule 2 to this Act; but this subsection does not prevent the court or arbitrator from holding, in accordance with any rule of law, that a term which purports to exclude or restrict any relevant liability is not a term of the contract.

(3) In relation to a notice (not being a notice having contractual effect), the requirement of reasonableness under this Act is that it should be fair and reasonable to allow reliance on it, having regard to all the circumstances obtaining when the liability arose or (but for the notice) would have arisen.

(4) Where by reference to a contract term or notice a person seeks to restrict liability to a specified sum of money, and the question arises (under this or any other Act) whether the term or notice satisfies the requirement of reasonableness, regard shall be had in particular (but without prejudice to subsection (2) above in the case of contract terms) to –

(a) the resources which he could expect to be available to him for the purpose of meeting the liability should it arise; and
(b) how far it was open to him to cover himself by insurance.

(5) It is for those claiming that a contract term or notice satisfies the requirement of reasonableness to show that it does.

12 'Dealing as consumer' [723]

(1) A party to a contract 'deals as consumer' in relation to another party if –

(a) he neither makes the contract in the course of a business nor holds himself out as doing so; and
(b) the other party does make the contract in the course of a business; and
(c) in the case of a contract governed by the law of sale of goods or hire-purchase, or by section 7 of this Act, the goods passing under or in pursuance of the contract are of a type ordinarily supplied for private use or consumption.

(2) But on a sale by auction or by competitive tender the buyer is not in any circumstances to be regarded as dealing as consumer.

(3) Subject to this, it is for those claiming that a party does not deal as consumer to show that he does not.

13 Varieties of exemption clause [724]

(1) To the extent that this Part of this Act prevents the exclusion or restriction of any liability it also prevents –

(a) making the liability or its enforcement subject to restrictive or onerous conditions;

(b) excluding or restricting any right or remedy in respect of the liability, or subjecting a person to any prejudice in consequence of his pursuing any such right or remedy;

(c) excluding or restricting rules of evidence or procedure; and (to that extent) sections 2 and 7 also prevent excluding or restricting liability by reference to terms and notices which exclude or restrict the relevant obligation or duty.

(2) But an agreement in writing to submit present or future differences to arbitration is not to be treated under this Part of this Act as excluding or restricting any liability.

14 Interpretation of Part I [725]

In this Part of this Act –

'business' includes a profession and the activities of any government department or local or public authority;

'goods' has the same meaning as in the Sale of Goods Act 1979;

'hire-purchase agreement' has the same meaning as in the Consumer Credit Act 1974; 'negligence' has the meaning given by section 1(1);

'notice' includes an announcement, whether or not in writing, and any other communication or pretended communication; and

'personal injury' includes any disease and any impairment of physical or mental condition.

PART III

PROVISIONS APPLYING TO WHOLE OF UNITED KINGDOM

26 International supply contracts [726]

(1) The limits imposed by this Act on the extent to which a person may exclude or restrict liability by reference to a contract term do not apply to liability arising under such a contract as is described in subsection (3) below.

(2) The terms of such a contract are not subject to any requirement of reasonableness under section 3 or 4 ...

(3) Subject to subsection (4), that description of contract is one whose characteristics are the following --

(a) either it is a contract of sale of goods or it is one under or in pursuance of which the possession or ownership of goods passes; and

(b) it is made by parties whose places of business (or, if they have none, habitual residences) are in the territories of different States (the Channel Islands and the Isle of Man being treated for this purpose as different States from the United Kingdom).

(4) A contract falls within subsection (3) above only if either:

(a) the goods in question are, at the time of the conclusion of the contract, in the course of carriage, or will be carried, from the territory of one State to the territory of another; or

(b) the acts constituting the offer and acceptance have been done in the territories of different States; or

(c) the contract provides for the goods to be delivered to the territory of a State other than that within whose territory those acts were to be done.

27 Choice of law clauses   [727]

(1) Where the law applicable to a contract is the law of any part of the United Kingdom only by choice of the parties (and apart from that choice would be the law of some country outside the United Kingdom) sections 2 to 7 and 16 to 21 of this Act do not operate as part of the law applicable to the contract.

(2) This Act has effect notwithstanding any contract term which applies or purports to apply the law of some country outside the United Kingdom, where (either or both) –

(a) the term appears to the court, or arbitrator or arbiter to have been imposed wholly or mainly for the purpose of enabling the party imposing it to evade the operation of this Act; or

(b) in the making of the contract one of the parties dealt as consumer, and he was then habitually resident in the United Kingdom, and the essential steps necessary for the making of the contract were taken there, whether by him or by others on his behalf.

29 Saving for other relevant legislation   [728]

(1) Nothing in this Act removes or restricts the effect of, or prevents reliance upon, any contractual provision which –

(a) is authorised or required by the express terms or necessary implication of an enactment; or

(b) being made with a view to compliance with an international agreement to which the United Kingdom is a party, does not operate more restrictively than is contemplated by the agreement.

(2) A contract term is to be taken –

(a) for the purposes of Part I of this Act, as satisfying the requirement of reasonableness ...

if it is incorporated or approved by, or incorporated pursuant to a decision or ruling of, a competent authority acting in the exercise of any statutory jurisdiction or function and is not a term in a contract to which the competent authority is itself a party.

(3) In this section:

'competent authority' means any court, arbitrator or arbiter, government department or public authority;

'enactment' means any legislation (including subordinate legislation) of the United Kingdom or Northern Ireland and any instrument having effect by virtue of such legislation; and

'statutory' means conferred by an enactment.

SCHEDULE 1   **[729]**

SCOPE OF SECTIONS 2 TO 4 AND 7

1. Sections 2 to 4 of this Act do not extend to

(a) any contract of insurance (including a contract to pay an annuity on human life);

(b) any contract so far as it relates to the creation or transfer of an interest in land, or to the termination of such an interest, whether by extinction, merger, surrender, forfeiture or otherwise;

(c) any contract so far as it relates to the creation or transfer of a right or interest in any patent, trade mark, copyright or design right, registered design, technical or commercial information or other intellectual property, or relates to the termination of any such right or interest;

(d) any contract so far as it relates –

(i) to the formation or dissolution of a company (which means any body corporate or unincorporated association and includes a partnership), or

(ii) to its constitution or the rights or obligations of its corporators or members;

(e) any contract so far as it relates to the creation or transfer of securities or of any right or interest in securities.

2. Section 2(1) extends to

(a) any contract of marine salvage or towage;

(b) any charterparty of a ship or hovercraft; and

(c) any contract for the carriage of goods by ship or hovercraft;

but subject to this sections 2 to 4 and 7 do not extend to any such contract except in favour of a person dealing as consumer.

3. Where goods are carried by ship or hovercraft in pursuance of a contract which either –

(a) specifies that as the means of carriage over part of the journey to be covered, or

(b) makes no provision as to the means of carriage and does not exclude that means,

then sections 2(2), 3 and 4 do not, except in favour of a person dealing as consumer, extend to the contract as it operates for and in relation to the carriage of the goods by that means.

4. Section 2(1) and (2) do not extend to a contract of employment, except in favour of the employee.

5. Section 2(1) does not affect the validity of any discharge and indemnity given by a person, on or in connection with an award to him of compensation for pneumoconiosis attributable to employment in the coal industry, in respect of any further claim arising from his contracting that disease.

SCHEDULE 2   **[730]**

'GUIDELINES' FOR APPLICATION OF REASONABLENESS TEST

The matters to which regard is to be had in particular for the purposes of sections 6(3), 7(3) and (4), 20 and 21 are any of the following which appear to be relevant –

(a) the strength of the bargaining positions of the parties relative to each other, taking into account (among other things) alternative means by which the customer's requirements could have been met;

(b) whether the customer received an inducement to agree to the term, or in accepting it had an opportunity of entering into a similar contract with other persons, but without having to accept a similar term;

(c) whether the customer knew or ought reasonably to have known of the existence and extent of the term (having regard, among other things, to any custom of the trade and any previous course of dealing between the parties);

(d) where the term excludes or restricts any relevant liability if some condition is not complied with, whether it was reasonable at the time of the contract to expect that compliance with that condition would be practicable;

(e) whether the goods were manufactured, processed or adapted to the special order of the customer.

[As amended by the Sale of Goods Act 1979, s63, Schedule 2, paras 19, 20; Supply of Goods and Services Act 1982, s17(2), (3); Occupiers' Liability Act 1984, s2; Copyright, Designs and Patents Act 1988, s303(1), Schedule 7, para 24; Contracts (Applicable Law) Act 1990, Schedule 4, para 4.]

SALE OF GOODS ACT 1979
(1979 c 54)

2 Contract of sale   [731]

(1) A contract of sale of goods is a contract by which the seller transfers or agrees to transfer the property in goods to the buyer for a money consideration, called the price.

(2) There may be a contract of sale between one part owner and another.

(3) A contract of sale may be absolute or conditional.

(4) Where under a contract of sale the property in the goods is transferred from the seller to the buyer the contract is called a sale.

(5) Where under a contract of sale the transfer of the property in the goods is to take place at a future time or subject to some condition later to be fulfilled the contract is called an agreement to sell.

(6) An agreement to sell becomes a sale when the time elapses or the conditions are fulfilled subject to which the property in the goods is to be transferred.

3 Capacity to buy and sell   [732]

(1) Capacity to buy and sell is regulated by the general law concerning capacity to contract and to transfer and acquire property.

(2) Where necessaries are sold and delivered to a minor or to a person who by reason of mental incapacity or drunkenness is incompetent to contract, he must pay a reasonable price for them.

(3) In subsection (2) above 'necessaries' means goods suitable to the condition in life of the minor or other person concerned and to his actual requirements at the time of the sale and delivery.

4 How contract of sale is made   [733]

(1) Subject to this and any other Act, a contract of sale may be made in writing (either with or without seal), or by word of mouth, or partly in writing and partly by word of mouth, or may be implied from the conduct of the parties.

(2) Nothing in this section affects the law relating to corporations.

5 Existing or future goods [734]

(1) The goods which form the subject of a contract of sale may be either existing goods, owned or possessed by the seller, or goods to be manufactured or acquired by him after the making of the contract of sale, in this Act called future goods.

(2) There may be a contract for the sale of goods the acquisition of which by the seller depends on a contingency which may or may not happen.

(3) Where by a contract of sale the seller purports to effect a present sale of future goods, the contract operates as an agreement to sell the goods.

6 Goods which have perished [735]

Where there is a contract for the sale of specific goods, and the goods without the knowledge of the seller have perished at the time when the contract is made, the contract is void.

7 Goods perishing before sale but after agreement to sell [736]

Where there is an agreement to sell specific goods and subsequently the goods, without any fault on the part of the seller or buyer, perish before the risk passes to the buyer, the agreement is avoided.

8 Ascertainment of price [737]

(1) The price in a contract of sale may be fixed by the contract, or may be left to be fixed in a manner agreed by the contract, or may be determined by the course of dealing between the parties.

(2) Where the price is not determined as mentioned in subsection (1) above the buyer must pay a reasonable price.

(3) What is a reasonable price is a question of fact dependent on the circumstances of each particular case.

9 Agreement to sell at valuation [738]

(1) Where there is an agreement to sell goods on the terms that the price is to be fixed by the valuation of a third party, and he cannot or does not make the valuation, the agreement is avoided; but if the goods or any part of them have been delivered to and appropriated by the buyer he must pay a reasonable price for them.

(2) Where the third party is prevented from making the valuation by the fault of the seller or buyer, the party not at fault may maintain an action for damages against the party at fault.

10 Stipulations about time [739]

(1) Unless a different intention appears from the terms of the contract, stipulations as to time of payment are not of the essence of a contract of sale.

(2) Whether any other stipulation as to time is or is not of the essence of the contract depends on the terms of the contract.

(3) In a contract of sale 'month' prima facie means calendar month.

11 When condition to be treated as warranty ...   [740]

(2) Where a contract of sale is subject to a condition to be fulfilled by the seller, the buyer may waive the condition, or may elect to treat the breach of the condition as a breach of warranty and not as a ground for treating the contract as repudiated.

(3) Whether a stipulation in a contract of sale is a condition, the breach of which may give rise to a right to treat the contract as repudiated, or a warranty, the breach of which may give rise to a claim for damages but not to a right to reject the goods and treat the contract as repudiated, depends in each case on the construction of the contract; and a stipulation may be a condition, though called a warranty in the contract.

(4) Subject to section 35A below where a contract of sale is not severable and the buyer has accepted the goods or part of them, the breach of a condition to be fulfilled by the seller can only be treated as a breach of warranty, and not as a ground for rejecting the goods and treating the contract as repudiated, unless there is an express or implied term of the contract to that effect.

(6) Nothing in this section affects a condition or warranty whose fulfilment is excused by law by reason of impossibility or otherwise.

12 Implied terms about title, etc   [741]

(1) In a contract of sale, other than one to which subsection (3) below applies, there is an implied term on the part of the seller that in the case of a sale he has a right to sell the goods, and in the case of an agreement to sell he will have such a right at the time when the property is to pass.

(2) In a contract of sale, other than one to which subsection (3) below applies, there is also an implied term that –

    (a) the goods are free, and will remain free until the time when the property is to pass, from any charge or encumbrance not disclosed or known to the buyer before the contract is made, and
    (b) the buyer will enjoy quiet possession of the goods except so far as it may be disturbed by the owner or other person entitled to the benefit of any charge or encumbrance so disclosed or known.

(3) This subsection applies to a contract of sale in the case of which there appears from the contract or is to be inferred from its circumstances an intention that the seller should transfer only such title as he or a third person may have.

(4) In a contract to which subsection (3) above applies there is an implied term that all charges or encumbrances known to the seller and not known to the buyer have been disclosed to the buyer before the contract is made.

(5) In a contract to which subsection (3) above applies there is also an implied term that none of the following will disturb the buyer's quiet possession of the goods, namely –

    (a) the seller;
    (b) in a case where the parties to the contract intend that the seller should transfer only such title as a third person may have, that person;
    (c) anyone claiming through or under the seller or that third person otherwise than under a charge or encumbrance disclosed or known to the buyer before the contract is made.

(5A) As regards England and Wales and Northern Ireland, the term implied by subsection (1) above is a condition and the terms implied by subsections (2), (4) and (5) above are warranties.

13 Sale by description [742]

(1) Where there is a contract for the sale of goods by description, there is an implied term that the goods will correspond with the description.

(1A) As regards England and Wales and Northern Ireland, the term implied by subsection (1) above is a condition.

(2) If the sale is by sample as well as by description it is not sufficient that the bulk of the goods corresponds with the sample if the goods do not also correspond with the description.

(3) A sale of goods is not prevented from being a sale by description by reason only that, being exposed for sale or hire, they are selected by the buyer.

14 Implied terms about quality or fitness [743]

(1) Except as provided by this section and section 15 below and subject to any other enactment, there is no implied term about the quality or fitness for any particular purpose of goods supplied under a contract of sale.

(2) Where the seller sells goods in the course of a business, there is an implied term that the goods supplied under the contract are of satisfactory quality.

(2A) For the purposes of this Act, goods are of satisfactory quality if they meet the standard that a reasonable person would regard as satisfactory, taking account of any description of the goods, the price (if relevant) and all the other relevant circumstances.

(2B) For the purposes of this Act, the quality of goods includes their state and condition and the following (among others) are in appropriate cases aspects of the quality of goods –

(a) fitness for all the purposes for which goods of the kind in question are commonly supplied,
(b) appearance and finish,
(c) freedom from minor defects,
(d) safety, and
(e) durability.

(2C) The term implied by subsection (2) above does not extend to any matter making the quality of goods unsatisfactory –

(a) which is specifically drawn to the buyer's attention before the contract is made,
(b) where the buyer examines the goods before the contract is made, which that examination ought to reveal, or
(c) in the case of a contract for sale by sample, which would have been apparent on a reasonable examination of the sample.

(3) Where the seller sells goods in the course of a business and the buyer, expressly or by implication, makes known –

(a) to the seller, or
(b) where the purchase price or part of it is payable by instalments and the goods were previously sold by a credit-broker to the seller, to that credit-broker,

any particular purpose for which the goods are being bought, there is an implied term that the goods supplied under the contract are reasonably fit for that purpose, whether or not that is a purpose for which such goods are commonly supplied, except where the circumstances show that the buyer does not rely, or that it is unreasonable for him to rely, on the skill or judgment of the seller or credit-broker.

(4) An implied term about quality or fitness for a particular purpose may be annexed to a contract of sale by usage.

(5) The preceding provisions of this section apply to a sale by a person who in the course of a business is acting as agent for another as they apply to a sale by a principal in the course of a business, except where that other is not selling in the course of a business and either the buyer knows that fact or reasonable steps are taken to bring it to the notice of the buyer before the contract is made.

(6) As regards England and Wales and Northern Ireland, the terms implied by subsections (2) and (3) above are conditions. ...

15 Sale by sample   [744]

(1) A contract of sale is a contract for sale by sample where there is an express or implied term to that effect in the contract.

(2) In the case of a contract for sale by sample there is an implied term –

(a) that the bulk will correspond with the sample in quality;
(c) that the goods will be free from any defect, making their quality unsatisfactory, which would not be apparent on reasonable examination of the sample.

(3) As regards England and Wales and Northern Ireland, the term implied by subsection (2) above is a condition. ...

15A Modification of remedies for breach of condition   [745]
in non-consumer cases

(1) Where in the case of a contract of sale –

(a) the buyer would, apart from this subsection, have the right to reject goods by reason of a breach on the part of the seller of a term implied by sections 13, 14 or 15 above, but
(b) the breach is so slight that it would be unreasonable for him to reject them,

then, if the buyer does not deal as consumer, the breach is not to be treated as a breach of condition but may be treated as a breach of warranty.

(2) This section applies unless a contrary intention appears in, or is to be implied from, the contract.

(3) It is for the seller to show that a breach fell within subsection (1)(b) above. ...

16 Goods must be ascertained   [746]

Subject to section 20A below where there is a contract for the sale of unascertained goods no property in the goods is transferred to the buyer unless and until the goods are ascertained.

17 Property passes when intended to pass   [747]

(1) Where there is a contract for the sale of specific or ascertained goods the property in them is transferred to the buyer at such time as the parties to the contract intend it to be transferred.

(2) For the purpose of ascertaining the intention of the parties regard shall be had to the terms of the contract, the conduct of the parties and the circumstances of the case.

18 Rules for ascertaining intention [748]

Unless a different intention appears, the following are rules for ascertaining the intention of the parties as to the time at which the property in the goods is to pass to the buyer.

Rule 1. – Where there is an unconditional contract for the sale of specific goods in a deliverable state the property in the goods passes to the buyer when the contract is made, and it is immaterial whether the time of payment or the time of delivery, or both, be postponed.

Rule 2. – Where there is a contract for the sale of specific goods and the seller is bound to do something to the goods for the purpose of putting them into a deliverable state, the property does not pass until the thing is done and the buyer has notice that it has been done.

Rule 3. – Where there is a contract for the sale of specific goods in a deliverable state but the seller is bound to weigh, measure, test, or do some other act or thing with reference to the goods for the purpose of ascertaining the price, the property does not pass until the act or thing is done and the buyer has notice that it has been done.

Rule 4. – When goods are delivered to the buyer on approval or on sale or return or other similar terms the property in the goods passes to the buyer: –

(a) when he signifies his approval or acceptance to the seller or does any other act adopting the transaction;

(b) if he does not signify his approval or acceptance to the seller but retains the goods without giving notice of rejection, then, if a time has been fixed for the return of the goods, on the expiration of that time, and, if no time has been fixed, on the expiration of a reasonable time.

Rule 5. – (1) Where there is a contract for the sale of unascertained or future goods by description, and goods of that description and in a deliverable state are unconditionally appropriated to the contract, either by the seller with the assent of the buyer or by the buyer with the assent of the seller, the property in the goods then passes to the buyer; and the assent may be express or implied, and may be given either before or after the appropriation is made.

(2) Where, in pursuance of the contract, the seller delivers the goods to the buyer or to a carrier or other bailee or custodier (whether named by the buyer or not) for the purpose of transmission to the buyer, and does not reserve the right of disposal, he is to be taken to have unconditionally appropriated the goods to the contract.

(3) Where there is a contract for the sale of a specified quantity of unascertained goods in a deliverable state forming part of a bulk which is identified either in the contract or by subsequent agreement between the parties and the bulk is reduced to (or to less than) that quantity, then, if the buyer under that contract is the only buyer to whom goods are then due out of the bulk –

(a) the remaining goods are to be taken as appropriated to that contract at the time when the bulk is so reduced; and
(b) the property in those goods then passes to that buyer.

(4) Paragraph (3) above applies also (with the necessary modifications) where a bulk is reduced to (or to less than) the aggregate of the quantities due to a single buyer under separate contracts relating to that bulk and he is the only buyer to whom goods are then due out of that bulk.

211

19 Reservation of right of disposal   [749]

(1) Where there is a contract for the sale of specific goods or where goods are subsequently appropriated to the contract, the seller may, by the terms of the contract or appropriation, reserve the right of disposal of the goods until certain conditions are fulfilled; and in such a case, notwithstanding the delivery of the goods to the buyer, or to a carrier or other bailee or custodier for the purpose of transmission to the buyer, the property in the goods does not pass to the buyer until the conditions imposed by the seller are fulfilled.

(2) Where goods are shipped, and by the bill of lading the goods are deliverable to the order of the seller or his agent, the seller is prima facie to be taken to reserve the right of disposal.

(3) Where the seller of goods draws on the buyer for the price, and transmits the bill of exchange and bill of lading to the buyer together to secure acceptance or payment of the bill of exchange, the buyer is bound to return the bill of lading if he does not honour the bill of exchange, and if he wrongfully retains the bill of lading the property in the goods does not pass to him.

20 Risk prima facie passes with property   [750]

(1) Unless otherwise agreed, the goods remain at the seller's risk until the property in them is transferred to the buyer, but when the property in them is transferred to the buyer the goods are at the buyer's risk whether delivery has been made or not.

(2) But where delivery has been delayed through the fault of either buyer or seller the goods are at the risk of the party at fault as regards any loss which might not have occurred but for such fault.

(3) Nothing in this section affects the duties or liabilities of either seller or buyer as a bailee or custodier of the goods of the other party.

20A Undivided shares in goods forming part of a bulk   [751]

(1) This section applies to a contract for the sale of a specified quantity of unascertained goods if the following conditions are met –

    (a) the goods or some of them form part of a bulk which is identified either in the contract or by subsequent agreement between the parties; and
    (b) the buyer has paid the price for some or all of the goods which are the subject of the contract and which form part of the bulk.

(2) Where this section applies, then (unless the parties agree otherwise), as soon as the conditions specified in paragraphs (a) and (b) of subsection (1) above are met or at such later time as the parties may agree –

    (a) property in an undivided share in the bulk is transferred to the buyer, and
    (b) the buyer becomes an owner in common of the bulk.

(3) Subject to subsection (4) below, for the purposes of this section, the undivided share of a buyer in a bulk at any time shall be such share as the quantity of goods paid for and due to the buyer out of the bulk bears to the quantity of goods in the bulk at that time.

(4) Where the aggregate of the undivided shares of buyers in a bulk determined under subsection (3) above would at any time exceed the whole of the bulk at that time, the undivided share in the bulk of each buyer shall be reduced proportionately so that the aggregate of the undivided shares is equal to the whole bulk.

(5) Where a buyer has paid the price for only some of the goods due to him out of a bulk, any delivery to the buyer out of the bulk shall, for the purposes of this

section, be ascribed in the first place to the goods in respect of which payment has been made.

(6) For the purposes of this section payment of part of the price for any goods shall be treated as payment for a corresponding part of the goods.

20B Deemed consent by co-owner to dealings **[752]**
in bulk goods

(1) A person who has become an owner in common of a bulk by virtue of section 20A above shall be deemed to have consented to –

(a) any delivery of goods out of the bulk to any other owner in common of the bulk, being goods which are due to him under his contract;
(b) any dealing with or removal, delivery or disposal of goods in the bulk by any other person who is an owner in common of the bulk in so far as the goods fall within that co-owner's undivided share in the bulk at the time of the dealing, removal, delivery or disposal.

(2) No cause of action shall accrue to anyone against a person by reason of that person having acted in accordance with paragraph (a) or (b) of subsection (1) above in reliance on any consent deemed to have been given under that subsection.

(3) Nothing in this section or section 20A above shall –

(a) impose an obligation on a buyer of goods out of a bulk to compensate any other buyer of goods out of that bulk for any shortfall in the goods received by that other buyer;
(b) affect any contractual arrangement between buyers of goods out of a bulk for adjustments between themselves; or
(c) affect the rights of any buyer under his contract.

21 Sale by person not the owner **[753]**

(1) Subject to this Act, where goods are sold by a person who is not their owner, and who does not sell them under the authority or with the consent of the owner, the buyer acquires no better title to the goods than the seller had, unless the owner of the goods is by his conduct precluded from denying the seller's authority to sell.

(2) Nothing in this Act affects –

(a) the provisions of the Factors Acts or any enactment enabling the apparent owner of goods to dispose of them as if he were their true owner;
(b) the validity of any contract of sale under any special common law or statutory power of sale or under the order of a court of competent jurisdiction.

23 Sale under voidable title **[754]**

When the seller of goods has a voidable title to them, but his title has not been avoided at the time of the sale, the buyer acquires a good title to the goods, provided he buys them in good faith and without notice of the seller's defect of title.

24 Seller in possession after sale **[755]**

Where a person having sold goods continues or is in possession of the goods, or of the documents of title to the goods, the delivery or transfer by that person, or by a mercantile agent acting for him, of the goods or documents of title under any sale, pledge, or other disposition thereof, to any person receiving the same in good faith and without notice of the previous sale, has the same effect as if the person making the delivery or transfer were expressly authorised by the owner of the goods to make the same.

25 Buyer in possession after sale [756]

(1) Where a person having bought or agreed to buy goods obtains, with the consent of the seller, possession of the goods or the documents of title to the goods, the delivery or transfer by that person, or by a mercantile agent acting for him, of the goods or documents of title, under any sale, pledge, or other disposition thereof, to any person receiving the same in good faith and without notice of any lien or other right of the original seller in respect of the goods, has the same effect as if the person making the delivery or transfer were a mercantile agent in possession of the goods or documents of title with the consent of the owner.

(2) For the purposes of subsection (1) above –

(a) the buyer under a conditional sale agreement is to be taken not to be a person who has bought or agreed to buy goods, and

(b) 'conditional sale agreement' means an agreement for the sale of goods which is a consumer credit agreement within the meaning of the Consumer Credit Act 1974 under which the purchase price or part of it is payable by instalments, and the property in the goods is to remain in the seller (notwithstanding that the buyer is to be in possession of the goods) until such conditions as to the payment of instalments or otherwise as may be specified in the agreement are fulfilled.

(3) Paragraph 9 of Schedule 1 below applies in relation to a contract under which a person buys or agrees to buy goods and which is made before the appointed day.

(4) In subsection (3) above and paragraph 9 of Schedule 1 below references to the appointed day are to the day appointed for the purposes of those provisions by an order of the Secretary of State made by statutory instrument.

26 Supplementary to sections 24 and 25 [757]

In sections 24 and 25 above 'mercantile agent' means a mercantile agent having in the customary course of his business as such agent authority either –

(a) to sell goods, or
(b) to consign goods for the purpose of sale, or
(c) to buy goods, or
(d) to raise money on the security of goods.

PART IV

PERFORMANCE OF THE CONTRACT

27 Duties of seller and buyer [758]

It is the duty of the seller to deliver the goods, and of the buyer to accept and pay for them, in accordance with the terms of the contract of sale.

28 Payment and delivery are concurrent conditions [759]

Unless otherwise agreed, delivery of the goods and payment of the price are concurrent conditions, that is to say, the seller must be ready and willing to give possession of the goods to the buyer in exchange for the price and the buyer must be ready and willing to pay the price in exchange for possession of the goods.

29 Rules about delivery [760]

(1) Whether it is for the buyer to take possession of the goods or for the seller to send them to the buyer is a question depending in each case on the contract, express or implied, between the parties.

(2) Apart from any such contract, express or implied, the place of delivery is the seller's place of business if he has one, and if not, his residence; except that, if the contract is for the sale of specific goods, which to the knowledge of the parties when the contract is made are in some other place, then that place is the place of delivery.

(3) Where under the contract of sale the seller is bound to send the goods to the buyer, but no time for sending them is fixed, the seller is bound to send them within a reasonable time.

(4) Where the goods at the time of sale are in the possession of a third person, there is no delivery by seller to buyer unless and until the third person acknowledges to the buyer that he holds the goods on his behalf; and nothing in this section affects the operation of the issue or transfer of any document of title to goods.

(5) Demand or tender of delivery may be treated as ineffectual unless made at a reasonable hour; and what is a reasonable hour is a question of fact.

(6) Unless otherwise agreed, the expenses of and incidental to putting the goods into a deliverable state must be borne by the seller.

30 Delivery of shortfall or excess [761]

(1) Where the seller delivers to the buyer a quantity of goods less than he contracted to sell, the buyer may reject them, but if the buyer accepts the goods so delivered he must pay for them at the contract rate.

(2) Where the seller delivers to the buyer a quantity of goods larger than he contracted to sell, the buyer may accept the goods included in the contract and reject the rest, or he may reject the whole.

(2A) A buyer who does not deal as consumer may not –

(a) where the seller delivers a quantity of goods less than he contracted to sell, reject the goods under subsection (1) above, or
(b) where the seller delivers a quantity of goods larger than he contracted to sell, reject the whole under subsection (2) above,

if the shortfall or, as the case may be, excess is so slight that it would be unreasonable for him to do so.

(2B) It is for the seller to show that a shortfall or excess fell within subsection (2A) above. ...

(3) Where the seller delivers to the buyer a quantity of goods larger than he contracted to sell and the buyer accepts the whole of the goods so delivered he must pay for them at the contract rate.

(5) This section is subject to any usage of trade, special agreement, or course of dealing between the parties.

31 Instalment deliveries [762]

(1) Unless otherwise agreed, the buyer of goods is not bound to accept delivery of them by instalments.

(2) Where there is a contract for the sale of goods to be delivered by stated instalments, which are to be separately paid for, and the seller makes defective deliveries in respect of one or more instalments, or the buyer neglects or refuses to take delivery of or pay for one or more instalments, it is a question in each case depending on the terms of the contract and the circumstances of the case whether the breach of contract is a repudiation of the whole contract or whether it is a severable breach giving rise to a claim for compensation but not to a right to treat the whole contract as repudiated.

32 Delivery to carrier   [763]

(1) Where, in pursuance of a contract of sale, the seller is authorised or required to send the goods to the buyer, delivery of the goods to a carrier (whether named by the buyer or not) for the purpose of transmission to the buyer is prima facie deemed to be a delivery of the goods to the buyer.

(2) Unless otherwise authorised by the buyer, the seller must make such contract with the carrier on behalf of the buyer as may be reasonable having regard to the nature of the goods and the other circumstances of the case; and if the seller omits to do so, and the goods are lost or damaged in course of transit; the buyer may decline to treat the delivery to the carrier as a delivery to himself or may hold the seller responsible in damages.

(3) Unless otherwise agreed, where goods are sent by the seller to the buyer by a route involving sea transit, under circumstances in which it is usual to insure, the seller must give such notice to the buyer as may enable him to insure them during their sea transit; and if the seller fails to do so, the goods are at his risk during such sea transit.

33 Risk where goods are delivered at distant place   [764]

Where the seller of goods agrees to deliver them at his own risk at a place other than that where they are when sold, the buyer must nevertheless (unless otherwise agreed) take any risk of deterioration in the goods necessarily incident to the course of transit.

34 Buyer to have opportunity to examine goods   [765]

Unless otherwise agreed, when the seller tenders delivery of goods to the buyer, he is bound on request to afford the buyer a reasonable opportunity of examining the goods for the purpose of ascertaining whether they are in conformity with the contract and, in the case of a contract for sale by sample, of comparing the bulk with the sample.

35 Acceptance   [766]

(1) The buyer is deemed to have accepted the goods subject to subsection (2) below –

(a) when he intimates to the seller that he has accepted them, or
(b) when the goods have been delivered to him and he does any act in relation to them which is inconsistent with the ownership of the seller.

(2) Where goods are delivered to the buyer, and he has not previously examined them, he is not deemed to have accepted them under subsection (1) above until he has had a reasonable opportunity of examining them for the purpose –

(a) of ascertaining whether they are in conformity with the contract, and

(b) in the case of a contract for sale by sample, of comparing the bulk with the sample.

(3) Where the buyer deals as a consumer or (in Scotland) the contract of sale is a consumer contract, the buyer cannot lose his right to rely on subsection (2) above by agreement, waiver or otherwise.

(4) The buyer is also deemed to have accepted the goods when after the lapse of a reasonable time he retains the goods without intimating to the seller that he has rejected them.

(5) The questions that are material in determining for the purposes of subsection (4) above whether a reasonable time has elapsed include whether the buyer has had a reasonable opportunity of examining the goods for the purpose mentioned in subsection (2) above.

(6) The buyer is not by virtue of this section deemed to have accepted the goods merely because –

(a) he asks for, or agrees to, their repair by or under an arrangement with the seller, or
(b) the goods are delivered to another under a sub-sale or other disposition.

(7) Where the contract is for the sale of goods making one or more commercial units, a buyer accepting any goods included in a unit is deemed to have accepted all the goods making the unit; and in this subsection 'commercial unit' means a unit division of which would materially impair the value of the goods or the character of the unit ...

35A Right of partial rejection [767]

(1) If the buyer –

(a) has the right to reject the goods by reason of a breach on the part of the seller that affects some or all of them, but
(b) accepts some of the goods, including, where there are any goods unaffected by the breach, all such goods,

he does not by accepting them lose his right to reject the rest.

(2) In the case of a buyer having the right to reject an instalment of goods, subsection (1) above applies as if references to the goods were references to the goods comprised in the instalment.

(3) For the purposes of subsection (1) above, goods are affected by breach if by reason of the breach they are not in conformity with the contract.

(4) This section applies unless a contrary intention appears in, or is to be implied from, the contract.

36 Buyer not bound to return rejected goods [768]

Unless otherwise agreed, where goods are delivered to the buyer, and he refuses to accept them, having the right to do so, he is not bound to return them to the seller, but it is sufficient if he intimates to the seller that he refuses to accept them.

37 Buyer's liability for not taking delivery of goods [769]

(1) When the seller is ready and willing to deliver the goods, and requests the buyer to take delivery, and the buyer does not within a reasonable time after such request take delivery of the goods, he is liable to the seller for any loss occasioned by his neglect or refusal to take delivery, and also for a reasonable charge for the care and custody of the goods.

(2) Nothing in this section affects the rights of the seller where the neglect or refusal of the buyer to take delivery amounts to a repudiation of the contract.

PART V

RIGHTS OF UNPAID SELLER AGAINST THE GOODS

38 Unpaid seller defined [770]

(1) The seller of goods is an unpaid seller within the meaning of this Act –

(a) when the whole of the price has not been paid or tendered;
(b) when a bill of exchange or other negotiable instrument has been received as conditional payment, and the condition on which it was received has not been fulfilled by reason of the dishonour of the instrument or otherwise.

(2) In this Part of this Act 'seller' includes any person who is in the position of a seller, as, for instance, an agent of the seller to whom the bill of lading has been indorsed, or a consignor or agent who has himself paid (or is directly responsible for) the price.

39 Unpaid seller's rights [771]

(1) Subject to this and any other Act, notwithstanding that the property in the goods may have passed to the buyer, the unpaid seller of goods, as such, has by implication of law –

(a) a lien on the goods or right to retain them for the price while he is in possession of them;
(b) in case of the insolvency of the buyer, a right of stopping the goods in transit after he has parted with the possession of them;
(c) a right of re-sale as limited by this Act.

(2) Where the property in goods has not passed to the buyer, the unpaid seller has (in addition to his other remedies) a right of withholding delivery similar to and co-extensive with his rights of lien or retention and stoppage in transit where the property has passed to the buyer.

41 Seller's lien [772]

(1) Subject to this Act, the unpaid seller of goods who is in possession of them is entitled to retain possession of them until payment or tender of the price in the following cases –

(a) where the goods have been sold without any stipulation as to credit;
(b) where the goods have been sold on credit but the term of credit has expired;
(c) where the buyer becomes insolvent.

(2) The seller may exercise his lien or right of retention notwithstanding that he is in possession of the goods as agent or bailee or custodier for the buyer.

42 Part delivery [773]

Where an unpaid seller has made part delivery of the goods, he may exercise his lien or right of retention on the remainder, unless such part delivery has been made under such circumstances as to show an agreement to waive the lien or right of retention.

43 Termination of lien [774]

(1) The unpaid seller of goods loses his lien or right of retention in respect of them –

(a) when he delivers the goods to a carrier or other bailee or custodier for the purpose of transmission to the buyer without reserving the right of disposal of the goods;
(b) when the buyer or his agent lawfully obtains possession of the goods;
(c) by waiver of the lien or right of retention.

(2) An unpaid seller of goods who has a lien or right of retention in respect of them does not lose his lien or right of retention by reason only that he has obtained judgment or decree for the price of the goods.

44 Right of stoppage in transit [775]

Subject to this Act, when the buyer of goods becomes insolvent the unpaid seller who has parted with the possession of the goods has the right of stopping them in transit, that is to say, he may resume possession of the goods as long as they are in course of transit, and may retain them until payment or tender of the price.

45 Duration of transit [776]

(1) Goods are deemed to be in course of transit from the time when they are delivered to a carrier or other bailee or custodier for the purpose of transmission to the buyer, until the buyer or his agent in that behalf takes deliver of them from the carrier or other bailee or custodier.

(2) If the buyer or his agent in that behalf obtains delivery of the goods before their arrival at the appointed destination, the transit is at an end.

(3) If, after the arrival of the goods at the appointed destination, the carrier or other bailee or custodier acknowledges to the buyer or his agent that he holds the goods on his behalf and continues in possession of them as bailee or custodier for the buyer or his agent, the transit is at an end, and it is immaterial that a further destination for the goods may have been indicated by the buyer.

(4) If the goods are rejected by the buyer, and the carrier or other bailee or custodier continues in possession of them, the transit is not deemed to be at an end, even if the seller has refused to receive them back.

(5) When goods are delivered to a ship chartered by the buyer it is a question depending on the circumstances of the particular case whether they are in the possession of the master as a carrier or as agent to the buyer.

(6) Where the carrier or other bailee or custodier wrongfully refuses to deliver the gods to the buyer or his agent in that behalf, the transit is deemed to be at an end.

(7) Where part delivery of the goods has been made to the buyer or his agent in that behalf, the remainder of the goods may be stopped in transit, unless such part delivery has been made under such circumstances as to show an agreement to give up possession of the whole of the goods.

46 How stoppage in transit is effected [777]

(1) The unpaid seller may exercise his right of stoppage in transit either by taking actual possession of the goods or by giving notice of his claim to the carrier or other bailee or custodier in whose possession the goods are.

(2) The notice may be given either to the person in actual possession of the goods or to his principal.

(3) If given to the principal, the notice is ineffective unless given at such time and under such circumstances that the principal, by the exercise of reasonable diligence, may communicate it to his servant or agent in time to prevent a delivery to the buyer.

(4) When notice of stoppage in transit is given by the seller to the carrier or other bailee or custodier in possession of the goods, he must re-deliver the goods to, or according to the directions of, the seller; and the expenses of the re-delivery must be borne by the seller.

47 Effect of sub-sale, etc by buyer [778]

(1) Subject to this Act, the unpaid seller's right of lien or retention or stoppage in transit is not affected by any sale or other disposition of the goods which the buyer may have made, unless the seller has assented to it.

(2) Where a document of title to goods has been lawfully transferred to any person as buyer or owner of the goods, and that person transfers the document to a person who takes it in good faith and for valuable consideration, then –

(a) if the last-mentioned transfer was by way of sale the unpaid seller's right of lien or retention or stoppage in transit is defeated; and
(b) if the last-mentioned transfer was made by way of pledge or other disposition for value, the unpaid seller's right of lien or retention or stoppage in transit can only be exercised subject to the rights of the transferee.

48 Rescission: and re-sale by seller [779]

(1) Subject to this section, a contract of sale is not rescinded by the mere exercise by an unpaid seller of his right of lien or retention or stoppage in transit.

(2) Where an unpaid seller who has exercised his right of lien or retention or stoppage in transit re-sells the goods, the buyer acquires a good title to them as against the original buyer.

(3) Where the goods are of a perishable nature, or where the unpaid seller gives notice to the buyer of his intention to re-sell, and the buyer does not within a reasonable time pay or tender the price, the unpaid seller may re-sell the goods and recover from the original buyer damages for any loss occasioned by his breach of contract.

(4) Where the seller expressly reserves the right of re-sale in case the buyer should make default, and on the buyer making default re-sells the goods, the original contract of sale is rescinded but without prejudice to any claim the seller may have for damages.

PART VI

ACTIONS FOR BREACH OF THE CONTRACT

49 Action for price [780]

(1) Where, under a contract of sale, the property in the goods has passed to the buyer and he wrongfully neglects or refuses to pay for the goods according to the terms of the contract, the seller may maintain an action against him for the price of the goods.

(2) Where, under a contract of sale, the price is payable on a day certain irrespective of delivery and the buyer wrongfully neglects or refuses to pay such

price, the seller may maintain an action for the price, although the property in the goods has not passed and the goods have not been appropriated to the contract. ...

50 Damages for non-acceptance [781]

(1) Where the buyer wrongfully neglects or refuses to accept and pay for the goods, the seller may maintain an action against him for damages for non-acceptance.

(2) The measure of damages is the estimated loss directly and naturally resulting, in the ordinary course of events, from the buyer's breach of contract.

(3) Where there is an available market for the goods in question the measure of damages is prima facie to be ascertained by the difference between the contract price and the market or current price at the time or times when the goods ought to have been accepted or (if no time was fixed for acceptance) at the time of the refusal to accept.

51 Damages for non-delivery [782]

(1) Where the seller wrongfully neglects or refuses to deliver the goods to the buyer, the buyer may maintain an action against the seller for damages for non-delivery.

(2) The measure of damages is the estimated loss directly and naturally resulting, in the ordinary course of events, from the seller's breach of contract.

(3) Where there is an available market for the goods in question the measure of damages is prima facie to be ascertained by the difference between the contract price and the market or current price of the goods at the time or times when they ought to have been delivered or (if no time was fixed) at the time of the refusal to deliver.

52 Specific performance [783]

(1) In any action for breach of contract to deliver specific or ascertained goods the court may, if it thinks fit, on the plaintiff's application, by its judgment or decree direct that the contract shall be performed specifically, without giving the defendant the option of retaining the goods on payment of damages.

(2) The plaintiff's application may be made at any time before judgment or decree.

(3) The judgment or decree may be unconditional, or on such terms and conditions as to damages, payment of the price and otherwise as seem just to the court. ...

53 Remedy for breach of warranty [784]

(1) Where there is a breach of warranty by the seller, or where the buyer elects (or is compelled) to treat any breach of a condition on the part of the seller as a breach of warranty, the buyer is not by reason only of such breach of warranty entitled to reject the goods; but he may –

(a) set up against the seller the breach of warranty in diminution or extinction of the price, or
(b) maintain an action against the seller for damages for the breach of warranty.

(2) The measure of damages for breach of warranty is the estimated loss directly and naturally resulting, in the ordinary course of events, from the breach of warranty.

(3) In the case of breach of warranty of quality such loss is prima facie the difference between the value of the goods at the time of delivery to the buyer and the value they would have had if they had fulfilled the warranty.

(4) The fact that the buyer has set up the breach of warranty in diminution or extinction of the price does not prevent him from maintaining an action for the same breach of warranty if he has suffered further damage. ...

54 Interest   [785]

Nothing in this Act affects the right of the buyer or the seller to recover interest or special damages in any case where by law interest or special damages may be recoverable, or to recover money paid where the consideration for the payment of it has failed.

PART VII

SUPPLEMENTARY

55 Exclusion of implied terms   [786]

(I) Where a right, duty or liability would arise under a contract of sale of goods by implication of law, it may (subject to the Unfair Contract Terms Act 1977) be negatived or varied by express agreement, or by the course of dealing between the parties, or by such usage as binds both parties to the contract.

(2) An express term does not negative a term implied by this Act unless inconsistent with it. ...

57 Auction sales   [787]

(1) Where goods are put up for sale by auction in lots, each lot is prima facie deemed to be the subject of a separate contract of sale.

(2) A sale by auction is complete when the auctioneer announces its completion by the fall of the hammer, or in other customary manner; and until the announcement is made any bidder may retract his bid.

(3) A sale by auction may be notified to be subject to a reserve or upset price, and a right to bid may also be reserved expressly by or on behalf of the seller.

(4) Where a sale by auction is not notified to be subject to a right to bid by or on behalf of the seller, it is not lawful for the seller to bid himself or to employ any person to bid at the sale, or for the auctioneer knowingly to take any bid from the seller or any such person.

(5) A sale contravening subsection (4) above may be treated as fraudulent by the buyer.

(6) Where, in respect of a sale by auction, a right to bid is expressly reserved (but not otherwise) the seller or any one person on his behalf may bid at the auction.

59 Reasonable time a question of fact   [788]

Where a reference is made in this Act to a reasonable time the question what is a reasonable time is a question of fact.

60 Rights, etc enforceable by action   [789]

Where a right, duty or liability is declared by this Act, it may (unless otherwise provided by this Act) be enforced by action.

61 Interpretation [790]

(1) In this Act, unless the context or subject matter otherwise requires –

'action' includes counterclaim and set-off, and in Scotland condescendence and claim and compensation;

'bulk' means a mass or collection of goods of the same kind which –

(a) is contained in a defined space or area; and
(b) is such that any goods in the bulk are interchangeable with any other goods therein of the same number or quantity;

'business' includes a profession and the activities of any government department (including a Northern Ireland department) or local or public authority;

'buyer' means a person who buys or agrees to buy goods;

'consumer contract' has the same meaning as in section 25(1) of the Unfair Contract Terms Act 1977; and for the purposes of this Act the onus of proving that a contract is not to be regarded as a consumer contract shall lie on the seller;

'contract of sale' includes an agreement to sell as well as a sale;

'credit-broker' means a person acting in the course of a business of credit brokerage carried on by him, that is a business of effecting introductions of individuals desiring to obtain credit –

(a) to persons carrying on any business so far as it relates to the provision of credit, or
(b) to other persons engaged in credit brokerage;

'delivery' means voluntary transfer of possession from one person to another except that in relation to sections 20A and 20B above it includes such appropriation of goods to the contract as results in property in the goods being transferred to the buyer;

'document of title to goods' has the same meaning as it has in the Factors Acts;

'Factors Acts' means the Factors Act 1889, the Factors (Scotland) Act 1890, and any enactment amending or substituted for the same;

'fault' means wrongful act or default;

'future goods' means goods to be manufactured or acquired by the seller after the making of the contract of sale;

'goods' includes all personal chattels other than things in action and money, and in Scotland all corporeal moveables except money; and in particular 'goods' includes emblements, industrial growing crops, and things attached to or forming part of the land which are agreed to be severed before sale or under the contract of sale and includes an undivided share in goods;

'plaintiff' includes pursuer, complainer, claimant in a multiplepoinding and defendant or defender counter-claiming;

'property' means the general property in goods, and not merely a special property;

'sale' includes a person who sells or agrees to sell goods;

'specific goods' means goods identified and agreed on at the time a contract of sale is made and includes an undivided share, specified as a fraction or percentage, of goods identified and agreed on as aforesaid;

'warranty' (as regards England and Wales and Northern Ireland) means an agreement with reference to goods which are the subject of a contract of sale, but collateral to the main purpose of such contract, the breach of which gives rise to a claim for damages, but not to a right to reject the goods and treat the contract as repudiated.

(3) A thing is deemed to be done in good faith within the meaning of this Act when it is in fact done honestly, whether it is done negligently or not.

(4) A person is deemed to be insolvent within the meaning of this Act if he has either ceased to pay his debts in the ordinary course of business or he cannot pay his debts as they become due.

(5) Goods are in a deliverable state within the meaning of this Act when they are in such a state that the buyer would under the contract be bound to take delivery of them.

(5A) References in this Act to dealing as consumer are to be construed in accordance with Part I of the Unfair Contract Terms Act 1977; and, for the purposes of this Act, it is for a seller claiming that the buyer does not deal as consumer to show that he does not.

62 Savings: rules of law, etc [791]

(1) The rules in bankruptcy relating to contracts of sale apply to those contracts, notwithstanding anything in this Act.

(2) The rules of the common law, including the law merchant, except in so far as they are inconsistent with the provisions of this Act,and in particular the rules relating to the law of principal and agent and the effect of fraud, misrepresentation, duress or coercion, mistake, or other invalidating cause, apply to contracts for the sale of goods.

(3) Nothing in this Act or the Sale of Goods Act 1893 affects the enactments relating to bills of sale, or any enactment relating to the sale of goods which is not expressly repealed or amended by this Act or that.

(4) The provisions of this Act about contracts of sale do not apply to a transaction in the form of a contract of sale which is intended to operate by way of mortgage, pledge, charge, or other security. ...

NB The repeal of s22(1) (market overt) by s1 of the Sale of Goods (Amendment) Act 1994 applies to any contract for sale of goods made after the 1994 Act came into force, ie 3 January 1995.

[As amended by the Insolvency Act 1985, s235(3), Schedule 10, Part III; Sale and Supply of Goods Act 1994, ss1–4, 7(1), Schedule 2, para 5, Schedule 3 (with effect from 3 January 1995); Sale of Goods (Amendment) Act 1995, ss1(1), (2), (3), 2 (with effect from 19 September 1995).]

LIMITATION ACT 1980
(1980 c 58)

PART I

ORDINARY TIME LIMITS FOR DIFFERENT CLASSES OF ACTION

1 Time limits under Part I subject to extension or exclusion under Part II [792]

(1) This Part of this Act gives the ordinary time limits for bringing actions of the various classes mentioned in the following provisions of this Part.

(2) The ordinary time limits given in this Part of this Act are subject to extension or exclusion in accordance with the provisions of Part 11 of this Act.

5 Time limit for actions founded on simple contract   **[793]**

An action founded on simple contract shall not be brought after the expiration of six years from the date on which the cause of action accrued.

6 Special time limit for actions in respect of certain loans   **[794]**

(1) Subject to subsection (3) below, section 5 of this Act shall not bar the right of action on a contract of loan to which this section applies.

(2) This section applies to any contract of loan which –

(a) does not provide for repayment of the debt on or before a fixed or determinable date; and

(b) does not effectively (whether or not it purports to do so) make the obligation to repay the debt conditional on a demand for repayment made by or on behalf of the creditor or on any other matter;

except where in connection with taking the loan the debtor enters into any collateral obligation to pay the amount of the debt or any part of it (as, for example, by delivering a promissory note as security for the debt) on terms which would exclude the application of this section to the contract of loan if they applied directly to repayment of the debt.

(3) Where a demand in writing for repayment of the debt under a contract of loan to which this section applies is made by or on behalf of the creditor (or, where there are joint creditors, by or on behalf of any one of them) section 5 of this Act shall thereupon apply as if the cause of action to recover the debt had accrued on the date on which the demand was made.

(4) In this section 'promissory note' has the same meaning as in the Bills of Exchange Act 1882.

7 Time limit for actions to enforce certain awards   **[795]**

An action to enforce an award, where the submission is not by an instrument under seal, shall not be brought after the expiration of six years from the date on which the cause of action accrued.

8 Time limit for actions on a specialty   **[796]**

(1) An action upon a specialty shall not be brought after the expiration of twelve years from the date on which the cause of action accrued.

(2) Subsection (1) above shall not affect any action for which a shorter period of limitation is prescribed by any other provision of this Act.

11 Special time limit for actions in respect of   **[797]** personal injuries

(1) This section applies to any action for damages for negligence, nuisance or breach of duty (whether the duty exists by virtue of a contract or of provision made by or under a statute or independently of any contract or any such provision) where the damages claimed by the plaintiff for the negligence, nuisance or breach of duty consist of or include damages in respect of personal injuries to the plaintiff or any other person.

(2) None of the time limits given in the preceding provisions of this Act shall apply to an action to which this section applies.

(3) An action to which this section applies shall not be brought after the expiration of the period applicable in accordance with subsection (4) or (5) below.

(4) Except where subsection (5) below applies, the period applicable is three years from –

>   (a) the date on which the cause of action accrued; or
>   (b) the date of knowledge (if later) of the person injured.

(5) If the person injured dies before the expiration of the period mentioned in subsection (4) above, the period applicable as respects the cause of action surviving for the benefit of his estate by virtue of section 1 of the Law Reform (Miscellaneous Provisions) Act 1934 shall be three years from –

>   (a) the date of death; or
>   (b) the date of the personal representative's knowledge;

whichever is the later.

(6) For the purposes of this section 'personal representative' includes any person who is or has been a personal representative of the deceased, including an executor who has not proved the will (whether or not he has renounced probate) but not anyone appointed only as a special personal representative in relation to settled land; and regard shall be had to any knowledge acquired by any such person while a personal representative or previously.

(7) If there is more than one personal representative, and their dates of knowledge are different, subsection (5)(b) above shall be read as referring to the earliest of those dates.

11A Actions in respect of defective products   [798]

(1) This section shall apply to an action for damages by virtue of any provision of Part I of the Consumer Protection Act 1987.

(2) None of the time limits given in the preceding provisions of this Act shall apply to an action to which this section applies.

(3) An action to which this section applies shall not be brought after the expiration of the period of ten years from the relevant time, within the meaning of section 4 of the said Act of 1987; and this subsection shall operate to extinguish a right of action and shall do so whether or not that right of action had accrued, or time under the following provisions of this Act had begun to run, at the end of the said period of ten years.

(4) Subject to subsection (5) below, an action to which this section applies in which the damages claimed by the plaintiff consist of or include damages in respect of personal injuries to the plaintiff or any other person or loss of or damage to any property, shall not be brought after the expiration of the period of three years from whichever is the later of –

>   (a) the date on which the cause of action accrued; and
>   (b) the date of knowledge of the injured person or, in the case of loss of or damage to property, the date of knowledge of the plaintiff or (if earlier) of any person in whom his cause of action was previously vested.

(5) If in a case where the damages claimed by the plaintiff consist of or include damages in respect of personal injuries to the plaintiff or any other person the injured person died before the expiration of the period mentioned in subsection (4) above, that subsection shall have effect as respects the cause of action surviving for the benefit of his estate by virtue of section 1 of the Law Reform (Miscellaneous Provisions) Act 1934 as if for the reference to that period there were substituted a reference to the period of three years from whichever is the later of –

>   (a) the date of death; and

(b) the date of the personal representative's knowledge.

(6) For the purposes of this section 'personal representative' includes any person who is or has been a personal representative of the deceased, including an executor who has not proved the will (whether or not he had renounced probate) but not anyone appointed only as a special personal representative in relation to settled land; and regard shall be had to any knowledge acquired by any such person while a personal representative or previously.

(7) If there is more than one personal representative and their dates of knowledge are different, subsection (5)(b) above shall be read as referring to the earliest of those dates.

(8) Expressions used in this section or section 14 of this Act and in Part I of the Consumer Protection Act 1987 have the same meanings in this section or that section as in that Part; and section 1(1) of that Act (Part I to be construed as enacted for the purpose of complying with the product liability Directive) shall apply for the purpose of construing this section and the following provisions of this Act so far as they relate to an action by virtue of any provision of that Part as it applies for the purpose of construing that Part.

12 Special time limit for actions under Fatal Accidents legislation [799]

(1) An action under the Fatal Accidents Act 1976 shall not be brought if the death occurred when the person injured could no longer maintain an action and recover damages in respect of the injury (whether because of a time limit in this Act or in any other Act, or for any other reason).

Where any such action by the injured person would have been barred by the time limit in section 11 or 11A of this Act, no account shall be taken of the possibility of that time limit being overridden under section 33 of this Act.

(2) None of the time limits given in the preceding provisions of this Act shall apply to an action under the Fatal Accidents Act 1976, but no such action shall be brought after the expiration of three years from –

(a) the date of death; or
(b) the date of knowledge of the person for whose benefit the action is brought;

whichever is the later.

(3) An action under the Fatal Accidents Act 1976 shall be one to which sections 28, 33 and 35 of this Act apply, and the application to any such action of the time limit under subsection (2) above shall be subject to section 39; but otherwise Parts II and III of this Act shall not apply to any such action.

14 Definition of date of knowledge for purposes of sections 11 and 12 [800]

(1) Subject to subsection (1A) below, in sections 11 and 12 of this Act references to a person's date of knowledge are references to the date on which he first had knowledge of the following facts –

(a) that the injury in question was significant; and
(b) that the injury was attributable in whole or in part to the act or omission which is alleged to constitute negligence, nuisance or breach of duty; and
(c) the identity of the defendant; and
(d) if it is alleged that the act or omission was that of a person other than the defendant, the identity of that person and the additional facts supporting the bringing of an action against the defendant;

227

and knowledge that any acts or omissions did or did not, as a matter of law, involve negligence, nuisance or breach of duty is irrelevant.

(1A) In section 11A of this Act and in section 12 of this Act so far as that section applies to an action by virtue of section 6(1)(a) of the Consumer Protection Act 1987 (death caused by defective produce) references to a person's date of knowledge are references to the date on which he first had knowledge of the following facts –

(a) such facts about the damage caused by the defect as would lead a reasonable person who had suffered such damage to consider it sufficiently serious to justify his instituting proceedings for damages against a defendant who did not dispute liability and was able to satisfy a judgment; and
(b) that the damage was wholly or partly attributable to the facts and circumstances alleged to constitute the defect; and
(c) the identity of the defendant;

but, in determining the date on which a person first had such knowledge there shall be disregarded both the extent (if any) of that person's knowledge on any date of whether particular facts or circumstances would or would not, as a matter of law, constitute a defect and, in a case relating to loss of or damage to property, any knowledge which that person had on a date on which he had no right of action by virtue of Part I of that Act in respect of the loss or damage.

(2) For the purposes of this section an injury is significant if the person whose date of knowledge is in question would reasonably have considered it sufficiently serious to justify his instituting proceedings for damages against a defendant who did not dispute liability and was able to satisfy a judgment.

(3) For the purposes of this section a person's knowledge includes knowledge which he might reasonably have been expected to acquire –

(a) from facts observable or ascertainable by him; or
(b) from facts ascertainable by him with the help of medical or other appropriate expert advice which it is reasonable for him to seek;

but a person shall not be fixed under this subsection with knowledge of a fact ascertainable only with the help of expert advice so long as he has taken all reasonable steps to obtain (and, where appropriate, to act on) that advice.

PART II

EXTENSION OR EXCLUSION OF ORDINARY TIME LIMITS

28 Extension of limitation period in case of disability   [801]

(1) Subject to the following provisions of this section, if on the date when any right of action accrued for which a period of limitation is prescribed by this Act, the person to whom it accrued was under a disability, the action may be brought at any time before the expiration of six years from the date when he ceased to be under a disability or died (whichever first occurred) notwithstanding that the period of limitation has expired.

(2) This section shall not affect any case where the right of action first accrued to some person (not under a disability) through whom the person under a disability claims.

(3) When a right of action which has accrued to a person under a disability accrues, on the death of that person while still under a disability, to another person under a disability, no further extension of time shall be allowed by reason of the disability of the second person.

(4) No action to recover land or money charged on land shall be brought by virtue of this section by any person after the expiration of thirty years from the date on which the right of action accrued to that person or some person through whom he claims.

29 Fresh accrual of action on acknowledgment or part payment [802]

(5) Subject to subsection (6) below, where any right of action has accrued to recover –

(a) any debt or other liquidated pecuniary claim; or

(b) any claim to the personal estate of a deceased person or to any share or interest in any such estate;

and the person liable or accountable for the claim acknowledges the claim or makes any payment in respect of it the right shall be treated as having accrued on and not before the date of the acknowledgment or payment.

(6) A payment of a part of the rent or interest due at any time shall not extend the period for claiming the remainder then due, but any payment of interest shall be treated as a payment in respect of the principal debt.

(7) Subject to subsection (6) above, a current period of limitation may be repeatedly extended under this section by further acknowledgements or payments, but a right of action, once barred by this Act, shall not be revived by any subsequent acknowledgment or payment.

30 Formal provisions as to acknowledgments and part payments [803]

(1) To be effective for the purposes of section 29 of this Act, an acknowledgment must be in writing and signed by the person making it.

(2) For the purposes of section 29, any acknowledgment or payment –

(a) may be made by the agent of the person by whom it is required to be made under that section; and

(b) shall be made to the person, or to an agent of the person, whose title or claim is being acknowledged or, as the case may be, in respect of whose claim the payment is being made.

31 Effect of acknowledgement or part payment on persons other than the maker or recipient [804]

(6) An acknowledgement of any debt or other liquidated pecuniary claim shall bind the acknowledgor and his successors but not any other person.

(7) A payment made in respect of any debt or other liquidated pecuniary claim shall bind all persons liable in respect of the debt or claim.

(8) An acknowledgement by one of several personal representatives of any claim to the personal estate of a deceased person or to any share or interest in any such estate, or a payment by one of several personal representatives in respect of any such claim, shall bind the estate of the deceased person.

(9) In this section 'successor', in relation to any mortgagee or person liable in respect of any debt or claim, means his personal representatives and any other person on whom the rights under the mortgage or, as the case may be, the liability in respect of the debt or claim devolve (whether on death or bankruptcy or the disposition of property or the determination of a limited estate or interest in settled property or otherwise).

32 Postponement of limitation period in case of fraud, [805] concealment or mistake

(1) Subject to subsection (3) below, where in the case of any action for which a period of limitation is prescribed by this Act, either –

(a) the action is based upon the fraud of the defendant; or
(b) any fact relevant to the plaintiff's right of action has been deliberately concealed from him by the defendant; or
(c) the action is for relief from the consequences of a mistake;

the period of limitation shall not begin to run until the plaintiff has discovered the fraud, concealment or mistake (as the case may be) or could with reasonable diligence have discovered it.

References in this subsection to the defendant include references to the defendant's agent and to any person through whom the defendant claims and his agent.

(2) For the purposes of subsection (1) above, deliberate commission of a breach of duty in circumstances in which it is unlikely to be discovered for some time amounts to deliberate concealment of the facts involved in that breach of duty.

(3) Nothing in this section shall enable any action –

(a) to recover, or recover the value of, any property; or
(b) to enforce any charge against, or set aside any transaction affecting, any property;

to be brought against the purchaser of the property or any person claiming through him in any case where the property has been purchased for valuable consideration by an innocent third party since the fraud or concealment or (as the case may be) the transaction in which the mistake was made took place.

(4) A purchaser is an innocent third party for the purposes of this section –

(a) in the case of fraud or concealment of any fact relevant to the plaintiff's right of action, if he was not a party to the fraud or (as the case may be) to the concealment of that fact and did not at the time of the purchase know or have reason to believe that the fraud or concealment had taken place, and
(b) in the case of mistake, if he did not at the time of the purchase know or have reason to believe that the mistake had been made.

(4A) Subsection (1) above shall not apply in relation to the time limit prescribed by section 11A(3) of this Act or in relation to that time limit as applied by virtue of section 12(1) of this Act.

33 Discretionary exclusion of time limit for actions [806] in respect of personal injuries or death

(1) If it appears to the court that it would be equitable to allow an action to proceed having regard to the degree to which –

(a) the provisions of section 11 or 11A or 12 of this Act prejudice the plaintiff or any person whom he represents; and
(b) any decision of the court under this subsection would prejudice the defendant or any person whom he represents;

the court may direct that those provisions shall not apply to the action, or shall not apply to any specified cause of action to which the action relates.

(1A) The court shall not under this section disapply –

(a) subsection (3) of section 11A; or

(b) where the damages claimed by the plaintiff are confined to damages for loss of or damage to any property, any other provision in its application to an action by virtue of Part I of the Consumer Protection Act 1987.

(2) The court shall not under this section disapply section 12(1) except where the reason why the person injured could no longer maintain an action was because of the time limit in section 11 or subsection (4) of section 11A.

If, for example, the person injured could at his death no longer maintain an action under the Fatal Accidents Act 1976 because of the time limit in Article 29 in Schedule 1 to the Carriage by Air Act 1961, the court has no power to direct that section 12(1) shall not apply.

(3) In acting under this section the court shall have regard to all the circumstances of the case and in particular to –

(a) the length of, and the reasons for, the delay on the part of the plaintiff;

(b) the extent to which, having regard to the delay, the evidence adduced or likely to be adduced by the plaintiff or the defendant is or is likely to be less cogent than if the action had been brought within the time allowed by section 11, by section 11A or (as the case may be) by section 12;

(c) the conduct of the defendant after the cause of action arose, including the extent (if any) to which he responded to requests reasonably made by the plaintiff for information or inspection for the purpose of ascertaining facts which were or might be relevant to the plaintiff's cause of action against the defendant;

(d) the duration of any disability of the plaintiff arising after the date of the accrual of the cause of action;

(e) the extent to which the plaintiff acted promptly and reasonably once he knew whether or not the act or omission of the defendant, to which the injury was attributable, might be capable at that time of giving rise to an action for damages;

(f) the steps, if any, taken by the plaintiff to obtain medical, legal or other expert advice and the nature of any such advice he may have received.

(4) In a case where the person injured died where, because of section 11 or subsection (4) of section 11A, he could no longer maintain an action and recover damages in respect of the injury, the court shall have regard in particular to the length of, and the reasons for, the delay on the part of the deceased.

(5) In a case under subsection (4) above, or any other case where the time limit, or one of the time limits, depends on the date of knowledge of a person other than the plaintiff, subsection (3) above shall have effect with appropriate modifications, and shall have effect in particular as if references to the plaintiff included references to any person whose date of knowledge is or was relevant in determining a time limit.

(6) A direction by the court disapplying the provisions of section 12(1) shall operate to disapply the provisions to the same effect in section 1(1) of the Fatal Accidents Act 1976.

(7) In this section 'the court' means the court in which the action has been brought.

(8) References in this section to section 11 or 11A include references to that section as extended by any of the preceding provisions of this Part of this Act or by any provision of Part III of this Act.

PART III

MISCELLANEOUS AND GENERAL

36 Equitable jurisdiction and remedies   [807]

(1) The following time limits under this Act, that is to say –

    (b) the time limit under section 5 for actions founded on simple contract;
    (c) the time limit under section 7 for actions to enforce awards where the submission is not by an instrument under seal;
    (d) the time limit under section 8 for actions on a specialty;

shall not apply to any claim for specific performance of a contract or for an injunction or for other equitable relief; except in so far as any such time limit may be applied by the court by analogy in like manner as the corresponding time limit under any enactment repealed by the Limitation Act 1939 was applied before 1 July 1940.

(2) Nothing in this Act shall affect any equitable jurisdiction to refuse relief on the ground of acquiescence or otherwise.

38 Interpretation   [808]

(1) In this Act, unless the context otherwise requires –

    'action' includes any proceeding in a court of law, including an ecclesiastical court;
    'land' includes corporeal hereditaments, tithes and rentcharges and any legal or equitable estate or interest therein, including an interest in the proceeds of the sale of land held upon trust for sale, but except as provided above in this definition does not include any incorporeal hereditament;
    'personal estate' and 'personal property' do not include chattels real;
    'personal injuries' includes any disease and any impairment of a person's physical or mental condition, and 'injury' and cognate expressions shall be construed accordingly;
    'rent' includes a rentcharge and a rentservice;
    'rentcharge' means any annuity or periodical sum of money charged upon or payable out of land, except a rent service or interest on a mortgage on land;
    'settled land', 'statutory owner' and 'tenant for life' have the same meanings respectively as in the Settled Land Act 1925;
    'trust' and 'trustee' have the same meanings respectively as in the Trustee Act 1925; and
    'trust for sale' has the same meaning as in the Law of Property Act 1925.

(2) For the purposes of this Act a person shall be treated as under a disability while he is an infant, or of unsound mind.

(3) For the purposes of subsection (2) above a person is of unsound mind if he is a person who, by reason of mental disorder within the meaning of the Mental Health Act 1983, is incapable of managing and administering his property and affairs.

(4) Without prejudice to the generality of subsection (3) above, a person shall be conclusively presumed for the purposes of subsection (2) above to be of unsound mind –

    (a) while he is liable to be detained or subject to guardianship under the Mental Health Act 1983 (otherwise than by virtue of section 35 or 89); and

(b) while he is receiving treatment as an in-patient in any hospital within the meaning of the Mental Health Act 1983 or mental nursing home within the meaning of the Nursing Homes Act 1975 without being liable to be detained under the said Act of 1983 (otherwise than by virtue of section 35 or 89), being treatment which follows without any interval a period during which he was liable to be detained or subject to guardianship under the Mental Health Act 1959, or the said Act of 1983 (otherwise than by virtue of section 35 or 89) or by virtue of any enactment repealed or excluded by the Mental Health Act 1959.

(5) Subject to subsection (6) below, a person shall be treated as claiming through another person if he became entitled by, through, under, or by the act of that other person to the right claimed, and any person whose estate or interest might have been barred by a person entitled to an entailed interest in possession shall be treated as claiming through the person so entitled.

(6) A person becoming entitled to any estate or interest by virtue of a special power of appointment shall not be treated as claiming through the appointor.

(7) References in this Act to a right of action to recover land shall include references to a right to enter into possession of the land or, in the case of rentcharges and tithes, to distrain for arrears of rent or tithe, and references to the bringing of such an action shall include references to the making of such an entry or distress.

(8) References in this Act to the possession of land shall, in the case of tithes and rentcharges, be construed as references to the receipt of the tithe or rent, and references to the date of dispossession or discontinuance of possession of land shall, in the case of rentcharges, be construed as references to the date of the last receipt of rent.

(9) References in Part II of this Act to a right of action shall include references to –

(a) a cause of action;
(b) a right to receive money secured by a mortgage or charge on any property;
(c) a right to recover proceeds of the sale of land; and
(d) a right to receive a share or interest in the personal estate of a deceased person.

(10) References in Part II to the date of the accrual of a right of action shall be construed –

(a) in the case of an action upon a judgment, as references to the date on which the judgment became enforceable; and
(b) in the case of an action to recover arrears of rent or interest, or damages in respect of arrears of rent or interest, as references to the date on which the rent or interest became due.

39 Saving for other limitation enactments [809]

This Act shall not apply to any action or arbitration for which a period of limitation is prescribed by or under any other enactment (whether passed before after the passing of this Act), or to any action or arbitration to which the Crown is a party and for which, if it were between subjects, a period of limitation would be prescribed by or under any such other enactment.

[As amended by the Mental Health Act 1983, s148, Schedule 4, para 55; Consumer Protection Act 1987, s6(b), Schedule 1, paras 1, 2, 3, 4, 5, 6.]

PUBLIC PASSENGER VEHICLES ACT 1981
(1981 c 14)

29 Avoidance of contracts so far as restrictive of liability in respect of death of or injury to passengers in public service vehicles [810]

A contract for the conveyance of a passenger in a public service vehicle shall, so far as it purports to negative or to restrict the liability of a person in respect of a claim which may be made against him in respect of the death of, or bodily injury to, the passenger while being carried in, entering or alighting from the vehicle, or purports to impose any conditions with respect to the enforcement of any such liability, be void.

SUPREME COURT ACT 1981
(1981 c 54)

49 Concurrent administration of law and equity [811]

(1) Subject to the provisions of this or any other Act, every court exercising jurisdiction in England or Wales in any civil cause or matter shall continue to administer law and equity on the basis that, wherever there is any conflict or variance between the rules of equity and the rules of the common law with reference to the same matter, the rules of equity shall prevail.

(2) Every such court shall give the same effect as hitherto –

(a) to all equitable estates, titles, rights, reliefs, defences and counterclaims, and to all equitable duties and liabilities; and
(b) subject thereto, to all legal claims and demands and all estates, titles, rights, duties, obligations and liabilties existing by the common law or by any custom or created by any statute,

and, subject to the provisions of this or any other Act, shall so exercise its jurisdiction in every cause or matter before it as to secure that, as far as possible, all matters in dispute between the parties are completely and finally determined, and all multiplicity of legal proceedings with respect to any of these matters is avoided.

50 Power to award damages as well as, or in substitution for, injunction or specific performance [812]

Where the Court of Appeal or the High Court has jurisdiction to entertain an application for an injunction for specific performance, it may award damages in addition to or in substitution for an injunction for specific performance.

SUPPLY OF GOODS AND SERVICES ACT 1982
(1982 c 29)

PART I

SUPPLY OF GOODS

1 The contracts concerned   [813]

(1) In this Act in its application to England and Wales and Northern Ireland a 'contract for the transfer of goods' means a contract under which one person transfers or agrees to transfer to another the property in goods, other than an excepted contract.

(2) For the purposes of this section an excepted contract means any of the following –

   (a) a contract of sale of goods;
   (b) a hire-purchase agreement;
   (c) a contract under which the property in goods is (or is to be) transferred in exchange for trading stamps on their redemption;
   (d) a transfer or agreement to transfer which is made by deed and for which there is no consideration other than the presumed consideration imported by the deed;
   (e) a contract intended to operate by way of mortgage, pledge, charge or other security.

(3) For the purposes of this Act in its application to England and Wales and Northern Ireland a contract is a contract for the transfer of goods whether or not services are also provided or to be provided under the contract, and (subject to subsection (2) above) whatever is the nature of the consideration for the transfer or agreement to transfer.

2 Implied terms about title, etc   [814]

(1) In a contract for the transfer of goods, other than one to which subsection (3) below applies, there is an implied condition on the part of the transferor that in the case of a transfer of the property in the goods he has a right to transfer the property and in the case of an agreement to transfer the property in the goods he will have such a right at the time when the property is to be transferred.

(2) In a contract for the transfer of goods, other than one to which subsection (3) below applies, there is also an implied warranty that –

   (a) the goods are free, and will remain free until the time when the property is to be transferred, from any charge or encumbrance not disclosed or known to the transferee before the contract is made, and
   (b) the transferee will enjoy quiet possession of the goods except so far as it may be disturbed by the owner or other person entitled to the benefit of any charge or encumbrance so disclosed or known.

(3) This subsection applies to a contract for the transfer of goods in the case of which there appears from the contract or is to be inferred from its circumstances an intention that the transferor should transfer only such title as he or a third person may have.

(4) In a contract to which subsection (3) above applies there is an implied warranty that all charges or encumbrances known to the transferor and not known to the transferee have been disclosed to the transferee before the contract is made.

(5) In a contract to which subsection (3) above applies there is also an implied warranty that none of the following will disturb the transferee's quiet possession of the goods, namely –

(a) the transferor;

(b) in a case where the parties to the contract intend that the transferor should transfer only such title as a third person may have, that person;

(c) anyone claiming through or under the transferor or that third person otherwise than under a charge or encumbrance disclosed or known to the transferee before the contract is made.

3 Implied terms where transfer is by description [815]

(1) This section applies where, under a contract for the transfer of goods, the transferor transfers or agrees to transfer the property in the goods by description.

(2) In such a case there is an implied condition that the goods will correspond with the description.

(3) If the transferor transfers or agrees to transfer the property in the goods by sample as well as by description it is not sufficient that the bulk of the goods corresponds with the sample if the goods do not also correspond with the description.

(4) A contract is not prevented from falling within subsection (1) above by reason only that, being exposed for supply, the goods are selected by the transferee.

4 Contracts for transfer: quality or fitness [816]

(1) Except as provided by this section and section 5 below and subject to the provisions of any other enactment, there is no implied condition or warranty about the quality or fitness for any particular purpose of goods supplied under a contract for the transfer of goods.

(2) Where, under such a contract, the transferor transfers the property in goods in the course of a business, there is an implied condition that the goods supplied under the contract are of satisfactory quality.

(2A) For the purposes of this section and section 5 below, goods are of satisfactory quality if they meet the standard that a reasonable person would regard as satisfactory, taking account of any description of the goods, the price (if relevant) and all the other relevant circumstances.

(3) The condition implied by subsection (2) above does not extend to any matter making the quality of goods unsatisfactory –

(a) which is specifically drawn to the transferee's attention before the contract is made,

(b) where the transferee examines the goods before the contract is made, which that examinatiion ought to reveal, or

(c) where the property in the goods is transferred by reference to a sample, which would have been apparent on a reasonable examination of the sample.

(4) Subsection (5) below applies where, under a contract for the transfer of goods, the transferor transfers the property in goods in the course of a business and the transferee, expressly or by implication, makes known –

(a) to the transferor, or

(b) where the consideration or part of the consideration for the transfer is a sum payable by instalments and the goods were previously sold by a credit-broker to the transferor, to that credit-broker

any particular purpose for which the goods are being acquired.

(5) In that case there is (subject to subsection (6) below) an implied condition that the goods supplied under the contract are reasonably fit for that purpose, whether or not that is a purpose for which such goods are commonly supplied.

(6) Subsection (5) above does not apply where the circumstances show that the transferee does not rely, or that it is unreasonable for him to rely, on the skill or judgment of the transferor or credit-broker.

(7) An implied condition or warranty about quality or fitness for a particular purpose may be annexed by usage to a contract for the transfer of goods.

(8) The preceding provisions of this section apply to a transfer by a person who in the course of a business is acting as agent for another as they apply to a transfer by a principal in the course of a business, except where that other is not transferring in the course of a business and either the transferee knows that fact or reasonable steps are taken to bring it to the transferee's notice before the contract concerned is made.

5 Transfer by sample [817]

(1) This section applies where, under a contract for the transfer of goods, the transferor transfers or agrees to transfer the property in the goods by reference to a sample.

(2) In such a case there is an implied condition

(a) that the bulk will correspond with the sample in quality; and
(b) that the transferee will have a reasonable opportunity of comparing the bulk with the sample; and
(c) that the goods will be free from any defect, making their quality unsatisfactory, which would not be apparent on reasonable examination of the sample.

(4) For the purposes of this section a transferor transfers or agrees to transfer the property in goods by reference to a sample where there is an express or implied term to that effect in the contract concerned.

5A Modification of remedies for breach of statutory [818] condition in non-consumer cases

(1) Where in the case of a contract for the transfer of goods –

(a) the transferee would, apart from this subsection, have the right to treat the contract as repudiated by reason of a breach on the part of the transferor of a term implied by sections 3, 4 or 5(2)(a) or (c) above, but
(b) the breach is so slight that it would be unreasonable for him to do so,

then, if the transferee does not deal as consumer, the breach is not to be treated as a breach of condition but may be treated as a breach of warranty.

(2) This section applies unless a contrary intention appears in, or is to be implied from, the contract.

(3) It is for the transferor to show that a breach fell within subsection (1)(b) above.

6 The contracts concerned [819]

(1) In this Act in its application to England and Wales and Northern Ireland a 'contract for the hire of goods' means a contract under which one person bails or agrees to bail goods to another by way of hire, other than an excepted contract.

(2) For the purposes of this section an excepted contract means any of the following: –

(a) a hire-purchase agreement;

(b) a contract under which goods are (or are to be) bailed in exchange for trading stamps on their redemption.

(3) For the purposes of this Act in its application to England and Wales and Northern Ireland a contract is a contract for the hire of goods whether or not services are also provided or to be provided under the contract, and (subject to subsection (2) above) whatever is the nature of the consideration for the bailment or agreement to bail by way of hire.

7 Implied terms about right to transfer possession, etc   [820]

(1) In a contract for the hire of goods there is an implied condition on the part of the bailor that in the case of a bailment he has a right to transfer possession of the goods by way of hire for the period of the bailment and in the case of an agreement to bail he will have such a right at the time of the bailment.

(2) In a contract for the hire of goods there is also an implied warranty that the bailee will enjoy quiet possession of the goods for the period of the bailment except so far as the possession may be disturbed by the owner or other person entitled to the benefit of any charge or encumbrance disclosed or known to the bailee before the contract is made.

(3) The preceding provisions of this section do not affect the right of the bailor to repossess the goods under an express or implied term of the contract.

8 Implied terms where hire is by description   [821]

(1) This section applies where, under a contract for the hire of goods, the bailor bails or agrees to bail the goods by description.

(2) In such a case there is an implied condition that the goods will correspond with the description.

(3) If under the contract the bailor bails or agrees to bail the goods by reference to a sample as well as a description it is not sufficient that the bulk of the goods corresponds with the sample if the goods do not also correspond with the description.

(4) A contract is not prevented from falling within subsection (1) above by reason only that, being exposed for supply, the goods are selected by the bailee.

9 Contracts for hire: quality or fitness   [822]

(1) Except as provided by this section and section 10 below and subject to the provisions of any other enactment, there is no implied condition or warranty about the quality or fitness for any particular purpose of goods bailed under a contract for the hire of goods.

(2) Where, under such a contract, the bailor bails goods in the course of a business, there is an implied condition that the goods supplied under the contract are of satisfactory quality.

(2A) For the purposes of this section and section 10 below, goods are of satisfactory quality if they meet the standard that a reasonable person would regard as satisfactory, taking account of any description of the goods, the consideration for the bailment (if relevant) and all the other relevant circumstances.

(3) The condition implied by subsection (2) above does not extend to any matter making the quality of goods unsatisfactory –

(a) which is specifically drawn to the bailee's attention before the contract is made,

(b) where the bailee examines the goods before the contract is made, which that examination ought to reveal, or

(c) where the goods are bailed by reference to a sample, which would have been apparent on a reasonable examination of the sample.

(4) Subsection (5) below applies where, under a contract for the hire of goods, the bailor bails goods in the course of a business and the bailee, expressly or by implication, makes known –

(a) to the bailor in the course of negotiations conducted by him in relation to the making of the contract, or

(b) to a credit-broker in the course of negotiations conducted by that broker in relation to goods sold by him to the bailor before forming the subject matter of the contract,

any particular purpose for which the goods are being bailed.

(5) In that case there is (subject to subsection (6) below) an implied condition that the goods supplied under the contract are reasonably fit for that purpose, whether or not that is a purpose for which such goods are commonly supplied.

(6) Subsection (5) above does not apply where the circumstances show that the bailee does not rely, or that it is unreasonable for him to rely, on the skill or judgment of the bailor or credit-broker.

(7) An implied condition or warranty about quality or fitness for a particular purpose may be annexed by usage to a contract for the hire of goods.

(8) The preceding provisions of this section apply to a bailment by a person who in the course of a business is acting as agent for another as they apply to a bailment by a principal in the course of a business, except where that other is not bailing in the course of a business and either the bailee knows that fact or reasonable steps are taken to bring it to the bailer's notice before the contract concerned is made.

10 Hire by sample [823]

(1) This section applies where, under a contract for the hire of goods, the bailor bails or agrees to bail the goods by reference to a sample.

(2) In such a case there is an implied condition –

(a) that the bulk will correspond with the sample in quality; and

(b) that the bailee will have a reasonable opportunity of comparing the bulk with the sample; and

(c) that the goods will be free from any defect, making their quality unsatisfactory, which would not be apparent on reasonable examination of the sample.

(4) For the purposes of this section a bailor bails or agrees to bail goods by reference to a sample where there is an express or implied term to that effect in the contract concerned.

10A Modification of remedies for breach of statutory [824] condition in non-consumer cases

(1) Where in the case of a contract for the hire of goods –

(a) the bailee would, apart from this subsection, have the right to treat the contract as repudiated by reason of a breach on the part of the bailor of a term implied by sections 8, 9 or 10(2)(a) or (c) above, but

(b) the breach is so slight that it would be unreasonable for him to do so,

then, if the bailee does not deal as consumer, the breach is not to be treated as a breach of condition but may be treated as a breach of warranty.

(2) This section applies unless a contrary intention appears in, or is to be implied from, the contract.

(3) It is for the bailor to show that a breach fell within subsection (1)(b) above.

11 Exclusion of implied terms, etc [825]

(1) Where a right, duty or liability would arise under a contract for the transfer of goods or a contract for the hire of goods by implication of law, it may (subject to subsection (2) below and the 1977 Act) be negatived or varied by express agreement, or by the course of dealing between the parties, or by such usage as binds both parties to the contract.

(2) An express condition or warranty does not negative a condition or warranty implied by the preceding provisions of this Act unless inconsistent with it.

(3) Nothing in the preceding provisions of this Act prejudices the operation of any other enactment or any rule of law whereby any condition or warranty (other than one related to quality or fitness) is to be implied in a contract for the transfer of goods or a contract for the hire of goods.

PART II

SUPPLY OF SERVICES

12 The contracts concerned [826]

(1) In this Act a 'contract for the supply of a service' means, subject to subsection (2) below, a contract under which a person ('the supplier') agrees to carry out a service.

(2) For the purposes of this Act, a contract of service or apprenticeship is not a contract for the supply of a service.

(3) Subject to subsection (2) above, a contract is a contract for the supply of a service for the purposes of this Act whether or not goods are also

    (a) transferred or to be transferred, or
    (b) bailed or to be bailed by way of hire,

under the contract, and whatever is the nature of the consideration for which the service is to be carried out.

(4) The Secretary of State may by order provide that one or more of sections 13 to 15 below shall not apply to services of a description specified in the order, and such an order may make different provision for different circumstances.

(5) The power to make an order under subsection (4) above shall be exercisable by statutory instrument subject to annulment in pursuance of a resolution of either House of Parliament.

13 Implied term about care and skill [827]

In a contract for the supply of a service where the supplier is acting in the course of a business, there is an implied term that the supplier will carry out the service with reasonable care and skill.

14 Implied term about time for performance   [828]

(1) Where, under a contract for the supply of a service by a supplier acting in the course of a business, the time for the service to be carried out is not fixed by the contract, left to be fixed in a manner agreed by the contract or determined by the course of dealing between the parties, there is an implied term that the supplier will carry out the service within a reasonable time.

(2) What is a reasonable time is a question of fact.

15 Implied term about consideration   [829]

(1) Where, under a contract for the supply of a service, the consideration for the service is not determined by the contract, left to be determined in a manner agreed by the contract or determined by the course of dealing between the parties, there is an implied term that the party contracting with the supplier will pay a reasonable charge.

(2) What is a reasonable charge is a question of fact.

16 Exclusion of implied terms, etc   [830]

(1) Where a right, duty or liability would arise under a contract for the supply of a service by virtue of this Part of this Act, it may (subject to subsection (2) below and the 1977 Act) be negatived or varied by express agreement, or by the course of dealing between the parties, or by such usage as binds both parties to the contract.

(2) An express term does not negative a term implied by this Part of this Act unless inconsistent with it.

(3) Nothing in this Part of this Act prejudices –

(a) any rule of law which imposes on the supplier a duty stricter than that imposed by section 13 or 14 above; or
(b) subject to paragraph (a) above, any rule of law whereby any term not inconsistent with this Part of this Act is to be implied in a contract for the supply of a service.

(4) This Part of this Act has effect subject to any other enactment which defines or restricts the rights, duties or liabilities arising in connection with a service of any description.

PART III

SUPPLEMENTARY

18 Interpretation: general   [831]

(1) In the preceding provisions of this Act and this section –

'bailee', in relation to a contract for the hire of goods means (depending on the context) a person to whom the goods are bailed under the contract, or a person to whom they are to be so bailed, or a person to whom the rights under the contract of either of those persons have passed;

'bailor', in relation to a contract for the hire of goods, means (depending on the context) a person who bails the goods under the contract, or a person who agrees to do so, or a person to whom the duties under the contract of either of those persons have passed;

'business' includes a profession and the activities of any government department or local or public authority;

'credit-broker' means a person acting in the course of a business of credit brokerage carried on by him;

'credit brokerage' means the effecting of introductions –

(a) of individuals desiring to obtain credit to persons carrying on any business so far as it relates to the provision of credit; or

(b) of individuals desiring to obtain goods on hire to persons carrying on a business which comprises or relates to the bailment ... of goods under a contract for the hire of goods; or

(c) of individuals desiring to obtain credit, or to obtain goods on hire, to other credit-brokers;

'enactment' means any legislation (including subordinate legislation) of the United Kingdom or Northern Ireland;

'goods' include all personal chattels (including emblements, industrial growing crops, and things attached to or forming part of the land which are agreed to be severed before the transfer or bailment concerned or under the contract concerned), other than things in action and money;

'hire-purchase agreement' has the same meaning as in the 1974 Act;

'property', in relation to goods, means the general property in them and not merely a special property;

'redemption', in relation to trading stamps, has the same meaning as in the Trading Stamps Act 1964 or, as respects Northern Ireland, the Trading Stamps Act (Northern Ireland) 1965;

'trading stamps' has the same meaning as in the said Act of 1964 or, as respects Northern Ireland, the said Act of 1965;

'transferee', in relation to a contract for the transfer of goods, means (depending on the context) a person to whom the property in the goods is transferred under the contract, or a person to whom the property is to be so transferred, or a person to whom the rights under the contract of either of those persons have passed;

'transferor', in relation to a contract for the transfer of goods, means (depending on the context) a person who transfers the property in the goods under the contract, or a person who agrees to do so, or a person to whom the duties under the contract of either of those persons have passed.

(2) In subsection (1) above, in the definitions of bailee, bailor, transferee and transferor, a reference to rights or duties passing is to their passing by assignment, ... operation of law or otherwise.

(3) For the purposes of this Act, the quality of goods includes their state and condition and the following (among others) are in appropriate cases aspects of the quality of goods –

(a) fitness for all the purposes for which goods of the kind in question are commonly supplied;

(b) appearance and finish;

(c) freedom from minor defects,

(d) safety, and

(e) durability.

(4) References in this Act to dealing as consumer are to be construed in accordance with Part I of the Unfair Contract Terms Act 1977; and, for the purposes of this Act, it is for the transferor or bailor claiming that the transferee or bailee does not deal as consumer to show that he does not.

19 Interpretation: references to Acts [832]

In this Act –

'the 1973 Act' means the Supply of Goods (Implied Terms) Act 1973;

'the 1974 Act' means the Consumer Credit Act 1974;

'the 1977 Act' means the Unfair Contract Terms Act 1977; and

'the 1979 Act' means the Sale of Goods Act 1979.

20 Commencement [833]

(3) Part I of this Act together with section 17 and so much of sections 18 and 19 above as relates to that Part shall not come into operation until 4 January 1983; and Part II of this Act together with so much of sections 18 and 19 above as relates to that Part shall not come into operation until such day as may be appointed by an order made by the Secretary of State [ie, 4 July 1983].

(5) No provision of this Act applies to a contract made before the provision comes into operation.

[As amended by the Sale and Supply of Goods Act 1994, s7, Schedule 2, para 6, Schedule 3 (with effect from 3 January 1995).]

COMPANIES ACT 1985
(1985 c 6)

14 Effect of memorandum and articles [834]

(1) Subject to the provisions of this Act, the memorandum and articles, when registered, bind the company and its members to the same extent as if they respectively had been signed and sealed by each member, and contained covenants on the part of each member to observe all the provisions of the memorandum and of the articles.

(2) Money payable by a member to the company under the memorandum or articles is a debt due from him to the company, and in England and Wales is of the nature of a specialty debt.

35 A company's capacity not limited by its memorandum [835]

(1) The validity of an act done by a company shall not be called into question on the ground of lack of capacity by reason of anything in the company's memorandum.

(2) A member of a company may bring proceedings to restrain the doing of an act which but for subsection (1) would be beyond the company's capacity; but no such proceedings shall lie in respect of an act to be done in fulfilment of a legal obligation arising from a previous act of the company.

(3) It remains the duty of the directors to observe any limitations on their powers flowing from the company's memorandum; and action by the directors which but for subsection (1) would be beyond the company's capacity may only be ratified by the company by special resolution.

A resolution ratifying such action shall not affect any liability incurred by the directors or any other person; relief from any such liability must be agreed to separately by special resolution ...

(4) The operation of this section is restricted by section 65(1) of the Charities Act 1993 and section 112(3) of the Companies Act 1989 in relation to companies which

are charities; and section 322A below (invalidity of certain transactions to which directors or their associates are parties) has effect notwithstanding this section.

35A Power of directors to bind the company [836]

(1) In favour of a person dealing with a company in good faith, the power of the board of directors to bind the company, or authorise others to do so, shall be deemed to be free of any limitation under the company's constitution.

(2) For this purpose –

(a) a person 'deals with' a company if he is a party to any transaction or other act to which the company is a party;

(b) a person shall not be regarded as acting in bad faith by reason only of his knowing that an act is beyond the powers of the directors under the company's constitution; and

(c) a person shall be presumed to have acted in good faith unless the contrary is proved.

(3) The references above to limitations on the directors' powers under the company's constitution include limitations deriving –

(a) from a resolution of the company in general meeting or a meeting of any class of shareholders, or

(b) from any agreement between the members of the company or of any class of shareholders.

(4) Subsection (1) does not affect any right of a member of the company to bring proceedings to restrain the doing of an act which is beyond the powers of the directors; but no such proceedings shall lie in respect of an act to be done in fulfilment of a legal obligation arising from a previous act of the company.

(5) Nor does that subsection affect any liability incurred by the directors, or any other person, by reason of the directors' exceeding their powers ...

(6) The operation of this section is restricted by section 65(1) of the Charities Act 1993 and section 112(3) of the Companies Act 1989 in relation to companies which are charities; and section 322A below (invalidity of certain transactions to which directors or their associates are parties) has effect notwithstanding this section.

35B No duty to enquire as to capacity of company [837]
or authority of directors

A party to a transaction with a company is not bound to enquire as to whether it is permitted by the company's memorandum or as to any limitation on the powers of the board of directors to bind the company or authorise others to do so.

36 Company contracts: England and Wales [838]

Under the law of England and Wales a contract may be made –

(a) by a company, by writing under its common seal, or

(b) on behalf of a company, by any person acting under its authority, express or implied;

and any formalities required by law in the case of a contract made by an individual also apply, unless a contrary intention appears, to a contract made by or on behalf of a company.

36A Execution of documents: England and Wales   [839]

(1) Under the law of England and Wales the following provisions have effect with respect to the execution of documents by a company.

(2) A document is executed by a company by the affixing of its common seal.

(3) A company need not have a common seal, however, and the following subsections apply whether it does or not.

(4) A document signed by a director and the secretary of a company, or by two directors of a company, and expressed (in whatever form of words) to be executed by the company has the same effect as if executed under the common seal of the company.

(5) A document executed by a company which makes it clear on its face that it is intended by the person or persons making it to be a deed has effect, upon delivery, as a deed; and it shall be presumed, unless a contrary intention is proved, to be delivered upon its being so executed.

(6) In favour of a purchaser a document shall be deemed to have been duly executed by a company if it purports to be signed by a director and the secretary of the company, or by two directors of the company, and, where it makes it clear on its face that it is intended by the person or persons making it to be a deed, to have been delivered upon its being executed.

A 'purchaser' means a purchaser in good faith for valuable consideration and includes a lessee, mortgagee or other person who for valuable consideration acquires an interest in property.

36C Pre-incorporation contracts, deeds and obligations   [840]

(1) A contract which purports to be made by or on behalf of a company at a time when the company has not been formed has effect, subject to any agreement to the contrary, as one made with the person purporting to act for the company or as agent for it, and he is personally liable on the contract accordingly.

(2) Subsection (1) applies –

(a) to the making of a deed under the law of England and Wales ...

as it applies to the making of a contract.

[As substituted by the Companies Act 1989, ss108(1) and 130(1), (2), (4) and amended by the Charities Act 1993, s98(1), Schedule 6, para 20(1), (2).]

INSOLVENCY ACT 1986
(1986 c 45)

345 Contracts to which bankrupt is a party   [841]

(1) The following applies where a contract has been made with a person who is subsequently adjudged bankrupt.

(2) The court may, on the application of any other party to the contract, make an order discharging obligations under the contract on such terms as to payment by the applicant or the bankrupt of damages for non-performance or otherwise as appear to the court to be equitable.

(3) Any damages payable by the bankrupt by virtue of an order of the court under this section are provable as a bankruptcy debt.

(4) Where an undischarged bankrupt is a contractor in respect of any contract jointly with any person, that person may sue or be sued in respect of the contract without the joinder of the bankrupt.

MINORS' CONTRACTS ACT 1987
(1987 c 13)

1 Disapplication of Infants Relief Act 1874, etc   [842]

The following enactments shall not apply to any contract made by a minor after the commencement of this Act –

(a) the Infants Relief Act 1874 (which invalidates certain contracts made by minors and prohibits actions to enforce contracts ratified after majority); and
(b) section 5 of the Betting and Loans (Infants) Act 1892 (which invalidates contracts to repay loans advanced during minority).

2 Guarantees   [843]

Where –

(a) a guarantee is given in respect of an obligation of a party to a contract made after the commencement of this Act, and
(b) the obligation is unenforceable against him (or he repudiates the contract) because he was a minor when the contract was made,

the guarantee shall not for that reason alone be unenforceable against the guarantor.

3 Restitution   [844]

(1) Where –

(a) a person ('the plaintiff') has after the commencement of this Act entered into a contract with another ('the defendant'), and
(b) the contract is unenforceable against the defendant (or he repudiates it) because he was a minor when the contract was made,

the court may, if it is just and equitable to do so, require the defendant to transfer to the plaintiff any property acquired by the defendant under the contract or any property representing it.

(2) Nothing in this section shall be taken to prejudice any other remedy available to the plaintiff.

4 Consequential amendment and repeals   [845]

(2) The Infants Relief Act 1874 and the Betting and Loans (Infants) Act 1892 are hereby repealed (in accordance with section 1 of this Act).

CONSUMER PROTECTION ACT 1987
(1987 c 43)

7 Prohibition on exclusions from liability   [846]

The liability of a person by virtue of this Part to a person who has suffered damage caused wholly or partly by a defect in a product, or to a dependant or relative of such a person, shall not be limited or excluded by any contract term, by any notice or by any other provision.

ROAD TRAFFIC ACT 1988
(1988 c 52)

148 Avoidance of certain exceptions to policies **[847]**
or securities

(1) Where a certificate of insurance or certificate of security has been delivered under section 147 of this Act to the person by whom a policy has been effected or to whom a security has been given, so much of the policy or security as purports to restrict –

(a) the insurance of the persons insured by the policy, or
(b) the operation of the security,

(as the case may be) by reference to any of the matters mentioned in subsection (2) below shall, as respects such liabilities as are required to be covered by a policy under section 145 of this Act, be of no effect.

(2) Those matters are –

(a) the age or physical or mental condition of persons driving the vehicle,
(b) the condition of the vehicle,
(c) the number of persons that the vehicle carries,
(d) the weight or physical characteristics of the goods that the vehicle carries,
(e) the time at which or the areas within which the vehicle is used,
(f) the horsepower or cylinder capacity or value of the vehicle,
(g) the carrying on the vehicle of any particular apparatus, or
(h) the carrying on the vehicle of any particular means of identification other than any means of identification required to be carried by or under the Vehicle Excise and Registration Act 1994.

(3) Nothing in subsection (1) above requires an insurer or the giver of a security to pay any sum in respect of the liability of any person otherwise than in or towards the discharge of that liability.

(4) Any sum paid by an insurer or the giver of a security in or towards the discharge of any liability of any person which is covered by the policy or security by virtue only of subsection (1) above is recoverable by the insurer or giver of the security from that person.

(5) A condition in a policy or security issued or given for the purposes of this Part of this Act providing –

(a) that no liability shall arise under the policy or security, or
(b) that any liability so arising shall cease,

in the event of some specified thing being done or omitted to be done after the happening of the event giving rise to a claim under the policy or security, shall be of no effect in connection with such liabilities as are required to be covered by a policy under section 145 of this Act.

(6) Nothing in subsection (5) above shall be taken to render void any provision in a policy or security requiring the person insured or secured to pay to the insurer or the giver of the security any sums which the latter may have become liable to pay under the policy or security and which have been applied to the satisfaction of the claims of third parties.

(7) Notwithstanding anything in any enactment, a person issuing a policy of insurance under section 145 of this Act shall be liable to indemnify the persons or classes of persons specified in the policy in respect of any liability which the policy purports to cover in the case of those persons or classes of persons.

149 Avoidance of certain agreements as to liability [848]
towards passengers

(1) This section applies where a person uses a motor vehicle in circumstances such that under section 143 of this Act there is required to be in force in relation to his use of it such a policy of insurance or such a security in respect of third-party risks as complies with the requirements of this Part of this Act.

(2) If any other person is carried in or upon the vehicle while the user is so using it, any antecedent agreement or understanding between them (whether intended to be legally binding or not) shall be of no effect so far as it purports or might be held –

(a) to negative or restrict any such liability of the user in respect of persons carried in or upon the vehicle as is required by section 145 of this Act to be covered by a policy of insurance, or
(b) to impose any conditions with respect to the enforcement of any such liability of the user.

(3) The fact that a person so carried has willingly accepted as his the risk of negligence on the part of the user shall not be treated as negativing any such liability of the user.

(4) For the purposes of this section –

(a) references to a person being carried in or upon a vehicle include references to a person entering or getting on to, or alighting from, the vehicle, and
(b) the reference to an antecedent agreement is to one made at any time before the liability arose.

[As amended by the Vehicle Excise and Registration Act 1994, s63, Schedule 3, para 24(1).]

LAW OF PROPERTY (MISCELLANEOUS PROVISIONS) ACT 1989
(1989 c 34)

1 Deeds and their execution [849]

(1) Any rule of law which –

(a) restricts the substances on which a deed may be written;
(b) requires a seal for the valid execution of an instrument as a deed by an individual; or
(c) requires authority by one person to another to deliver an instrument as a deed on his behalf to be given a deed,

is abolished.

(2) An instrument shall not be a deed unless –

(a) it makes it clear on its face that it is intended to be a deed by the person making it or, as the case may be, by the parties to it (whether by describing itself as a deed or expressing itself to be executed or signed as a deed or otherwise); and
(b) it is validly executed as a deed by that person or, as the case may be, one or more of those parties.

(3) An instrument is validly executed as a deed by an individual if, and only if –

(a) it is signed –

(i) by him in the presence of a witness who attests the signature; or

(ii) at his direction and in his presence and the presence of two witnesses who each attest the signature; and

(b) it is delivered as a deed by him or a person authorised to do so on his behalf.

(4) In subsections (2) and (3) above 'sign', in relation to an instrument, includes making one's mark on the instrument and 'signature' is to be construed accordingly.

(5) Where a solicitor, duly certificated notary public or licensed conveyancer, or an agent or employee of a solicitor, duly certified notary public or licensed conveyancer, in the course of or in connection with a transaction involving the disposition or creation of an interest in land, purports to deliver an instrument as a deed on behalf of a party to the instrument, it shall be conclusively presumed in favour of a purchaser that he is authorised so to deliver the instrument.

(6) In subsection (5) above –

'disposition' and 'purchaser' have the same meanings as in the Law of Property Act 1925;

'duly certified notary public' has the same meaning as it has in the Solicitors Act 1974 by virtue of section 87 of that Act; and

'interest in land' means any estate, interest or charge in or over land or in or over the proceeds of sale of land.

(7) Where an instrument under seal that constitutes a deed is required for the purposes of an Act passed before this section comes into force, this section shall have effect as to signing, sealing or delivery of an instrument by an individual in place of any provision of that Act as to signing, sealing or delivery....

(9) Nothing in subsection (1)(b), (2), (3), (7) or (8) above applies in relation to deeds required or authorised to be made under –

(a) the seal of the county palatine of Lancaster;

(b) the seal of the Duchy of Lancaster; or

(c) the seal of the Duchy of Cornwall.

(10) The references in this section to the execution of a deed by an individual do not include execution by a corporation sole and the reference in subsection (7) above to signing, sealing or delivery by an individual does not include signing, sealing or delivery by such a corporation.

(11) Nothing in this section applies in relation to instruments delivered as deeds before this section comes into force.

2 Contracts for sale, etc of land to be made by signed writing   [850]

(1) A contract for the sale or other disposition of an interest in land can only be made in writing and only by incorporating all the terms which the parties have expressly agreed in one document or, where contracts are exchanged, in each.

(2) The terms may be incorporated in a document either by being set out in it or by reference to some other document.

(3) The document incorporating the terms or, where contracts are exchanged, one of the documents incorporating them (but not necessarily the same one) must be signed by or on behalf of each party to the contract.

(4) Where a contract for the sale or other disposition of an interest in land satisfies the conditions of this section by reason only of the rectification of one or more documents in pursuance of an order of a court, the contract shall come into being, or be deemed to have come into being, at such time as may be specified in the order.

(5) This section does not apply in relation to –

(a) a contract to grant such a lease as is mentioned in section 54(2) of the Law of Property Act 1925 (short leases);
(b) a contract made in the course of a public auction; or
(c) a contract regulated under the Financial Services Act 1986;

and nothing in this section affects the creation or operation of resulting, implied or constructive trusts.

(6) In this section –

'disposition' has the same meaning as in the Law of Property Act 1925;
'interest in land' means any estate, interest or charge in or over land or in or over the proceeds of sale of land.

(7) Nothing in this section shall apply in relation to contracts made before this section comes into force.

(8) Section 40 of the Law of Property Act 1925 (which is superseded by this section) shall cease to have effect.

3 Abolition of rule in Bain v Fothergill   **[851]**

The rule of law known as the rule in Bain v Fothergill is abolished in relation to contracts made after this section comes into force.

NB Sections 2 and 3 of this Act came into force on 27 September 1989, s1 on 31 July 1990.

[As amended by the Courts and Legal Services Act 1990, s125(2), Schedule 17, para 20(1), (2).]

COMPANIES ACT 1989
(1989 c 40)

155 Market contracts   **[852]**

(1) This Part applies to the following descriptions of contract connected with a recognised investment exchange or recognised clearing house.

The contracts are referred to in this Part as 'market contracts'.

(2) Except as provided in subsection (2A), in relation to a recognised investment exchange this Part applies to –

(a) contracts entered into by a member or designated non-member of the exchange which are either

(i) contracts made on the exchange or on an exchange to whose undertaking the exchange has succeeded whether by amalgamation, merger or otherwise; or
(ii) contracts in the making of which the member or designated non-member was subject to the rules of the exchange or of an exchange to whose undertaking the exchange has succeeded whether by amalgamation, merger or otherwise; and

(b) contracts subject to the rules of the exchange entered into by the exchange for the purposes of or in connection with the provision of clearing services.

A 'designated non-member' means a person in respect of whom action may be taken under the default rules of the exchange but who is not a member of the exchange.

(2A) This Part does not apply to contracts falling within paragraph (a) of subsection (2) above where the exchange in question is a recognised overseas investment exchange.

(3) In relation to a recognised clearing house, this Part applies to contracts subject to the rules of the clearing house entered into by the clearing house for the purposes of or in connection with the provision of clearing services for a recognised investment exchange ...

164 Disclaimer of property, rescission of contracts, &c [853]

(1) Sections 178, 186, 315 and 345 of the Insolvency Act 1986 (power to disclaim onerous property and court's power to order rescission of contracts, etc) do not apply in relation to –

(a) a market contract, or
(b) a contract effected by the exchange or clearing house for the purpose of realising property provided as margin in relation to market contracts ...

[As amended by the Financial Markets and Insolvency Regulations 1991.]

CHILDREN ACT 1989
(1989 c 41)

2 Parental responsibility for children [854]

(1) Where a child's father and mother were married to each other at the time of his birth, they shall each have a parental responsibility for the child.

(2) Where a child's father and mother were not married to each other at the time of his birth –

(a) the mother shall have parental responsibility for the child;
(b) the father shall not have parental responsibility for the child, unless he acquires it in accordance with the provisions of this Act.

(3) References in this Act to a child whose father and mother were, or (as the case may be) were not, married to each other at the time of his birth must be read with section 1 of the Family Law Reform Act 1987 (which extends their meaning).

(4) The rule of law that a father is the natural guardian of his legitimate child is abolished.

(5) More than one person may have parental responsibility for the same child at the same time.

(6) A person who has parental responsibility for a child at any time shall not cease to have that responsibility solely because some other person subsequently acquires parental responsibility for the child.

(7) Where more than one person has parental responsibility for a child, each of them may act alone and without the other (or others) in meeting that responsibility; but nothing in this Part shall be taken to affect the operation of any enactment which requires the consent of more than one person in a matter affecting the child.

(8) The fact that a person has parental responsibility for a child shall not entitle him to act in any way which would be incompatible with any order made with respect to the child under this Act.

(9) A person who has parental responsibility for a child may not surrender or transfer any part of that responsibility to another but may arrange for some or all of it to be met by one or more persons acting on his behalf.

(10) The person with whom any such arrangement is made may himself be a person who already has parental responsibility for the child concerned.

(11) The making of any such arrangement shall not affect any liability of the person making it which may arise from any failure to meet any part of his parental responsibility for the child concerned.

3 Meaning of 'parental responsibility'   [855]

(1) In this Act 'parental responsibility' means all the rights, duties, powers, responsibilities and authority which by law a parent of a child has in relation to the child and his property.

(2) It also includes the rights, powers and duties which a guardian of the child's estate (appointed, before the commencement of section 5, to act generally) would have had in relation to the child and his property.

(3) The rights referred to in subsection (2) include, in particular, the right of the guardian to receive or recover in his own name, for the benefit of the child, property of whatever description and wherever situated which the child is entitled to receive or recover.

(4) The fact that a person has, or does not have, parental responsibility for a child shall not affect –

(a) any obligation which he may have in relation to the child (such as a statutory duty to maintain the child); or
(b) any rights which, in the event of the child's death, he (or any other person) may have in relation to the child's property.

(5) A person who –

(a) does not have parental responsibility for a particular child; but
(b) has care of the child,

may (subject to the provisions of this Act) do what is reasonable in all the circumstances of the case for the purpose of safeguarding or promoting the child's welfare.

CONTRACTS (APPLICABLE LAW) ACT 1990
(1990 c 36)

1 Meaning of 'the Conventions'   [856]

In this Act –

(a) 'the Rome Convention' means the Convention on the law applicable to contractual obligations opened for signature in Rome on 19th June 1980 and signed by the United Kingdom on 7th December 1981;
(b) 'the Luxembourg Convention' means the Convention on the accession of the Hellenic Republic to the Rome Convention signed by the United Kingdom in Luxembourg on 10th April 1984; and
(c) 'the Brussels Protocol' means the first Protocol on the interpretation of the Rome Convention by the European Court signed by the United Kingdom in Brussels on 19th December 1988;
(d) 'the Funchal Convention' means the Convention on the accession of the Kingdom of Spain and the Portuguese Republic to the Rome Convention and the Brussels Protocol, with adjustments made to the Rome Convention by the Luxembourg Convention, signed by the United Kingdom in Funchal on 18th May 1992;

and these Conventions and the Protocol are together referred to as 'the Conventions'.

2 Conventions to have force of law [857]

(1) Subject to subsections (2) and (3) below, the Conventions shall have the force of law in the United Kingdom.

(1A) The internal law for the purposes of Article 1(3) of the Rome Convention is whichever of the following are applicable, namely –

(a) the provisions of Schedule 3A to the Insurance Companies Act 1982 (law applicable to certain contracts of insurance with insurance companies), and

(b) the provisions of Schedule 20 to the Friendly Societies Act 1992 as applied by subsections (1)(a) and (2)(a) of section 101 of that Act (law applicable to certain contracts of insurance with friendly societies).

(2) Articles 7(1) and 10(1)(e) of the Rome Convention shall not have the force of law in the United Kingdom.

(3) Notwithstanding Article 19(2) of the Rome Convention, the Conventions shall apply in the case of conflicts between the laws of different parts of the United Kingdom.

(4) For ease of reference there are set out in Schedules 1, 2, 3 and 3A to this Act respectively the English texts of –

(a) the Rome Convention;

(b) the Luxembourg Convention;

(c) the Brussels Protocol; and

(d) the Funchal Convention.

3 Interpretation of Conventions [858]

(1) Any question as to the meaning or effect of any provision of the Conventions shall, if not referred to the European Court in accordance with the Brussels Protocol, be determined in accordance with the principles laid down by, and any relevant decision of, the European Court.

(2) Judicial notice shall be taken of any decision of, or expression of opinion by, the European Court on any such question.

(3) Without prejudice to any practice of the courts as to the matters which may be considered apart from this subsection –

(a) the report on the Rome Convention by Professor Mario Giuliano and Professor Paul Lagarde which is reproduced in the Official Journal of the Communities of 31st October 1980 may be considered in ascertaining the meaning or effect of any provision of that Convention; and

(b) any report on the Brussels Protocol which is reproduced in the Official Journal of the Communities may be considered in ascertaining the meaning or effect of any provision of that Protocol.

[As amended by the Friendly Societies (Amendment) Regulations 1993, reg 6(5); Contracts (Applicable Law) Act 1990 (Amendment) Order 1994, arts 3–6.]

COURTS AND LEGAL SERVICES ACT 1990
(1990 c 41)

61 Right of barrister to enter into contract for the provision of his services   [859]

(1) Any rule of law which prevents a barrister from entering into a contract for the provision of his services as a barrister is hereby abolished.

(2) Nothing in subsection (1) prevents the General Council of the Bar from making rules (however described) which prohibit barristers from entering into contracts or restricts their right to do so.

62 Immunity of advocates from actions in negligence and for breach of contract   [860]

(1) A person –

(a) who is not a barrister; but
(b) who lawfully provides any legal services in relation to any proceedings,

shall have the same immunity from liability for negligence in respect of his acts or omissions as he would have if he were a barrister lawfully providing those services.

(2) No act or omission on the part of any barrister or other person which is accorded immunity from liability for negligence shall give rise to an action for breach of any contract relating to the provision by him of the legal services in question.

PROPERTY MISDESCRIPTIONS ACT 1991
(1991 c 29)

1 Offence of property misdescription   [861]

(1) Where a false or misleading statement about a prescribed matter is made in the course of an estate agency business or a property development business, otherwise than in providing conveyancing services, the person by whom the business is carried on shall be guilty of an offence under this section.

(2) Where the making of the statement is due to the act or default of an employee the employee shall be guilty of an offence under this section; and the employee may be proceeded against and punished whether or not proceedings are also taken against his employer.

(3) A person guilty of an offence under this section shall be liable –

(a) on summary conviction, to a fine not exceeding the statutory maximum, and
(b) on conviction on indictment, to a fine.

(4) No contract shall be void or unenforceable, and no right of action in civil proceedings in respect of any loss shall arise, by reason only of the commission of an offence under this section ...

(5) For the purposes of this section –

(a) 'false' means false to a material degree,
(b) a statement is misleading if (though not false) what a reasonable person may be expected to infer from it, or from any omission from it, is false,

(c) a statement may be made by pictures or any other method of signifying meaning as well as by words and, if made by words, may be made orally or in writing,

(d) a prescribed matter is any matter relating to land which is specified in an order made by the Secretary of State,

(e) a statement is made in the course of an estate agency business if (but only if) the making of the statement is a thing done as mentioned in subsection (1) of section 1 of the Estate Agents Act 1979 and that Act either applies to it or would apply to it but for subsection (2)(a) of that section (exception for things done in course of profession by practising solicitor or employee),

(f) a statement is made in the course of a property development business if (but only if) it is made –

(i) in the course of a business (including a business in which the person making the statement is employed) concerned wholly or substantially with the development of land, and

(ii) for the purpose of, or with a view to, disposing of an interest in land consisting of or including a building, or a part of a building, constructed or renovated in the course of the business, and

(g) 'conveyancing services' means the preparation of any transfer, conveyance, writ, contract or other document in connection with the disposal or acquisition of an interest in land, and services ancillary to that, but does not include anything done as mentioned in section 1(1)(a) of the Estate Agents Act 1979.

(6) For the purposes of this section any reference in this section or section 1 of the Estate Agents Act 1979 to disposing of or acquiring an interest in land –

(a) in England and Wales and Northern Ireland shall be construed in accordance with section 2 of that Act ...

TIMESHARE ACT 1992
(1992 c 35)

1 Application of the Act   [862]

(1) In this Act –

(a) 'timeshare accommodation' means any living accommodation, in the United Kingdom or elsewhere, used or intended to be used, wholly or partly, for leisure purposes by a class of persons (referred to below in this section as 'timeshare users') all of whom have rights to use, or participate in arrangements under which they may use, that accommodation, or accommodation within a pool of accommodation to which that accommodation belongs, for intermittent periods of short duration, and

(b) 'timeshare rights' means rights by virtue of which a person becomes or will become a timeshare user, being rights exercisable during a period of not less than three years.

(2) For the purposes of subsection (1)(a) above –

(a) 'accommodation' means accommodation in a building or in a caravan (as defined in section 29(1) of the Caravan Sites and Control of Development Act 1960), and

(b) a period of not more than one month, or such other period as may be prescribed, is a period of short duration.

(3) Subsection (1)(b) above does not apply to a person's rights –

(a) as the owner of any shares or securities,

(b) under a contract of employment (within the meaning of the Employment Rights Act 1996) or a policy of insurance, or

(c) by virtue of his taking part in a collective investment scheme (as defined in section 75 of the Financial Services Act 1986),

or to such rights as may be prescribed.

(4) In this Act 'timeshare agreement' means, subject to subsection (6) below, an agreement under which timeshare rights are conferred or purport to be conferred on any person and in this Act, in relation to a timeshare agreement –

(a) references to the offeree are to the person on whom timeshare rights are conferred, or purport to be conferred, and

(b) references to the offeror are to the other party to the agreement,

and, in relation to any time before the agreement is entered into, references in this Act to the offeree or the offeror are to the persons who become the offeree and offeror when it is entered into.

(5) In this Act 'timeshare credit agreement' means, subject to subsection (6) below, an agreement, not being a timeshare agreement –

(a) under which a person (referred to in this Act as the 'creditor') provides or agrees to provide credit for or in respect of a person who is the offeree under a timeshare agreement, and

(b) when the credit agreement is entered into, the creditor knows or has reasonable cause to believe that the whole or part of the credit is to be used for the purpose of financing the offeree's entering into a timeshare agreement.

(6) An agreement is not a timeshare agreement or a timeshare credit agreement if, when entered into, it may be cancelled by virtue of section 67 of the Consumer Credit Act 1974.

(7) This Act applies to any timeshare agreement or timeshare credit agreement if –

(a) the agreement is to any extent governed by the law of the United Kingdom or of a part of the United Kingdom, or

(b) when the agreement is entered into, one or both of the parties are in the United Kingdom.

(8) In the application of this section to Northern Ireland –

(a) for the reference in subsection (2)(a) above to section 29(1) of the Caravan Sites and Control of Development Act 1960 there is substituted a reference to section 25(1) of the Caravans Act (Northern Ireland) 1963, and

(b) for the reference in subsection (3)(b) above to the Employment Rights Act 1996 there is substituted a reference to article 2(2) of the Industrial Relations (Northern Ireland) Order 1976.

2 Obligation to give notice of right to cancel timeshare agreement [863]

(1) A person must not in the course of a business enter into a timeshare agreement to which this Act applies as offeror unless the offeree has received, together with a document setting out the terms of the agreement or the substance of those terms, notice of his right to cancel the agreement.

(2) A notice under this section must state –

(a) that the offeree is entitled to give notice of cancellation of the agreement to the offeror at any time on or before the date specified in the notice, being a day falling not less than fourteen days after the day on which the agreement is entered into, and

(b) that if the offeree gives such a notice to the offeror on or before that date he will have no further rights or obligations under the agreement, but will have the right to recover any sums paid under or in contemplation of the agreement ...

3 Obligation to give notice of right to cancel timeshare credit agreement [864]

(1) A person must not in the course of a business enter into a timeshare credit agreement to which this Act applies as creditor unless the offeree has received, together with a document setting out the terms of the agreement or the substance of those terms, notice of his right to cancel the agreement.

(2) A notice under this section must state –

(a) that the offeree is entitled to give notice of cancellation of the agreement to the creditor at any time on or before the date specified in the notice, being a day falling not less than fourteen days after the day on which the agreement is entered into, and
(b) that, if the offeree gives such notice to the creditor on or before that date, then –

(i) so far as the agreement relates to repayment of credit and payment of interest, it shall have effect subject to section 7 of this Act, and
(ii) subject to sub-paragraph (i) above, the offeree will have no further rights or obligations under the agreement.

4 Provisions supplementary to sections 2 and 3 [865]

(1) Sections 2 and 3 of this Act do not apply where, in entering into the agreement, the offeree is acting in the course of a business.

(2) A notice under section 2 or 3 must be accompanies by a blank notice of cancellation and any notice under section 2 or 3 of this Act or blank notice of cancellation must –

(a) be in such form as may be prescribed, and
(b) comply with such requirements (whether as to type, size, colour or disposition of lettering, quality or colour of paper, or otherwise) as may be prescribed for securing that the notice is prominent and easily legible.

(3) An agreement is not invalidated by reason of a contravention of section 2 or 3.

5 Right to cancel timeshare agreement [866]

(1) Where a person –

(a) has entered, or proposes to enter, into a timeshare agreement to which this Act applies as offeree, and
(b) has received the notice required under section 2 of this Act before entering into the agreement,

the agreement may not be enforced against him on or before the date specified in the notice in pursuance of subsection (2)(a) of that section and he may give notice of cancellation of the agreement to the offeror at any time on or before that date.

(2) Subject to subsection (3) below, where a person who enters into a timeshare agreement to which this Act applies as offeree has not received the notice required under section 2 of this Act before entering into the agreement, the agreement may not be enforced against him and he may give notice of cancellation of the agreement to the offeror at any time.

(3) If in a case falling within subsection (2) above the offeree affirms the agreement at any time after the expiry of the period of fourteen days beginning with the day on which the agreement is entered into –

(a) subsection (2) above does not prevent the agreement being enforced against him, and
(b) he may not at any subsequent time give notice of cancellation of the agreement to the offeror.

(4) The offeree's giving, within the time allowed under this section, notice of cancellation of the agreement to the offeror at a time when the agreement has been entered into shall have the effect of cancelling the agreement.

(5) The offeree's giving notice of cancellation of the agreement to the offeror before the agreement has been entered into shall have the effect of withdrawing any offer to enter into the agreement.

(6) Where a timeshare agreement is cancelled under this section, then, subject to subsection (9) below –

(a) the agreement shall cease to be enforceable, and
(b) subsection (8) below shall apply.

(7) Subsection (8) below shall also apply where giving a notice of cancellation has the effect of withdrawing an offer to enter into a timeshare agreement.

(8) Where this subsection applies –

(a) any sum which the offeree has paid under or in contemplation of the agreement to the offeror, or to any person who is the offeror's agent for the purpose of receiving that sum, shall be recoverable from the offeror by the offeree and shall be due and payable at the time the notice of cancellation is given, but
(b) no sum may be recovered by or on behalf of the offeror from the offeree in respect of the agreement.

(9) Where a timeshare agreement includes provision for providing credit for or in respect of the offeree, then, notwithstanding the giving of notice of cancellation under this section, so far as the agreement relates to repayment of the credit and payment of interest –

(a) it shall continue to be enforceable, subject to section 7 of this Act, and
(b) the notice required under section 2 of this Act must also state that fact.

6 Right to cancel timeshare credit agreement   [867]

(1) Where a person –

(a) has entered into a timeshare credit agreement to which this Act applies as offeree, and
(b) has received the notice required under section 3 of this Act before entering into the agreement,

he may give notice of cancellation of the agreement to the creditor at any time on or before the date specified in the notice in pursuance of subsection (2)(a) of that section.

(2) Subject to subsection (3) below, where a person who enters into a timeshare credit agreement to which this Act applies as offeree has not received the notice required under section 3 of this Act before entering into the agreement, he may give notice of cancellation of the agreement to the creditor at any time.

(3) If in a case falling within subsection (2) above the offeree affirms the agreement at any time after the expiry of the period of fourteen days beginning

with the day on which the agreement is entered into, he may not at any subsequent time give notice of cancellation of the agreement to the creditor.

(4) The offeree's giving, within the time allowed under this section, notice of cancellation of the agreement to the creditor at a time when the agreement has been entered into shall have the effect of cancelling the agreement.

(5) Where a timeshare credit agreement is cancelled under this section –

(a) the agreement shall continue in force, subject to section 7 of this Act, so far as it relates to repayment of the credit and payment of interest, and
(b) subject to paragraph (a) above, the agreement shall cease to be enforceable.

7 Repayment of credit and interest. [868]

(1) This section applies following –

(a) the giving of notice of cancellation of a timeshare agreement in accordance with section 5 of this Act in a case where subsection (9) of that section applies, or
(b) the giving of notice of cancellation of a timeshare credit agreement in accordance with section 6 of this Act.

(2) If the offence repays the whole or a portion of the credit –

(a) before the expiry of one month following the giving of the notice, or
(b) in the case of a credit repayable by instalments, before the date on which the first instalment is due,

no interest shall be payable on the amount repaid.

(3) If the whole of a credit repayable in instalments is not repaid on or before the date specified in subsection (2)(b) above, the offeree shall not be liable to repay any of the credit except on receipt of a request in writing in such form as may be prescribed, signed by or on behalf of the offeror or (as the case may be) creditor, stating the amounts of the remaining instalments (recalculated by the offeror or creditor as nearly as may be in accordance with the agreement and without extending the repayment period), but excluding any sum other than principal and interest.

12 General provisions [869]

(1) For the purposes of this Act, a notice of cancellation of an agreement is a notice (however expressed) showing that the offeree wishes unconditionally to cancel the agreement, whether or not it is in a prescribed form.

(2) The rights conferred and duties imposed by sections 2 to 7 of this Act are in addition to any rights conferred or duties imposed by or under any other Act.

(3) For the purposes of this Act, if the offeree sends a notice by post in a properly addressed and pre-paid letter the notice is to be treated as given at the time of posting.

(4) This Act shall have effect in relation to any timeshare agreement or timeshare credit agreement notwithstanding any agreement or notice.

(5) For the purposes of the Consumer Credit Act 1974, a transaction done under or for the purposes of a timeshare agreement is not, in relation to any regulated agreement (within the meaning of that Act), a linked transaction.

(6) In this Act –

'credit' includes a cash loan and any other form of financial accommodation,

'notice' means notice in writing,

'order' means an order made by the Secretary of State, and

'prescribed' means prescribed by an order ...

[As amended by the Employment Rights Act 1996, s240, Schedule 1, para 53.]

TRADE UNION AND LABOUR RELATIONS
(CONSOLIDATION) ACT 1992
(1992 c 52)

236 No compulsion to work   [870]

No court shall, whether by way of –

(a) an order for specific performance or specific implement of a contract of employment, or

(b) an injunction or interdict restraining a breach or threatened breach of such a contract.

compel an employee to do any work or attend at any place for the doing of any work.

SALE AND SUPPLY OF GOODS ACT 1994
(1994 c 35)

8 Short title, commencement and extent ...   [871]

(3) This Act has effect in relation to contracts of sale of goods, hire-purchase agreements, contracts for the transfer of goods, contracts for the hire of goods and redemptions of trading stamps for goods (as the case may be) made after this Act comes into force. ...

NB This Act came into force on 3 January 1995. Its other provisions, so far as they are relevant, amended, inter alia, the Supply of Goods (Implied Terms) Act 1973, the Sale of Goods Act 1979 and the Supply of Goods and Services Act 1982, and these amendments have been included in the text of these Acts.

SALE OF GOODS (AMENDMENT) ACT 1995
(1995 c 28)

3 Short title, commencement and extent ...   [872]

(2) This Act shall come into force at the end of the period of two months beginning with the day on which it is passed; but nothing in this Act shall have effect in relation to any contract concluded before the coming into force of this Act. ...

NB This Act came into force on 19 September 1995. It amended the Sale of Goods Act 1979 and those amendments have been included in the text of that Act.

EMPLOYMENT RIGHTS ACT 1996
(1996 c 18)

203 Restrictions on contracting out [873]

(1) Any provision in an agreement (whether a contract of employment or not) is void in so far as it purports –

(a) to exclude or limit the operation of any provision of this Act, or
(b) to preclude a person from bringing any proceedings under this Act before an industrial tribunal.

(2) Subsection (1) –

(a) does not apply [in certain situations] ...

Glossary
of Latin and other words and phrases

Ab extra. From outside.

Ab inconvenienti. *See* ARGUMENTUM

Ab initio. From the beginning.

Accessio. Addition; appendage. The combination of two chattels belonging to different persons into a single article.

Acta exteriora indicant interiora secreta. A man's outward actions are evidence of his innermost thoughts and intentions.

Acta jure imperii. Acts performed in the exercise of sovereign authority.

Actio personalis moritur cum persona. A personal right of action dies on the death of the person by or against whom it could be enforced.

Actio quanti minoris. Action for how much less.

Actor sequitur forum rei. The plaintiff follows the court of the country where the subject of the action is situated.

Actus non facit reum, nisi mens sit rea. The act itself does not make a man guilty, unless he does it with a guilty intention.

Ad colligenda bona. To collect the goods.

Ad hoc. Arranged for this purpose; special.

Ad idem. *See* CONSENSUS.

Ad infinitum. To infinity; without limit; for ever.

Ad litem. For the purpose of the law suit.

Ad opus. For the benefit of: on behalf of.

Ad referendum. For further consideration.,

Ad valorem. Calculated in proportion to the value or price of the property.

Adversus extraneos vitiosa possessio prodesse solet. Possession, though supported only by a defective title, will prevail over the claims of strangers other than the true owner.

A fortiori (ratione). For a stronger reason; by even more convincing reasoning.

Agrément. Approval; consent.

Aliter. Otherwise; the result would be different, if ...; (also, used of a judge who thinks differently from his fellow judges).

Aliud est celare; aliud est tacere; neque enim id est celare quicquid reticeas. Mere silence is one thing but active concealment is quite another thing; for it is not disguising something when you say nothing about it.

Aliunde. From elsewhere; from other sources.

A mensa et thoro. A separation from the 'table and bed' of one's spouse.

Amicus curiae. A friend of the court.

Animo contrahendi. With the intention of contracting.

Animo et facto. By act and intention.

Animo non revertendi. With the intention of not returning.

Animo revocandi. With the intention of revoking.

Animus deserendi. The intention of deserting.

Animus donandi. The intention of giving.

Animus manendi. The intention of remaining.

Animus possidendi. The intention of possessing.

Animus residendi. The intention of residing.

Animus revertendi. The intention of returning.

Animus testandi. The intention of making a will.

Ante. Before; (also used of a case referred to earlier on a page or in a book).

A posteriori. From effect to cause; inductively; from subsequent conclusions.

A priori. From cause to effect; deductively; from previous assumptions or reasoning.

Arguendo. In the course of the argument.

Argumentum ab inconvenienti. An argument devised because of the existence of an awkward problem so as to provide an explanation for it.

Asportatio. The act of carrying away.

Assensus. *See* CONSENSUS.

Assensus ad idem. Agreement as to the same terms.

Assumpsit (super se). He undertook.

Ats. (ad sectam). At the suit of. (The opposite of VERSUS.)

Autrefois acquit. Formerly acquitted.

Autrefois convict. Formerly convicted.

A vinculo matrimonii. From the bonds of matrimony.

Bis dat qui cito dat. He gives doubly who gives swiftly; a quick gift is worth two slow ones.

Bona fide. In good faith; sincere.

Bona vacantia. Goods without an owner.

Brutum fulmen. A silent thunderbolt; an empty threat.

Cadit quaestio. The matter admits of no further argument.

Caeterorum. Of the things which are left.

Capias ad satisfaciendum. A writ commanding the sheriff to take the body of the defendant in order that he may make satisfaction for the plaintiff's claim.

Causa causans (proxima). The immediate cause of something; the last link in the chain of causation.

Causa proxima non remota spectatur. Regard is paid to the immediate, not to the remote cause.

Causa sine qua non. A cause without which an event would not happen; a preceding link in the chain of causation without which the CAUSA CAUSANS could not be operative.

Caveat emptor. The buyer must look out for himself.

Caveat venditor. The seller must look out for himself.

Cessante ratione legis, cessat lex ipsa. When the reason for its existence ceases, the law itself ceases to exist.

Cestui(s) que trust. A person (or persons) for whose benefit property is held on trust; a beneficiary (beneficiaries).

Cestui que vie. Person for the duration of whose life an estate is granted to another person.

Chargé d'affaires ad interim. One charged with affairs in the mean time.

Chose in action. Intangible personal property or rights, which can be enjoyed or enforced only by legal action, and not by taking physical possession (eg debts).

Chose jugée. Thing it is idle to discuss.

Coitus interruptus. Interrupted sexual intercourse, i.e. withdrawal before emission.

Colore officii. Under the pretext of a person's official position.

Commorientes. Persons who die at the same time.

Confusio. A mixture; union. The mixture of things of the same nature, but belonging to different persons so that identification of the original things becomes impossible.

Consensu. By general consent; unanimously.

Consensus ad idem. Agreement as to the same thing.

Consortium. Conjugal relations with and companionship of a spouse.

Contra. To the contrary. (Used of a case in which the decision was contrary to the doctrine or cases previously cited; also of a judge who delivers a dissenting judgment.)

Contra bonos mores. Contrary to good morals.

Contra mundum. Against the world.

Contra proferentem. Against the party who puts forward a clause in a document.

Cor. (coram). In the presence of; before (a judge).

Coram non judice. Before one who is not a judge. Corpus. Body; capital.

Corpus. Body; capital.

Coverture. Marriage.

Cri de coeur. Heartfelt cry.

Cujus est solum, ejus est usque ad coelum et ad inferos. Whosoever owns the soil also owns everything above it as far as the heavens and everything below it as far as the lower regions of the earth.

Culpa. Wrongful default.

Cum onere. Together with the burden.

Cum testamento annexo. With the will annexed.

Cur. adv. vult. (curia advisari vult). The court wishes time to consider the matter.

Cy-pres. For a purpose resembling as nearly as possible the purpose originally proposed.

Damage feasant. *See* DISTRESS.

Damnosa hereditas. An insolvent inheritance.

Damnum. Loss; damage.

Damnum absque injuria. *See* DAMNUM SINE INJURIA.

Damnum emergens. A loss which arises.

Damnum fatale. Damage resulting from the workings of fate for which human negligence is not to blame.

Damnum sine (or absque) injuria. Damage which is not the result of a legally remediable wrong.

De bene esse. Evidence or action which a court allows to be given or done provisionally, subject to further consideration at a later stage.

Debitor non praesumitur donare. A debtor is presumed to give a legacy to a creditor to discharge his debt and not as a gift.

Debitum in praesenti. A debt which is due at the present time.

Debitum in futuro solvendum. A debt which will be due to be paid at a future time.

De bonis asportatis. Of goods carried away.

De bonis non administratis. Of the assets which have not been administered .

De cujus. The person about whom an issue is to be determined.

De die in diem. From day to day.

De facto. In fact.

De futuro. Regarding the future; in the future; about something which will exist in the future.

Dehors. Outside (the document or matter in question); irrelevant.

De integro. As regards the whole; entirely.

De jure. By right; rightful.

Del credere agent. An agent who for an extra commission guarantees the due performance of contracts by persons whom he introduces to his principal.

Delegatus non potest delegare. A person who is entrusted with a duty has no right to appoint another person to perform it in his place.

De minimis non curat lex. The law does not concern itself with trifles.

De momento in momentum. From moment to moment.

De novo. Anew; starting afresh.

Deodand. A chattel which caused the death of a human being and was forfeited to the Crown.

De praerogativa regis. Concerning the royal prerogative.

De son tort. Of his own wrong.

Deus est procurator fatuorum. God is the protector of the simpleminded.

Devastavit. Where an executor 'has squandered' the estate.

Dictum. Saying. *See* OBITER DICTUM.

Dies certus. Day certain, determined.

Dies non (jurisdicus). Day on which no legal business can be transacted.

Dissentiente. Delivering a dissenting judgment.

Distress damage feasant. The detention by a landowner of an animal or chattel while it is doing damage on his land.

Distringas. That you may distrain.

Doli incapax. Incapable of crime.

Dolus qui dat locum contractui. A deception which clears the way for the other party to enter into a contract.

Dominium. Ownership.

Dominus litis. The principal in a suit.

Dominus pro tempore. The master for the time being.

Donatio mortis causa. A gift made in contemplation of death and conditional thereon.

Dubitante. Doubting the correctness of the decision.

Durante absentia. During an absence abroad.

Durante minore aetate. While an infant; during minority.

Durante viduitate. During widowhood.

Ei incumbit probatio qui dicit, non qui negat. The onus of proving a fact rests upon the man who asserts its truth, not upon the man who denies it.

Ejusdem generis. General words following a list of specific things are construed as relating to things 'of the same kind' as those specifically listed.

Enceinte. Pregnant.

En ventre sa mère. Conceived but not yet born.

Eodem modo quo oritur, eodem modo dissolvitur. What has been created by a certain method may be extinguished by the same method.

Eo instanti. At that instant.

Escrow. A document delivered subject to a condition which must be fulfilled before it becomes a deed.

Estoppel. A rule of evidence which applies in certain circumstances and stops a person from denying the truth of a statement previously made by him.

Estoppel in pais. Estoppel by matter or conduct; equitable estoppel.

Et cetera (etc). And other things of that sort.

Et seq (et sequentes). And subsequent pages.

Ex. From; by virtue of.

Ex abundanti cautela. From an abundance of caution.

Ex aequo et bono. According to what is just and equitable.

Ex cathedra. From his seat of office: an authoritative statement made by someone in his official capacity.

Ex comitate et jure gentium. Out of comity (friendly recognition) and the law of nations.

Ex concessis. In view of what has already been accepted.

Ex contractu. Arising out of contract.

Ex converso. Conversely.

Ex debito justitiae. That which is

due as of right; which the court has no discretion to refuse.

Ex delicto. Arising out of a wrongful act or tort.

Ex dolo malo non oritur actio. No right of action arises out of a fraud.

Executor de son tort. One who 'of his own fault' has intermeddled with an estate, purporting to act as executor.

Exequatur. Governmental permission to an official of another state to enter upon the discharge of his functions.

Ex facie. On the face of it; ostensibly.

Ex gratia. Out of the kindness. Gratuitous; voluntary.

Ex hypothesi. In view of what has already been assumed.

Ex improviso. Unexpectedly, without forethought.

Ex officio. By virtue of one's official position.

Ex pacto illicito non oritur actio. No action can be brought on an unlawful contract.

Ex parte. Proceedings brought on behalf of one interested party without notice to, and in the absence of, the other.

Ex post facto. By reason of a subsequent act; acting retrospectively.

Ex relatione. An action instituted by the Attorney-General on behalf of the Crown on the information of a member of the public who is interested in the matter (the relator).

Expressio unius est exclusio alterius. When one thing is expressly specified, then it prevents anything else being implied.

Expressis verbis. In express words.

Expressum facit cessare tacitum. Where terms are expressed, no other terms can be implied.

Extra territorium. Outside the territory; extra territorial(ly).

Ex turpi causa non oritur actio. No action can be brought where the parties are guilty of illegal or immoral conduct.

Faciendum. Something which is to be done.

Factum. Deed; that which has been done; statement of facts or points in issue.

Fait accompli. An accomplished fact.

Falsa demonstratio non nocet cum de corpore constat. Where the substance of the property in question is clearly identified, the addition of an incorrect description of the property does no harm.

Falsus in ono, falsus in omnibus. False in one, false in all.

Fecundatio ab extra. Conception from outside, i.e. where there has been no penetration.

Feme covert. A married woman.

Feme sole. An unmarried woman.

Ferae naturae. Animals which are by nature dangerous to man.

Fieri facias. A writ addressed to the sheriff: 'that you cause to be made' from the defendant's goods the sum due to the plaintiff under the judgment.

Filius nullius. *See* NULLIUS FILIUS.

Force majeure. Irresistible compulsion.

Forum. Court; the court hearing the case.

Forum conveniens. The appropriate court to hear the case.

Forum domicilii. The court of the country of domicile.

Forum rei. The court of the country where the subject of the action is situated.

Fraude à la loi. Evasion of the law.

Fructus industriales. Cultivated crops.

Fructus naturales. Vegetation which grows naturally without cultivation.

Functus officio. Having discharged his duty; having exhausted its powers.

Furiosus. Frantic, mad.

Genus numquam perit. Particular goods which have been identified may be destroyed, but 'a category or type of article can never perish'.

Habeas corpus (ad subjiciendum). A writ addressed to one who detains another in custody, requiring him 'that you produce the prisoner's body to answer' to the court.

Habitue. A frequent visitor to a place.

Ibid. (ibidem). In the same place, book, or source.

Id certum est quod certum reddi potest. That which is capable of being reduced to a certainty is already a certainty.

Idem. The same thing, or person.

Ideo consideratum est per. Therefore it is considered by the court.

Ignorantia juris haud (neminem) (non) excusat, ignorantia facti excusat. A man may be excused for mistaking facts, but not for mistaking the law.

Ignorantia juris non excusat. Ignorance of the law is no excuse.

Imperitia culpae adnumeratur. Lack of skill is accounted a fault.

In aequali jure melior est conditio possidentis. Where the legal rights of the parties are equal, the party with possession is in the stronger position.

In articulo mortis. On the point of death.

In bonis. In the goods (or estate) of a deceased person.

In capite. In chief; holding as tenant directly under the Crown.

In consimili casu. In a similar case.

In custodia legis. In the keeping of the law.

Indebitatus assumpsit. A form of action in which the plaintiff alleges the defendant 'being already indebted to the plaintiff undertook' to do something.

In delicto. At fault.

Indicia. Signs; marks.

Indicium. Indication; sign; mark.

In esse. In existence.

In expeditione. On actual military service.

In extenso. At full length.

In fieri. In the course of being performed or established.

In flagrante delicto. In the act of committing the offence.

In forma pauperis. In the character of a poor person.

Infra. Below; lower down on a page; later in a book. In futuro. In the future.

In futuro. In the future.

In hac re. In this matter; in this particular aspect.

In jure non remota causa sed proxima spectatur. In law it is the immediate and not the remote cause which is considered.

Injuria. A wrongful act for which the law provides a remedy.

Injuria sine damno. A wrongful act unaccompanied by any damage yet actionable at law.

In lieu of. In place of.

In limine. On the threshold; at the outset.

In loco parentis. In the place of a parent.

In minore delicto. A person who is 'less at fault'.

In omnibus. In every respect.

Inops consilii. Lacking facilities for legal advice.

In pari delicto, potior est conditio defendentis (or possidentis). Where both parties are equally at fault, the defendant (or the party in possession) is in the stronger position.

In pari materia. In an analogous case or position.

In personam. *See* JUS IN PERSONAM.

In pleno. In full.

In praesenti. At the present time.

In propria persona. In his own capacity. In re. In the matter of. In rem. *See* JUS IN REM.

In re. In the matter of.

In rem. *See* JUS IN REM.

In situ. In its place.

In specie. In its own form; not converted into anything else.

In statu quo ante. In the condition in which it, or a person, was before.

Inter alia. Amongst other things.

Inter alios. Amongst other persons.

Interest reipublicae ut sit finis litium. It is in the interests of the community that every law suit should reach a final conclusion (and not be reopened later).

Interim. In the meanwhile; temporary.

Inter partes. Between (the) parties.

In terrorem. As a warning; as a deterrent.

Inter se. Between themselves.

Inter vivos. Between persons who are alive.

In toto. In its entirety; completely.

In transitu. In passage from one place to another.

Intra vires. Within the powers recognised by law as belonging to the person or body in question.

In utero. In the womb.

In vacuo. In the abstract; without considering the circumstances.

In vitro. In glass; in a test tube.

Ipsissima verba. 'The very words' of a speaker.

Ipso facto. By that very fact.

Jura. Rights.

Jura mariti. By virtue of the right of a husband to the goods of his wife.

Jus. A right which is recognised in law.

Jus accrescendi. The right of survivorship; the right of joint tenants to have their interests in the joint property increased by inheriting the interests of the deceased joint tenants until the last survivor inherits the entire property.

Jus actionis. Right of action.

Jus cogens. Law obliging.

Jus gentium. The law of nations.

Jus in personam. A right which can be enforced against a particular person only.

Jus in rem. A right which can be enforced over the property in question against all other persons.

Jus naturale. Natural justice.

Jus neque in re neque ad rem. A right which is enforceable neither over the property in question against all the world nor against specific persons only.

Jus quaesitum tertio. A right vested in a third party (who is not a party to the contract).

Jus regale. A right or privilege belonging to the Crown.

Jus spatiandi. A right to stray.

Jus tertii. *See* JUS QUAESITUM TERTIO

Laches. Slackness or delay in pursuing a legal remedy which disentitles a person from action at a later date.

Laesio fidei. Breach of faith.

Laissez faire. 'Let him do what he likes'; permissive.

Lapsus linguae. Slip of the tongue.

Lex actus. The law governing a legal act or transaction.

Lex causae. The law governing the case or a given issue therein.

Lex domicilii. The law of the country of domicile of a person.

Lex fori. The law of the court in which the case is being heard.

Lex loci actus. The law of the country where a legal act or transaction took place.

Lex loci celebrationis. The law of the place where the marriage was celebrated.

Lex loci contractus. The law of the place where the contract was made.

Lex loci delicti commissi. The law of the place where the wrong was committed.

Lex loci situs. *See* LEX SITUS.

Lex loci solutionis. The law of the place where the contract is to be performed.

Lex monetae. The law of the country in whose currency a debt or other financial obligation is expressed.

Lex nationalis. The law of the country of a person's nationality.

Lex patriae. *See* LEX NATIONALIS.

Lex pecuniae. *See* LEX MONETAE.

Lex situs. The law of the place where the thing in question is situated.

Lex successionis. The law governing the succession to a deceased's estate.

Lien. The rights to retain possession of goods, deeds or other property belonging to another as security for payment of money.

Lis alibi pendens. An action pending elsewhere.

Lis pendens. Pending action.

Loc. cit. (loco citato). In the passage previously mentioned.

Locus celebrationis. The place where the marriage was celebrated.

Locus classicus. Authoritative passage in a book or judgment; the principal authority or source for the subject.

Locus contractus. The place where the contract was made.

Locus delicti. The place where the wrong was committed.

Locus in quo. Scene of the event.

Locus poenitentiae. Scope or opportunity for repentance.

Locus regit actum. The law of the place where an act takes place governs that act.

Locus solutionis. The place where a contract is to be performed or a debt is to be paid.

Locus standi. Recognised position or standing; the right to appear in court.

Lucrum cessans. A benefit which is terminated.

Magnum opus. A great work of literature.

Mala fide(s). (In) bad faith.

Malitia supplet aetatem. Malice supplements the age of an infant wrongdoer who would (in the absence of malice) be too young to be responsible for his acts.

Malum in se. An act which in itself is morally wrong, e.g. murder.

Malum prohibitum. An act which is wrong because it is prohibited by human law but is not morally wrong.

Malus animus. Evil intent.

Mansuetae naturae. Animals which are normally of a domesticated disposition.

Mesne. Intermediate; middle; dividing.

Mesne profits. Profits of land lost by the plaintiff while the defendant remained wrongfully in possession.

Mobilia sequuntur personam. The domicile of movable property follows the owner's personal domicile.

Molliter manus imposuit. Gently laid his hand upon the other party.

Mutatis mutandis. With the necessary changes of detail being made.

Natura negotii. The nature of the transaction.

Negotiorum gestio. Handling of other people's affairs.

Nemo dat quod non habet. No one has power to transfer the ownership of that which he does not own.

Nemo debet bis vexari, si constat curiae quod sit pro una et eadem causa. No one ought to be harassed with proceedings twice, if it appears to the court that it is for one and the same cause.

Nemo est haeres viventis. No one

can be the heir of a person who is still living.

Nexus. Connection; bond.

Nisi. Unless; (also used of a decree or order which will later be made absolute 'unless' good cause be shown to the contrary); provisional.

Nisi prius. Cases which were directed to be tried at Westminster only if the justices of assize should 'not' have tried them in the country 'previously'.

Nocumenta infinita sunt. There is no limit to the types of situations which constitute nuisances.

Nomen collectivum. A collective name, noun or description; a word descriptive of a class.

Non compos mentis. Not of sound mind and understanding.

Non constat. It is not certain.

Non est factum. That the document in question was not his deed.

Non grata. Not acceptable.

Non haec in foedera veni. This is not the agreement which I came to sign.

Non omnibus dormio. I do not turn a blind eye on every instance of misconduct.

Non sequitur. It does not follow; an inconsistent statement.

Noscitur a sociis. The meaning of a word is known from the company it keeps (ie from its context).

Nova causa interveniens. An independent cause which intervenes between the alleged wrong and the damage in question.

Novus actus interveniens. A fresh act of someone other than the defendant which intervenes between the alleged wrong and the damage in question.

Nudum pactum. A bare agreement (unsupported by consideration).

Nullius filius. No man's son; a bastard.

Obiter dictum (dicta). Thing(s) said by the way; opinions expressed by judges in passing, on issues not essential for the decision in the case.

Obligatio quasi ex contractu. An obligation arising out of an act or event, as if from a contract, but independently of the consent of the person bound.

Omnia praesumuntur contra spoliatorem. Every presumption is raised against a wrongdoer.

Omnia praesumuntur rite et solemniter esse acta donec probetur in contrarium. All things are presumed to have been performed with all due formalities until it is proved to the contrary.

Omnis ratihabitio retrotrahitur et mandato priori aequiparatur. Every ratification of a previous act is carried back and made equivalent to a previous command to do it.

Onus probandi. The burden of proving.

Op. cit. (opere citato). In the book referred to previously.

Orse. Otherwise.

Pace. By permission of.

Pacta sunt servanda. Agreements are kept.

Par delictum. Equal fault.

Par in parem non habet imperium. An equal has no authority over an equal.

Parens patriae. Parent of the nation.

Pari materia. With equal substance.

Pari passu. On an equal footing; equally; in step with.

Pari ratione. By an equivalent process of reasoning.

Parol. By word of mouth, or unsealed document.

Participes criminis. Accomplices in the crime.

Passim. Everywhere; in various places.

Pater est quem nuptiae demonstrant. He is the father whom the marriage indicates to be so.

Patrimonium. Beneficial ownership.

Pendente lite. While a law suit is pending.

Per. By; through; in the opinion of a judge.

Per capita. Divided equally between all the persons filling the description.

Per curiam. In the opinion of the court.

Per formam doni. Through the form of wording of the gift or deed.

Per incuriam. Through carelessness or oversight.

Per quod. By reason of which.

Per quod consortium et servitium amisit. By reason of which he has lost the benefit of her company and services.

Per quod servitium amisit. By reason of which he has lost the benefit of his service.

Per se. By itself.

Persona non grata. A person not acceptable.

Persona(e) designata(e). A person(s) specified as an individual(s), not identified as a member(s) of a class nor as fulfilling a particular qualification.

Per stirpes. According to the stocks of descent; one share for each line of descendants; where the descendants of a deceased person (however many they may be) inherit between them only the one share which the deceased would have taken if alive.

Per subsequens matrimonium. Legitimation of a child 'by subsequent marriage' of the parents.

Plene administravit. A plea by an executor 'that he has fully administered' all the assets which have come into his hands and that no assets remain out of which the plaintiff's claim could be satisfied.

Plus quam tolerabile. More than can be endured.

Post. After; mentioned in a subsequent passage or page.

Post mortem. After death.

Post nuptial. Made after marriage.

Post obit bond. Agreement or bond by which a borrower agrees to pay the lender a sum larger than the loan on or after the death of a person on whose death he expects to inherit property.

Post obitum. After the death of a specified person.

Pour autrui. On behalf of another.

Prima facie. At first sight.

Primae impressionis. Of first impression.

Pro bono publico. For the public good.

Procès verbal. Verbal proceedings.

Profit a prendre. The right to enter the land of another and take part of its produce.

Pro hac vice. For this occasion.

Propositus. The person put forward; the person about whom a legal issue is to be determined.

Pro privato commodo. For private benefit.

Pro rata. In proportion.

Pro rata itineris. At the same rate per mile as was agreed for the whole journey.

Pro tanto. So far; to that extent.

Pro tempore. For the time being.

Publici juris. Of public right.

Puisne. Inferior; lower in rank; not secured by deposit of deeds; of the High Court.

Punctum temporis. Moment, or point of time.

Pur autre vie. During the life of another person.

Q.v. (quod vide). Which see.

Qua. As; in the capacity of.

Quaere. Consider whether it is correct.

Quaeritur. The question is raised.

Quantum. Amount; how much.

Quantum meruit. As much as he has earned.

Quantum valebant. As much as they were worth.

Quare clausum fregit. Because he broke into the plaintiff's enclosure.

Quasi. As if; seemingly.

Quasi ex contractu. *See* OBLIGATIO.

Quatenus. How far; in so far as; since.

Qui sentit commodum sentire debet et onus. He who takes the benefit must accept the burden.

Quia timet. Because he fears what he will suffer in the future.

Quicquid plantatur solo solo cedit. Whatever is planted in the soil belongs to the soil.

Quid pro quo. Something for something; consideration.

Qui elegit judicem elegit jus. He who chooses a judge chooses also the law which the judge administers.

Qui facit per alium facit per se. He who employs another person to do something does it himself.

Qui prior est tempore potior est jure. He who is earlier in point of time is in the stronger position in law.

Quoad. Until; as far as; as to.

Quoad hoc. As far as this matter is concerned.

Quo animo. With what intention.

Quot judices tot sententiae. There were as many different opinions as there were judges.

Quousque. Until the time when.

Ratio decidendi. The reason for a decision; the principle on which a decision is based.

Ratione domicilii. By reason of a person's domicile.

Ratione impotentiae et loci. By reason of weakness and of place.

Re. In the matter of; by the thing or transaction.

Reductio ad absurdum. Reduction to absurdity.

Refouler. To return, drive back.

Renvoi. Reference to or application of the rules of a foreign legal system in a different country's courts.

Res. Thing; affair; matter; circumstance.

Res extincta. The thing which was intended to be the subject matter of a contract but had previously been destroyed.

Res gestae. Things done; the transaction.

Res integra. A point not covered by the authority of a decided case which must therefore be decided upon principle alone.

Res inter alios acta alteri nocere non debet. A man ought not to be prejudiced by what has taken place between other persons.

Res ipsa loquitur. The thing speaks for itself, i.e. is evidence of negligence in the absence of an explanation by the defendant.

Res judicata. A matter on which a court has previously reached a binding decision; a matter which cannot be questioned.

Res nova. A matter which has not previously been decided.

Res nullius. Nobody's property.

Respondeat superior. A principal must answer for the acts of his subordinates.

Res sua. Something which a man believes to belong to another when it in fact is 'his own property'.

Restitutio in integrum. Restoration of a party to his original position; full restitution.

Res vendita. The article which was sold.

Rex est procurator fatuorum. The King is the protector of the simple minded.

Rigor aequitatis. The inflexibility of equity.

Sc. *See* SCILICET.

Sciens. Knowing.

Scienter. Knowingly; with knowledge of an animal's dangerous disposition.

Scienti non fit injuria. A man who is aware of the existence of a danger has no remedy if it materialises.

Scilicet. To wit; namely; that is to say.

Scintilla. A spark; trace; or moment.

Scire facias. A writ; that you cause to know.

Scriptum praedictum non est factum suum. A plea that the aforesaid document is not his deed.

Secundum formam doni. In accordance with the form of wording in the gift or deed.

Secus. It is otherwise; the legal position is different.

Sed. But.

Sed quaere. But inquire; look into the matter; consider whether the statement is correct.

Semble. It appears; apparently.

Sentit commodum et periculum rei. He both enjoys the benefit of the thing and bears the risk of its loss.

Seriatim. In series; one by one; point by point.

Serivitium. Service.

Sic. So; in such a manner; (also used to emphasise wording copied or quoted from another source: 'such was the expression used in the original source').

Sic utere tuo ut alienum non laedas. So use your own property as not to injure the property of your neighbour.

Similiter. Similarly; in like manner.

Simplex commendatio non obligat. Mere praise of goods by the seller imposes no liability upon him.

Simpliciter. Simply; merely; alone; without any further action; without qualification.

Sine animo revertendi. Without the intention of returning.

Sine die. Without a day being appointed; indefinitely.

Situs. The place where property is situated.

Solatium. Consolation; relief; compensation.

Sotto volce. In an undertone.

Specificatio. The making of a new article out of the chattel of one person by the labour of another.

Spes successionis. The hope of inheriting property on the death of another.

Spondes peritiam artis. If skill is inherent in your profession, you guarantee that you will display it.

Stare decisis. To stand by what has been dedided.

Status quo (ante). The previous position; the position in which things were before; unchanged position.

Stet. Let it stand; do not delete.

Stricto sensu. In the strict sense.

Sub colore officii. Under pretext of someone's official position.

Sub judice. Under judgment; being decided by the court.

Sub modo. Within limits; to a limited extent.

Sub nom. (sub nomine). Under the name of.

Sub silentio. In silence.

Sub tit. (sub titulo). Under the title of.

Suggestio falsi. The suggestion of something which is untrue.

Sui generis. Of its own special kind; unique.

Sui juris. Of his own right; possessed of full legal capacity.

Sup. *See* SUPRA.

Suppressio veri. The suppression of the truth.

Supra. (Sup.) Above; referred to higher up the page; previously.

Talis qualis. Such as it is.

Tam ... quam. As well ... as.

Tempore mortis. At the time of death.

Tempore testamenti. At the time when the will was made.

Toties quoties. As often as occasion shall require; as often as something happens.

Transit in rem judicatam. A right of action merges in the judgment recovered upon it.

Turpis causa. Immoral conduct which constitutes the subject matter of an action.

Uberrima fides. Most abundant good faith.

Ubi jus ibi remedium. Where there is a legally recognised right there is also a remedy.

Ubi supra. In the passage or reference mentioned previously.

Ultimus heres. The ultimate heir who is last in order of priority of those who may be entitled to claim the estate of an intestate.

Ultra vires. Outside the powers recognised by law as belonging to the person or body in question.

Uno flatu. With one breath; at the same moment.

Ut res magis valeat quam pereat. Words must be construed so as to support the validity of the contract rather than to destroy it.

v. (versus). Against.

Verba fortius accipiuntur contra proferentem. Ambiguous wording is construed adversely against the party who introduced it into the document.

Vera copula. True sexual unity.

Verbatim. Word by word; exactly; word for word.

Via media. Middle way; compromise.

Vice versa. The other way round; in turn.

Vide. See.

Vi et armis (et contra pacem domini regis). By force of arms (and in breach of the King's peace).

Vigilantibus et non dormientibus jura subveniunt (or jus succurrit). The law(s) assist(s) those who are vigilant, not those who doze over their rights.

Vinculum juris. Legal tie; that which binds the parties with mutual obligations.

Virgo intacta. A virgin with hymen intact.

Virtute officii. By virtue of a person's official position.

Vis-a-vis. Face to face; opposite to.

Vis major. Irresistible force.

Viva voce. Orally; oral examination.

Viz. (videlicet). Namely; that is to say.

Voir dire. Examination of a witness before he gives evidence, to ascertain whether he is competent to tell the truth on oath; trial within a trial.

Volens. Willing.

Volenti non fit injuria. In law no wrong is done to a man who consents to undergo it.

Index

The entry numbers refer to the paragraphs, not the pages.